D0536477

De Niro

BY THE SAME AUTHOR

The Cinema of Josef von Sternberg
The Gangster Film
Science Fiction in the Cinema
Hollywood in the Thirties
Hollywood in the Sixties
Sixty Years of Hollywood
Stunt: The Great Movie Stuntmen
The Hollywood Exiles
Ken Russell: An Appalling Talent
Buñuel
Fellini
Steven Spielberg: The Unauthorised Biography
Stanley Kubrick: A Biography
Woody Allen: A Biography
George Lucas: A Biography

De Niro

A BIOGRAPHY

JOHN BAXTER

HarperCollins*Publishers*

HarperCollins*Publishers*
77–85 Fulham Palace Road,
Hammersmith, London W6 8JB

www.fireandwater.com

Published by HarperCollins*Publishers* 2002

Copyright © John Baxter 2002

2 4 6 8 9 7 5 3 1

The author asserts the moral right to be
identified as the author of this work

A catalogue record for this book is
available from the British Library

ISBN 0 00 257196 X

Set in Sabon by
Rowland Phototypesetting Ltd,
Bury St Edmunds, Suffolk

Printed and bound in Great Britain by
Clays Ltd, St Ives plc

All rights reserved. No part of this publication may be
reproduced, stored in a retrieval system, or transmitted,
in any form or by any means, electronic, mechanical,
photocopying, recording or otherwise, without the
prior permission of the publishers.

Contents

Illustrations

With Irwin Winkler on the set of *Guilty by Suspicion*.
(© *1991 Le Studio Canal + and Warner Bros*)

Elia Kazan directs De Niro and Ingrid Boulting on *The Last Tycoon*. (© *1976 Academy Productions and Paramount Pictures*)

De Niro on location for *Ronin*, with producer Frank Mancuso Jr and director John Frankenheimer. (© *1998 FGM Entertainment, MGM and United Artists*)

De Niro endured repeated beatings as Jake La Motta in *Raging Bull*. (© *1980 United Artists and Chartoff-Winkler Productions*)

To prepare for the role of cab driver Travis Bickle in *Taxi Driver*, De Niro drove a taxi in New York and haunted cafés where drivers hung out. (© *1976 Columbia Pictures, Bill/Phillips and Italo/Judeo Productions*)

De Niro learned the saxophone – not very well – to play musician Jimmy Doyle in *New York, New York*. (© *1977 Chartoff-Winkler Productions, Metro-Goldwyn-Mayer and United Artists*)

Rehearsing barefoot on the stones of the Amazon for *The Mission*. (© *1986 Enigma Productions, Goldcrest Films, Kingmore Productions and Warner Bros*)

De Niro as dying baseball player Bruce Pearson in *Bang the Drum Slowly*. (© *1973 ANJS, Dibs Partnership and Paramount Pictures*)

De Niro and Gerard Depardieu in Bernardo Bertolucci's *Novecento*. (© *1976 Artémis Productions, Les Productions Artistes Associés, Produzioni Europee Associati (PEA) and Paramount Pictures*)

Betsy storms away from Travis Bickle after he has taken her to a porno film in *Taxi Driver*. (© *1976 Columbia Pictures, Bill/Phillips and Italo/Judeo Productions*)

De Niro as the psychopath Travis Bickle. (© *1976 Columbia Pictures, Bill/Phillips and Italo/Judeo Productions*)

'Are you talkin' to *me*?' (© *1976 Columbia Pictures, Bill/ Phillips and Italo/Judeo Productions*)

De Niro as Jimmy Doyle in *New York, New York*. (© *1977*

Chartoff-Winkler Productions, Metro-Goldwyn-Mayer and
United Artists)

As Michael Vronsky in Michael Cimino's *The Deer Hunter*.
(© 1978 EMI Films Ltd and Universal Pictures)

As gunman 'Noodles' Aaronson in Sergio Leone's *Once Upon
a Time in America*. (© 1984 Embassy International Pictures,
PSO International, Rafran Cinematografica, Warner Bros
and Wishbone)

Ex-slave trader and mercenary Rodrigo Mendoza in *The
Mission*. (© 1986 Enigma Productions, Goldcrest Films,
Kingmore Productions and Warner Bros)

De Niro as troubled bounty hunter Jack Walsh in *Midnight
Run*. (© 1988 City Light Films and Universal Pictures)

De Niro and Sean Penn as escaped convicts in *We're no
Angels*. (© 1989 Paramount Pictures)

As Stanley Cox in *Stanley and Iris*. (© 1990 Lantana and
MGM)

As screenwriter David Merrill in *Guilty by Suspicion*. (© 1991
Le Studio Canal + and Warner Bros)

De Niro in *Mad Dog and Glory*. (© 1992 Mad Dog
Productions and Universal Pictures)

Baseball fan Gil Renard in *The Fan*. (© 1996 Mandalay
Entertainment, Scott Free Productions and TriStar Pictures)

De Niro as political 'fixer' Conrad Brean in *Wag the Dog*.
(© 1997 Baltimore Pictures, New Line Cinema, Punch
Productions and Tribeca Productions)

De Niro as undercover CIA man Sam in *Ronin*. (© 1998 FGM
Entertainment, MGM and United Artists)

As gang boss Paul Vitti in *Analyze This*. (© 1999 Baltimore
Pictures, Face Productions, NPV Entertainment, Spring
Creek Productions, Tribeca Productions, Village Roadshow
Productions)

As Fearless Leader in *The Adventures of Rocky and
Bullwinkle*. (© 2000 Capella International, KC Medien AG
and Tribeca Productions)

Acknowledgments

For assistance with the writing of this book, I'm grateful to the many people who shared their memories of Robert De Niro. Charles Carshon provided information on teaching De Niro at the Stella Adler Academy of Dramatic Art, while Anton Gill generously shared his research on the place of Virginia Admiral and Robert Sr in the art scene of New York in the 1940s. Hans Peter Litscher added much useful information on the career of Valeska Gert and the erratic history of Beggars' Bar, and translated a number of documents. Michael Neal was, as always, encyclopedic, in this case about *White Stains* and Anaïs Nin's experiments with erotica.

Robert A. Wilson and Mitchell Clements described their early encounters with both Robert De Niro Sr and Jr in the Greenwich Village of the fifties. For information on De Niro's early days as an actor, I'm indebted to Annie Girardot, David Scott Milton, Robert Cordier, Gianni Bozzacchi, Fabio Testi, Barbara Johnson and Maggie Brammall. Among those who cast light on his later career were Sir David Puttnam, Don S. Davis, Charlotte Rampling, Chazz Palminteri, John Milius, David Noh, Jean Reno, Jay Holben, Patricia Hartwell, Roy Scheider, Lawrence Kasdan, Donald Pleasence, Roger Corman, Bernard Vorhaus and Bernardino Zapponi.

For invaluable help with research, and for their hospitality in Rome, London, New York and Los Angeles, I'm grateful to Tom Rudolph, Adrian Turner, David Thompson, Pat McGilligan, Jacques Boko of *Les Bains Douches*, David and Joanne Burke, Minor and Mary Knight, Bill Warren, Benjamin Sutherland, Shawn Bell and Mary Troath for picture assistance, and the staff of the André Malraux Library, Paris, and Charles Silver and Ron Magliozzi of the Museum of Modern Art, New York.

John Baxter, April 2002

CHAPTER ONE

The Last Actor Alive

Player (lost): *There we were – demented children mincing about in clothes that no one ever wore, speaking as no man ever spoke, swearing love in wigs and rhymed couplets, killing each other with wooden swords, hollow protestations of faith hurled after empty promises of vengeance – and every gesture, every pose, vanishing into the thin unpopulated air. We ransomed our dignity to the clouds, and the uncomprehending birds listened. (He rounds on them) Don't you see?! We're actors – we're the opposite of people!*

Tom Stoppard, *Rosencrantz and Guildenstern are Dead*

Valentine's Day, 14 February 1989.

From the offices along the Strip of Sunset Boulevard, there's a classic LA view. No palms, no lawns, no *art moderne* architecture; leave those to the glitzier residential suburbs closer to the Pacific: Beverly Hills, Westwood, Santa Monica.

Here, in the DMZ between Beverly Hills and Hollywood, everything is commerce. The very light and air are for sale – perhaps the only things Hollywood has to sell.

Film interfaces with the record business. The monuments are all to bad taste and the hard sell. Tonight, in Bill Gazzarri's Rock Club, with its self-aggrandising billboard portrait of its pouchy proprietor on the façade, and his boast of the groups launched here, the Hollywood porn-movie community is having its annual bash to present its Oscars, the Heart-Ons, with awards for Best Anal Love Scene and Best Blow Job.

But in Hollywood there's always a gaudier image, a louder voice. Opposite, higher, brighter, more strident, a billboard has been erected for the personal junk-lit industry of Jackie Collins, author of *Hollywood Husbands* and *Once is not Enough*. Ten times larger than life, she glares out over her domain. Underneath her image is the rubric of her reign. *More than a Hundred Million Sold*.

At Hollywood's smartest restaurants, Le Dôme and Spago, black stretch limos queue decorously to drop off their clients, then circle back into the dark. The drivers wait in empty parking lots, smoking and listening to the radio until the car phone burrs its summons.

One white chauffeured Cadillac limousine glides past Le Dôme, moving west on Sunset, heading for the 405 Freeway. LAX. The east.

In its air-conditioned hush, Robert De Niro takes a last look at Hollywood through smoky yellow glass. When he comes back, it will no longer be the same place.

It's said that every performing artist has ten years in which to make his or her mark. By that standard, De Niro had succeeded better than most. From *Taxi Driver* and his Best Supporting Actor Academy Award for *The Godfather II* in 1975 to the acclaim for *Awakenings* in 1987, he'd taken twelve years to create the benchmarks against which every other screen actor of his generation needs to measure himself.

But now he is turning his back on all that, leaving the febrile society he has always affected to despise, but whose blandishments he can never quite resist.

He has already passed Tower Records' gigantic Hollywood outlet, where anything that can be put on disc is for sale. He has passed On the Rox, the disco where he'd spent more than his share of white nights. He has passed below the Xanadu-like silhouette of the Château Marmont Hotel, in the grounds of which his friend John Belushi died.

As the sun sinks, Sunset comes alive with black leather, Spandex, studs. On Sunset Strip, the sidewalk is jammed with Harleys, and Porsches parked three-deep as, twittering like parakeets, the Valley Girls from Sherman Oaks and Encino, bums and tits compressed into tank tops and jeans tight and hard as lacquer, jostle for attention as they gather for a night of disco. Manes of moussed hair – male and female – shimmer in the streetlights, and down the gutters roll dusty skeins of tape from gutted cassettes. Sunset Tumbleweed.

Jackie's billboard ignites, neon outlining the imperious Collins silhouette.

Showtime.

De Niro's limo drives by, its passenger no longer noticing. He is forty-six, but feels ten years older. He has won the greatest honours his craft can bestow, but he believes himself without merit. He is returning to New York, where he thinks he belongs. But part of him knows he doesn't really belong anywhere. Nobody is waiting for him in New York. Nothing is waiting for him – except work.

'*You travel a lot?*' the girl in the bookstore will ask.

'*Yeah,*' he'll reply.

'*Does it make you lonely?*'

'*I am alone,*' he will say mildly. '*I'm not lonely.*'

Sure, Bobby.

The big Cadillac undulates silkily as it rolls over a hump in the shifting surface of the slide area that is Hollywood, and glides into the warm and scented dark.

To talk about 'performance' in movies at the beginning of the twenty-first century is to discuss an art as fossilised as Egyptian wall painting. Jack Nicholson has rightly called himself a member of the last generation of film performers. Already, the 'synthespians' who will replace him are crowding on camera. Electronics routinely resuscitate actors who die in mid-production, and raise long-dead stars from the grave. Joe Dante's threat in *Gremlins II* of an updated *Casablanca*, 'in colour, and with a happier ending', now sounds like next week's Fox-TV programming. As for the science-fictional proposal that old films might be cleansed of politically incorrect activities like smoking, Steven Spielberg showed the way in 2002 with a sanitised *E.T.* in which agents' guns became torches.

As he turns sixty, Robert De Niro, one of the most gifted screen performers of his generation, can be seen as also the last of a line in which he was already a throwback. Born a century too late, he belonged in the barnstorming theatre of the nineteenth and early twentieth centuries, the world of John Barrymore, Emil Jannings, Werner Krauss, Fritz Kortner. No six degrees of separation divide De Niro from a theatre of putty noses and crêpe hair, of rhetoric and speeches from the scaffold. Erwin Piscator of Berlin's pamphleteering Communist pre-war Volksbühne theatre was a childhood friend, and his teacher, Stella Adler, came from the Theater Guild of the thirties and the nineteenth-century Yiddish theatre.

Born to perform in a theatre that no longer existed, De Niro crammed the djinn of his skill into the constricted bottle of the movies. Watching him writhe and grimace through the glass, audiences imagined they were seeing great acting, when in fact they were watching great acting distorted.

'These days,' writes the British playwright and actor Alan Bennett, 'what the public calls Great Acting is often not even good acting. It's acting with a line around it, acting in inverted commas, acting which shows. The popular idea of Great Acting is a rhetorical performance (award-winning for choice) at the extremes, preferably the extremes of degradation and despair. Such a performance seems to the public to require all an actor has got. Actors know that this is a false assessment. The limit of an actor's ability is a spacious and fairly comfortable place to be; such parts require energy rather than judgment. Anything goes.'

At the start by force of circumstances, but later out of a need for reassurance, De Niro became the last star in this 'anything goes' school of screen performing. He could have done better by doing less, and by doing less with what he did do. A character actor by birth, he allowed himself to be made a leading man, and, born to play villains, agreed to play the hero; and a hero, moreover, in a medium littered with heroes – which, any actor will tell you, are far easier to play.

Robert Towne, screenwriter of *Chinatown* and *Shampoo*, has written, 'Gifted movie actors affect the most, I believe, not by talking, fighting, fucking, killing, cursing or cross-dressing. They do it by being photographed.

'It is said of such actors that the camera loves them. Whatever that means, I've always felt their features are expressive in a unique way; they seem to register swift and dramatic mood changes with no discernible change of expression . . . Great movie actors have features that are ruthlessly efficient. Efficiency that's been touched with a bit of lightning, perhaps. Certainly such actors have this in common with lightning; they can illuminate a moment with shock and scorching clarity. And virtually no dialogue.'

Robert De Niro is such an actor. To see him at his best is to be aware of a new capacity in the art of cinema. His gift is all the greater for the reticence with which it is exercised; like those Japanese painters who work with a heavily inked brush on wet paper, the slightest hesitation brings everything to naught. 'Great feeling shows itself in silence,' wrote the poet Marianne Moore – then corrected herself. 'No, not in silence, but restraint.'

When he chooses to restrain himself, to rely on silence, Robert De Niro is among the finest performers of his generation. That he has chosen so infrequently to exercise that control is his tragedy.

CHAPTER TWO

New York

I go to Paris, I go to London, I go to Rome, and I always say, 'There's no place like New York. It's the most exciting city in the world now. That's the way it is. That's it.'

Robert De Niro

Actors often come from homes that lack imaginative stimulus; the urge to dress up and play other characters is a form of flight from that environment. Yet De Niro's parents were both artists, and he grew up surrounded by artists. In that, he resembles Bernardo Bertolucci, who directed him in *Novecento*. Both are artists over whom an affection-filled childhood with creative parents exercised an ambiguous influence, at once stimulating and stifling.

De Niro's father, also Robert, was born in 1922 in Tipperary Hill, the predominantly Irish quarter of Syracuse in northern New York state. Robert Sr's mother, Bobby's grandmother, was Helen O'Reilly before she married Henry De Niro, a salesman and, later, a health inspector, but Robert Sr inherited the dark good looks and mystical temperament of his Italian father, which he passed on to his own son.

The De Niros came from Campobasso, near Naples, well south of the notional divide which separates the cooler northern Italians from the dark and fiery *meridionali*. A *penchant* for argument, depression and rage passed largely undiminished from the first of the De Niro name to arrive in the United States at the turn of the century to those members of the family born on American soil, as did an apparently genetic Italian rhythm of speech which became even more pronounced in adulthood.

Robert Sr started painting at five. 'Why? I don't know. I was very isolated,' he said later. By the time he was eleven he was attending art classes at the Syracuse Museum, and showing such ability that the directors gave him a studio of his own. When adolescence brought the usual soul-searching, he shocked his family by embracing atheism, though, in the best traditions of the lapsed Catholic, religious iconography preoccupied him for most of his life, the Crucifixion and other elements of his discarded faith recurring in his work.

He spent the summer of 1938 in Gloucester, Massachusetts, studying with Ralph Pearson, an artist best known for his landscapes. Pearson held his classes on a coal barge in Gloucester Harbour, which is where De Niro first read the plays of Eugene O'Neill. The grim picture of the emigrant experience in O'Neill's *Anna Christie* impressed him so much that he modelled a stage set for a possible production.

After Gloucester, De Niro gravitated to New York, studying by day and waiting tables at night. Much serious art discourse in New York at that time centred on Hans Hofmann, who had arrived from Munich via Paris, trailing an impressive record as a teacher and theoretician. Hofmann opened a school in 1933, and in the summer of 1935 started summer sessions in Provincetown, Rhode Island.

In the winter of 1938–39 Hofmann gave an influential series of six lectures in New York on new movements in European art. They were attended by the best emerging American artists, including Jackson Pollock, Arshile Gorky and Willem de Kooning, and future critics Clement Greenberg and Harold Rosenberg, all of whom, recognising that Surrealism was waning, were alert for the next new thing, Abstract Expressionism. The following summer, Pollock and some others followed Hofmann to Provincetown. He only accepted twenty-five students for his summer school. Among them in 1939 was Robert De Niro.

At the end of 1939, De Niro won a place at Black Mountain

College in Asheville, North Carolina, where one of the greatest of contemporary artists, Josef Albers, taught. Set up in 1933 by a group of liberal academics, Black Mountain admitted only fifty students, and gave them superior teaching and maximum freedom. De Niro spent most of 1939 and 1940 there – a frustrating time, since Albers found his work 'too emotional'. De Niro, then, as later, inclined to be argumentative, protested, 'A painting can't be too emotional. It can be controlled, but never too emotional.' After a year of trying to satisfy Albers, he returned to New York early in 1941, with only $5 in his pocket. That summer, he once again attended Hofmann's summer school.

A village of crackerbox cabins scattered among the dunes of the Atlantic coast, Provincetown had a reputation for bohemianism and political radicalism that went back to the turn of the century. The Provincetown Playhouse and Provincetown Players were co-founded by Communist ideologue John Reed, author of *Ten Days that Shook the World*, who scandalised the community by running off with Louise Bryant, art-struck wife of a local dentist. In 1916, Eugene O'Neill had his first play performed there. After that, painters and writers from New York and Boston, called sarcastically by the locals 'wash-ashores', found it a useful summer hangout, particularly when, thanks to Hofmann, it became a centre for avant-garde artists too.

Young playwright Tennessee Williams also turned up in Provincetown in 1941, hoping to have a play accepted at the Playhouse. He and De Niro met at Captain Jack's, a pier-end restaurant where both worked as waiters. It shared a building with a boarding house where two out-of-work dance students lived, one of whom, Kip Kiernan, also modelled for Hofmann. Tennessee Williams fell in love with Kiernan, the first man with whom he enjoyed a complete sexual relationship – celebrated in his long-suppressed play *Sometimes Cloudy, Sometimes Bright*. Williams, Kiernan and their friend Donald Windham made no secret of their activities, documenting them in nude photographs. Among Williams' lovers that summer was Jackson Pollock, whose alcoholism inflamed a taste for being promiscuously sodomised.

With his movie-star good looks – he resembled the actor Robert Stack – De Niro was not short of admirers, male and female, and it was during this period at Provincetown that he acknowledged his own homosexuality, and probably had his first homosexual experience. Williams and Kiernan may have initiated him, but it's equally possible that Pollock was among his first lovers.

Hofmann's classes that year also included a lively young woman from Dalles, Oregon. Even in a community where women were accustomed to speaking out and being heard, Virginia Admiral's voice was confident and committed. A Communist from her teens, she'd joined the Trotskyite Young People's Socialist League on the Berkeley campus of the University of California, and led its clashes with the Stalinist Young Communist League.

Admiral's closest friend on campus was Oakland-born poet Robert Duncan – 'a strikingly beautiful boy,' remembered the writer Anaïs Nin, 'who looked about seventeen, with regular features, abundant hair, a faunish expression and a slight deviation in one eye, which made him seem to be looking always beyond and around you.'

Already an outsider by virtue of his homosexuality, Duncan joined Admiral's radical circle, which also included Pauline Kael, future film critic of the *New Yorker*. At Admiral's urging, he quit obligatory Reserve Officer Training Corps military training, and eventually left UCLA altogether for Black Mountain. Politically advanced for the time, Black Mountain's faculty still wasn't sufficiently so for Duncan, who, after an argument with the administration about the Spanish Civil War, quickly exited, accompanied by his new lover, one of the instructors.

In 1939, Admiral decided to abandon literature for art. Her mother, fearful that she would never be able to support herself, demanded she at least earn a teaching credential before plunging into bohemia. Virginia acquiesced, but only if she could study at Columbia in New York. Her mother agreed, provided she live at the college's International House, in effect under supervision. Once in New York, Admiral did enrol in a teaching course of sorts, though it was a Masters programme in Art Education, which gave her plenty of opportunities to paint.

By then, Robert Duncan was living in Woodstock, New York, on 'Cooney's Farm', a commune-cum-artists' colony run by James Cooney and his wife Blanche. An enthusiast for D.H. Lawrence, Cooney published the *Phoenix*, a magazine dedicated to Lawrence's work. The farm was a log cabin in the woods; guests bunked down in the old woodshed. Admiral spent time there in 1940, and, with Duncan, edited the first and only issue of the literary magazine *Epitaph*, which would evolve into *Experimental Review*.

Among Cooney's visitors was Anaïs Nin. Eroticist, fabulist, lover and muse of Henry Miller, who dedicated *Tropic of Cancer* to her, the small, dark and seductive Nin had fled from Nazi-occupied Paris with banker husband Ian Hugo, and was now cutting a swathe through New York literary society.

Nin didn't think Virginia sufficiently awed by her tales of wild times in Paris. 'Virginia and her friends dress like schoolchildren,' she wrote pettishly in her diary. 'Baby shoes, little bows in their hair, little-girl dresses, little-boy clothes, orphan hats, schoolgirl short socks; they eat candy, sugar, ice cream. And some of the books they read are like schoolchildren's books; how to win friends, how to make love, how to do this or that. They prefer the radio, the movies, recordings, to hearing experiences directly. They are not curious about people, only their voices over a machine and their faces on the screen.'

After the farm, Virginia taught for six weeks at a summer camp in Maine. By the time she returned to New York, the tuition money borrowed from her father had run out. Quitting college, she settled down to paint, supporting herself by waiting tables in Greenwich Village, and sharing a loft with two friends on 14th Street, above Union Square, for a rent of $30 a month.

Meant as factory spaces, lofts were zoned for commercial use only. The high-beamed ceilings rested on massive wooden pillars. Floors were of wide planks, uneven and splintered. Few lofts had bathrooms, kitchens or heating. But for artists unconcerned about creature comfort, they offered a peerless working environment. Robert Duncan wrote in his journal, 'Virginia's studio opens out. We stand in the shadows above the lights of 14th St. The paintings move back into the walls like mirrors of our dreams – the dark stage of gathering forces. This is our last nursery – this is today's, 1941's projection of a Berkeley paradise where we go over again drawings by Virginia, by Mary, by Lillian, by Cecily, by me from the golden age – where I sit reading to Virginia and her fellow students.'

Anaïs Nin was less impressed when she visited. 'The first floor houses a shop, a hamburger bar, a shoe shop and a synthetic orange juice bar,' she recalled. 'I climb a bare wooden stairway painted a dusty gray. The place is cold, but the hallways and lofts are big and high-ceilinged and the only place possible and available to a painter. There is space for easels, canvases of any size. There is a lavatory outside, running water and washstand inside, and that is all. On weekends, the heat is turned off. The enormous windows which give on the deafening traffic noise of 14th St have to be kept closed. There are nails on the walls for clothes, a Sterno burner for making coffee. We drink sour wine out of paper cups. There Virginia and Janet paint, study acting and dancing, type when they need money.' This was the environment in which the young Robert Jr would be raised.

Surprisingly to Nin, given their apparent naïveté, Virginia and her friends were all in psychoanalysis. As émigrés flooded into America from Austria and Germany, New York had become a centre of psychotherapy. Most creative people regarded analysis as essential to their intellectual growth, not to mention, in the cases of gays or bisexuals like Robert Duncan and Jackson Pollock, a quick route to military deferment. The fact that Nin kept a journal attracted instant interest, and everybody started one. Their analyst sent her a letter of thanks, saying it made his work much easier.

Admiral's work impressed Hans Hofmann sufficiently for him to accept her as a student, and in the summer of 1941 she arrived in Provincetown, where she met the young Robert De Niro, back for his second year. Hofmann had appointed him class monitor, and she and the dramatically handsome young man instantly struck sparks.

Six years older than De Niro, Virginia was more sophisticated sexually, socially and politically. Though homosexuality would prove De Niro's lifetime sexual choice, he remained, for the moment, bisexual. Telling her nothing of his homosexual inclinations, he became Admiral's lover.

For a while, they enjoyed a bohemian existence, living in a shack on the dunes, picking blueberries for pocket money, painting by day and partying by night, often at an illegal bar run by legendary Berlin dancer, choreographer and actress Valeska Gert.

In 1925 Gert had appeared with Garbo in G.W. Pabst's *Joyless Street*, and she acted in a number of other movies in the course of a sensational career. When the Nazis came to power, Gert, damned three times over as a lesbian, a Communist and a Jew, divorced her gay husband, married a young English admirer, also gay, in order to get a British passport, and, when the Germans threatened to invade Britain, fled to America. Washing ashore in Provincetown, she ran her bar, queened it over the local gays, and modelled nude for Hofmann's classes, striking the eccentric poses from her Berlin cabaret act.

After summer school ended, De Niro and Admiral stayed on, Robert getting work in the local fish cannery. Robert Duncan and Anaïs Nin visited, Nin confessing that she was supporting herself by writing pornography for Oklahoma oil millionaire Roy M. Johnson, who paid $1 a page. She'd recruited Henry Miller and one-time Paris publisher Caresse Crosby to help, and De Niro too joined the round-robin of writers. 'Everyone is writing of their sexual experiences,' Nin wrote. 'Invented, overheard, researched from Krafft-Ebing and medical books. We have comical conversations. We tell a story and the rest of us have to decide whether it is true or false. Or plausible. Robert [Duncan] would offer to experiment, to test our inventions, to confirm or negate our fantasies.' De Niro didn't have the stamina of Nin, Duncan or Miller, however, nor the imagination. 'It was very hard work,' he recalled, 'so eventually I went back to the fishery.'

By the summer of 1941, he and Virginia had returned to New York and were sharing the 14th Street loft. Robert Duncan was a frequent visitor. Disinherited by his adoptive father, architect

Edwin Joseph Symmes, he'd become a homosexual hustler. As he explained to one friend, 'the ideal evening was to find a Scarsdale or Westchester husband who wanted a quick, anonymous fling before returning home to the wife and kids, and who would rent a hotel room in which you could spend the remainder of the night'.

If he had no luck, Duncan would sometimes 'crash' at De Niro and Virginia's loft. That he would seduce Robert was inevitable. They began having sex during one of Virginia's brief absences and continued to do so secretly until Duncan was drafted at the end of 1941.

Once he'd left, De Niro confessed everything to Virginia. The double betrayal enraged and astonished her. They argued through the night, forgetting the thinness of the partitions dividing their space from others on that floor. Suddenly, in a pause, they heard a voice through the wall from a neighbouring studio. 'I have been listening to you,' it said. 'I have been weighing all your arguments. I think that Virginia is absolutely fair and right, and the behaviour of Bob and Robert treacherous and ugly.'

Bob bolted out of the apartment and hammered on the nearest doors. There was no response from the three painters who lived there. For days, aghast that his secret was out, he 'walked', according to Anaïs Nin, 'with shoulders bowed. He was silent. He looked haunted.'

Duncan endured only six weeks in boot camp in San Antonio before declaring his homosexuality and winning a discharge on psychological grounds. 'I am an officially certified fag now,' he announced proudly when he arrived back in New York. Unaware of Robert's confession, he turned up at the 14th Street loft, only to be ordered out by a furious Virginia while a much-chastened De Niro looked on helplessly.

Like the rest of the 'wash-ashores', Valeska Gert also left Provincetown when the weather turned cold. In a basement at the corner of Morton and Bleecker Streets in Greenwich Village, she opened Beggars' Bar, which, despite having no liquor licence, became a hangout for gays, radicals and the criminal fringe. Show people from uptown often turned up there to see Gert perform, or to watch visiting artists like dancer Kadidja Wedekind, whose father Frank wrote *Lulu*. Judy Garland, a regular, called Beggars' Bar 'the only cabaret in New York worth visiting'.

De Niro waited tables there. So did Tennessee Williams. Williams doesn't refer to De Niro by name in his *Memoirs*, though one incident does offer glimpses of the lifestyle they shared.

'Towards the end of 1941,' writes Williams, 'I was companion to an abstract painter in the warehouse district of the West Village. The friend was, nervously speaking, a basket case. I mean he was a real freak-out before it was fashionable to be one.'

One night Gert announced that, henceforth, the waiters would have to pool their tips, and share them with her. In the resulting fracas, the painter began hurling beer bottles. Gert went to hospital with a head wound, and Williams was out of a job. He moved in with the painter, who demanded that Williams cruise the streets for 'carefully specified kinds of visitors' as sex partners. Williams did so, helped by another friend, whom he identifies only as 'the pilot fish'. The arrangement continued until some of the 'visitors' left with the painter's valuables, and Williams was evicted.

Whatever his part in these events, De Niro was already committed to the gay lifestyle represented by Gert, Williams and their friends. He remained, however, attached to Virginia, even besotted by her.

Of the poems he wrote in this period, he chose to publish only six, all from 'about 1941'. Floridly sensual, they're reminiscent of Hart Crane (who committed suicide over his homosexuality) and Oscar Wilde.

> Light powdered her eyelashes, gilded her teeth
> lustered her hair
> but she refused to enter
> leaving in the doorway a pool from her milky body . . .
> Two nuns brought incense to cover
> the ends of her breasts
> Strange peacocks bloomed upon her thighs
> as only angels can . . .

The 'her' in De Niro's verse is usually ambiguous. Later, in a series inspired by George Cukor's *Camille*, he would write in the voice of Greta Garbo. But the sense of erotic fascination is palpable.

In December 1941, Robert and Virginia took the unexpected decision to marry. America's entry into the war that month may have played a part, since De Niro was of draft age, but the decision was probably more quixotic. In their circle, marriages between sexually mismatched partners were almost the norm. Jackson Pollock entered a stormy marriage with fellow artist Lee Krasner, and even Robert Duncan took a wife – Marjorie McKee, the first, and probably only, woman with whom he had sex. They divorced a few months later, after an early pregnancy and abortion – a pattern not far from that which the De Niros would follow.

Three people effectively ran contemporary art in New York in 1942. They alone had the funds to buy and show new work. One was Alfred Barr, head of the Museum of Modern Art. The other two were an uncle and niece, who, far from enjoying any family feeling, were usually at each other's throats.

Marguerite 'Peggy' Guggenheim had expected to inherit millions when her father died in the sinking of the *Titanic* in 1912. Instead the money went mostly to her uncles. She received only $450,000, which was held in trust. Although still a fortune, her comparatively meagre inheritance influenced Peggy to hoard every dime, and earned her, over the years, a reputation for cheapness. Her friend David Hare called her 'avaricious to the point of comedy: the kind of person who goes from place to place, looking for the cheapest bottle of milk, and argues about who pays for the coffee'.

Drawn to the art world, Peggy moved to Europe and plunged into the bohemia of Paris and London. In London, at the urging of her friend Marcel Duchamp, she opened a gallery, Guggenheim Jeune, which showcased mostly Surrealist art. Few of its shows made money, but Peggy insisted artists sign a contract agreeing to let her buy any unsold pictures at $100 each – supposedly to encourage the artists but actually to build up a collection cheap.

In 1939 she fled to New York, towing the painter Max Ernst, whom she later married. Providently, she'd sent ahead her collection, part of which she put on show in 1942 at the gallery called Art of This Century which she'd had built on West 57th Street. Art of This Century had curved wooden walls, and lighting of startling originality. The paintings, unframed, hung on metal cantilever arms, each surmounted with a photograph of the eyes of the artist. Other canvases circulated on a conveyor belt, popping into sight for a few moments only.

Only a few blocks away, at 24 East 54th Street, Peggy's uncle, Solomon R. Guggenheim, had established the Guggenheim Foundation. It, and Guggenheim himself, were dominated by the Baroness Hilla Rebay von Ehrenwisen, his mistress.

Thirty years younger than he, Rebay relished the power conferred by her lover's wealth. Dressed like a Hollywood columnist in amazing hats and outfits that were like theatrical costumes, Hilla Rebay queened it over the Foundation and its shows, which mostly exhibited her own work and that of her friends. It was also Rebay's idea to christen their New York headquarters 'The Museum of Non-Objective Painting', a reproof to the Museum of Modern Art, which was just round the corner.

Shrewd artists played Barr, Rebay and Peggy Guggenheim against one another. Peggy could present shows, recommend artists to other gallery-owners, and even buy paintings – Jackson Pollock painted a mural for her Manhattan home – but she was notoriously slow to spend actual money. Rebay, on the other hand, had none of Peggy's taste, but offered cash to anyone who pledged allegiance to the Guggenheim Foundation. She funded the school set up on 8th Street by Hans Hofmann, who made no secret of his scorn for Peggy's speciality, Surrealism.

Rebay also disbursed monthly grants of $15 a head to Hofmann's best students, including De Niro and Admiral, for canvas and paints. The sum seems derisory today, but few modern artists in New York then made any money at all. Max Ernst's son Jim was considered lucky to be earning $25 a week in the Museum of Modern Art's stock room. Clement Greenberg, the country's most perceptive critic of emerging art, worked as a postal clerk, and wrote in his spare time. Jackson Pollock dressed department-store windows, silk-screened designs on scarves and umbrellas, and painted dials for aircraft instruments (with Elaine, the wife of Willem de Kooning, working next to him).

In 1942, Rebay offered both Pollock and De Niro full-time work at the Foundation, answering queries from the public. She even paid for the black suits the job required. The men sometimes had to sleep in the poorly-secured building overnight, but both were glad of the $35 a week.

Even aside from their sexual disparity, Robert and Virginia, each at the start of a career, and with little in common socially, politically or intellectually, were hardly credible as husband and wife, and even less likely parents. But towards the end of 1942 Virginia briefly took care of an infant cousin, and the experience, she explained later, stirred a maternal impulse she'd never suspected. Gripped briefly by this urge, she became pregnant, and on 17 August 1943 her first and only child, Robert Jr, was born. To avoid confusion with his father, he soon became 'Bobby', and carried that name all his life.

The 14th Street studio was no place to bring up a baby, so the De Niros found another loft at 220 Bleecker Street, in the heart of Greenwich Village, between McDougal Street and 6th Avenue. It occupied the entire top floor and, once a wall was knocked out to create two big studio spaces and a bedroom, made a comfortable, if draughty home. Scavenged radiators softened the chill. Baths were taken in a tin tub in the kitchen.

Young Bobby became used to being picked up, played with, but put down as the novelty palled. Family friends remember a child who was 'never coddled'. He was already marking out his own territory. There was plenty for him to discover in the cavernous space, and, left to his own devices, he probed every cranny. Curiosity became his strongest motivation. It would make him, in adulthood, supremely inquisitive, ready to spend months probing, observing, imitating.

Bobby never lost his enthusiasm for his parents' style of life, nor for the district where they raised him. He lives in a loft himself, and in 1997 boasted of his parents' prescience. 'They were aware of lofts, of industrial . . . whatever ya wanna call it; culture, blah blah . . . way before they became fashionable. SoHo was a lot different [then]. It was just a total industrial area that nobody thought of as a place to live. Warehouses, factories; stuff like that.'

Whatever the material drawbacks, the Village and its environs was *the* place to live if you were involved in the arts. 'Except for the museums, theatres and opera,' wrote the critic Lionel Abel, 'all that was humanly essential to the city was bounded by Bleecker and 14th Streets, by 2nd Avenue and Greenwich Street. There was no other residential section in New York.'

Bobby absorbed the same belief. Accepting the 1997 Municipal Art Society's Jacqueline Kennedy Onassis Medal for his efforts to help revive TriBeCa, the downtown Manhattan neighbourhood where he'd opened a pair of restaurants and established a film centre, De Niro told the audience, 'I just want to thank the Municipal Art Society for holding this downtown, because I really don't like to go above 14th Street.'

It's surprising that the marriage of the De Niros lasted as long as it did. On top of his sexual incompatibility with Virginia, Robert could be a trying companion. ' "Affability" is not a word that applies to Bob,' said his friend Barbara Guest, 'nor is "social".' Art critic Thomas Hess remembers him as 'tall, saturnine, given to black trenchcoats, his face sharp as a switchblade, with a temperament to match'. His moods swung between elation and black depression. 'Since I was a child,' he confessed later, 'I have felt in my heart two contradictory feelings, the horror of life and the ecstasy of life.'

Admiral, though equally intense, was more social. Friends, both artistic and political, thronged the apartment day and night, arguing, gossiping, flirting, plotting. She attracted men, in particular writers Manny Farber and Clement Greenberg. The most authoritative voice in American cinema criticism, Farber was always dropping in, since he was writing a screenplay with James

Agee, who had a fourth-floor walk-up apartment at 172 Bleecker Street.

In 1942, Peggy Guggenheim included some of Admiral's work in the Spring Salon for Young Artists at Art of This Century, and Alfred Barr bought one of her canvases, *Composition*, for the Museum of Modern Art. He only paid $100, but nobody else in her group had sold anything at all. Though Jackson Pollock was widely acknowledged as the brightest of the emerging New York School, it would be 1944 before Barr bought anything by him.

Virginia's success, coming at a time when Robert had sold nothing himself, strained the marriage still more. He succumbed increasingly to depression. On the wall of his studio, he scribbled two lines from a poem by nineteenth-century poet and photographer Charles Cros, friend of Rimbaud and Verlaine: '*Je suis un homme mort depuis plusiers années/Mes os sont recouvert par les roses fanées*' ('I have been a dead man many years/My bones are clothed in faded roses').

His resentment grew as it became clear that, despite her sale to MoMA, Virginia didn't seriously contemplate a career in art. After the birth of Bobby, she concentrated on making a living. Robert had no such concerns. He lived for painting, unworried whether he sold his canvases or not. He wouldn't achieve any kind of reputation until 1946, when Peggy Guggenheim gave him his first one-man show at Art of This Century, and another didn't come along until 1950.

As if the social and sexual differences between Robert and Virginia were not enough, they also faced the classic artistic gulf between the figurative and the abstract. 'For virtually his entire career,' wrote critic Peter Frank, 'Robert De Niro Sr painted recognisable images; still life objects, interiors, landscapes, the occasional religious subject, and, above all, figures.' *Composition* and the rest of Admiral's work was entirely abstract, and, given the prevailing movement away from Surrealism, more fashionable.

Being figurative placed De Niro, as one friend remarked, 'on the wrong side of the commercial divide'. In 1949, Clement

Greenberg would list De Niro, Pollock, de Kooning and Robert Motherwell as artists who 'must still waste valuable energy in the effort to survive as working artists in the face of a public whose indifference consigns them to neglect and poverty'. By then, however, Robert's finances were of less concern to Virginia, and to Bobby, because the De Niros were no longer living together.

CHAPTER THREE

My Father's Business

They are not girls. They are not boys. They can't help it.
They was born that way. Something in de throat.

Two old ladies commenting on homosexuals in Joel Schumacher's
screenplay for his film *Flawless* (1999), in which De Niro starred

As tensions increased in their marriage, Robert and Virginia
began seeing a Freudian therapist. 'Many artists who knew Hans
Hofmann,' recalls Barbara Guest, 'went to a particular shrink
whose patients (eventually) had terrible crises and breakdowns.
But he couldn't help them. He was a frustrated man – a failed
artist, who meddled.'

The therapist may have been Dr Lawrence Kubie, who claimed
to 'cure' homosexuals, and whose patients included such showbiz
figures as bisexual playwright and director Moss Hart. Following
their 'treatment', the De Niros agreed to separate, though since
adultery still represented the main grounds for divorce, they
decided, rather than air their sexual incompatibility in the courts,
to delay a formal dissolution of the marriage.

While his parents worked out new domestic arrangements,
Bobby was sent to his father's parents in Syracuse, where, despite
Robert's hostility towards Catholicism, Bobby's grandparents
had him baptised. Though Robert was furious, the gesture had
little real effect, since Bobby was almost immediately returned
to New York, and to his mother. Nevertheless, being 'officially'

Catholic would cement him even more firmly into the Italo-American culture.

Robert moved into a Greenwich Village studio, and immersed himself in the principles of Abstract Expressionism. What those principles were depended on who taught them. Art historian Lee Hall calls Abstract Expressionism 'an attitude, if not a proper philosophy, of art [which] pits the lonely and searching individual against the unknown (possibly unknowable) first forces of the universe, casting the painter in the role of voyager and seeker after truth. By courting accidents resulting from the manipulated collision of materials, by taking risks with the surprising imagery that results, and by exploring that imagery to discover new vision, the painter creates an order that embodies his or her quest. To the Abstract Expressionist, the process of painting is more valued than the product, the finished painting.' As an actor, Bobby would also conceive himself as a 'voyager and seeker after truth' whose work embodied the 'manipulated collision of materials' to achieve 'surprising imagery'.

Always a slow worker, Robert became slower still. For every canvas completed, he threw out a hundred, then reworked the survivors, often erasing the entire design before starting over. Despite this, his work changed little over the years. He shared Matisse's enthusiasm for North African subjects, and, when a magazine photograph of Moorish women posed in an elaborate interior caught his eye, began painting his own versions of it – but, with characteristic obsessiveness, continued to do so for twenty years. A driven search for 'perfect' colours gradually made his pictures brighter, but his canvases of the late forties feature the same roughly painted figures as those he exhibited four decades later.

'He had a few friends,' says Barbara Guest, 'but mostly was alone in the tremendously cluttered place in which he painted. Sometimes I saw him out walking, and a scene plays across the screen of my mind of the day I saw him, standing on the sidewalk, talking to a woman friend while he held his mongrel dog on a leash. It was a typical encounter, a repeated scene in his life. There was no social life of dinners etc. There were many parties he did not attend, or at which he showed up as if out walking the dog.' When he did arrive at a party, he was seldom a social asset. 'He was given to acid comments about the art scene,' says Guest. 'He preferred provocative conversations.' If he found a subject uninteresting, half-finished sentences would tail off into silence.

Virginia and Bobby remained in the Bleecker Street apartment. As long as Bobby was too young for nursery school, she took paying work she could do at home. For a while, she framed pictures at $1.25 an hour – not enough to maintain the loft, which in any event was about to be taken over by The Little Red Schoolhouse, an elementary school launched to give the children of Greenwich Village the sort of education demanded by radical parents. Virginia moved to a smaller apartment, at 521 Hudson Street, a building mostly of studios, where many painter friends rented space. She stayed there until she found a better place at 219 West 14th Street. The rent was high, at $50 a month, but the two-room apartment with its parquet floors and central heating was too tempting. Bobby would grow up and live most of his young adult life here.

When he was old enough, Virginia placed Bobby in the nursery school attached to Greenwich House on Barrow Street. Set up to provide arts training and a social centre to the downtown area, Greenwich House included music and pottery schools, as well as its kindergarten, which charged working mothers only $1.25 a month.

Starting at the nursery brought De Niro into contact for the first time with the Ethical Culture Movement, which ran a free kindergarten and various humanitarian projects in and around New York. Founded by Felix Adler in 1876, Ethical Culture offered a substitute for organised religion, founded on ethics and morality rather than dogma. Adler spelled out its four principles: '1. Every person has inherent worth; each person is unique. 2. It is our responsibility to improve the quality of life for ourselves and others. 3. Ethics are derived from human experience. 4. Life is sacred, interrelated and interdependent.' Though never particularly religious, De Niro, with Virginia's encouragement, would grow away from his grandparents' Catholicism towards the principles of Ethical Culture. When he married in 1976, it would be at the group's New York headquarters, and he remains an enthusiastic supporter of its activities.

Able to get out of the house for the first time since her separation from Robert, Virginia applied for work through the welfare system. Since employment offices routinely directed out-of-work artists to any job which, under the loosest possible definition, involved painting, she found herself decorating fabrics and assembling jewellery. Before she was married she had made pin money typing, and now she started again, typing manuscripts for writers, and editing and typing theses for students at the New School for Social Research, just around the corner on 12th Street.

With its left-wing ideology and funding from wealthy liberals like the Rockefellers, the New School was a haven for European intellectuals fleeing Hitler. Its University in Exile, founded in 1934, accommodated four hundred of them, including German theatre director Erwin Piscator and his wife, the Viennese dancer Maria Ley.

In Berlin, Piscator had directed the Volksbühne theatre, supported by the labour unions. His productions of Meyerhold and Brecht, often using a bare stage, or a few sets in the Constructivist style pioneered in Soviet Russia, with the addition of film or projected images, attracted much attention, not least from the Nazis, who dubbed his work 'degenerate'. (Piscator always claimed this charge, plus his Communism, led to his exile from Germany, though in fact the impetus was a paternity suit he looked certain to lose.)

Alvin Johnson, director of the New School, invited the couple to launch a programme of drama. Piscator immediately began hiring teachers, while his wife started dancing classes and a Saturday-morning theatre course for children.

Piscator was in his element at the New School. Dressed always in the most expensive silk and cashmere, white hair swept back to emphasise his leonine profile, he ruled the theatre department like a duke. Mel Brooks, later one of his students, parodied him in his film *The Producers* as the manic Nazi composer of the musical *Springtime for Hitler*.

Herbert Berghof, one of Max Reinhardt's actors who'd arrived in America during the thirties and worked with the Theater Guild, managed the acting course. Other teachers included theatre historian John Gassner, editor of the *Best Plays of the Year* anthologies, Leo Kertz, Lisa Jalowitz, Theresa Helburn, James Light and, most notably, Stella Adler, who would become the most powerful influence on the young De Niro when he decided to become an actor.

When Piscator, under investigation in America for his Communist sympathies, returned to Germany in 1946, Maria Ley Piscator ran the New School's drama workshop until 1949. Virginia typed her manuscripts and, through her, got similar work from other foreign writers, notably military historian Ladislas Farago. She also found time to paint, and, like Robert, had a solo show at Art of This Century in 1946. Peggy Guggenheim also included some of Virginia's work at the 1947 Biennale in Venice, where she would shortly relocate permanently, along with her collection.

There was no money in art, however, and Virginia turned increasingly to writing. Her market was the most accessible one, the 'true detective' magazines. Lurid monthlies that filled the vacuum created by the demise of the old pulp crime magazines, they published accounts of real crimes, illustrated with original police photographs, augmented with gaudy art or posed photos, usually of terrified girls.

Detective World and *Underworld Detective* were edited by Lionel White, who wrote *Clean Break*, the novel on which Stanley Kubrick would base his first major success, *The Killing*, in 1956. (White's pseudonymous contributors included hard-boiled crime novelist Jim Thompson, who scripted Kubrick's film.) A typical *Detective World* article began: 'It was Wednesday, October 2, and deep autumnal tints were already visible in the foliage surrounding Harrison's aged courthouse.' This line, in fact, comes from 'Who Killed the 2 Sisters?' in *Detective World* for April 1952, credited to one 'Virgil E. La Marre', a near-anagram for 'Virginia Admiral'.

*   *   *

Robert's first solo show in May 1946 at Art of This Century attracted critical attention, and he even sold some paintings, though insisting the proceeds go straight to Virginia. Not that there was much, since he refused to sell to people whom he felt wouldn't appreciate his pictures. As late as 1989, when his son wanted to give Francis Coppola two canvases for his fiftieth birthday, Robert quizzed him at length about Coppola's character. 'You give it to someone, they put it in a closet,' he grumbled before relinquishing the pictures, which Coppola hung in the hotel suite he maintained permanently at New York's Plaza Hotel.

Virginia insisted that father and son spend as much time together as they wished. By osmosis, Bobby acquired many of his father's traits, including the tendency to leave sentences dangling, or to descend into moody silence. Neither set much store by what he wore, where he lived or how he behaved. And watching his father discard version after version of a composition instilled Bobby's conviction that 'near enough' was never good enough.

Years later, talking about her friendship with De Niro, Shelley Winters would create something of a furore by telling the *New York Times*, 'Bobby will never talk about what made him the way he is, but I suspect he must have been a lonely kid, that somewhere along the line he was brutalised.' If any psychological damage was inflicted on the young Bobby, his father's sexuality and depression must have played a central part in it. Acting may well have been a form of self-therapy, as well as an attempt to come to terms with his ambivalent feelings towards Robert.

'His father was important to him,' says French actor and director Robert Cordier, who knew the young De Niro, 'and his father was not recognised, and I think Bob got to thinking, "I owe him one." I think becoming famous was very important to him to pay back his father. That has a lot to do with his drive. I think that has a lot to do with Bob's will to succeed.'

Asked as an adult if he was close to his father, De Niro said, 'Close? In some ways I was very close to him, but then . . .' He was unable to go on, and his eyes filled with tears. When Robert died, Bobby preserved his studio as a shrine, in exactly the same disorder as when his father was working there. He still visits it from time to time. De Niro also dedicated his first film as director, *A Bronx Tale*, to his father, who died in 1993, the year it was released.

Uninterested in comfort, Robert moved frequently as space became vacant north and south of Houston Street, on Great Jones Street, West Broadway or Bleecker. 'He had these dank lofts in NoHo and SoHo at a time when nobody wanted to live in those areas,' says his son. 'Often he was the only tenant who wanted to live in the building.'

Bobby got used to being sent out to Washington Square with a book if his father wanted to work. On occasion he'd take him along if he was teaching; his students were sometimes Wall Street brokers, and the class took place in a loft in the business district. On such occasions, he'd give Bobby paints and brushes. 'He'd paint,' said Robert shortly. 'He had a good sense of colour.' From time to time he'd ask him to pose – 'but when you're a kid,' recalled Bobby, 'the last thing you want to do is sit still for a long time.' Rigorous even about pictures of his own son, Robert preserved only one image of Bobby, a superficially casual charcoal sketch.

When they did go out together, it was often to Washington Square, where they would rollerskate or play ball games. But Robert's real enthusiasm emerged when the two went to the movies. First-run cinemas were too expensive, so they generally saw films at Variety Photoplay in the East Village, Loew's Commodore at 6th Street and 2nd Avenue, or the Academy of Music on 14th Street – all second-run and revival houses offering two features for only fifty cents. *Camille* or *Ninotchka* was usually showing in at least one of them, and Bobby got to see these and other Garbo performances a number of times. Back home, he acted out his favourite scenes for his mother.

Camille fascinated Robert – not the first gay artist to find it inspirational: Jean Cocteau called it 'a bad film raised to the heights by the extraordinary presence of Miss Greta Garbo'. To

Robert, its impassive star embodied a spiritual purity. She was like a secular version of the Madonna he'd rejected with his abandonment of Catholicism. He made sculptures of Garbo, and devoted a series of canvases to her first sound film, *Anna Christie*, while lines from *Camille* inspired a dozen poems, and stills from the same film a decade of drawings.

Later, Bobby acknowledged that his idea of great acting derived from watching performers like Robert Mitchum and particularly Montgomery Clift, while his influences for comedy were knockabout ex-vaudeville comics Bud Abbott and Lou Costello. He admired Walter Huston, particularly as the half-crazy old prospector in *The Treasure of the Sierra Madre*, though he disliked Humphrey Bogart, in that film and almost everything else; always playing himself, Bogart seemed the antithesis of everything Bobby thought an actor should be.

Instead, De Niro followed the path of those protean Hollywood stars of the thirties who won their reputations, and their Oscars, by transforming themselves for each role, losing themselves behind heavy accents, crêpe whiskers, wigs, tattoos, scars, false noses, heavy glasses, a shuffle, a limp, a stoop.

Every generation throws up one or two of these performers. Lon Chaney fulfilled this role for Hollywood in the twenties. Christened 'The Man of a Thousand Faces', he created definitive versions of *The Hunchback of Notre Dame* and *The Phantom of the Opera*, and a gallery of scarred pirates, grinning Asians, clowns, crooks and cripples. 'Don't tread on a spider!' ran one Hollywood slogan. 'It might be Lon Chaney.'

De Niro probably never saw Chaney. He did, however, see Muni Weisenfreund, alias Paul Muni, the graduate from New York's Yiddish theatre who could play an Italian emigrant gangster in *Scarface*, a gaudy Chicano club-owner in *Bordertown* and a crusading miner in *Black Legion*, but just as easily transform himself into a French author for *The Life of Emile Zola* or Benito Juarez, the politician of Indian descent who founded the modern Mexican state, for *Juarez*.

Once De Niro became an actor, he scorned Muni, calling his performance in Howard Hawks' 1932 *Scarface* 'awful. He's the biggest ham. It was so hammy. You could say he was possibly a great stage actor, but a lot of his movies were over the top. Like *I am a Fugitive From a Chain Gang*.' Yet Muni remains the thirties screen actor whom De Niro resembles most.

Like Chaney and Muni, De Niro would always avoid period pictures or the great classical roles. To play Othello or Don Juan would be like putting on a costume thousands had worn before. But to transform yourself into someone entirely new – that was genius. Chaney's insistence on strapping his calf to the back of a thigh to simulate amputation, on duplicating blindness by pressing the membrane of an egg to his eyeball, or screwing wire rings into his eye sockets to create the crazy glare of a burned face in *The Phantom of the Opera*, would all find resonances in De Niro's work. His Jake La Motta in *Raging Bull* is a Chaney performance. And the comment a contemporary writer made of Chaney, 'To endure pain for his art gave him a strange pleasure,' applies equally well to De Niro.

'He developed a thick-muscled neck and a fighter's body,' Pauline Kael wrote of De Niro in *Raging Bull*, 'and for the scenes of the broken, drunken La Motta he put on so much weight that he seems to have sunk into the fat with hardly a trace of himself left. What De Niro does in this picture isn't acting, exactly. I'm not sure what it is. Though it may at some level be awesome, it definitely isn't pleasurable.'

Impressive as she found the effort, Kael felt it failed in what it set out to achieve. 'De Niro seems to have emptied himself out to become the part he's playing and then not got enough material to refill himself with: his La Motta is a swollen puppet with only bits and pieces of a character inside, and some semi-religious, semi-abstract concepts of guilt.'

Marcello Mastroianni dismissed De Niro's performances as the opposite of true acting: 'By nature, the actor is a kind of wonder who can allow himself to change personalities. If you don't know how to do this, it's better to change professions. I think it's ridiculous to imagine that to play a taxi driver or a boxer you have to spend months and months "studying" the life of cabdrivers and the weight of fighters.'

But 'Chaney' roles appeal to shy actors, because the performer plays them effectively alone. And there was no doubting De Niro's shyness. Speaking about his days as an acting student, he remarked, 'An actor is sensitive as it is – shy – and the whole point of you doing this [acting] is that you want to express yourself. There's a kind of thread there as to why people become actors.' De Niro would become famous, or notorious, as an actor with whom there was little or no give-and-take. 'I think playing opposite De Niro is a challenge for any actor,' says Cybill Shepherd, 'because he is a master of underplaying.' Actors strain to make some contact with him in a scene, and usually fail. Without any way of knowing what goes on in his mind while the camera rolls, they emerge from the experience aware only that they have come off second-best.

De Niro never socialises with fellow actors between scenes, and they in turn avoid him, instinctively giving him the space justified by his huge investment in the created personality. Over the years, De Niro learned to encourage this reaction by only appearing on the set for his own scenes, and remaining aloof from the rest of the cast, who are instructed not to talk to him or even meet his eye. Paradoxically, he found anonymity in the least likely of all places – the spotlight.

In 1954, Jean-Paul Sartre published *Kean*, updating Alexandre Dumas's play about the early-nineteenth-century actor of whom Coleridge had said that to see him act was 'like reading Shakespeare by flashes of lightning'. Sartre's Edmund Kean has become a victim of his virtuosity, and can no longer distinguish between real life and acting. Halfway through a performance as Othello, he scrapes off his make-up and roars his frustration to the audience in an outpouring of the anger that is never far below the surface of any actor's performance.

Such rage was a crucial component of all the roles played by actors like Chaney and Muni. Adopting the character of another man gave one a licence to unleash one's darker impulses. To play Quasimodo without swinging madly from the bells of Notre Dame, or to embody the phantom without burning down the Opera, was inconceivable. Though Muni would always be remembered for the machine-gun shootout that ended *Scarface*, even his roles as Zola, Juarez and Louis Pasteur demanded a final scene in which, occupying centre stage, the actor stormed, ranted or cajoled for ten bravura minutes.

Rage is Robert De Niro's gift to the cinema. Without it, he would be little more than the proficient performer of *The Last Tycoon*, *Falling in Love*, *We're no Angels* and his many other flops. But it is when he injects into such roles the fury unleashed in *Taxi Driver*, *Raging Bull* or *The Deer Hunter* that we see De Niro at his most effective.

'He appears to have a tremendous potential for violence,' says Kenneth Branagh. 'He is one of the more frightening people I have met in my life, and you seriously wouldn't want to cross him. It's just that moment where perhaps you've said something and his eyes just "go". It's not so much the physical threat as the potential for him to be very, very free with whatever aggression he might feel. You wouldn't want to get in the way of that. I've seen him in a couple of situations where the smile just drops, and you really don't want to be there when that happens. You would imagine that you would basically just get thumped.'

Greenwich Village provided a rich environment for the maturing Bobby. Instead of grocers and butchers, the shops at street level were jazz clubs and cafés. In summer, music poured from open windows. Cultural diversity ruled. Émigrés and refugees from Germany and Austria mingled with Italians and Jews who were migrating from the old ghettos into the Village. None of this was lost on the young Bobby, who would develop an instinct for the styles of speech, clothing and movement that differentiated one class, race or calling from another.

For the summer holidays, he went upstate to Syracuse, to stay with his father's family, acquiring the cadences of Italian English that he would employ in so many of his films. Coaching him for his role in *Cape Fear*, an expert in accents would label his natural way of speaking 'Italian-American', and his career would be hampered when, playing an Italian in his first major Hollywood film, he would be so convincing that people assumed he was imported from Italy for the role.

In Syracuse, he also brushed against organised crime – an Italian industry in the US. In 1950, Senator Estes Kefauver, enquiring into the rackets, made public the already widely-acknowledged existence of 'a nationwide crime syndicate, a loosely organised but cohesive coalition of autonomous crime "locals" which work together for mutual profit. Behind the local mobs that make up the national crime syndicate is a shadowy criminal organisation known as the Mafia.' None of this came as news to the large Italian communities of Syracuse and Rome, where Mafia *caporegimes* milked the construction and restaurant businesses in which so many Italians worked. When De Niro got round to playing the young Vito Corleone in *The Godfather II*, he didn't need to look far for inspiration.

Back in New York, Bobby started in the public school system, at PS.41, just round the corner on West 11th Street. He stayed there until the fifth grade, when he was about eleven. Through her work for Maria Ley Piscator, Virginia got him into the Saturday-morning acting classes of what was now called the Erwin Piscator Workshop. It was here, aged ten, that he played his first dramatic role, the Cowardly Lion in a production of *The Wizard of Oz*. He also appeared in a version of Chekhov's *The Bear* which toured some New York schools. But there was no over-night conversion to acting. 'I stayed for a few years,' De Niro says off-handedly of the Workshop. 'I wasn't interested.'

At eleven, he would normally have moved from PS.41 to IS.71. Instead, Virginia enrolled him in the Elizabeth Irwin High School on Charlton Street, the high school of the Little Red Schoolhouse. The 'Red' in Little Red Schoolhouse uncompromisingly indicated its political leanings. Many of its teachers were blacklisted. Fire-brand folk-singer Woody Guthrie performed there. A typical school excursion was a week in a steel town. Parents and children marched in the May Day parade, sometimes with a red flag fluttering from the pram that carried their youngest child.

To counter accusations that its curriculum was too 'liberal', Elizabeth Irwin pushed to get its students into reputable colleges.

For Bobby, this was bad news. School bored him. He disliked books, preferring comics, from which he learned to read. Virginia didn't dissuade him. She felt children should develop at their own speed, finding naturally the things that interested them. From the age of ten, Bobby was allowed to choose his own clothes. Virginia also sent him briefly to Boy Scout camp, but he disliked the experience so much he never repeated it.

Virginia was busy with her work, her political activities – she continued to write, edit and produce left-wing propaganda – and her personal life. Though she never remarried, she had a succession of lovers, among them the film critic Manny Farber, who wrote for the *Nation*, the *New Republic*, the *New Leader* and other left-wing magazines. Both painter and writer, Farber, unlike Robert, was charismatic, politically savvy, and un-ashamedly heterosexual. Bobby deeply resented the relationship. Years later, when Farber approached him at a party and reminded him he'd once been his mother's boyfriend, De Niro fled.

Bobby remained at Elizabeth Irwin through seventh and eighth grades, but never looked a likely candidate for college. Though he was not stupid, his perfectionist nature drove him to recopy his work over and over, as his father did his canvases, while the rest of the class moved on.

Virginia volunteered him as a model for an article she was writing for *Glamour* magazine on the differences between public and private schooling in New York – Bobby representing the 'funky' face of the public-school system. A photograph illustrating the article shows a slightly dumpy Bobby with tousled hair in a zippered leather jacket, crumpled trousers, shirt pulled outside the belt, hands shoved in the pockets. He regards the camera sideways with a gaze not so much belligerent as indifferent.

As he entered adolescence and shed his childish plumpness, other aspects of life in Greenwich Village attracted Bobby's attention. The area was changing. In particular, Italians moving in from the West Side were squeezing the Anglo community of the downtown area, just as they, in turn, would be squeezed by the invading Chinese two decades later.

Despite a solitary nature, Bobby was drawn to the Italian and Sicilian youth gangs now appearing on the streets. Though his skin was pale, he could have been one of them. The gangs also radiated superiority and power. Being in the headlines made the street kids bolder. Knives and guns became more evident, the swagger more pronounced.

De Niro affected the gang members' silk shirts, their slim-cut leather jackets, the hat tilted on the back of the head. His friends nicknamed him 'Bobby Milk' because of his pallor. At seventeen, he was recognisably a cadet version of Johnny Boy, the street punk he would play in *Mean Streets*.

Johnny Boy likes explosions. He blows up a mailbox, and throws dynamite from the rooftops. As a kid, Bobby acted as a 'steerer' for one of the Chinese firecracker vendors across Mott Street. Kids in the Village preyed on boys who turned up from the suburbs in search of the giant cherry bombs and other danger-ously large fireworks employed by the Chinese at their festivals. In *Mean Streets*, Martin Scorsese would show two of these inno-cents being ripped off by a couple of streetwise Village guys.

On Christmas Day 1970, when Brian De Palma introduced De Niro to Scorsese, each would recognise the other from his teenage gang affiliations. But De Niro was never part of a gang, any more than was Scorsese, who only moved to the Lower East Side in 1949, when his garment-maker father went broke, and who, as a lifelong asthmatic, observed street life mainly from his bedroom window.

That said, both recognised and respected the reality of street crime. When he made *Sleepers* in 1996, De Niro still recalled Hell's Kitchen, the tough area near the intersection of 42nd Street and Broadway: 'It was Italian, Irish, Latin, Puerto Rican. When I was growing up downtown, it was a neighbourhood where you would get hassled, where you wouldn't go.' Both he and Scorsese were accustomed to being beaten up, and knew better than to complain to the law. Only by enduring punishment and saying nothing could they earn the respect of the tough guys who ran the streets.

As a kind of protective coloration, De Niro began going to

Sunday mass with his new friends at the old St Patrick's Cathedral on Mulberry Street. For the new generation of Italian-Americans, that church had a special significance, reflected in the way their film-makers would adopt it as a location. Scorsese, who served there as altar boy, used it for the climax of his first film, *Who's that Knocking at my Door?*, as did Francis Coppola for the christening that closes *The Godfather*.

It incensed Robert to see his son embracing both the religion he'd abandoned and a lifestyle he thought dangerous. 'When I was about thirteen,' recalled Bobby, 'we ran into each other in Washington Square Park. I was with a group of street kids, and he got fairly worked up, going on and on about bad influences.'

De Niro relived the moment years later when he made his debut as director with *A Bronx Tale*, about a man trying to prevent his young son idolising a career criminal. As Ray Vitti, the gang boss in *Analyze This*, he also cites a similar event from his own fictitious childhood.

As if to prove that her artistic ambitions had never been more than infatuation with Greenwich Village bohemia, Virginia thrived as a businesswoman. She started a small service, called Academy, which turned manuscripts into camera-ready copy for printers. Half of the 14th Street apartment became her office, where she installed a couple of typewriters and a Varitype machine. Before long, she had a staff of ten, most of whom, in defiance of the lease, worked in the apartment. Bobby became so angry with the noise of the machines that he threatened to throw them out the window. Virginia took the hint, and in 1957 moved everything into an office at 68 7th Street.

In 1953, the De Niros finally divorced. Bobby continued to spend time in Robert's studio, but, inevitably, both recognised a growing gap. At this time they sometimes browsed Village bookshops, like Robert Wilson's Phoenix Bookstore on Cornelia Street, which specialised in literary first editions. Wilson, a friend of W.H. Auden and the bibliographer of Gertrude Stein, was a congenial conversationalist, and De Niro Sr relaxed in his company, even drawing a cover for one of Wilson's catalogues.

'I saw him often,' recalls Wilson. 'He was shy more than anti-social. He came into the shop often, at least once with the teenage son. He was gay, and came in quite often, mainly, I think, because he had an obvious crush on my then-assistant Marshall Clements. He was not a collector of rare books, but was a reader of Gertrude Stein's works, and often bought one of her books for reading purposes.'

Marshall Clements too remembers De Niro Sr well. 'I first met Bob Sr and Virginia Admiral in 1960 or '61, along with others of their circle, through the painter, Nell Blaine, who often gave parties for her old friends, mostly fellow painters. So by the time I started working at the Phoenix Book Shop with Bob Wilson in 1968, Bob De Niro and I were old acquaintances. He lived nearby in the Village, and when he found out I was working at the shop, he frequently stopped by to visit.

'Bob Wilson always thought this was because of some sexual interest in me, but I doubt this. What he was interested in, other than simply friendly chat, was using me as a model. I had been a dancer in the years 1950–1960 and was still in pretty good physical shape. I admired his work and found him a very pleasant, gentle and intelligent man, one completely focused on his painting. If he had any problems with his sexuality, they were never evident to me, and though we were both gay and obviously knew this about one another, the subject never came up in our conversations. He also had a wonderfully subtle wit and was childishly pleased when one "got" it and laughed. There was an air of sadness about him, and as far as I know, he was a lonely man, which I believe was also a reason for his frequent visits to the bookshop.'

Through the early fifties, Robert came to feel he'd reached an impasse in his work. Though the Charles Egan Gallery in New York City gave him one-man shows in 1952, 1953 and 1954, after which he switched to the Poindexter Gallery, which showed him in 1954, 1955 and 1956, he became convinced his career was marking time. He needed fresh inspiration, and friends like Tennessee Williams urged him to look for it in Europe.

Paris exercised a special attraction for De Niro. During his friendship with Anaïs Nin, he'd pumped her for information about the French capital and her meetings with artists like Picasso. In the spring of 1959, he arrived at the apartment of his friend Barbara Guest with a box of books, mostly French poetry. He was going to Paris, he explained, and wanted her to take care of them until he returned. Something final in his tone convinced her, however, that he believed the move to be permanent. Before his departure, friends threw a party on the boat that took him to France in April 1959, and Bobby attended – with what feelings one can imagine.

Bobby's grades at Elizabeth Irwin weren't good enough to keep him there, but since he showed some artistic talent, and had spent some months in the Piscator Workshop, the faculty suggested he apply for a scholarship to New York's High School of Music and Art. Students were required to submit some example of their creativity, and De Niro got in on his acting ability, but stayed only one sparsely-attended semester in 1959. He claimed that the phoniness of his fellow students, 'wearing sandals and playing guitars in Washington Square Park', repelled him. But such people can hardly have been strange to a kid born and raised in Greenwich Village. Probably he disliked having to travel uptown to school when all his life he'd been able to walk. He would also have found it demanding to take classes both in academic subjects and one's chosen creative area. After that, De Niro spent one semester at the Rhodes School on West 54th Street, but passed only three subjects then dropped out, his only explanation that 'it was a bad scene'.

After the High School of Music and Art, Virginia resignedly put him into IS.71, where he had been intended to go in the first place. But he did no better there, responding to the discipline and rigour of public education with truancy, inattention and a threat to strike a teacher. 'His idea of school,' his mother later complained, 'was just not to show up.'

She switched him to the fee-paying McBurney School on 23rd Street, attached, improbably, to the YMCA. Run like a British prep school, McBurney had an excellent reputation, but its curriculum and discipline didn't suit everyone. (Among those who'd found it uncongenial was J.D. Salinger, who flunked out of McBurney just before World War II. His experience there would find its way into *The Catcher in the Rye*.)

Having lagged behind, De Niro found himself in a class of younger kids, which made him feel even more of an outsider. When summer arrived, and he was told to attend a catch-up school if he wanted to come back in 1960, he rebelled. Instead, he told his mother, he wanted to spend summer in Europe, visiting his father. On his return, he promised, he would tell her what he'd decided to do with his life. She would not, he assured her, be disappointed.

Before he left, Bobby set the pattern of his future life when he made a brief appearance in television drama, his first experience of the media that were to fill his adult life. The soap opera *Search for Tomorrow* was broadcast live from New York, and the six-teen-year-old De Niro became one of many kids who had bit parts and walk-ons that season.

De Niro spent four months hitching around Europe, starting in Paris. His father painted him a sign in English and Italian: 'Student Wants Ride'. The sign, and his charm, took him to Venice, Rome and Capri, where he met French actress Michele Morgan. Bobby told her his father was a famous artist in Paris who was eager to paint her portrait, but De Niro Sr gruffly turned down the job: 'I wasn't interested in doing her portrait, or anyone else's.'

Back in New York in March 1960, Bobby saw the Cole Porter/ Frank Sinatra musical *Can Can* with a friend. As they left the cinema, De Niro surprised his companion by telling him, 'I'm going to do that.'

'What?' his friend asked.

'Act in the movies.'

The friend laughed, and thought nothing of it. But, months earlier, when Bobby returned from Europe, he'd surprised Virginia with the news that, rather than going to college or even graduating from high school, he had decided to train as an actor instead.

CHAPTER FOUR

Stella

I've never been one of those actors who has touted myself as
a fascinating human being. I had to decide early on whether
I was to be an actor or a personality.

Robert De Niro

Why did De Niro decide at the age of seventeen to become an
actor?

Withdrawn, ill-educated, physically unremarkable, he was
nobody's idea of a stage or screen star. And it's perhaps there
that the answer lies. How does a timid person express himself
except by taking on another personality? Lon Chaney's parents
were deaf-mutes, with whom he could communicate only via
sign language – a situation analogous to De Niro's upbringing
by two people preoccupied with their own agendas.

Theatre was undergoing drastic redefinition when De Niro
entered it. Acting and writing, regarded as professions before
World War II, with formal structures, standards and requirements, were being invaded by people stronger on feeling than
technique. The new writers, in the words of Jack Kerouac to
Truman Capote, 'didn't want to get it right; just get it *written*'.
Capote's scornful response, 'That's not writing, Jack. That's *type*
writing,' summed up the horror of classical stylists at such *ad*
hoc creativity; but they were in the minority. By the early fifties,
anyone who felt they'd like to try acting, singing or writing could
usually find a platform.

Performance in particular became a magnet to the maladjusted. The actor was no longer the rock-jawed hero of Victorian melo-drama, but a human being, weak and fallible. Producers and writers began to speak of 'American' and 'European' acting. American acting stressed flair and feeling, European acting text and technique. 'The big difference is that in England we have a great tradition of theatre,' says Kenneth Branagh, who in 1993 directed, produced and acted with De Niro in *Mary Shelley's Frankenstein*. 'Most actors work through many different styles, from Shakespeare to Noël Coward to Harold Pinter, so you learn technique. The Americans are wonderful at being ordinary, at being real and gritty, and yet they have difficulty when technique is required. You ask an American actor to immediately turn on the tears and play a very emotional scene, and he will find it difficult.'

Working at the Moscow Art Theatre through the 1920s, Kon-stantin Stanislavski developed a system of mental exercises and games for actors to help them access the feelings that paralleled the emotions of the characters they played. Books like *Building a Character* elaborated his system. It never had a formal name, but came to be called in theatre circles just 'the Method'.

Until 1949, while the Piscators remained in charge at the New School, two of his teachers were edgy, vivacious Stella Adler, daughter of a distinguished family in the Yiddish theatre, and an irascible and opinionated little man named Lee Strasberg. Adler and Strasberg shared a rivalry that went back to 1931, when three producer/directors, Strasberg, Howard Clurman and Cheryl Crawford, broke away from New York's conservative Theater Guild to launch the Group Theater. The Group Theater presented plays in repertory, like European companies, playing them in rotation with the same company of actors who, as in Europe, worked to achieve a unified style of performance. Stella Adler, who married its co-founder Howard Clurman, became a star with the Group, of which Lee Strasberg was the acting ideologue.

In Strasberg's version of the Method, the performer built up a role by 'affective memory', tapping deep emotions and 'sense memories', which he or she used to create the character. To play comedy, one accessed happy memories; for tragedy, childhood traumas. Not everyone in the Group cared for this self-analysis. An actor in the grip of a primal Oedipal conflict, they argued, could hardly be expected to give a sensitive portrayal of Hamlet.

Convinced that Strasberg had got it wrong, Adler went to Paris in 1934 to study under Stanislavski. Her description of Strasberg's system surprised him. This was a version of the Method he'd long since abandoned. 'Affective memory', he explained, endangered both the mental health of the actor and the validity of the performance. Adler returned to New York in triumph with the news, but Strasberg shrugged. 'I don't teach the Stanislavski Method,' he said. 'I teach the *Strasberg* Method.'

In 1947, Cheryl Crawford, with director Elia Kazan and producer Robert Lewis, bought a converted Orthodox church on West 44th Street and opened the Actors Studio, where performers could practise 'American acting'. Here, with an audience of professional colleagues, they could try new things, and, probably, fail. But in the process of failure they would learn and grow. It was exactly the *milieu* Strasberg needed, and he jumped at the chance to become the Actors Studio's director.

From the start, Strasberg imposed a strict regime. Only performers could attend. It would be years before producers and directors were allowed in as guests. Doors were ritually locked before each session. All applicants had to audition, and most didn't make it. In 1955, out of the two thousand who tried, only two were admitted: Martin Landau and Steve McQueen. Once in, however, membership was for life, and the eight hundred 'anointed' members were regarded as a theatrical elite.

Adler set up in opposition at the New School, where she taught her version of the Method. Tennessee Williams was a student. So were Rod Steiger, Shelley Winters, Ben Gazzara and Marlon Brando, who became Adler's lover, as he had been the lover of almost every other woman in the school.

While Piscator remained, he preached Expressionism: exaggerated gestures, symbolic poses, movements that externalised emotion – 'Be big!'. Meanwhile, Stella in the basement was screaming at her students, 'Don't act! Stop acting!' But once Piscator returned to East Germany, Adler inherited undisputed control, pointedly renaming the school 'The Stella Adler Conservatory of Acting'. Her pronouncements became more dogmatic. 'You act with your soul,' she said. 'That's why you all want to be actors, because your souls are not used up by life.' At times, she approached *folie de grandeur*. Asked during a May Day parade if she could imagine living in a Communist state, she said she'd be happy to, providing it would crown her its queen.

Bobby drifted into classes with Luther James, an African-American director – hardly an obvious choice, given the racial tensions still persisting even in Manhattan. His mother didn't try to dissuade him from his decision. 'They were both supportive,' he says of his parents. 'They would never tell me, "No."'

De Niro's choice of a teacher clearly resonates with his subsequent preference for African-American wives and girlfriends. He'd been impressed by a 1960 Broadway stage version of Kyle Onstott's trashy sex-and-slavery novel *Mandingo*. Franchot Tone played opposite the young Dennis Hopper, whom De Niro had seen in *Rebel Without a Cause* with James Dean. Bobby went backstage to meet him. As the two were introduced for the first time, a beautiful girl came up to Hopper and asked a question about acting. Acting as a way of meeting girls? De Niro had never thought of that.

Bobby returned to the New School in 1960, where Stella Adler was totally in charge. By then, her *bête noire* was the Actors Studio, where Strasberg was expounding his version of the Method to an increasingly mesmerised acting community. 'She was always putting down the Actors Studio,' says De Niro. 'The Method thing – as opposed to the Conservatory of Acting.'

Unlike the Actors Studio, where people dressed as they liked, Adler's male students were required to wear white shirts, black trousers and black shoes, while the girls wore skirts, blouses with high collars, shoes with heels, and hair pulled back from their faces. When she entered each day, usually late, dressed in black, made up as if for a stage appearance, and flanked by two assistants, the students stood and recited, 'Good morning, Miss Adler. We are pleased to meet you and look forward to embarking with you on our journey to discover our art.' This ritual over, Adler took her place in a leather chair at the centre of the stage, with her assistants on either side, and the class began.

'She would be inspirational as a teacher for me,' De Niro said. 'There was a lot of pomp and splendour with her, but ... she was a good teacher. Very good. I always give her credit for having a big effect on me. [She talked a lot about] Stanislavski. *Building a Character*. I think that that was really very important. I thought it was important for any actor. I couldn't see how you wouldn't be made aware of that. [Acting] is not about neurosis; playing on your neuroses. It's about the character, and about doing that first: the tasks of the character. Not going on about it as if it was all about you and how *you* would do it. It was more about the character, being faithful to the text, the script.'

Adler cleansed the Method of psychoanalysis. 'Affective memory' was used sparingly, and only when the actor could find the character in no other way. Above all, the 'given circumstances' of a play, its plot and character, were the actor's fundamental concerns. Real acting, she stressed, lay in making choices – not in imposing your psychology on the character but finding the character and choosing the way you explored and illuminated that character. 'The talent is in the choices' became not only her catchphrase but that of the generations of students she trained.

Between 1960 and 1963, the Conservatory of Acting totally occupied De Niro. He had no right to be there, since he hadn't graduated from high school, but, subdued and diffident, he was conveniently invisible in the Conservatory's large classes. Charles Carshon, who taught 'Sight Reading', a class in audition techniques which De Niro later singled out as particularly useful, says, 'While I am very gratified that Robert De Niro remembered me, it is true that he was so self-effacing in those days that I had to confirm with a student with whom I am still in contact that he had indeed studied with me.' The most memorable thing about

De Niro to most people was his habit of getting around town on a bicycle.

'Stella Adler had a very good script-breakdown-and-analysis class that nobody else was teaching,' De Niro recalled. 'It was just a way of making people aware of character, style, period, and so on.' It appealed particularly to De Niro because it didn't involve getting up and performing in front of the class, as at the Actors Studio. 'People could sit down in a classroom as opposed to having to get up and demonstrate it,' he said.

De Niro loathed being forced to perform in public until he'd totally grasped a character, and reserved a particular distaste for a feature of the Actors Studio curriculum called 'Private Moment', when a student was asked to perform some trivial task as if doing so in the privacy of his home and not in front of a critical audience. At its worst, a 'Private Moment' could involve removing all one's clothes. Even at best, it usually made one look foolish.

'It was hard to get up,' De Niro said. 'You had to try to overcome that.' Teachers like Carshon helped him do so. 'At the end of the day, you've got to get up and do it. And the sooner you get to knowing you've got to get up and do it, the quicker you'll do it. I had this problem, where I was afraid to make a move. "You have to *feel* it," and all that. Carshon would say, "You've got to, sometimes, just . . . *jump in*," and that was true. If I just jumped in, took the leap, I'd arrive at the place where you thought you'd have to go.'

Echoes of Stella Adler's teaching ring through De Niro's work. Writer David Scott Milton, who went through the Conservatory about the same time, recalls, 'When we were at Stella Adler's, she had an acting exercise that went like this: she would call on each student and the student would have this line: "Are you talking to me?" She would have each student do it with several different adjustments: "Are *you* talking to me?" "Are you talking to *me*?" Not line readings, but adjustments; that is, character attitudes that determined the line reading. When I saw *Taxi Driver*, the De Niro in the mirror scene, it appeared to me that he was doing a reprise of the Stella Adler exercise, "Are you talking to *me*?"'

*   *   *

Among the people for whom De Niro auditioned in his last year at the Conservatory was a film student from Sarah Lawrence College casting his first feature. A film with New York actors, not Hollywood imports, was sufficiently novel to attract attention, even if, as was the case with *The Wedding Party*, both project and film-makers were erratic.

Though Sarah Lawrence was a women's college, the director was the dark, glowering Brian De Palma. De Palma, whose shark-like smile and aggressive manner telegraphed his inner torments – 'His sense of outrage is limitless,' said his mentor, Wilford Leach – came to film late. His first love was physics, but in 1958 he saw Hitchcock's *Vertigo*, which transformed his life.

As a student at Columbia, De Palma was accosted on campus by a courteous Southerner who asked if he'd ever thought of acting. Wilford Leach taught drama at Sarah Lawrence, and had come to Columbia looking for males to balance his all-female casts. Leach offered to let De Palma make films to use in his plays if he agreed to come, and De Palma signed up to do an MA at Sarah Lawrence after graduating from Columbia in 1962.

De Palma's Byronic character and taste for film violence drew many of the college's students to him, and he used some of them in his films. They included Jennifer Salt, daughter of blacklisted Hollywood screenwriter Waldo Salt; a wealthy young woman named Cynthia Munroe; and leggy, neurotic Jill Clayburgh. The product of a wealthy but dysfunctional family, Clayburgh was in psychoanalysis from the age of nine. De Palma also roped in his Columbia roommates Jared Martin and William Finley, and a handsome young blond actor named Gerrit Graham, who would figure in his career for many years.

In 1963, America's student film-makers were besotted with the *nouvelle vague*. De Palma suggested making a *film à sketches*, as some young French directors had done, each contributing a segment. De Palma planned a fantasy called *Fairy Tale*, while Munroe's contribution would be a story based on the riotous wedding of De Palma's friend Jared Martin. 'Then the whole thing fell apart,' recalls De Palma. 'Cynthia's story was basically the best, and we decided to do that one as a movie all by itself.' They called it *The Wedding Party*.

De Palma, Munroe and Leach boosted the screenplay to feature length, though most of it would be improvised. Munroe raised the money – often quoted as $100,000, though, from the look of the film, shot on black-and-white 16mm with a hand-held camera, a small cast and almost no crew, the real figure was probably a tenth of that.

The budget didn't allow for the best actors, so De Palma advertised in *Billboard* and *Variety*. Among those who turned up to audition was De Niro.

'He was very mild, very shy and very self-effacing,' De Palma recalls. 'Nobody knew him, he was only a kid of about nineteen. [He] came in about nine or ten at night. We gave him some material to read. He did it well and then we asked him to improvise, and he was extraordinary. Then he said he had something else he wanted to show us, something he was working on. He left the room and was gone about twenty minutes. We thought he'd changed his mind and gone home. Then the door flies open and he bursts in from nowhere and he does a scene from a play by Clifford Odets. It was like watching Lee J. Cobb. Personally De Niro may be shy and soft-spoken, but in character he could be anybody.'

The Odets monologue came from *Waiting for Lefty*. As cabbies at a union meeting argue and wait for their leader, Lefty, news comes that he's been murdered by management goons. Periodically, the narrative flashes away to examples of class oppression, including one manifestation of it that Odets knew well from his days on Broadway – a young actor auditioning for an indifferent producer. De Niro knew the play, since Stella Adler insisted her students study it. She'd starred in the Group Theater's production, of which Harold Clurman said ecstatically, 'It was the birth cry of the thirties. Our youth had found its voice.' De Niro too found his voice in Odets' words. De Palma was instantly convinced, and offered him the part for $50 – not, as De Niro assumed, $50 a week, but, as his mother confirmed when she read the contract, $50 for the entire role. The contract also promised a percentage of the profits, but as usual there were none.

The Wedding Party started shooting in the spring of 1963, on an estate on Shelter Island, at the eastern end of Long Island. The plot resembles *Meet the Parents*, in which De Niro was to have a hit almost forty years later. Charlie (Charles Pfluger), a Harvard student about to marry his rich fiancée Josephine Fish (Jill Clayburgh), arrives at her estate by ferry with his two friends, Cecil (De Niro) and Baker (John Quinn), who will act as ushers at the wedding.

Neither can understand why the tomcatting Charlie wants to get married, and one look at his prospective in-laws, a horde of elderly ladies in unfortunate hats, has Charlie doubting too. Invading Josephine's bedroom on the first night, he discovers her in neck-to-ankle flannel. When he suggests she slip into something lacy, she tells him, 'If you want lace, I'll give you a hankie.' Interruptions by an aged nanny also ruin the mood.

Half-convinced now that his friends are right, Charlie tries to sneak off the island, and when one of Josephine's old lovers, a wealthy Indian with a penchant for sail-planing, turns up, coaxes him to take her off his hands, even at the cost of going gliding with him. When this fails, he makes a drunken pass at a pretty cousin, but gets cold feet when she responds with enthusiasm. Finally, after being chased all over the island by his friends, he gives up and says yes.

As Munroe finished writing each scene, she and De Palma recorded it on tape. The actors used the tapes as the basis for improvisation, then passed back their versions for her to rewrite. When she wasn't writing, Munroe cooked the team's meals. De Palma doubled as runner, calling up people in his capacity as producer, then putting on a cap and mounting a motorbike to collect the item he'd demanded. The cast were asked to supply their own clothing, and even props. Neither Clayburgh nor Salt minded, but De Niro felt exploited, particularly when one such prop, a new suitcase, fell off the top of a car as it pulled into the mansion, and was damaged.

Leach and De Palma directed, with Leach having the deciding vote, usually after argument from the combative De Palma. Leach, later highly successful on Broadway with an updated version of Gilbert and Sullivan's *The Pirates of Penzance* and his productions of Shakespeare, strove for high production values, which the amateur crew and inexperienced cast could seldom achieve. De Palma felt Pfluger played Charlie in a superficial manner. For his part, Leach disliked the occasional references to movies, from *Singin' in the Rain* to *Psycho*, and the decision to introduce each segment with a silent-movie-style title card quoting from an imaginary marriage guide, 'The Compleat Bridegroom'. He also disliked De Palma's decision to undercrank the camera in the chase and driving scenes, giving the movie a Keystone Kops jerkiness.

As Cecil, comic relief of the trio of friends, De Niro had little to do. Arriving on the island struggling with a pile of sporting equipment, he bumbles about in the background, periodically taking part in rambling improvised conversations in which he and Baker first try to talk Charlie out of marriage, then into it. A drunken speech at the pre-wedding banquet that might have been his chance to shine is so badly post-synched that his words are mostly inaudible.

Periodically, production stopped as Leach returned to teaching. In one such break, in the summer of 1964, De Niro made another trip to Europe to see his father. De Niro Sr hadn't lingered in Paris, but had moved to Gravigny, west of the city, then to Saint-Just-en-Chevalet, in the centre of France, near Clermont-Ferrand, and finally to Baren, above the resort of Luchon, near the Spanish border, his base for excursions into Spain and to North Africa. But France hadn't proved the stimulant he'd hoped for, and Virginia could tell from his infrequent letters that her ex-husband was in trouble. She financed Bobby's trip, with the idea that he would bring him back.

Bobby spent an enjoyable few weeks in Paris, where he could lose himself in the small hotels of the Left Bank around the Odeon and the *Quartier Latin*. He took language classes at the Alliance Française and met his share of local expatriates, but had little success with the French, whose reserve almost equalled his own.

Convincing his father to return to New York was an uphill task. Though Robert had been shipping his canvases back to American galleries, sales were meagre. Bobby urged him to look for a gallery in Paris, but his father refused; the market for his work, he insisted, was in New York.

After that, Bobby took off on an extended search for his roots. He hitchhiked around Ireland for a fortnight, looking for his mother's family, but the country was thick with O'Reillys and he had no luck. Italy proved more fruitful, and he found cousins in Campobasso, sixty miles north-east of Naples. He also penetrated the Iron Curtain to visit Erwin and Marie Ley Piscator in East Berlin. When he returned to New York, it was with his father reluctantly in tow. Of that aspect of the trip, Bobby later told a friend, 'It was an absolute nightmare.'

CHAPTER FIVE

Sally, Candy, Andy and the Others

He can't do Shakespeare and he can't do comedy. How can you even begin to compare him with Brando?

Mario Puzo, author of *The Godfather*, on De Niro's acting ability

Editing *The Wedding Party* took years. Cynthia Munroe died, bequeathing the uncompleted film to Wilford Leach. Despite the delay, De Palma and De Niro remained friendly, even though De Niro was reticent, withdrawn, while De Palma, loud, sarcastic, with a genius for undiplomatic remarks, was the opposite.

Both came from Italian Catholic families but were raised in another faith, in De Palma's case Presbyterian. Both fell under the influence of charismatic fathers, in De Palma's case an orthopaedic surgeon. Just as De Niro had spent many hours watching his father work, De Palma sat in on his father's operations, establishing a lifelong preoccupation with blood and flesh. In both cases, the marriage of their parents collapsed, though De Palma's reaction to the break-up was characteristically extreme. He stalked his father, observing and recording his assignations with his mistress – an episode that appeared in his 1980 film *Dressed to Kill*.

In 1965 De Niro scored a role in a film which, though he is barely visible in his one scene, and the film was shown almost entirely in France, would reach the screen quickly, giving him his first official movie appearance.

Marcel Carné's great days had been in the thirties and during World War II, near the end of which he had made *Les Enfants du Paradis*. In 1965, with his career running down, he was happy to take on an adaptation of Georges Simenon's 1946 novel *Trois chambres à Manhattan*, which Jean Renoir had just abandoned after working at it, on and off, for a decade. Its hero, François, an actor, goes to New York to work on a television film after breaking up with his wife. In a bar he meets Kay, another lost soul whose flatmate has just left her. François and Kay start an affair. Maurice Ronet played François and Annie Girardot Kay.

Carné was given a week in New York to film some exteriors and 'atmosphere', including a scene in a Greenwich Village bar. Among the extras hired for a day was De Niro. It was not a particularly agreeable experience. 'I remember a bunch of other young actors hanging around,' he said, 'moaning and bitching, all made-up, with pieces of tissue in their collars; it was the kind of thing you always hear about actors – where they're just silly or vain, complaining back and forth, walking around primping, not wanting to get the make-up on their suits.'

But something about De Niro caught Girardot's eye. 'We chatted a little,' says the actress. 'And later, someone else on the film told me he had said I was "a good little guy". Years later, I was surprised when I met him at a party in Paris, and he reminded me that we knew each other already, from *Trois chambres*.'

In 1963, seventeen-year-old Jimmy Slattery from Massapequa Park, Long Island, began a course of hormone shots that would turn him into a woman. Taking the name Hope Slattery, he began haunting Manhattan's gay bars, and fell for Jackie Curtis, who, despite his cross-dressing, insisted truculently, 'I got balls under my ballgown and I don't care who knows it.' Curtis completed Jimmy's make-over with a new name, Candy Darling.

In 1968 Candy played a bit part in Andy Warhol's *Flesh*, then starred in *Women in Revolt*, contributing the unforgettable line,

'I'm young, I'm rich, I'm beautiful. Why shouldn't I sleep with my brother?'

Lou Reed immortalised Candy in his anthem of the Warhol years, 'Walk on the Wild Side', and Jackie, recognising star quality, volunteered to create a vehicle for her. Working day and night for a week, high on amphetamines, and inspired by the Hollywood stars of the forties whom Candy revered, in particular Lana Turner, he wrote a high-camp musical satire called *Glory, Glamour and Gold*, subtitled 'The Life and Legend of Nola Noonan, Goddess and Star'. Candy would play Nola, enduring every indignity men could inflict, including rape. Curtis also wrote parts for prominent drag queens like Holly Woodlawn, another graduate of the Andy Warhol *atelier*.

Ten men contributed to Nola's rise and fall, but nobody thought all of them could be played by the same actor until Bobby De Niro volunteered. Curtis claimed he 'begged' to be cast. 'He came over to the director's apartment where Candy, Holly Woodlawn and I were sitting around, and you would have thought he was crazy – *we* did.

'"I gotta be in the play! I gotta be in the play! Please! I'll do anything!"' he kept pleading.

'I said to him, "Ten roles?"'

'He said, "Yes. And I'll do the posters too – my mother has a printing press."'

The play perfectly suited a chameleon like De Niro. Curtis and Candy persuaded Warhol and his entourage to attend the opening at the tiny Bastiano's Cellar Studio in Greenwich Village on 7 August 1968. Andy called De Niro's performance 'a tour de force'. The *Village Voice* would write, 'De Niro made clean, distinct character statements in a series of parts which many actors would have fused into a general mush. De Niro is new on the scene and deserves to be welcomed.'

Actress Sally Kirkland was in Warhol's group at the opening, and went backstage to compliment De Niro. 'Do you know that you are going to be the most incredible star?' she told him.

To De Niro, Kirkland, tall, busty and blonde, seemed to live in the headlines. She'd just become the first actress to appear totally nude in a 'legitimate' play, the off-Broadway production of *Sweet Eros* by Terrence McNally. With 'Yippies' Abbie Hoffman and Jerry Rubin, she'd invaded the New York Stock Exchange and showered incredulous brokers with dollar bills. She also appeared naked on the cover of *Screw* magazine, riding a pig. Later, she moved to California, was ordained as a minister of the Church of the Movement of Spiritual Inner Awareness, and started teaching acting and relaxation technique, as well as playing occasional small roles in movies.

'He was unbelievably shy,' Kirkland says of De Niro. 'I thought perhaps I was embarrassing him. But I could tell that, more than anything, he wanted to believe it.' De Niro was still reticent with women. Traditionally, 85 per cent of theatre students are female, a fact which his most distinguished predecessor at the Conservatory, Marlon Brando, had exploited without scruple, but De Niro felt uncomfortable around his fellow students, and had no regular girlfriends. All his energy was directed towards performance. As one friend of the time, Diane Ladd, remarked, 'Bobby was hell-bent on being a success but not just a movie star. He didn't want to be a star. He wanted to be an actor.'

But Kirkland's compliments fell on fertile ground. Thereafter, De Niro would ring up and ask her, 'Do you really think I'm any good? Do you really?' His naked need for reassurance shocked some friends. A few years later, when his mentor Shelley Winters confessed she hadn't seen a preview of his film *Bang the Drum Slowly*, De Niro hung up on her.

The acquaintance with Kirkland ripened into a friendship that would influence De Niro's career. 'We were very, very close friends then in that whole time frame,' Kirkland says. 'I think he liked me because I had always been very social and he was always shy. I really thought he was a genius and I told everyone. I was always telling people, "Hire Robert De Niro." He was always very intense. If you pushed his buttons, you'd know it. He's Italian. He has that caution. He seemed to know that because of my work with Strasberg and Shelley Winters, I could match his intensity, and I was forgiving of it.'

Both ambitious, they spent hours in the De Niros' 14th Street apartment rehearsing, mostly in the kitchen. Kirkland's eccentricity resonated with the fury on which De Niro drew for his best work. 'We had so much rage and energy in us,' she says. 'We would go at each other, have knockdown fights – kitchen-sink-drama-style.'

Already De Niro had formulated his theory that one had to 'earn the right' to play a role, either by detailed research or by transforming one's appearance. When a scene demanded a costume, he had plenty to choose from. 'Bobby had this walk-in closet,' says Kirkland. 'It was like going into a costume room backstage of a theatre. He had every conceivable kind of get-up imaginable – and the hats! Derbies, straw hats, caps, homburgs.'

Well into the eighties, De Niro browsed the flea markets and thrift shops of the Lower East Side, collecting all sorts of clothing – because 'costumes can look too created'. It was to pay off – notably on *Raging Bull*, where a cheap two-toned jacket gave him the clue to the character of Jake La Motta.

De Niro got interested in photography, and offered to make a photographic record of his father's canvases. He also took a professional interest in his own portraits. 'Bobby had this composite [photograph] he'd carry around with him to auditions,' recalls Sally Kirkland. 'Twenty-five pictures of himself in various disguises. In one, he was like this IBM executive, in another, a professor with glasses and a goatee, in another a cab driver – to prove to casting directors he wasn't an exotic. And he'd always have a stack of paperback novels with him too – ideas for characters he might play, might turn into screenplays for himself. He was totally focused on his work.'

Casting director Marion Dougherty, a friend of many years, also remembers De Niro's portfolio of pictures. 'One of them, I remember, was particularly striking. He was made-up as an eighty-year-old man. In other shots, he was wearing costumes of all kinds. I had never seen anything like that in any of the portfolios young actors carry around, which are for the most part glamour shots.'

De Niro's degree of preparation went well beyond simply putting on costume and make-up to have his portrait taken. David

Scott Milton, who created the original material for the 1971 film *Born to Win*, in which De Niro had a small part, remembered how he turned up for his first interview with a thick 'character' book, an album of pictures showing him in various make-ups and outfits.

'Now, it was common practice for actors in those days – as it's done even today – to work up a series of character photos. But Bobby had done more than that: he had actually worked on the characters. He told me he had done this for Stella Adler's classes, worked up fully-drawn characters, not just character photos: dozens of them.'

Just how much costume and make-up meant to De Niro emerged more than thirty years later, when he revealed that he'd hoarded every major item of wardrobe from all his films, a collection that, in the year 2000, comprised 2600 costumes and five hundred items of make-up and props.

To find inspiration in a costume isn't in itself odd, but to hoard them distinguishes De Niro from the majority of movie actors, who attempt to remove barriers between themselves and the audience rather than erecting them. Once again, it's behaviour one would expect from actors of an earlier tradition, like Chaney, Muni and such character comics as Bert Lahr. John Lahr wrote of his father, 'Our small, sunless 5th Avenue apartment was full of Dad's disguises, which he'd first used onstage and in which he now occasionally appeared on TV. The closet contained a woodsman's props (axe, jodhpurs, and boots); a policeman's suit and baton; a New York Giants baseball outfit, with cap and cleats. The drawers of an apothecary's cabinet, which served as a wall-length bedroom bureau, held his toupees, starting pistol, monocle, putty noses, and make-up.' In an odd coincidence, De Niro's first acting role was also the one that made Lahr famous – the Cowardly Lion in *The Wizard of Oz*.

De Niro's interest in costumes and transformation, as well as demonstrating again his roots in nineteenth-century theatre and the Hollywood of the thirties, shows how much, despite his many friends at the Actors Studio, his sympathy lay with Adler's theory, not Strasberg's. Strasberg performers shunned costumes. Nor did his Method stress physical transformation. Marlon Brando, whether playing the Emperor Napoleon or a beat-up-boxer-turned-dockworker, was always recognisably Brando.

Actors Studio performers spoke of their body as their 'instrument' – a device which, though capable of many tunes, remained physically untransformed. De Niro, by contrast, thrived on transformation. None of his outfits, however, were costumes that might be used in classical roles: no doublets, no cloaks, no togas. Except for the reformed eighteenth-century slaver Mendoza in *The Mission*, De Niro has never played a period role. Even Martin Scorsese couldn't persuade him to play Jesus in *The Last Temptation of Christ*, De Niro explaining that he would always feel uncomfortable in robes.

In his early twenties, De Niro spent some time in psychoanalysis, the better to understand his conflicted attitude to his parents and his need to hide himself in invented characters. He was also helped by Kirkland to deal with his anger. 'I taught him yoga,' she said, 'even though I have no idea if he ever practised it again. We had a group of actors, sort of an actors' co-op group, with him, Raul Julia, James Keach, myself; we all hung out at Raul's house with his wife in the late sixties.' Many years later, when Kirkland joined the West Coast branch of the Actors Studio in Los Angeles as a teacher, De Niro appeared as a guest speaker. A student asked, 'Mr De Niro, how do you relax?', and De Niro pointed to Kirkland and said, 'Talk to her.' But Bobby was seldom relaxed. When Kirkland asked Virginia what drove her son, she was in no doubt. 'Will,' she said shortly. 'Force of will.'

Despite his success in *Glory, Glamour and Gold*, De Niro didn't find it any easier to get parts. He went on the road through the Southern states in 'dinner theatre', where the audience sat at tables and ate a meal before the show, with the performers acting as waiters and, also like waiters, dividing up their tips. De Niro always passed this off as 'good experience', but it must have galled him, as it galled most actors.

French actor/director/writer Robert Cordier met De Niro through Barry Primus, another New York actor, a few years older than De Niro, who became, and has remained, one of Bobby's closest friends. Cordier was casting an off-Broadway play. 'I had a friend called Steve McQueen,' he says, 'who had been unknown in Greenwich Village, and I thought he would be great to play the lead. I went to parties with Steve. He wangled himself into the Actors Studio. Then somebody said, "There's this kid. He's wonderful. He takes classes with Stella Adler. He's the son of this painter Bob De Niro, and he's quite a comer." I was seeing actors, and Barry Primus took an audition. Then he said, "I have this friend, Bob De Niro, do you want to see him too?"'

Cordier didn't audition De Niro on that occasion. 'I had done the play,' he says. 'It had gotten good reviews and Barry had been noticed and signed up for the lead in *The Changeling* at Lincoln Center. I was at Max's Kansas City and this guy came and tapped on my shoulder and said, "You never called me for the play that Barry was in." It was Bob De Niro, and he said, "I'm gonna give you my phone number and I want you to call me the next time there's something."'

Well-known Living Theater actor Warren Finidy initially played the lead in Cordier's play, but Cordier fired him for drinking, despite the fact that he'd appeared in Jack Gelber's *The Connection*, to considerable acclaim. 'Bob thought it was funny that I had fired the actor of the year, a year after his award,' says Cordier. 'Then Warren walked up and said, "Hey Bob, Robert!", and Bob said, "Well, you guys are still on very good terms." I think he was impressed, and he said "Let's work together sometime."'

De Niro cultivated Cordier, as he did anybody who might push his career. 'He used to call me to ask what was up. We went to parties; you know, kicking around at parties, but the main social life was going to cafés, bars and restaurants. We all went practically every night either to the Cedar Bar, to Bradley or to Max's Kansas City, or Elaine's uptown, you know, we went to these few places.'

Meanwhile, De Niro won another film role in a New York independent production, but *Sam's Song* was to haunt him for the next twenty years, and provide, through no fault of his, one of his least distinguished credits. Directed by editor and underground film-maker Jordan Leondopoulos, it was shot, very professionally and in colour, by Alex Phillips Jr, who would go on to light Sam Peckinpah's *Bring me the Head of Alfredo Garcia*. The film was meant as a 'calling card', intended, like Steven Spielberg's *Amblin'*, to win the director a job in features, though, by scattering fashionable *hommages* to the *nouvelle vague*, Leondopoulos also hoped for an art-house release.

Most of the action takes place in the grounds of a Long Island mansion like the one in *The Wedding Party*, with a further sequence at sea on a cabin cruiser. Young film-maker Sam (De Niro) is invited to join a house party thrown by friends of the wealthy Erica (Jennifer Warren) and Andrew (Jarred Mickey). The three drive up in the couple's convertible, Sam reading Andre Bazin's film criticism and Erica quoting from the book by Louis Ferdinand Céline which she's translating.

When they arrive, they find their hosts have invited some people to an impromptu birthday party. They include the glamorous and very available Carol (Terrayne Crawford), who, to the chagrin of Erica and the envy of Andrew, sneaks off with Sam to have sex. When the party transfers to a boat, Carol disappears into a cabin, this time with Andrew, and a furious Erica asks to be taken back to shore on a conveniently passing launch. Sam joins her. Back on the beach, they act out their own version of a scene from Jean-Luc Godard's *Pierrot le fou*, an imaginary gunfight using pointed fingers, with Sam improvising a series of facetious slow-motion death scenes.

De Niro, behind a heavy moustache, makes a believable New York movie-maker, and Jennifer Warren, who later had a solid career in films (*Night Moves*), TV and, more recently, as a director (*Partners in Crime*), is equally convincing, if dressed unflatteringly and forced to deliver some ridiculous lines. At the time, however, nobody saw either of them, since the film had almost no release, and would languish in a New York warehouse for more than a decade.

*   *   *

In 1969, De Palma's *The Wedding Party* finally screened in a single small cinema downtown, drawing little attention. To De Niro's irritation, the credits mis-spelled his name 'DeNero'. Small as his role was, however, it admitted him to the select group of young New York actors with feature-film experience.

Another of these was a short, intense Actors Studio alumnus named Al Pacino. 'I had seen Robert in *The Wedding Party*,' Pacino said later, 'and was very impressed by him.' In Pacino's version of their first meeting, he stopped De Niro on 14th Street and introduced himself. It's more likely, however, that they met at Jimmy Ray's, a bar on 8th Avenue where young out-of-work performers could drink on credit. Another hang-out where they would almost certainly have run into one another was the Bear Garden, an all-night restaurant on the Upper East Side run by playwright David Scott Milton.

De Niro became a regular at the Bear Garden, an establishment which, Milton recalls with some pride, 'attracted a number of strong-arm men, gangsters, whores, junkies. Our luncheon waitress was Jill Clayburgh, dinner waiter Frederick Forrest. Peter Boyle worked for us for a short while. Louise Lasser, who was married to Woody Allen at the time, was our late-night waitress. Waldo Salt, who later wrote *Midnight Cowboy*, was a regular; his daughter, Jennifer, worked there occasionally. Norman Wexler, screenwriter of *Joe* and *Saturday Night Fever*, was also a regular. William Saroyan's son, Aram, a writer and a poet, also mis-spent much of his youth there.'

Films were so rarely shot in New York that the same actors, including Christopher Walken, Ralph Waite, Allen Garfield and Charles Durning, as well as De Niro and Pacino, often found themselves competing for roles. De Niro auditioned for Jerry Schatzberg's 1971 *Panic in Needle Park*, but Pacino won the part, and made his movie debut.

Pacino, devoted to Lee Strasberg both personally and professionally, pressed De Niro to audition for the Actors Studio, about which De Niro had begun to change his mind. Pacino's experience showed that Studio members got first shot at the best roles. Robert Cordier, then in the Studio's Directors' Unit, recalls,

'Bob was not at the Actors Studio then, but he was trying to get in. He called me a few times and said, "What's up, what's going on? I'm trying to get into the Actors Studio."'

His chance came, indirectly, though Sally Kirkland, who one afternoon at Jimmy Ray's introduced him to her godmother, Shelley Winters. Winters had passed through Stella Adler's Conservatory *en route* to a Hollywood career that culminated in her 1951 Academy Award nomination for *A Place in the Sun*. She'd hoped for better things after this success, but her subsequent films were largely routine, and following some roles in Britain, she returned to New York, determined to relaunch herself as a stage actress and playwright. In 1955, she found a niche at the Actors Studio.

Strasberg, as part of an infatuation with Hollywood which many Studio members viewed with alarm, now admitted 'observers', who could watch but not participate. Paul Newman and Marilyn Monroe attended regularly, as did Charles Laughton, who had a particularly close relationship with Al Pacino. Winters, by virtue of her movie career, was appointed one of the 'Moderators' who guided discussions when Strasberg wasn't present. At the same time, resigning herself to the onset of middle age, she began taking character roles, and even won a Best Supporting Actress Academy Award in 1959 for *The Diary of Anne Frank*.

De Niro impressed Winters instantly. 'He was skinny and very gentle, with dark watchful eyes,' she recalled. 'He didn't say much. He had very little money at that point and he used to ride around town on a rickety old bike.' She later implied a romance between them – almost certainly wishful thinking. Despite his involvements with Kirkland and the actress Susan Tyrrell, De Niro was immature, still living at home and very much under the thumb of the assertive Virginia.

Winters did, however, have an ulterior motive for wanting to meet him. In 1959, in the throes of redefining herself, she had written a play, *Gestations of a Weather Man*. Not surprisingly, it portrayed three incidents in the life of an Oscar-winning actress. The third section called for a charismatic young actor, and from what Kirkland had told her, De Niro seemed ideal. Pulling strings, she got him into the Studio. 'She got permission for he and I to work on scenes as working observers,' recalls Kirkland. 'She had just made me a member; talked Lee Strasberg into allowing my audition to get me in. Bobby was very good and we worked almost every week for a period of time.'

Though Strasberg would retrospectively claim De Niro as a product of the Studio, and display among his trophies a photograph of the two embracing, Bobby never auditioned for the Studio, and though he spent seven years as occasional observer and performer, remains circumspect about the worth of Strasberg's teaching, which he calls 'another thing' from Stella Adler's system. Many actors, Pacino among them, accepted the professional value of membership of the Actors Studio without necessarily embracing its ideas, and De Niro, like Pacino, may well have 'blocked his ears' to the discussions that followed each student performance; Pacino admitted he would count numbers mentally rather than listen.

'It was beneficial and helpful,' De Niro said of his Strasberg experience, choosing his words carefully. 'What I thought was better was when a director would come up and have a session. Because a director had a mixture of experience and practical doing. A director would get up and say, "We'll do this and do that." At the end of the day you've got to get up and do it. And the sooner you get to knowing you've got to get up and do it, the quicker you'll do it.'

Once her two protégés were established at the Studio, Winters tried to persuade her agency, ICM, to represent them, but it was a bridge too far. Kirkland says, 'The higher-ups at ICM said, "Who are they?" We both got turned down by ICM in 1968.' But shortly after, De Niro acquired an agent, in Richard Bauman, who would represent him through the first part of a fast-accelerating career.

CHAPTER SIX

Shelley and the Boys

I met a man in filmland, a patron of the arts,
He bought my scheme to turn my dream into a peeping art.

From title song of the film *Hi, Mom!*

As he approached twenty-five, De Niro felt that his working life
hadn't really begun. He had little commitment to acting as a
career. 'I didn't want to act for a while,' he later told Chris
Hodenfield of *Rolling Stone* magazine. 'I was afraid that I would
get wrapped up in it so much that I wouldn't have time to do what
I wanted.' He still thought he might return to Europe, and spend
more time in Paris, where he'd enjoyed the sense of anonymity.
For the moment, he did the next best thing, playing in occasional
off-Broadway plays, just another obscure fringe performer.

But 1968 marked his definitive decision to take acting seriously. 'When I was about twenty-four or twenty-five,' he said,
'I committed; started to look for stuff, go out on auditions, sent
out résumés. The whole thing.'

The change had much to do with Brian De Palma, who, having
graduated from Sarah Lawrence, continued to make short films.
Their voyeuristic undertone was increasingly obvious, particularly in the 1966 *Murder à la Mod*, a three-part fantasy with a
middle section much influenced by Hitchcock. The film attracted
interest, but no distributor, so De Palma used his earnings from
working in a Village restaurant to hire the Gate Cinema in the
East Village and show it himself.

One person who saw it was Charles Hirsch, who had a vague job scouting new talent for Universal, which was toying with the idea of investing in some low-budget features to cash in on the student audience and the art-house boom. Through Hirsch, De Palma got a small development grant from Universal's parent company, MCA, but they rejected all his ideas as too radical.

De Palma and Hirsch became friends, however, and sat around Universal's New York office for days on end, talking movies. 'Out of that frustration,' says De Palma, 'smoking cigarettes and waiting for someone to return our calls, we came up with the idea for *Greetings*.'

The inspiration was Jean-Luc Godard's *Masculine Feminine*, a film in fifteen fragments during which Jean-Pierre Léaud moves in with a girl he meets in a café, then spends the rest of the film wandering Paris, quizzing her and her friends about politics and their way of life.

Writing their screenplay, De Palma and Hirsch addressed a similar ragbag of topical issues: marijuana, pornography and censorship, computer dating, the underground press, the new climate of tolerance for homosexuality, the Kennedy assassination; but particularly Vietnam and its manifestations on TV. The three lead characters, Paul, Jon and Lloyd, are all pre-occupied with avoiding the draft: the title comes from the pre-amble of the draft notice – 'From the President of the United States, Greetings.'

Nobody in Hollywood found the script very funny, so Hirsch offered to produce it, finding the $43,000 budget himself. De Palma rounded up a cast, mostly of old friends prepared to work for little or nothing. Gerrit Graham played Lloyd, the conspiracy theorist, and De Niro, with nothing particular on the horizon, agreed to be the voyeur and De Palma *alter ego* Jon Rubin. Not yet confident enough to leave his day job, Hirsch waited until his paid vacation, during the thirteen days of which he and De Palma shot the film.

Greetings announced its topicality from the first scene. Audiences accustomed to the kneejerk patriotism of films like *The Green Berets* hooted as Paul, hoping to be so badly beaten up the army won't accept him, walks into a tough bar and demands, 'Which one of you niggers wants to take me on?' He escapes with only a few cuts and bruises, however, and Lloyd and Jon urge him to think more imaginatively – pretending, for instance, to be homosexual, or part of the fascist underground.

In any event, they decide he should arrive at the recruitment office exhausted, to which end they keep him awake for two nights, dragging him around New York city and involving him in their own obsessions, in Lloyd's case the Kennedy killing and in Jon's sex, in particular voyeurism. Lloyd chats with an artist about the way in which photographs, enlarged, can reveal unexpected truths, and even uses the nude body of a girl to mark Kennedy's wounds and argue that a single bullet couldn't have caused them. Another conspiracy freak contacts him in the bookshop where he and Jon work, warning him that shadowy forces threaten any who discover The Truth. In the end, a sniper's bullet makes Lloyd the eighteenth victim of the Kennedy conspiracy.

Meanwhile, Paul tries dating by computer, which matches him with a series of unsatisfactory partners. Jon follows women around New York, filming them. Trailing one to the Whitney Museum, he's sold a 16mm porn film by a man in the forecourt, who assures him it's a work of art. He also picks up a shoplifter and persuades her to undress while he films her through a window – supposedly for an art piece. All this ends when he's drafted, though the last scene shows him as a sniper in Vietnam, less interested in the TV reporter trying to interview him than in the pretty Viet Cong girl glimpsed through his telescopic sight.

While *Greetings* did imitate the apparent randomness of the *nouvelle vague*, large sections were as contrived as any Hollywood film. As the three friends, hanging round a clothing shop, discuss ways of ducking the draft, their hats and scarves change arbitrarily from shot to shot, and the client in the foreground suddenly switches places with the seller on the other side of the counter. Gerrit Graham and English pop artist Richard Hamilton sit in a New York park as Hamilton explains how he used photo enlargement in one of his recent works to create an ambiguous image of reality – music to the ears of someone who spends most of his time staring at the Zapruder film of Kennedy's death.

De Palma shuns stylistic consistency. The three men cavort around Manhattan as if in a New York version of *A Hard Day's Night*, and De Palma drops in a speeded-up sex scene which may have inspired Stanley Kubrick to insert a similar sequence into *A Clockwork Orange*. As in *The Wedding Party*, titles introduce sub-sections. In one, titled 'Two Views of Vietnam', the maker of a Vietnam documentary describes how it was shot, and a man at a party explains in lubricious details the sex and drugs available in Saigon.

But the film's naïveté is deceptive. Shot by shot, De Palma transforms the audience into voyeurs, luring us, as does Hitchcock in *Rear Window*, from casual curiosity to an obsessive interest in what's happening through the window opposite. He opens the film with a TV speech by Lyndon Johnson to the American labour organisation AFL/CIO, urging America to fight in Vietnam to protect the American Way. It's shot from a TV screen, and in a domestic interior, as if we're watching over someone's shoulder (a copy of the book *Six Seconds in Dallas* sits prominently next to the set). De Palma filmed some scenes with a hidden camera, including the long conversation between De Niro and the pornographer, and others, the framing slightly off-centre, with people wandering in and out of the background, *as if* the actors weren't aware of the camera.

De Niro worked on the role of Jon with the zeal that became his trademark. 'It was make-up and clothes that changed his look,' said De Palma, 'but it was more than that. He had *inhabited* the character, and become different physically.' Picking up on De Niro's enthusiasm, Alan Goorwitz, a friend from the Village who'd joined the Actors Studio and changed his name to Allen Garfield, agreed to come up to the Whitney Museum and improvise the scene as the pornographer. De Niro also improvised most of his scenes with Rutanya Alda as the shoplifter who strips on film for him. As she peels, he keeps up a running commentary that is also a parody of Strasberg's Method, explaining that this is a 'private moment' and that she should behave naturally, as if unaware of an audience.

Unexpectedly, *Greetings* was a commercial success, in part because its nudity won it an X certificate, which brought people flocking. Its sarcastic view of Vietnam also harmonised with the prevailing cynicism. The film opened on 16 December 1968. Four days earlier, the embarrassed incoming administration of Richard Nixon, who'd squeaked to a narrow election win in November, announced that American fatalities in Vietnam, now the longest war in American history, numbered 30,007, almost ten thousand of them killed in the first six months of that year.

To De Niro, *Greetings* didn't look like the kind of film likely to launch him in movies, even if that had been his ambition. Like Pacino and his other friends and competitors, he thought of himself as pre-eminently a stage performer. The best theatre on the east coast was being done by regional repertory companies like the Long Wharf and the Boston Theater Company, and in 1969 De Niro signed up to work with the latter under its innovative producer David Wheeler – only, paradoxically, to receive almost immediately an invitation to make his first Hollywood film.

1967 had been the year of Arthur Penn's *Bonnie and Clyde*, and half of Hollywood seemed intent on trying to repeat its enormous success. Among the first out of the gate was Roger Corman at American-International Pictures, the king of exploitation movies, who announced *Bloody Mama*, based on the exploits of 1930s gangster 'Ma' Barker and her four homicidal sons. Warren Beatty and Faye Dunaway had re-invented Bonnie Parker and Clyde Barrow as star-crossed lovers driven by sexual passion and a lust for fame. In case anyone missed the point, the poster copy read, 'They're Young. They're in Love. They Rob Banks. They Kill People.' The teenage drive-in cinema audience that was AIP's biggest market lapped it up. James Nicholson and Samuel Z. Arkoff, AIP's owners, instantly understood the lesson of *Bonnie and Clyde* – that some Hollywood stars would now appear in what had formerly been ghetto genres. Known until then almost entirely for biker pictures and cheap science-fiction and horror films, particularly a series of Edgar Allan Poe fantasies directed by Corman, the company branched out into crime films. In 1967, Jason Robards Jr, then reviving his career between bouts of alcoholism, let himself be miscast as Al Capone in Corman's *The St Valentine's Day Massacre*. The following year, someone at the company saw Shelley Winters playing in two episodes of the spoof *Batman* TV series as 'Ma Parker', a twenties-style gang boss. AIP made her an offer she couldn't refuse.

With Don Peters, Oscar-nominated for his screenplay for Cornel Wilde's 1966 *The Naked Prey*, Robert Thom, an AIP regular, wrote a treatment based on the Barkers' career, but Corman found 'some of the sequences . . . simply crazy'.

The writers erred by sticking too closely to the unglamorous facts. Notwithstanding the notice at the start of the film that 'Any similarity to Kate Barker and her sons is intentional', Thom's revised screenplay had little to do with reality. The real Arizona Clark Barker was anything but a criminal mastermind. 'The old woman couldn't plan breakfast,' complained one gang member. 'When we'd sit down to plan a bank job, she'd go in the other room and listen to *Amos and Andy* or hillbilly music on the radio.'

Nor was her family the tight criminal unit shown in the film. Her eldest son, Herman, killed himself in 1927 after being wounded by police. Both Lloyd and Arthur, alias 'Dock', drew long jail sentences in the late twenties. Lloyd, the character De Niro played in the film, stayed in jail until 1938, after which he managed a bar and grill in Denver, Colorado, until 1949, when his wife murdered him. He wasn't anywhere near Lake Weir, Florida, where Freddie, Ma, Arthur Dunlop and Alvin 'Creepy' Karpis died in a furious machine-gun battle in January 1935.

Determined to outdo *Bonnie and Clyde*, Corman ladled on violence, with a sixties spicing of incest, nudity and drugs. Kate, now younger, more intelligent and attractive than the real Ma Barker, dominates the story, living and stealing with all her boys, three of whom survive to die with her at Lake Weir. Freddie and Herman do get sent to jail, but Ma robs enough banks to hire a good lawyer and have them released. Lloyd isn't present at the shootout, but not because he's in jail. The film turns him into a drug addict, a glue-sniffer who graduates to heroin and dies of an overdose.

Corman assembled the usual AIP cast of wannabes and has-beens, anchored by a few pros. This produced a family oddly mismatched in height, build and hair colour. Don Stroud, 190cm tall, an ex-surfer and nightclub bouncer, towered over Clint Kimbrough and Robert Walden, who played Arthur and Fred. In 1968 Stroud had been the heavy in *Coogan's Bluff* opposite Clint Eastwood, but Kimbrough and Warden had almost no film experience, though Walden would later become familiar in TV series like *Lou Grant*.

To back them up, AIP veteran Bruce Dern played an invented character, Kevin Dirkman, while the part of Herman's girlfriend Mona went unexpectedly to a classic Hollywood casualty, Diane Varsi. After an Oscar nomination in 1958 for her role as Lana Turner's daughter in *Peyton Place*, Varsi's career nose-dived when she broke her contract in 1959 and fled Hollywood, supposedly to 'retire' but actually to keep the illegitimate child she wasn't prepared to abort or adopt. In 1969, she'd just returned to films and was taking any roles she could get.

Into this mix, Winters introduced her protégé, Bobby De Niro. Corman says he'd watched at least some of De Niro's work before casting him, but it would hardly have mattered if he hadn't. On paper, Winters and Stroud dominated the film. The remaining meat of the script went to Robert Walden's Fred and his masochistic relationship with the bisexual sadist Dirkman, whom he meets in prison and brings home to join the gang, and to oust Herman as Ma's lover. De Niro as Lloyd looked to be just along for the ride.

Having Shelley Winters in the cast inspired AIP to spend more money than usual. Most of the performers, including Winters, had Los Angeles homes and so didn't need hotels, but De Niro was put up at the Beverly Hilton, a luxury he didn't expect or demand; he'd have been just as happy in a tent. By then, however, Winters doted on her protégé no less than did Ma on her boys. 'Bobby needs someone to watch over him,' she announced. 'He doesn't even know enough to wear a coat in the winter time. When we did *Bloody Mama*, he didn't even know how much they were paying him. I found out how little it was and insisted they at least give him some expense money. He was broke all the time, but wouldn't take money from anybody. So I figured out ways of giving him money without him even knowing about it.'

'Location shooting' for AIP normally meant driving up to Vasquez Rocks with a box lunch, but *Bloody Mama* would be shot in Arkansas, and on a generous schedule, at least by AIP standards. 'It was a four-week picture,' Corman says, 'and that was long for me. I don't think I'd ever done one before that ever required more than a three-week shoot. But I had looked at the script and I said, "This is going to be very tough. We're filming all over the state. We're going to be in the Ozarks in northern Arkansas, then we're going to be filming around Little Rock and various other places. I really need four weeks." And they gave them to me.'

In deference to the Method-trained Winters, Walden and De Niro, Corman agreed to rehearse some scenes and even accept a little improvisation – a novelty for a film-maker who once shot an entire feature in one weekend. Mostly, however, *Bloody Mama* proceeded on the well-worn grooves of the gangster genre. Undeterred, De Niro researched his part with dedication. Arriving a few days early in Arkansas, he loitered round the locals until he learned their speech rhythms – learned them so well, in fact, that Corman suggested he coach the rest of the cast. That was a waste of time, since those who bothered with any accent chose the standard Southern drawl.

In response, and to make his character more memorable, De Niro adopted the most distinctive voice in the film, a murmured sing-song, shot through with echoes of a giggle that harmonised with the snatches of hymns he quotes. This, and an infantile innocence, would characterise his performance, as Shelley Winters discovered when she started the first scene, in which she has to give her boys a bath.

Seeing her hesitation, De Niro came over to her. 'What's the matter, Shelley?'

'I'm upset because I have to bathe five grown men in this scene, and I don't even know all of you.'

'But Shelley,' De Niro said dreamily, 'we're all your babies.'

Lloyd's gentleness makes him unquestionably the most sinister of the Barker boys. Mona, Herman's mistress, is ready to pleasure his brothers if that's what he wants, but she draws the line at Lloyd. Watching her through a screen door as she strolls naked around the room, smoking a cigarette, an aggrieved Lloyd whines, 'Everyone knows what she can do. She can do it even better than Ma.'

Piqued, Mona taunts, 'You should try my pie crust, little boy. It would melt in your mouth.'

In the end, however, Lloyd prefers dope. Corman, who the year before directed *The Trip*, an apologia for LSD, not surprisingly drew Lloyd as a holy fool on a permanent high. There's a goofy domesticity in the way he sniffs glue in the parlour, watched by an uncomprehending Ma ('When you're working on those model airplanes, you get to acting *awful* silly'). The first time we see him shooting up, he's in the depths of shrubbery, Corman pulling back to show him framed by flowers. When he dies, it's curled up, smiling and apparently asleep, in the plants at the edge of a lake – 'Like Moses,' says his brother.

Such religious references pepper Lloyd's lines. When Rembrandt (Pamela Dunlap) swims up to him while he's enjoying a high at the end of a pier, his feet with their two-toned shoes immersed in the water, he murmurs, 'Jesus, lover of my soul!' in surprise.

Even though it copies Clyde Barrow's meditation on his sexual dysfunction from *Bonnie and Clyde*, the subsequent scene is one of De Niro's best in the film. 'Sometimes I can make it. Sometimes I can't,' Lloyd muses as he sprawls on top of the complaisant Rembrandt. 'You can't hit the jackpot every time.' He confesses that 'everything frightens me', and shows her his needle-marked arms. Spooked, she tries to escape, but the rest of the family drag her inside, tie her to the bed and rape her, after which Herman and Ma drown her in the bath.

De Niro's involvement in *Bloody Mama* has gathered an extensive mythology, with Winters the largest contributor. 'I thought he was concentrating too much on externals,' she has said. 'I mean, the things he did to his body! He was a wizard, though. He can blush or turn white just like that! But he broke out in sores. He refused to eat, and drank only water. He must've lost thirty pounds. Just to *look* like an addict.'

Corman denies most of this. De Niro did diet, but not to excess, and indeed doesn't look any thinner on film than Walden, Kimbrough or Dern. However, Corman confirms that, on location, De Niro, as he would do habitually for the rest of his career, remained in character as the perennially stoned Lloyd even after hours, and stayed largely aloof from the rest of the cast.

In particular, Winters' description of filming Lloyd's burial is cemented into the De Niro legend. 'On the day we were to shoot the burial scene,' she's said, 'I walked over to the open grave, looked down and got the shock of my life. "Bobby!" I screamed. "I don't believe this! You get out of that grave this minute!" To see the character through to the end, he had actually got down into the pit and half covered himself with dirt so that his fellow actors would look down and get an honest reaction.'

This would not have been out of character for De Niro, but, unfortunately for Winters' story, there is no burial in *Bloody Mama*, and no grave. De Niro agreed he did 'play dead' in one scene, but it was the one in which he's found curled up in the grass.

'I was just lying in that state, without getting up,' he explained later. 'It seemed like an easy thing to do and I wanted to help the actors, because once they saw me like that, they were forced to deal with it.' Which they do, staring down at him, apparently asleep, then gradually coming to the understanding that Lloyd is dead – followed by the thought, 'How do we tell Ma?'

This was Winters' cue to enter. The day before, she'd announced that she would find inspiration for the scene by spending the morning in a Little Rock funeral parlour, fully made-up and costumed as Ma. Corman was not to bring her to the location until they needed her.

When she arrived on the set, it was in the grip of a creative jag verging on hysteria. Finding that Herman and Kevin aren't even there, but out in a boat machine-gunning a famous local alligator (a true incident), she stands at the edge of the water and bellows for them to come and mourn their brother. There follows some desultory grave-digging by Fred and Arthur, watched by Mona, then a hysterical outburst from Ma. Corman tried to rein Winters back, but Robert Walden dissuaded him. 'Be very careful,' he warned. 'She's in the part. Don't do anything that might take her out.' Deferring to someone who knew the needs of the Method, Corman went along. The result was high-adrenalin emoting on the Strasberg model, and hilariously false.

Whatever its limitations, De Niro's performance is one of the few in the film that aspires to go beyond cliché. Only Diane Varsi as Mona creates anything like the same sense of personality. Her anachronistically curly hair and small breasts with their tweaked nipples, her puzzled confessions of love for Herman and her sense of 'How did I get into this?' breathe the perfume of regret that also permeates the films of James Dean. Under a different director and in a better project, she and De Niro could have made beautiful music together, but, one on his way up, the other on her way down, they were destined never to do so.

If *Bloody Mama* did nothing else, it opened De Niro's eyes to the possibilities of film acting. Since there was no 'real' Lloyd Barker, it had been necessary to invent one, and in doing so he found that Stella Adler's training prepared him well. Once he had visualised the character completely and understood his motivations, he could make informed choices about Lloyd's tone of voice, his way of dressing and moving. The technique operated creakily in *Bloody Mama*, but Lloyd is as recognisable a De Niro character as Vito Corleone in *The Godfather II* and Max Cady in *Cape Fear*.

Like the great impersonating actors of the twenties and thirties whom he increasingly resembled, De Niro came to believe that creating a convincing character demanded detailed research and physical effort, even suffering. One had to 'earn the right' to play that person. The theory would cause him considerable discomfort, but would produce his best work.

*   *   *

De Niro and Winters returned to New York, Bobby scuffling for the same jobs with Pacino, who was increasingly regarded, with some judicious promotion from his friends at the Actors Studio, as *the* coming young actor. He had even gone to the Boston Theater Company and scored the success that might have been De Niro's.

Pacino was then living with Jill Clayburgh, whom he'd met in Boston. They shared a hard-drinking lifestyle. Pacino and De Niro shared something too, since both had been involved with Susan Tyrrell, a minor actress and major party animal who'd appeared in films like *Andy Warhol's Bad*, and at the time was Sally Kirkland's flatmate. Tyrrell, shortly to earn an Academy Award nomination in John Huston's *Fat City*, radiated a sensuality that was echoed in her activities off-screen, which she made the subject of a sour one-woman show in 1990 called *My Rotten Life*. Shelley Winters has described an incident from the period that almost certainly refers to De Niro's relationship with Tyrrell and its conclusion. 'I gave a Thanksgiving party. Invited all my theatrical waifs, my babies. Bobby was there, waiting for his date, a young actress he had a crush on. She didn't show up until dessert. She sort of floated in. "Oh, hi, Bobby . . ." He went into the bedroom and pounded on the headboard with his fist. He was crying. He never talked to her again.'

Editing on *Bloody Mama* finished at the end of 1969 but the film didn't open until March 1970. To reinforce the thirties look, not very well realised, Corman inserted old newsreels, with a voice-over from Winters to remind people when the story was set. By the time it was ready, the Actors Playhouse on 7th Avenue in the Village had accepted Winters' play for production, and De Niro was headed for another stage role that might, he hoped, launch him into the same orbit as Brando.

Much rewritten, with the injection of more sex and profanity, the piece, originally called 'Gestations of a Weather Man', had become *One Night Stands of a Noisy Passenger*. The three one-act plays, each with a different cast, depicted stages in the life of an actress not a million miles from the author. In the first, Sally Kirkland was the actress and Richard Lynch the man who arouses her latent leftist tendencies. Joanna Miles played her in the second segment, located in Paris, against the background of the Korean War and the anti-Communist blacklist. The third and longest section, called *Last Stand*, took place in the present. The actress was played by Diane Ladd, married to Bruce Dern and even then pregnant with the young Laura Dern.

In the play, Ladd's character has just won her Academy Award, and meets an arrogant young actor at the celebratory party. He spikes her drink with LSD, and after a dazed candle-lit seduction during which the actor is revealed as a karate fanatic *and* bisexual, they end up in bed.

Winters pleased De Niro by offering him this role. He learned to splinter planks with his bare hand, and worked diligently with Ladd on developing his character, despite the interference of Winters, who doubled as director, and insisted on De Niro appearing mostly in a pair of abbreviated floral briefs. But the opening on 17 November 1970 became a debacle when Actors' Equity walked out of seventeen off-Broadway theatres, the Actors Playhouse among them, in a dispute over wages. Winters wept as those few actors in the piece who weren't old friends refused to appear. The curtain didn't rise, and stayed down until 30 December, by which time Joanna Miles had taken another job.

The few people who saw the play when it did finally open felt De Niro succeeded in his melodramatic role, though Winters, with her usual hyperbole, said it was 'like watching sexual lightning on stage. Every night was a different performance.' Some were more different than others. On one occasion, De Niro, without alerting Ladd, placed additional lighted candles on stage for their love scene. As Ladd got out of bed and began to dress, a sleeve caught fire. An anguished Winters rushed down the aisle, but Ladd had enough presence of mind to snuff the flames out and carry on.

The following morning Ladd abused both De Niro and Winters for their lack of professionalism, but by then catastrophic reviews had condemned the piece to death. One critic found it a 'foolish and vulgar affair'. Another compared it to 'an evening of audition material'. To a third, it was 'a trio of tawdry peepshows' which 'makes sex so ugly and dull that even the most ardent voyeur would be turned off'. The *Village Voice*, in an otherwise negative review, rated De Niro 'stunning', but that wasn't enough to save the play, which closed after seven performances. Winters was in tears. 'I've been clobbered, and I'm in a daze,' she sobbed. 'Nobody understands my plays.'

De Niro quickly put the failure of *One Night Stands of a Noisy Passenger* behind him. He continued to make brief stage appearances, mostly off-Broadway or in short repertory seasons, but the action was moving to Hollywood as the best young directors, writers and performers in live TV drama and the stage followed their audience to the movies. In 1967, one film, *The Graduate*, earned more money than the whole Broadway season combined.

With the New York pond smaller, those actors who remained there had to struggle harder for work. The atmosphere drove De Niro's already furious ambition. Roy Scheider remembers going up against him for a part on Broadway. 'I got it,' he recalled. 'And a couple of days later I was in Joe Allan's, and De Niro was at another table. He stared across at me, and I thought, "Wow, this guy really *means* it."'

Unable to shake off the characters of *Greetings*, De Niro started writing a screenplay about a man based on an amalgam of Jon and Lloyd – a young drifter in New York, fascinated with assassinations. He found writing was harder than it looked. Non-verbal, he was non-literate too. Years later, he would admit, 'I couldn't sit down and write – I had ideas, I'd always be making notes about things, but I just couldn't have the discipline to sit down and write. It's another type of discipline, that's hard. I could co-write something, collaborate in a certain way, but not really the way you have to in order to come up with a screenplay.'

He would later show what he'd written of this screenplay to Paul Schrader, the eventual screenwriter of *Taxi Driver*. Schrader remembers the incident well. 'I said to him, "Do you know what the gun in your script represents?" I said it was obvious to me that it was his talent, which was like a loaded gun hidden in him that nobody would let him shoot, and that if somebody would just let him fire once, the whole world would see the enormous impact his talent would have.'

CHAPTER SEVEN

The Year of the Turkey

Miracle Pictures. If it's a good movie, it's a Miracle

Traditional Hollywood studio sign

Greetings made almost $1 million, though De Niro saw nothing but his salary. For Hirsch and De Palma, it was the breakthrough. Filmways, the company of ex-TV producer Martin Ransohoff, guilty of creating *The Beverly Hillbillies*, *The Addams Family* and *Mr Ed*, commissioned another film from them, this time with a budget of $100,000. As a title, Ransohoff suggested – no surprise – *Son of Greetings*, but De Palma, as much out of stubbornness as invention, preferred *Hi, Mom!*, a title that meant nothing to audiences until the last shot of the film, and not much even then.

History remembers 1969 as the year of *Easy Rider*, but Peter Fonda and Dennis Hopper's film hadn't broken when Filmways bought *Greetings*. Ransohoff saw De Palma as the first American *nouvelle vague* film-maker, a saleable mating of Jean-Luc Godard and Alfred Hitchcock. To ensure the film's counter-cultural credentials, he preferred, even insisted, that *Hi, Mom!* be shot in New York, and with a non-union crew.

Unacknowledged but implicit was the assumption that *Greetings* had succeeded not because of its anti-war stance or its cinematically playful discourse, but its sex, of which Ransohoff wanted a lot more in the sequel. De Palma, characteristically, couldn't wait to bite the Hollywood hand that fed him. *Hi, Mom!*

would have some nudity, but also a core of violence and social comment, and an apocalyptic conclusion. 'The message of *Hi, Mom!*,' said the director cheerfully, 'was that you can't beat them so you have to annihilate them.'

Between *Greetings* and *Hi, Mom!*, De Palma filmed a play in which the performers left the stage and mingled with the audience. The idea went back to early stagings of Clifford Odets' *Waiting for Lefty*, and even Max Reinhardt toyed with it in the twenties in Vienna, but De Palma added a new wrinkle by filming the play with split screen, half showing the audience, the other half the cast. The logical extension of this idea – that cast and audience become interchangeable – would inspire the last half of *Hi, Mom!*

For *Hi, Mom!*, De Palma encouraged De Niro to both widen and deepen the character of Jon Rubin, back from Vietnam but no less the Peeping Tom than before. In the opening shot, the camera prowls with his point of view through a ruined Lower East Side tenement, finally discovering the janitor, who shows him truculently through filthy rooms filled with collapsing furniture. The place has nothing to recommend it until Jon, pulling back a curtain, sees the picture windows of the block opposite, all invitingly open to his gaze, and that of his camera. 'I'll take it,' he says impulsively.

One of the gang from Jimmy Ray's, an almost unrecognisably thin Charles Durning (mis-credited as 'Durnham'), played the janitor. Another old friend of De Niro's, Allen Garfield, reprised his *Greetings* role as pornographer Joe Banner, who hires Rubin to record the activities of his neighbours for a film. The improvised dialogue with Garfield and also the stratagem Rubin uses to meet Judy Bishop, most attractive of the girls opposite – he arrives at her door claiming to have been sent by a computer dating agency – both recall *Greetings*. And, like Rutanya Alda in *Greetings*, who herself has a small role in *Hi, Mom!*, Judy, played by yet another De Palma alumna, Jennifer Salt, becomes a willing, or at least complaisant, subject for his camera.

After a long and contrived farcical sequence where Jon tries to film his seduction of Judy, only to be frustrated by the weakness of the tripod head, which causes the camera to droop at the crucial moment, he swaps his equipment for a TV set. Its arrival sets up the last part of the film, which De Palma casts as a fake 'National Intellectual TV' documentary about black power, featuring a radical theatrical piece called *Be Black, Baby*, performed by a group led by another neighbour from the building opposite, Gerrit Graham.

De Palma, framing the image in a fake TV fascia, shot the 'documentary' with a hand-held camera in black and white, only reverting to colour when Jon auditions for the role of a policeman in the play. The group, all black except for Graham, are sceptical; he doesn't look like a cop. De Palma then cuts abruptly to a shot of De Niro, dressed now in New York police 'blues', pounding with his baton on the door of a men's room, and yelling about perversions going on inside. He kicks a garbage can down a flight of stairs, then, still clutching his baton and standing in a narrow corridor, addresses an aluminium ladder and a mop leaning against the wall as if they are a tall suspect and his shorter female companion. A demand to see their street-demonstration permit builds in seconds, through a succession of belligerent questions – 'You got a permit? . . . What are you lookin' at? . . . You touch my baton? . . . Make love, not war?' – into a litany of fury until, overcome with rage, he lashes the ladder with his baton, then turns on the mop and strangles it.

The scene is a sketch for De Niro's famous 'You talkin' to *me*?' conversation with the mirror in *Taxi Driver*. For the first time, he tapped into the rage that would power his best work. The effect wasn't lost on either actor or director. De Palma drew on the same sense of barely-suppressed violence in the extraordinary sequence that follows, as middle-class theatregoers, mostly white, attend a 'performance' of *Be Black, Baby*.

In murky monochrome, they're hustled onto a tenement staircase, forced to feel up their black hosts, choke down 'soul food', and submit to having their faces blacked up, then threatened at gunpoint with robbery and rape. The 'audience' seem genuinely terrified, up to the point where De Niro appears in cop uniform to 'rescue' them. After that, they spill into the street, praising the show and promising to send their friends.

Like *Greetings*, *Hi, Mom!* doesn't so much conclude as run out of steam. Married to a now-pregnant Judy, Jon, weary of her demands, reads up on terrorism in a copy of *The Urban Guerrilla*, plants dynamite in the laundry room of the apartment block, and flees. When the building collapses, he's one of the crowd which gathers around the TV crews. After delivering a profane tirade against the dangers of New York, he asks to send a message to his mother. 'Hi, Mom!' he grins into the camera.

Once he had finished *Hi, Mom!*, De Niro felt alarmed by what it revealed of himself. Years later, asked by a London journalist how he felt about a retrospective screening, he confessed he'd avoided watching again a film he found 'a little scary. I didn't want to look at it because it would remind me of things – like the first time you ever hear your own voice or the first time I ever saw myself in a film ... I don't need to see it.' And, in a real sense, *Hi, Mom!* is the film where we see the real De Niro for the first time.

Ransohoff's hopes for *Hi, Mom!* were never realised. Before it could be released, *Easy Rider*'s cocktail of civil disobedience and recreational pharmaceuticals jolted independent American cinema onto a new path, away from the *nouvelle vague* and back towards the Hollywood genre movie – albeit with new and updated concerns: now the cowboys had psychological problems, and the gangsters grappled with questions of national identity. Overnight, the mischievous bohemians of *Greetings* and *Hi, Mom!* were out of fashion.

After *Easy Rider*, which justified dealing drugs as a means of purchasing freedom, film-makers were suddenly interested in New York all over again, as a stage for drug stories. Hollywood crews flooded into the city, alarming the Californian movie unions, who saw work slipping away to the east coast as it had during the sixties to Europe. They began to enforce the regulation that a production working on location in New York, even with its own technicians, had to hire an additional local crew who would do nothing, but be paid full wages.

Actors had no such clout, however, and, while New York's

few grips and gaffers were never out of work, local performers like De Niro became accustomed to outsiders getting all the major acting roles. 'I was taking pretty much anything that came along,' De Niro said of those days. 'There wasn't that much.' But he remained optimistic. 'I never became disillusioned,' he said later. 'I knew that, if I kept at it, I would at least make a decent living. If you are halfway decent at what you do, by the law of averages in five or ten years you will make enough money to do what you want to.'

For evidence of this, he had only to look to his parents. Virginia's company was flourishing, while Robert had won a Guggenheim Fellowship in 1968 and now spent summers teaching at colleges all over New York state and in San Francisco, which became a second home.

But Bobby still lived in the $75 a week fourth-floor walk-up apartment on 14th Street, now turned over to him by Virginia, and arrived at auditions by bicycle. Socially, he rivalled his father in elusiveness, avoiding parties, and even when he did turn up, maintaining a reserve that chilled anyone who tried to get close. As one friend put it, 'He was the only man I ever knew who seemed as if he had to think before he smiled, as if he was saying to himself, "Is that funny? Shall I laugh or what?" His laughter never seemed spontaneous.'

The musical *Hair* was still causing a sensation on Broadway when Bernard Schwartz, president of Joseph M. Schenck Enterprises, called a press conference to announce he'd just paid $50,000 for the film rights to *Heir* – not the Ragni and Rado show, he hastened to explain, but a novel by the unknown Roger Simon about two rich and beautiful kids on drugs, one of whom dies young. (Ragni and Rado, on the advice of their guru, refused to sell the film rights to *Hair* for another decade.) United Artists put up $2 million to make the film, which Schwartz, having milked the coincidence of titles of all possible publicity, rushed into production as *Jennifer on my Mind*, with director Noel Black.

To script it, he recruited Erich Segal, author of the seminal weepie *Love Story* – also about two young and beautiful people, one of whom dies young. For *Jennifer*, Segal made it the story of Marcus (Michael Brandon), rich heir of a Jewish gangster, who meets and falls for the appealing and equally wealthy but oddly disconnected Jenny (Tippy Walker) in Venice, California, and follows her to New Jersey, only to find she's heavily into drugs. Marijuana gives way to hashish and then heroin, on which she overdoses, with Marcus's connivance, and dies. A fortuitous car accident disposes of her body, leaving Marcus, sadder and wiser, free to return to California. *Jennifer* was, in fact, *Love Story* on heroin. As Kevin Thomas wrote sarcastically in the *Los Angeles Times*, the film 'could just as easily have been called *Drug Story* and been hyped with the slogan, "Love Means Never Having to Ask for a Fix"'.

Black cast De Niro as Madrigian, the driver of an unlicensed 'gypsy' cab painted with the truculent message 'We Are Not Yellow. We Go Anywhere'. Inspired by the character's Middle Eastern name, Bobby grew a moustache and small pointed beard, and affected vaguely Middle Eastern hand-woven clothing, including a head scarf. He looked good as a cab driver. That wisecracking lawlessness suited his style: you felt he might do and say almost anything. Picking up Brandon, he tells him as he pulls out, 'Hey man, I think I should warn you – I'm very high.' Startled, Brandon blurts, 'I am too.'

Some magazines, including the *Hollywood Reporter*, singled De Niro out for praise. The camera liked him, and, increasingly, he liked the camera. But the film was panned by its preview audience, and United Artists hastily demanded cuts to remove the dead wood, which included some of De Niro's scenes. He ended up nineteenth in the acting credits, as lost as the film itself, which was dumped into the desert of double-bills, never to be seen again.

Despite this, the drug cycle still had some time to run, and De Niro was now on the list of young performers who looked convincing in that world. Or so Ivan Passer thought when he gave him the script for what would become *Born to Win*.

In Czechoslovakia in the early sixties, Passer and Milos Forman had collaborated on the screenplays of Forman's most successful films, while in 1966 Passer had directed the highly-regarded *Intimate Lighting*. When the Russians invaded in 1968, both fled to America. Forman joined the queue of people who wanted to film *Hair*, but, like the rest, floundered in the swamp of hippie mysticism surrounding its creators. Shelving the project for a decade, he made *Taking Off*, the kind of social comedy with which he'd built his reputation back in the Old Country.

Re-enter David Scott Milton, proprietor of the Bear Garden, who had developed a play, 'Scraping Bottom', based on characters he knew from the restaurant. Ivan Passer liked it, and persuaded United Artists to fund Milton's sourly comic story of J – for Jerome – a once-successful hairdresser now feeding a $100-a-day heroin habit on the streets of New York.

Just back from eighteen months in jail, J finds that his wife has become a prostitute, and mistress of a smooth dealer, the Geek, for whom J runs errands. Despite everything, he still fosters the optimism symbolised by the tattoo on his arm, 'Born to Win'. Things look up when he meets Parm, a romantic innocent, but two cops target him to entrap the Geek, and, when he fails, plant drugs on Parm and arrest her. Falling foul of a dealer he's tried to rob, J is given the choice of being thrown off a building or committing suicide by 'hot shot' – an injection of battery acid. Handing him the poisoned dope, the Geek offers him the dubious consolation that it will the best high he'll ever experience, as well as the last. The film ends with J sitting in a wintry park, knowing that, sooner or later, he'll use it.

Abandoning 'Scraping Bottom' as a title, Passer called the film *Born to Win*. In a style more common in Europe than America, the film would cynically alternate tragedy with farce. J covers the theft of a safe from a restaurant by engaging the cashier in a long comic conversation about enemas, meets his new girlfriend when he tries to steal her car, escapes from his enemies dressed only in a frilly pink negligée, and, fleeing from a cop and his partner, hides in a clothes drier; amused, the cop puts a coin in the slot and watches J revolve.

Alerted by Milton, De Niro auditioned for Passer, who liked

to work improvisationally. 'He paired Bobby up [as the cop] with Ed Madsen, a former Mafia enforcer turned actor, and the combination worked,' says Milton.

Once he'd finished casting, Passer began shooting on the streets and in the clubs and restaurants of New York – and almost immediately ran into problems with De Niro. 'Ivan and George Segal [who was playing J] began to have second thoughts,' says Milton. 'Bobby was inventive and imaginative, and because of that a pain in the ass. George and Ivan felt he was trying to make more out of his part than the part called for. They began to talk of replacing him. The fact that he and I had both studied with Stella gave us a common background and vocabulary. I defended him; his passion for what he was doing – he was a real Stella Adler actor, relentlessly pursuing his craft. If he seemed to be making more of his part than they thought was right for the film, it was out of passion, of caring, a real actor's love of his calling.

'There was a scene in the film where Bobby and Ed Madsen are interrogating George in their unmarked detective car. They were putting pressure on George's character to set up a drug dealer, the Geek, played by Hector Elizondo. Bobby had a tooth-pick in his mouth. Ivan asked him not to move the toothpick from side to side during the scene because it would be impossible to cut away: the toothpick would seem to leap from cut to cut when he went back to Bobby. Bobby agreed with Ivan, but then ignored him, and it became a problem in the editing room. I'm not sure if Bobby did it on purpose or he just couldn't comply with what Ivan wanted because he was so involved in the scene.

'At the time, I had the sense that Bobby was very shrewd. He would nod and nod and "Yes, Ivan," and act as though he knew exactly what Ivan (or George) wanted, but ultimately he would do what he had intended doing from the beginning. Ivan would call him on this and he would play dumb. "Oh, is that what you wanted! Ah. OK. I can do that..." And, again, he would do exactly what he wanted to do.'

De Niro also clashed with Passer on another scene, in which his character has persuaded J to introduce him to the Geek as a potential buyer of a large quantity of heroin. They shot it in the Horn and Hardart Automat restaurant on 57th Street.

'De Niro arrived dressed like a high-rolling Mafia hood,' says Milton. 'Flashy suit, slicked-down hair, fancy shoes. Ivan didn't like it. It may have had something to do with Bobby bringing undue attention to what was essentially a secondary character.'

Milton defended De Niro's choice, but the film's technical advisor, a former narcotics officer, sided with Passer. De Niro changed his clothes for something less flamboyant. 'I thought Bobby's approach was right, logically and theatrically,' says Milton. 'Ivan's concern was that this subsidiary part not become so interesting that it overshadowed the main thrust of the film. Bobby couldn't think this way. To him every part was a lead part.'

In time, *Born to Win*, re-released first as *Born to Lose* and later as *The Addict*, would earn grudging respect, though, ironically, the factor that put it back into circulation was the growing reputation of De Niro, whose role could have been played by anyone. As J, George Segal gave a career-best performance. The film also launched Karen Black, who played Parm, to the eventual Hollywood heights of *Airplane*. De Niro, long-haired and looking too young for the role, had four scenes as one of the cops. Even had the part been bigger, it would have done him little good, since an appalled United Artists first recut *Born to Win* to emphasise its comic elements, then barely released it. 'They didn't open it,' said Pauline Kael. 'They just let it out.'

Of fifty-six Broadway shows that opened in the 1970–71 season, only four – *Home, Miss Reardon Drinks a Little, Oh! Calcutta!* and *Sleuth* – earned back their costs. Off-Broadway fared little better. Theatregoers, facing the prospect of being mugged, having their car stolen and being accosted by drug dealers or whores, preferred staying home in front of the television, which was booming with the launching of series like *All in the Family* and *Columbo*. Hollywood didn't help. The three major movies with New York settings, *The French Connection, Klute* and *Shaft*, showed the city as a sewer of drugs and crime, while a fourth, *The Hospital*, suggested that, if you survived a mugging or shooting, you might not live through the medical treatment.

With growing alarm, De Niro watched other New York actors, only a few years older than him, like Dustin Hoffman and Jon Voight, make their reputations and go on to major careers in movies. What was worse, actors of his own age like Christopher Walken were edging into the limelight. He sensed a real risk that he would be left behind. The lesson was driven home when his major competitor, Al Pacino, won a big role in the film of Mario Puzo's Mafia epic *The Godfather*.

In retrospect, *The Godfather* was the film De Niro had been waiting for. A crime story with an Italian-American background, it invited the sort of operatic performance of which he was uniquely capable. When the project passed to Francis Ford Coppola to direct, it looked even more promising. An Italian-American himself, with New York roots, Coppola announced early that he would shoot the film in and around the city, and with local performers, ideally Italian-American.

Behind the scenes, however, the project was already in trouble. A dozen directors, including Arthur Penn, Fred Zinnemann, Sidney Furie, Peter Yates, Richard Brooks and Constantin Costa Gavras, turned it down before it arrived on the desk of Coppola, a director with a couple of flops on his record who had, however, just scripted *Patton*, already $9 million into profit after nine months. Paramount were desperate enough to send executive Peter Bart to San Francisco to beg Coppola to both write and direct *The Godfather*, but he did so reluctantly, seeing it as just another potboiler, cashing in on a best-selling novel.

Almost immediately, Coppola clashed with Paramount over locations and casting. The studio preferred that he shoot in Hollywood, not New York, and with well-known actors, not the unknowns he auditioned in Manhattan through the spring and summer of 1971.

Ethnicity became a big issue in *The Godfather*'s casting. 'What about Robert Redford for the character of Michael Corleone?' the studio suggested. Coppola responded that, among other things, Redford was blond. 'He could be from *northern* Italy,' they coaxed.

Both Coppola and producer Al Ruddy wanted the glowering Al Pacino to play Michael Corleone, but Paramount's head of production Robert Evans vetoed him. *Anyone*, drawled the WASP executive, would be better than this short, muttering, impassive, ethnic unknown. Wearily, Coppola filmed tests for Michael with Martin Sheen and his old friend James Caan, already pencilled in to play Michael's quick-tempered elder brother Sonny. With black wigs and dark Sicilian make-up, both looked ridiculous. Marcia Lucas, wife of George Lucas, was cutting the tests. 'Use Pacino,' she urged Coppola. 'He's the only one whose eyes address the camera.'

Coppola agreed, but he still had to kowtow to Evans. Thinking two moves ahead, he started testing other actors for the role of Sonny, just in case Caan had to take over from Pacino. Among them was De Niro.

Sally Kirkland takes credit for suggesting Bobby, though he was far from the only person up for the part. 'I was one of the four hundred . . . well, more like four *thousand*, who tested,' said De Niro. 'They were all over the place, sitting on the cement floor . . . Foreigners, amateurs, guys who spoke like "deez and doze" . . .'

As an audition piece, Coppola asked everyone to do the scene where Sonny mocks Michael for offering to assassinate a crooked cop and his gangster confederate. The war hero who didn't want any part in the family business now proposes to kill two men at point-blank range. 'It isn't like the war,' sneers Sonny. 'You don't shoot people from a hundred yards away. You put the gun against their head and get brains on your nice new suit.'

For his test, De Niro tucked back his long hair with a woman's hairclip and selected a hat from his collection, narrow-brimmed and faintly comic. He looked, in fact, like Gene Hackman's 'Pop-eye' Doyle in *The French Connection*. His reading of Sonny was equally eccentric – mocking but manic. Coppola called the test 'electric', but De Niro's concept didn't fit the part. 'This was Sonny as a killer,' said Coppola. 'It wasn't anything you could sell. But I never forgot it, and when I did *Godfather II*, I thought he could play the young Brando.'

Reluctantly, Evans accepted Pacino. '$400,000 spent on tests,' says Caan sarcastically, 'and Paramount ends up with four corned-beef sandwiches.' To complicate matters, Pacino, assured by Al Ruddy that he had no chance of being in *The Godfather*, had signed to appear in MGM's *The Gang that Couldn't Shoot Straight*, about to begin filming across the river in the Redhook district of Brooklyn. Even worse for Paramount, MGM refused to cancel Pacino's contract. Evans claims he had to pull strings with his criminal contacts inside the construction unions to get MGM to release Pacino, and even then had to hand over the screen rights to one of Harold Robbins' novels as well.

Coppola, meanwhile, hoping to hang onto De Niro, signed him for a small role. Coppola remembers it as that of Carlo Rizzi, the handsome turncoat whose marriage to Connie, the only Corleone daughter, opens the film. Others claim it was Paulie Gatto, the young driver who also betrays the family and ends up dead on the New Jersey flatlands, a bullet in the back of his head. Neither character had more than a few minutes on screen, though one of Rizzi's scenes looks like a refined version of De Niro's cop audition in *Hi, Mom!* To lure Sonny out of his hideout, Carlo thrashes the pregnant Connie around their apartment with his belt, leaving a trail of broken china and smashed furniture.

Whichever role he was offered, De Niro took it, even though each had only two or three brief scenes, but kept his eye out for something better. He found it, paradoxically, in *The Gang that Couldn't Shoot Straight*, which Pacino had abandoned to make *Godfather*. Director James Goldstone needed a convincing Italian-American actor to take over, and De Niro was ready and willing.

Based on a novel by the columnist and humorist Jimmy Breslin, the story was latter-day Damon Runyon, with comic mobsters in bad suits and worse accents squabbling over territory. Breslin simply fictionalised the shenanigans of 'Crazy' Joey Gallo, the not-very-bright *capo* of a Brooklyn family which hoped to take over the territory of the much more powerful Colombo family.

Breslin's gangsters, including 'Kid Sally' Palumbo, the Gallo character, are small-time businessmen with the brains of turtles. To make some quick money, one gang stages a lottery based on the outcome of a six-day bicycle race, for which they import a group of Italian riders. These include Mario Trantino (De Niro), a handsome but kleptomaniac young Calabrian more interested in staying in the United States than in competing; but so strong is his urge to steal that, even at the reception held in the riders' honour, he's emptying bowls of peanuts into his pockets. In the battles that follow as rival gangs try to hijack the project, Mario meets and falls in love with Angela, Kid Sally's sister.

An early project of Robert Chartoff and Irwin Winkler, later the producers of the *Rocky* series, *The Gang that Couldn't Shoot Straight* had all the hallmarks of a quick money-maker: Breslin's laconic newspaper pieces had won him a national following; New York crime was hot; Waldo Salt, the screenwriter, had just had a hit with his adaptation of *Midnight Cowboy*; and MGM had an option on the services of Italian star Marcello Mastroianni to make his first American film.

The film hit its first snag when Pacino left. Then Mastroianni, pencilled in to play Kid Sally, confessed he couldn't speak English and was too busy to learn. He was replaced by little-known New York actor Jerry Orbach. Veteran Jo Van Fleet played Sally's black-clad mother, full of Sicilian imprecations, and Lionel Stander rival gang boss Baccala. All were grossly miscast, though not so spectacularly as Hervé Villechaize, the 119cm French midget who was revoiced in Brooklyn-ese throughout. The only performer with anything like star quality was the lion which Kid Sally keeps in his cellar as a pet. Its occasional eruptions into the action are handled with considerable flair, which may have inspired Martin Scorsese to introduce two tiger cubs into his movie *Mean Streets* a few years later.

De Niro's agent Richard Bauman cut a reasonable deal for De Niro, though he had to give MGM and Chartoff/Winkler an option to make two more films with him over the next two years.

They did, however, persuade the Screen Actors' Guild to waive its usual restrictions on non-members. With memories of the starvation conditions under which he'd made *Bloody Mama*, De Niro also had them agree in writing to provide him with reasonable accommodation while he was working away from home.

De Niro was enough of a newcomer to be impressed by big-time studio film-making. Years later, he was still calling *The Gang that Couldn't Shoot Straight* 'my first big-deal movie'. For the first time, he was lit in Hollywood style: to director of photography Owen Roizman went the honour of shooting the first real close-ups of De Niro, who didn't protest when Goldstone suggested he grow his hair long, and let it hang in a fringe over his forehead. The look transformed him into something closer to the standard Hollywood *jeune premier* – a near-clone of eighties leading man James Spader.

Leigh Taylor-Young, once a star in the TV soap *Peyton Place*, had abandoned showbiz entirely after the collapse of her marriage to Ryan O'Neal, and was living in New Mexico when her agent offered her the role of Angela. Busty, tall and red-headed, she was hardly obvious casting for a Sicilian teenager. 'I took the job on faith, to keep myself busy,' she says.

Goldstone, like many directors, rehearsed the film at New York's Stanhope Hotel. 'They asked me to gain fifteen pounds, dye my hair black, and learn the accent "fluently",' says Taylor-Young. 'This panicked me. I had a good ear for sound, but no confidence with accents.' It was worse when she met De Niro. 'Bobby's Italian accent was impeccable almost immediately.' No wonder, since between auditioning for *The Godfather* and taking the role of Mario, he'd made a quick trip to Sicily. The visit was supposedly to polish up his accent for *Gang*, but since Mario is Calabrian, not Sicilian, and anyway speaks broken English throughout the film, it's more likely that De Niro was preparing for a possible *Godfather* call-back.

'He came into rehearsal seemingly very ordinary,' recalls Taylor-Young, 'quiet and "mumbly" and with a very endearing sweet, shy way about him. His eyes didn't make direct contact for very long.'

After a week of grappling with the accent, Goldstone sent them on an excursion. They were to spend the day, in character, exploring New York, during which Taylor-Young, pretending to be Angela and speaking in a Brooklyn accent, would introduce De Niro to New York as if he were the newly arrived Mario. 'We were to be spontaneous,' says Taylor-Young, 'take the bus, and go wherever, as long as we never stepped out of character. I was a bit horrified, because I was now aware I was working with a great talent who had a perfect accent, and I felt I didn't have a clue yet about my character, let alone a proper Brooklyn accent.

'Off we went on the 5th Avenue bus. We got off near the Empire State Building. I was stone silent for almost the whole ride, for fear of demonstrating my ineptitude. Slowly as we walked west toward Macy's I plunged into behaviour that began to feed my sense of this girl, and my terror eased.' Not for long. As they left the department store, Young felt a hand on her arm. A large man had grabbed her with one hand and De Niro with the other. De Niro's jacket fell open and two shirts fell out; taking Goldstone's directions literally, he'd given in to Mario's kleptomania.

'We were pushed back into Macy's,' says Taylor-Young, 'up the elevator to a floor that was nothing but a jail! [The detective] was not at all interested in the fact that we were actors rehearsing a film. As far as he was concerned we were partners in crime and he arrested us. I was amazed to see Bobby's response to all of this, with him being a true New Yorker. He was scared.'

Finally a cop recognised Taylor-Young from *Peyton Place* and accepted that she and De Niro were just creating characters. The experience broke the ice between the two, and during the film they enjoyed, in Taylor-Young's words, 'a tempestuous love affair'.

With her showgirl body and long legs, Taylor-Young was the sort of trophy companion De Niro would increasingly prefer. Statuesque, even stately, with heels higher than their IQs, these women held his interest until the pursuit ended, after which the relationship descended into public bickering, then indifference.

If De Niro or Goldstone hoped the affair would improve Taylor-Young's performance, they were disappointed. She never did manage a Brooklyn accent, or any accent at all, and her newly-assumed fifteen pounds, accentuated by unflatteringly short skirts, merely made her look dumpy. Every critic trashed the film, though one person at least liked it. Just stupid enough to take Jerry Orbach's characterisation as a compliment, 'Crazy' Joey Gallo befriended the actor, who was partying with him at Umberto's Clam House in Greenwich Village in 1972 when an anonymous assassin shot the gangster dead.

CHAPTER EIGHT

Boyz of the 'Hood

*You don't make up for your sins in church. You do it in the
street. You do it at home. The rest is bullshit, and you know it.*

Charlie in *Mean Streets*. Script by Martin Scorsese and Mardik
Martin

While De Niro was launching his film career, Martin Scorsese,
his neighbour from the Village, had been making a niche for
himself on the other side of the camera. Like all the New York
film directors and actors, he'd headed for Hollywood, where
he found work as an editor on films like Michael Wadleigh's
documentary *Woodstock*. He also acquired a girlfriend, Sandy
Weintraub, whose father was one of the triumvirate running a
re-energised Warner Brothers under the suave and devious Steve
Ross.

A company town, Hollywood was accustomed to burying its
failures, suppressing its scandals and showing a bland face to the
world. The new arrivals from New York stampeded into this
orderly culture like bank robbers. Brian De Palma with his new
pal Steven Spielberg would turn up to double-date a couple of
starlets carrying one of the new portable video cameras on his
shoulder, and record everything that followed. Screenwriter John
Milius, preoccupied with weaponry, took payment in antique
guns for screenplays like *Jeremiah Johnson*, and ritually exchanged a weapon with his director on any new film. Most of
the newcomers learned to enjoy cocaine, then to rely on it.

Even in this dysfunctional group Scorsese stood out, in that it often looked as if he wouldn't survive the Sunshine State. 'Stress would disable him,' said one-time girlfriend, producer Dawn Steel. 'Smog would disable him. Cigarette smoke would cripple him. I would hear Marty downstairs at three o'clock in the morning, wheezing, hacking, barely able to breathe.'

Many of these newcomers to Hollywood could trace their dysfunction to childhood traumas, often religious in nature, and Scorsese was no exception. He brought to Los Angeles an impressive portfolio of obsessive behaviour. Terrified of flying, he clutched a crucifix every moment he spent in the air. He couldn't function without the pouch of lucky charms he wore around his neck. Regarding the number '11' as unlucky, he not only wouldn't enter a building of that number or put his car in space 11; he even shunned anything the numbers of which added up to eleven. On top of this, he refused to go out by day in California, convinced sunlight exacerbated his asthma. Not surprisingly, colleagues nicknamed him 'Dracula'.

But Scorsese knew an enormous amount about movies, and, what's more, could apply that knowledge to make new ones. A friendship with John Cassavetes led him into directing, and the low-budget 1970 *Who's that Knocking at my Door?* persuaded Roger Corman to offer him an even lower-budget project, *Box-Car Bertha*, another in the lengthening series of *Bonnie and Clyde* rip-offs begun with *Bloody Mama*.

When it was finished, Corman suggested Scorsese make a cheap version of *Papillon* called *I Escaped from Devil's Island*. Scorsese was all set to do so when he screened *Bertha* to Cassavetes, who gave him what's been called 'a sound three-hour talking to'. 'Now that you've made a piece of shit,' Cassavetes told him, 'why don't you make a movie about something you really care about?'

What Scorsese cared about was guilt and gangs. They were the subject of 'Season of the Witch', a script he'd first written in 1966, the last part of a projected trilogy that began with 'Jerusalem, Jerusalem', which was never filmed, and continued with the fifty-eight-minute *Who's that Knocking at my Door?*. He dusted it off, and asked his friend Mardik Martin to help him rewrite it. Without an apartment in which to work, they cruised Manhattan in Scorsese's old Valiant, pulling in periodically to put their ideas on paper.

At the suggestion of screenwriter/critic Jay Cocks, they renamed the script *Mean Streets*, from Raymond Chandler's essay 'The Simple Art of Murder'. Describing the moral hero who acts in all crime stories as a counterbalance and corrective to the criminal anarchy of the city, Chandler wrote, 'down these mean streets a man must go who is not himself mean'.

In Scorsese's story, based on people with whom he'd grown up, the man 'not himself mean' is Charlie Cappa, a young man on the fringes of organised crime who's torn between his inclination to a moral life and his loyalty to the Mafia into which he has been born. The conflict is embodied in his friendship with 'Johnny Boy' Cervello, a borderline psychopath with a penchant for random violence. Charlie's friends Michael, a local hood on the rise, and Tony, owner of the bar where they hang out, barely tolerate Johnny Boy for Charlie's sake, and when Michael, enraged over Johnny Boy's refusal to pay off a debt, decides to have him killed, Charlie must choose between his family and his friend. To make the point that such decisions don't always follow the Hollywood line, Scorsese would himself play the gunman who shoots Johnny Boy.

Mardik Martin acknowledged that Charlie and Johnny Boy comprised a dual portrait of Scorsese. 'One is the guilt-ridden nice guy who's basically a coward. The other is a crazy doer who doesn't care how he destroys himself.' When Scorsese formed his own film company in the eighties, he called it Cappa Films, after Charlie.

De Niro knew of Scorsese, and had seen *Who's that Knocking at my Door?*, but they'd never met. Nor, as it turned out, had Scorsese seen any of De Niro's films. Brian De Palma introduced them at Christmas 1972 at the home of Jay Cocks and his actress wife Verna Bloom.

Their first conversation was, predictably, about the Old Neighbourhood. Once De Niro saw the little man with the greasy pageboy haircut, rat-trap mouth and machine-gun voice, he realised he'd glimpsed him before – at dances, for instance, in a Latin-American club on 14th Street, and at Webster Hall, where Scorsese would shoot some of the scenes in *Raging Bull*.

'I know you,' said De Niro in the slightly hooting baritone that could seem almost a parody of Italian-American diction. 'You used to hang out with Joe Morali and Kurdy on Elizabeth Street.'

'And you used to hang out in Kenmare Street and Grand,' snapped back Scorsese.

They were soon deep in conversation. 'De Niro found in Martin the one person who would talk for fifteen minutes on the way a character would tie a knot,' says Scorsese's second wife, Julia Cameron. 'That's what drew them together, and since then I have seen them go at it for ten hours virtually non-stop.'

'We were both brought up in the same area,' explains Scorsese, 'and we see things the same way. I think, also, we both had the sense of being outsiders.'

But neither was as tough as he played it. They'd purchased admittance to the society of the streets by being alert, funny, and sensitive to the play of power behind the apparently featureless façade of the gangs. It took Scorsese very little time talking to Bobby to see in him a performer who could play his characters at least as well as he could write them. A virtuoso had found his instrument.

But it would take Scorsese more than a year to find the money for *Mean Streets*. Meanwhile, De Niro went back to the hand-to-mouth life of a minor-league New York actor, starting with a few days in two one-act plays by Merle Molofsky, presented under the title *Kool-Aid* by Lincoln Center Repertory in 1971.

Despite its critical and box-office failure, *The Gang that Couldn't Shoot Straight* should have gained De Niro some attention. He played his role so convincingly, however, that casting agents thought he was an Italian imported for the movie. As a result, his next film part, and one of the most important in his career, came about just like the role in *The Wedding Party* – from a cattle-call audition.

The project was *Bang the Drum Slowly*, from Mark Harris's novel about the friendship of two professional baseball players in the fictional New York Mammoths. Henry Wiggen is their star pitcher, while rookie catcher Bruce Pearson, no asset, socially or professionally, to the team, looks sure to be sent back to the minor leagues. Despite this, and even though Pearson, as Wiggen explains in a weary voice-over, 'chews tobacco, pisses in the sink, and is almost too dumb to play a joke on', the pitcher befriends him.

The revelation that Pearson has a fatal blood disease brings them even closer (the film's title comes from the lachrymose ballad 'Streets of Laredo', about a cowboy dying young). Wiggen accompanies Pearson to Georgia to meet his family, loyally hides the diagnosis from the team manager, Dutch Schnell, and even keeps Pearson from being fired by tying his contract to that of his friend; if they want Wiggen, they have to keep Pearson. Schnell hires a detective to find out the truth, but by then the Mammoths have won the title and Pearson is ready to enter hospital to die. Even at this point, Wiggen is on hand to dissuade him from marrying a gold-digger who has her eye on his insurance.

In 1956 Paul Newman played Wiggen in a one-hour TV version of the story opposite Albert Salmi, but though someone optioned the movie rights, it never reached the screen. The eventual producer of the cinema feature, Maurice Rosenfield, was a Chicago lawyer who had defended *Playboy* editor Hugh Hefner and comic Lenny Bruce on obscenity charges, and who owned the liberal WAIT radio station. Recuperating from a heart attack, Rosenfield convalesced watching the Chicago Cubs play baseball. He also read Harris's novel, and, shortly after, at half-time in the annual Thanksgiving football broadcast, saw a short film by John Hancock called *Sticky my Fingers, Fleet my Feet*, about a group of young executives who meet to play touch football in imitation of the Kennedy clan. Rosenfield and his wife Lois raised the $1 million to make *Bang the Drum Slowly*, commissioned Harris to write a screenplay, and hired Hancock to direct.

For six weeks, almost every working actor in New York passed through Hancock's suite at the Warwick Hotel, one every fifteen minutes. 'We read everybody,' he says. 'We read James Woods and John Lithgow, Tommy Lee Jones. We were principally seeking the big parts. James Woods [impressed us] but not for either part. De Niro, I thought, "Oooh, he's good."'

But the decision to give De Niro the role of the dying Pearson was hardly instant. 'I read for the director seven times,' he complained later. 'I read first for the Michael Moriarty part [Wiggen], then I read for the part I played. I read for the director, the producer, the producer and his wife, and finally I got the part. I felt I deserved it after that.' The marathon audition wore out De Niro's patience. When Rosenfield suggested he might take a share of the profits rather than a flat salary, Bobby told him decisively, 'I don't work percentages any more.'

Nobody could accuse De Niro of not, in his terminology, 'earning the right' to play Pearson. 'There may be more talented people,' he assured Hancock when he landed the role, 'but no one will ever work harder.' He let his hair grow, leaving it unwashed so that it flopped greasily around his ears. Harder to acquire was Pearson's habit of chewing tobacco. Worried that it would turn his teeth yellow, De Niro tried various substitutes, from bubble gum and liquorice to tea leaves. Finally, a doctor assured him tobacco would, if anything, make his teeth look whiter, so he gave in and 'took a chaw', developing an alarming expertise in squirting tobacco juice and saliva through his front teeth.

De Niro spent three weeks in Georgia, picking up the drawl. Carrying a tape recorder, he sat in on conversations in hotel lobbies, cafés and at baseball games, and even asked people to read parts of the script out loud. With the shit-kicking Georgia cracker accent came a furtiveness of movement, an unwillingness to meet people's eyes. You knew why people would shrink from Pearson, and make the slow-thinking innocent the butt of their jokes.

Part of the character's appeal to De Niro lay in his stupidity. De Niro can play rage, cunning and most of the baser instincts, but, from his performances in *The Last Tycoon* and *True Con-*

fessions, he's uneasy with intelligence. Being dumb simply made Pearson more explicable to De Niro, and he was incensed when the wardrobe mistress joked about Pearson's stupidity and bad taste as she was fitting his uniforms. He told her not to make fun of the character, which, by now, he had come to inhabit like a second skin.

Just how much De Niro, and his method, differed from other actors of his generation was dramatised by Hancock's choice to play Henry Wiggen. Michael Moriarty was a collar ad of an actor. 193cm tall, handsome and self-effacing, an accomplished jazz pianist and singer who'd also published poetry, he'd trained at London's Royal Academy of Dramatic Art on a Fulbright scholarship, acted on stage in London, then returned to work with Stella Adler. The role of Henry Wiggen called on all his technique. Hampered, almost crippled by an over-developed sense of responsibility – he sells insurance to his fellow team-members in his spare time, and has published a book about the world of baseball – Wiggen is that hardest of all characters to make believable, a truly good person, and Moriarty never managed to bring him to life.

Hancock and his cast joined the Cincinnati Reds at their summer camp in Clearwater, Florida, but were mostly fobbed off by players preoccupied with perfecting their game. Resourcefully, De Niro worked with the automatic pitching machines to learn how to swing a bat. He'd never played baseball, and although, by the time they started shooting, he was proficient, this wasn't enough. 'We'd shoot all day,' says Hancock, 'and then he'd go take two or three hours of batting practice, run three or four miles, and then go learn his lines, and then, start the next day and shoot and do the same thing again.' On days when he didn't film, he'd practise in Central Park, or watch baseball on TV. 'I saw in every baseball game how relaxed the players were,' he said. 'I could just pick it up. I could practise in my room watching them do nothing.'

De Niro's often painful use of technique startled Mark Harris, who watched some of the film being shot. To induce tears, he thrust his fingers down his throat until he retched – not just on takes, but rehearsals also, as often as forty times in a single scene. To appear sick, he put his arms out straight from his shoulders, and spun until he was so dizzy he couldn't stand. Such punishment reflected just how much De Niro lacked the technique of European actors.

For all his effort, however, De Niro never took command of the film. Like Dustin Hoffman in *Midnight Cowboy*, his remained a supporting role. 'He reminded me very much of the way Alec Guinness submerged himself in his roles,' comments John Hancock. 'Guinness isn't a personality actor; he's a character actor who is also a star, and that's Bobby. The only difference is that De Niro also has evident sexuality, which Guinness never had.' But in *Bang the Drum Slowly*, the De Niro sexuality, like the De Niro rage, was not on show.

True to type, Bobby, still inhabited by the character of Pearson, avoided rushes, simply disappearing after the final take of the day. Mark Harris, for one, found this admirable. 'From De Niro's point of view,' he wrote, 'a roomful of tense people watching the rushes was the gateway to hell. He cared nothing for all that jabbering, all that speculation. Such a scene was pointless. Superfluous. Whether De Niro had sufficient confidence to ignore the rushes, or too little to risk exposure to torrents of talk, I could not decide. For whatever reason, he remained in his room studying. If not studying, alone. If not alone, fabulously discreet.'

De Niro was a lot less confident than Harris imagined. He would have liked to watch the rushes, since they could provide him with vital clues about his performance. But not to look at them was a sort of bravado – walking the tightrope without a net. 'Anybody who asks should be allowed to see them,' he said later of rushes, 'unless they're "flippo" and they're going to watch themselves and go crazy and change their whole performance.' However, he realised as well as any performer that nobody could change a performance simply because it didn't look perfect in the rushes. 'I mean, you still have to walk from here to there to get to the other side of the street. If you see yourself, just maybe you walk a little this way, or change your style of walk slightly. But you have enough sense to know that you're not going to

throw the thing out of whack, because then you're just screwing
it up for yourself.'

De Niro's ideal was to enter his character so completely that
he wouldn't *need* rushes; he would *know* he was making the
right moves. 'I do want to do something where I never look at
rushes,' he said, 'because you always get kind of disappointed.
You know every foot of the thing; you've seen everything. So
finally, it's hard to really be objective. I'd like to do one thing
where I feel so confident about what I'm doing that I'll just do
it and I won't look at any of the rushes. I'll just see the finished
film.'

Michael Moriarty, on the other hand, never missed rushes,
and afterwards could be found at the piano in a nearby bar,
singing and playing for cast and crew. But, where this film was
to represent a high-water-mark of Moriarty's career, De Niro
would shortly pull away from the rest of his contemporaries. A
few years later, Moriarty visited the set of *Taxi Driver*. Someone
offered to re-introduce the two men. 'Don't bother,' Moriarty
said, watching De Niro prowl the set like a predator. 'I don't
know that guy at all. I knew Bruce Pearson. I don't know Travis
Bickle or Bobby De Niro.'

Those closest to the production already knew that De Niro's
performance was exceptional. One was Jon Cutler, his stand-in.
'I watched Bob at first off-camera from the sidelines,' he says.
'He was totally unimpressive. Then, later on, I walked closer to
the camera. Finally I was sitting under the camera, on the crab
dolly. Crouching under the lens, I discovered a fascinating fact.
If I leaned my head three feet away from the lens, I didn't see
very much coming out of De Niro. He looked boring. But if I
stuck my head under the lens, I was watching a genius. He was
only brilliant when I sat under the lens. Bob is a guy the camera
loves.'

It wasn't only the camera that loved De Niro. For the first time
in his life, he had a regular girlfriend. Two years younger than
him, but vastly more worldly, Diahnne Abbott was an exotic
mixture of the African, Caribbean and Caucasian, with the same

piquant contrast of dark skin and European features which distinguished Lena Horne. 'She is black, and very tall,' wrote one awed
(if inaccurate) observer, 'with an aquiline nose and the carriage
of a Russian ballerina. A lavishly-coloured butterfly is tattooed
on her upper back.'

Abbott had a light singing voice, and ambitions to become a
model, but when De Niro spotted her she was waiting tables in
a Washington Square restaurant. He badgered her for a date,
but at first she could see little to admire in this little-known actor.
'At the end of our first month together,' De Niro said, 'we were
spending so much time in each other's company that I invited
her to move into my apartment, along with her daughter Drena.'
Not mentioned were Abbott's cats, which quickly became a problem wherever she lived.

'From the beginning, it was a fairly casual, open arrangement,'
said Abbott. 'We both had our own views on life, and they did
not mean we had to pin each other down.' For someone as
inclined to jealousy as De Niro, the arrangement carried the seeds
of its own destruction.

Abbott's affection for De Niro had little to do with his acting
ability. 'I'll be frank and say that when I first knew him I did
not expect him to become a star,' she says. 'But gradually, I
could see he was so obsessive about his work that he just had
to succeed.' Once he started playing Bruce Pearson he would
disappear for weeks, then turn up in character and, to Abbott's
astonishment, 'so wrapped up in the role that you would not
know him. He was capable of changing even his physical
appearance.'

Meanwhile, De Niro had also become involved – for life, as it
would later emerge – with Martin Scorsese, who'd finally found
the money to make *Mean Streets*. Roger Corman had offered a
budget of $150,000, but only if Scorsese would make all the
characters black and copy successful 'blaxploitation' films like
Shaft. Scorsese declined, not because he couldn't see his characters as black, but because he couldn't imagine people of such a
different ethnic background attending a Catholic church – and

the Catholic sense of guilt was fundamental to the piece. Verna
Bloom finally hit on the right source of funding when she intro-
duced Scorsese to Jonathan Taplin, ex-road manager for Bob
Dylan and The Band, who wanted to get into movies. At the end
of summer 1972, Taplin offered $300,000. Scorsese asked Paul
Rapp, *Boxcar Bertha*'s producer, if this was enough.

'To make this film for $300,000,' Rapp told him, 'you're going
to have it shoot it in Los Angeles.' In New York, Rapp explained,
Scorsese would need to build sets, square the unions, find stuntmen to manage the final car crash, and in general spend lots of
money on resources that were available for much less in California.

Scorsese was under pressure because he needed to shoot during
the October festival of San Gennaro. The most important event
of the Italian social calendar, it was a celebration both of piety,
with a statue of the Virgin paraded through the streets under
arches festooned with lights, and of the Italian community's solidarity. If he missed it in 1972, he'd have to wait twelve months.
He decided to start shooting in New York, then move to LA for
principal photography.

Scorsese wanted Jon Voight for Charlie, but his success in
Midnight Cowboy made the actor skittish, and on the eve of
shooting he decided he'd rather be an idealistic teacher in *Con-
rack* than a two-bit gangster in *Mean Streets*. At a few hours'
notice, Scorsese persuaded Harvey Keitel, who'd appeared in
Who's that Knocking at my Door?, to play Charlie. Short and
combative, with a sailor's belligerent rolling walk, Keitel came
from the Brighton Beach district of Brooklyn; but street life was
much the same there, and he understood the culture in which
Scorsese grew up. For four days, Keitel walked through exteriors
of the San Gennaro festival. Then Scorsese closed down production.

That Christmas, Scorsese met De Niro, and offered him a role
in the film, to start reshooting early in the new year in Hollywood.

'Which role?' De Niro asked.

'Take your pick,' said Scorsese. 'Only, not Charlie. I've already
shot some stuff with Harvey in that part.'

It rankled with De Niro that he wasn't free to choose. At this stage in his career, he felt he should only be playing leads. This might have been enough to drive him off the movie had not he and Keitel met in the street.

'We looked at each other,' recalls Keitel, 'and we just laughed. That was it. We just kept laughing. Looking back, I see that we recognised each other. I knew he was a great actor.'

Superficially, it was a precarious friendship – Keitel the Jew from Brighton Beach, De Niro the Italian from Little Italy; De Niro the disciple of the Actors Studio's arch-enemy Stella Adler, Keitel the fanatic for Strasberg (who, nevertheless, turned him down every year for full Studio membership – until *Mean Streets*). But each saw in the other a complementary nature, enviable but unattainable. Keitel would never achieve De Niro's sense of tension embedded in stillness, his ability to vibrate like a plucked piano string, while De Niro never quite matched Keitel's foam-mouthed manic fury.

Initially, De Niro so impressed Keitel that he was ready to give up Charlie. But Scorsese, seeing his painfully-won San Gennaro scenes going down the toilet, refused. De Niro could play Tony or Michael – or, Keitel told him, 'I can see you doing Johnny Boy.'

'I hadn't thought of playing him at all,' says De Niro. 'I had picked a role, and it wasn't Johnny Boy. I said, "I'm going to do *this* one." But Harvey made me somehow see it in another way. In a way, it was a good thing. When you play a role you don't see yourself doing at first, you can get things from yourself that you ordinarily wouldn't get.'

Keitel, De Niro, Richard Romanus, who played the gangster Michael, and David Proval as bar-owner Tony began improvisation sessions during which De Niro widened the character of Johnny Boy to include memories of people he'd known in the Village. They would tape the sessions, play them back, and start again. 'It had to build,' says De Niro. 'Working this way takes a lot of personal stuff.'

With his usual meticulousness, De Niro developed Johnny Boy's loopy style. Charlie, Tony and particularly Michael dress snappily, almost always in suits, with a collar and tie, but never a hat, so Johnny Boy always wears a hat, usually a pork pie, one size too small, and casual jackets, often over a knitted shirt that hangs outside his trousers. The first time he enters Tony's joint, he even lacks the trousers, having jokily taken them off and left them with the hat-check girl.

By the time De Niro had 'paid his dues' to play Johnny Boy, Scorsese was ready to move the cast to Los Angeles. Even though he revered the old directors of Hollywood, Scorsese had neither the money nor the inclination to make *Mean Streets* sharp and clean, in the studio style. But its rawness would shake audiences who'd just got used to Hollywood's new and more thoughtful crime films. A hybrid of John Cassavetes and the *11 O'Clock News*, it was shot on the streets, often with hand-held camera, in available light and with the actors improvising their lines. Mocking conversations turn to flailing scuffles and back to conversations again: violence, too common to be worth commenting on, oozes from everything these people do and say. A drunk is shot down in the men's room by a killer who flees into the night, identity and motive unknown. The bar-owner proudly displays a treasure kept in the back room – two tiger cubs, which he fondles like puppies, talking about William Blake. Johnny climbs on a roof, fires off a pistol and throws a stick of dynamite into the night, shrugging it off as a prank. On the run from Michael, Charlie takes Johnny to see a movie. It's one of Roger Corman's Poe adaptations, and they stare unblinking at Vincent Price being consumed in Hollywood flames. At the same time, Charlie's uncle, a Mafia don, relaxes watching Fritz Lang's tale of murder and revenge, *The Big Heat*.

Scorsese's autobiography litters *Mean Streets*. The two women Johnny brings into the bar are Scorsese's girlfriend Sandy Weintraub and her sister. The quotes with which Charlie and Johnny greet one another are from the Bible, which Scorsese had drummed into him as a boy. Charlie holds his hand in the flame of a candle as Scorsese had seen Jesuit priests do in his childhood to demonstrate the agonies of hell. He also spoke the voice-over.

De Niro retained enough of his father's atheism to find Scorsese's Catholicism unhealthy, but he enjoyed working with a director who knew and liked the movies of old Hollywood on which he'd been raised. 'We realised that we liked Abbott and Costello a great deal,' says Scorsese, 'their language routines with inverted word-meanings done with wonderful timing. We tried to keep as much of that as possible.' For all its playfulness, however, *Mean Streets* never strayed far from violence. In particular, the conclusion, shot at night, with cars crashing, gunfire echoing, metal tearing, and Johnny Boy lurching down a dark alley, blood pouring from a wound in his neck, prefigured *Taxi Driver* in its almost Jacobean thirst for blood. In Charlie's life, as in Catholicism itself, the impulse to do good dissolved in cruelty and slaughter.

In May, producer Jonathan Taplin paid to take Scorsese and Sandy Weintrub, De Niro and Diahnne Abbott to Cannes to show *Mean Streets*. Federico Fellini, though he hadn't seen the film, praised it as 'the greatest American film in the last ten years', and a number of countries picked up the rights.

Taplin threw a dinner at Le Moulin de Mougins, one of the most expensive restaurants on the Côte d'Azur. De Niro and Abbott quickly made a scene – typical of his relationships with women. 'He picked these incredibly strong girls, top chicks, always black,' says Taplin, 'and then he'd fight with them all the time. They would always be in tears the next morning, and he would buy them some perfume.'

At lunch, Abbott complained of being bothered by a bee. The waiter flicked it away with his hand towel, which sent the animal-loving Abbott into hysterics.

'He killed the bee!' she shrieked. 'A living thing! I can't believe this guy killed a bee.'

An angry De Niro told her, 'Shut the fuck up!' Abbott flounced out. Unconcerned, De Niro finished lunch, and called a cab. He caught up with Abbott about five miles down the road towards Cannes, and she silently climbed in. Next day, he placated her with the traditional bumper flagon of Chanel No. 5.

In the autumn, *Mean Streets* was chosen to close the 1973 New York Film Festival. The reaction was ecstatic, particularly to De Niro's performance. The reviews compensated De Niro for the slowness in the release of *Bang the Drum Slowly* by Paramount, who feared the subject would be thought a 'downer'. By the time it arrived in theatres, Al Pacino, having won a Best Supporting Actor Oscar nomination in 1972 for *The Godfather*, had also scored a Best Actor nomination in 1973 for *Serpico*, establishing him as the premier young actor of his generation. That his rival didn't win either Oscar was cold comfort to De Niro, particularly when the one actor to earn an Academy nomination for his work on *Bang the Drum Slowly* was Vincent Gardenia, who played coach Dutch Schnell.

Neither *Bang the Drum Slowly* nor *Mean Streets* made any money on its first release, despite excellent reviews and good houses in New York. 'We thought the New York Film Festival meant something in LA,' says Scorsese, 'but nobody even knew about the picture.' *Variety* reported an 'NY trade vet' commenting of *Drum*, 'It's a New York picture, and they hate us "out there".' More importantly, the films simply had the bad luck to appear in a remarkable year. *The Exorcist* opened the week before *Mean Streets*, and *A Clockwork Orange*, *Deliverance* and *The Sting* captured what headlines remained. De Niro had to console himself with the accolade of the New York Film Critics, who in January 1974 named his performance as Bruce Pearson the best of the year.

Until *Bang the Drum Slowly*, De Niro had been as anxious as any young actor to be recognised, but with this first success he began to develop the shell that became the keynote of his public persona.

Within a few years, he would become famous for his ability to pass unrecognised in a crowd. English Director Michael Powell, eating lunch with Martin Scorsese and friends, asked, 'When is Mr De Niro arriving?' when De Niro was sitting next to him. After appearing in the play *Cuba and his Teddy Bear* in 1986, he walked into a press conference with co-star Ralph Macchio at his side. A reporter waiting by the door asked Macchio,

'Where's De Niro?' 'He's coming along behind,' said Macchio, deadpan. De Niro's ability at self-effacement occasionally meets its match, however. He and French actress Isabelle Huppert once arranged to meet in a hotel lobby. After half an hour, both left, convinced the other had failed to turn up, though they had been staring past one another all that time.

'When he's not on screen,' Scorsese has said, 'Bob is so reserved that you just wouldn't know him. In a social situation, he's a completely different person, and that's one of his most endearing qualities' – 'endearing', of course, being a subjective term. With Scorsese, it was understood to mean 'happy to talk about movies and movie technique'. Since this was what De Niro also enjoyed doing above all else, theirs was a friendship made in heaven.

For anyone not willing to discuss the art of tying a knot for ten hours, De Niro's introspection held less charm. Anyone who spends time with actors knows of their ability, not necessarily anti-social, to 'turn themselves off' and appear almost transparent to the public. De Niro's ability to do so is less interesting than his decision to use the skill so aggressively. The most obvious explanation is also the most quotidian: less articulate than many, less able to express his thoughts – and often having no thoughts to express aside from those about the work in hand – he takes refuge in anonymity.

CHAPTER NINE

An Offer You Can't Refuse

I believe in America.

Opening line of the screenplay of *The Godfather*, by Francis Ford Coppola and Mario Puzo, from Puzo's novel

In 1973, De Niro tried out for Stanley Kowalski, Marlon Brando's old part in a Lincoln Center revival of *A Streetcar Named Desire*, but was humiliatingly turned down. Instead, he appeared at the Manhattan Theater Club's Stage 73 in a one-act comedy, *Schubert's Last Serenade*, written by the actress and acting teacher Julie Bovasso, an old friend who'd been on the faculty at Sarah Lawrence when De Palma was there, but whom Bobby had known since he was eight or nine years old.

In an Italian restaurant, construction worker De Niro tries to woo college student Laura Esterman. The setting offered plenty of props with which to experiment. 'He wanted to do one scene while chewing on breadsticks,' says Bovasso. 'Dubiously I let him, and for three days I didn't hear a word of my play – it was all garbled up in the breadsticks. But I could see something was happening, he was making a connection with something, a kind of clown element.'

At the dress rehearsal, De Niro showed up without the breadsticks. Bovasso asked where they were.

'I don't need them any more,' he told her.

In a sense he was right. While De Niro would never entirely abandon the need for props, *Mean Streets* and *Bang the Drum*

Slowly meant he would be working with more expensive and sophisticated tools.

Though these two films would transform his career, De Niro found them, at the time, an expensive luxury, as did everyone else involved. Maurice and Lois Rosenfield never backed another film, investing their energy and money in Broadway musicals like *Barnum* and *Singin' in the Rain*. Michael Moriarty disappeared into TV. So, for the moment, did Harvey Keitel, cast in the first episode of the new crime series *Kojak* with Telly Savalas, and in a segment of *The FBI*, but not much else. David Proval and Richard Romanus fared correspondingly poorly.

Scorsese, after wasting months with Brando trying to adapt Dee Brown's non-fiction account of a Native American massacre, *Bury my Heart at Wounded Knee*, agreed to direct *Alice Doesn't Live Here Any More*, a project set up by Ellen Burstyn, who exploited the clout earned with her Oscar for playing the mother in *The Exorcist*. An almost-comedy, it starred Burstyn as a widow who abandons Midwestern tedium to go on the road with her wiseacre young son in hopes of reviving her singing career. She wanted a director who was 'still hungry', and would take notice of her suggestions. Sandy Weintraub, who had metamorphosed from girlfriend to producer, persuaded her that Scorsese was her man.

De Niro went back to scuffling for work. Screenwriter James Toback had written a screenplay called *The Gambler*, about a college professor of literature whose gambling habit destroys him and everyone around him. De Niro wanted the role, and Toback wanted him to have it, but director Karel Reisz preferred James Caan. While they were discussing the project, De Niro and Toback got used to sharing a cab uptown from their homes in the Village. De Niro always asked for a receipt so that he could claim his half of the fare as a business expense. It was a long way from the bottomless coffers of Hollywood.

Scorsese also sent De Niro an original screenplay, *The King of Comedy*, written by Paul D. Zimmermann, *Newsweek* maga-zine's film critic, and a champion of the work being done by Scorsese and De Niro. It dealt with a would-be stand-up comedian who kidnaps Johnny Carson, offering to release him if he gives him a spot on his nightly TV talk show. Zimmermann developed it with Milos Forman, and, when Forman chose another project, rewrote it as a novel, but never found a publisher. De Niro like the idea well enough to buy the screenplay, but Scorsese felt that, for the joke to work, Carson must play himself. The discreet TV host, known in the trade as 'Doctor Novocaine', wasn't interested, and the project went on the shelf.

The Godfather had been the phenomenon of 1972. Even as Paramount previewed it in February of that year, it was obvious the film cried out for a sequel. Mario Puzo went to Sicily to write a screenplay, his right by contract, though nobody imagined it would be anything but a springboard for the rewrite by Coppola, who was placed on notice that Paramount wanted him shooting no later than July.

Coppola's screenplay incorporated an ingenious double story, paralleling the growing ruthlessness and isolation of Michael Corleone with the tale of his father's childhood, and the birth of the Corleone dynasty in the New York of the early 1900s. It showed Vito Corleone as a dapper urban Robin Hood, siding with widows against rapacious landlords, and even disposing of a local Mafia *capo* for the good of the community. For contrast, Michael in the modern sequences had to appear pitiless, scheming like a Borgia, and slaughtering even his own brother Fredo.

With Michael such a negative character, Coppola needed a winning personality to play the young Godfather. He remembered De Niro's tests from the first film, screened *Mean Streets*, and knew he'd found his Vito.

'I rang Paramount,' Coppola said. 'I told them the idea. They said no.'

They might have continued to say no had Brando not refused his Academy Award for the first film in March 1973, sending 'Indian maiden' Sacheen Littlefeather to explain to an incredulous audience and TV public that he was doing so as a protest at Hollywood's depiction of Native Americans.

For a while, Brando had seemed interested in slimming down

and playing himself as the young Vito, but after the Littlefeather incident a humiliated Frank Yablans, head of Paramount, snarled that he wouldn't accept Brando on any terms, fat or thin. Though negotiations continued almost to the start of production in September 1973, Brando didn't even play the brief walk-on which Coppola planned to conclude the film. Early versions of the script resurrected the whole family, including Brando, for a party scene. Coppola hurriedly rewrote it as a surprise birthday party for the Don, whom everyone greets off-screen.

Having done the first film for a paltry $25,000, Pacino was in no mood to compromise with the sequel, and extracted $500,000 from Paramount, plus 10 per cent of the profits. He also 'suggested' they offer the role of Hyman Roth, arch-intriguer against the Corleones, to his mentor Lee Strasberg, who hadn't acted on screen for decades. The Actors Studio guru accepted $58,000 for his few scenes, which were effective enough to win him a Supporting Actor Academy Award nomination. In the rush of penny-pinching that followed, Paramount dropped Richard Castellano, the genially ruthless Clemenza of the first film, who wanted not only much more money but a role for his girlfriend.

Since Pacino and De Niro never appear on screen together, Coppola prepared their stories as, in effect, two different films, shot in contrasting styles. Lighting cameraman Gordon Willis suffused the Sicilian and early New York sequences with a nostalgic mist, but imposed a glassy sharpness on the modern scenes, set mainly in Lake Tahoe, Las Vegas and Florida.

Coppola shot the Pacino scenes first, but took time off during preparation to tour Sicily with De Niro. In Rome, they visited Bernardo Bertolucci, still a hero to Coppola, who had screened *Il Conformista* repeatedly while making *Godfather*. Bertolucci and De Niro eyed one another, the director wondering if De Niro would be good for a role in his epic *Novecento*. He needed an American star, and though his first choice to play the hereditary landowner Alfredo Berlingheri had been Jack Nicholson, there was a quality about De Niro that he liked.

Coppola hired a Sicilian consultant, Romano Pianti, who travelled through Sicily with De Niro. They visited Pianti's relatives, spent some weeks in Scopello and Castellamare del Golfo, and finally visited Corleone, the village after which a careless American immigration official rechristens the young Vito Andolini on his arrival at Ellis Island. Following the trip, Pianti said admiringly, 'If you'd asked me if it was possible for an actor to master a language like Sicilian in such a short time, I would have said, "Never. Impossible." But this De Niro has done it.' Which raises the question of why he did so, since Vito says only a few words in the Sicilian dialect, and otherwise speaks Italian throughout the film, with occasional words of English.

At the end of 1973, Coppola still hadn't finished shooting the Pacino portion of the film, and the company was flagging. In Santo Domingo, doubling for Florida and Batista's Havana, it rained ceaselessly. Shooting continued through Christmas, but Pacino caught pneumonia. Closing down the shoot, already two months over schedule, Coppola returned to New York.

Still waiting to be called for the start of the New York scenes, De Niro celebrated the arrival of 1974 at the Hollywood home of Michael and Julia Phillips, producers of *Steelyard Blues* and *The Sting*.

No new arrivals in California more perfectly reflected the nature of New Hollywood than the Phillipses and their partner, actor Tony Bill. Their beach house became a social centre for talented but socially inept newcomers from New York and the Midwest, with Julia, sexy in hotpants and rose-coloured shades, an unlikely den mother. Cocaine was liberally dispensed, and casual sex not only permitted but encouraged. John Milius was free to discharge his .45 into the rising sun to celebrate the arrival of the new year, or to weave through the neighbourhood in the early hours and, standing up on the back seat of a convertible driven by a bare-breasted Margot Kidder, pulverise the streetlights with a shotgun.

Everyone recognised De Niro as too tightly wound for this laid-back community. Watching him hover nervously around Diahnne Abbott, laying his hand repeatedly on her arm and shoulder, shooting glares at any men who took an interest, he seemed a throwback to Victorian, indeed Sicilian concepts of the male/female relationship – unlike Abbott, who showed a lively interest in other male guests. There was general agreement that Bobby was in for a rough ride.

A few weeks later, the New York Film Critics presented De Niro with its Best Actor award for *Bang the Drum Slowly*. De Niro and Abbott attended the party at Manhattan's Ginger Man restaurant, where Abbott fell into conversation with an obviously appreciative François Truffaut. 'Bobby was very jealous,' recalls Sandy Weintraub. 'He saw them talking, and put a chair down behind Truffaut and straddled it. Truffaut finally realised there was somebody behind him, and got up and said, "Excuse me," and left. Bobby jumped up and said, "What did he want? What did he want?"'

These encounters with the fast-track movie establishment also introduced De Niro to cocaine, quickly becoming its ruling pre-occupation. Julia Phillips would blow almost all her profits from *Close Encounters* on the drug, and De Niro later figured in the death by overdose of actor John Belushi. 'The history of Holly-wood in the seventies and eighties,' wrote one authority, 'cannot be understood without reference to cocaine.'

While Coppola completed the Pacino scenes of *Godfather II*, his regular production designer, Dean Tavoularis, took over an entire block of 6th Street, between Avenues A and B, and trans-formed it into Little Italy at the end of World War I. Modern signs, TV antennae, even the road surface disappeared. The street became an open market where ancient trucks hooted vigorously as they steered around mud-filled potholes and pushed aside the mass of humanity.

De Niro would shoot there, on and off, until June, working himself into the character of the young Corleone. We see Vito meeting and cultivating the friends who would become his *capo-regimes* once he came to power. Bruno Kirby plays young Clemenza and Jon Aprea a youthful version of Abe Vigoda's horse-faced Tessio.

Coppola wanted to show Vito as just another Italian-American businessman making good, but Paramount flinched at the irony. Robert Duvall, who played Tom Hagen, the family *consigliere*, particularly regretted losing the line, 'What a gunman can steal with a .45 is nothing to what a lawyer can steal with a briefcase.' Some scenes dropped from the feature version were restored for the ten-hour TV 'omnibus' compilation, including the introduction of Hyman Roth as 'Johnny Lips', who makes himself useful mending the gangsters' cars. Others were never shot, including Vito's courtship of his wife, and a scene where Enrico Caruso visits Little Italy and sings 'Over There' to encourage men to enlist for World War I.

Except for some petty larceny, and the murder of the local *Mano Nero* big-shot Fanucci, played by Gastone Moschin from *Il Conformista*, Vito never kills, in contrast to Michael, who, pale, subdued, expressionless, malevolent, climbs to power over the bodies of the slaughtered. As a result, Vito Andolini is one of De Niro's least characteristic parts. We never see the fury that underlies Vito's success as a criminal. Neat, soft-spoken, usually smiling, he glides through life, making no waves, disturbing nobody. Susan Braudy of the *New York Times* spoke of 'the usual De Niro glances and body English, punctuated by meaningful silences – warm, lethal, even loony silences'. Even his gutting of the old Don who murdered his mother is achieved dispassionately, like a slaughterman slicing through the belly of a pig.

Influenced by the howls of protest after the first film, which suggested that the Italian-American community was overrun with criminals, Coppola gave them a soft ride in the sequel, a fact reflected in the lack of affect in the role of Vito Andolini. But Coppola's repentance had a sting in its tail: the lines praising Italian industry and integrity come from the mouth of corrupt Senator Pat Geary (G.D. Spradlin), whom the Corleones have in their pocket.

Coppola was more concerned not to offend his own family, which came to America in the same diaspora as Andolini. In a scene deleted from the film version, Vito, Clemenza and Tessio visit Augustino Coppola, the director's own grandfather, a gun-smith who fences stolen weapons for the gangsters. While

Augustino examines the guns they've brought, his son Carmine – Francis's father – wanders around the workshop, playing his flute. Carmine would share the Best Music Oscar with Nino Rota for the score to *Godfather II*.

Preparing to play Vito, De Niro worried that he would be reduced simply to aping Brando's performance. He confided his fears to a friend of Brando's, who passed them on. 'I can understand how he would want to do that,' said Brando smugly, 'but he won't be able to.' Finally, De Niro decided not to try too hard. He dutifully screened the first *Godfather* repeatedly – supposedly fifty times. He practised Brando's habit of lightly touching his left cheek with the tips of his fingers, and developed a version of Brando's rasping voice.

Trying out for the role of the Don, Brando had stuffed Kleenex into his cheeks, an effect later duplicated with a dental prosthesis. Once De Niro got to the scenes where Vito and his family return to Sicily, he had the same dentist fit a smaller version of the device. He also put on weight, the better to fill Vito's well-tailored grey suits. Still, he didn't look much like a young Brando, any more than James Caan, Al Pacino and John Cazale look like brothers.

Coppola never quite decided whether he wanted De Niro to resemble Brando or not. Tiny details assumed major significance. 'One of the things we were trying to decide was about the moustache,' says De Niro. 'Whether or not he should have a moustache. There was a whole thing, back and forth, about whether to make this commitment. Finally I said, "Why don't we flip a coin." We did, and so I got to have a moustache.'

Unable to find a sufficiently large space and enough Italian extras in America to duplicate Ellis Island of a century before, Coppola took the production to Italy and transformed an old fish market in Trieste into the Immigrant Reception Hall. After that, he moved to Sicily for the scenes where Vito, returning as a prosperous family man, greets his relatives, and exacts revenge for the death of his mother. For Vito's arrival in Palermo, Coppola chose a small railway station an hour by road from the crew's hotel. They all drove out every day, only to find it cloudy.

Since Sicily had to look sunny, they waited around for ten days, until someone explained that at this time of year the proximity of the volcano Mount Etna caused a permanent overcast. They had to return some weeks later, when the weather improved.

In the break, De Niro reacquainted himself with Bernardo Bertolucci, who was now ready to shoot *Novecento*. Jack Nicholson was out of the picture, and while Donald Sutherland had been hired for the supporting role of Attila, and young French actor Gerard Depardieu for Olmo, the working-class hero, Bertolucci still didn't have anyone to play Alfredo, who inherits the land on which Olmo and his family have worked for generations. When he met Bertolucci a year earlier, De Niro did not quite have the clout to satisfy *Novecento*'s financiers, but the promise of *Godfather II* was guarantee enough, and Paramount, 20th Century-Fox and United Artists put up $2 million each, enough for Bertolucci to start the film; but not, as it turned out, to complete it.

Shooting on *Godfather II* finished in June 1974, and Coppola retired into the cutting room, conscious that he had to have a completed film before year's end if it was to qualify for Oscar contention.

Meanwhile, the film that was to make De Niro's career was slouching towards some sort of birth. The script for *Taxi Driver* was already at least a decade old. Its antecedents included the screenplay De Niro himself started to write at the time of *Greetings*, the story a New York drifter fascinated by assassinations, based on the Lloyd Clay character played in the film by Gerrit Graham.

The earliest pages of Paul Schrader's first draft are dated May 1972, though he continued to revise it until July 1976. Along with Robert Towne and Lawrence Kasdan, Schrader would prove the laureate of his generation of film-makers. He shared the religious and psychiatric hang-ups of Scorsese and De Niro, and had experienced at first hand the kind of urban alienation they only observed from their apartment windows. The product of a fundamentalist Christian sect which forbade attending movies, he evolved, perversely, into a film critic, fascinated with the intense, slow-moving, hypnotic cinema – he called it 'transcendental' – of Yasujiro Ozu, Carl Dreyer and Robert Bresson.

When he began writing screenplays, Schrader ordered the camera to linger, observing actions in detail, as did Robert Bresson in his classic *Pickpocket*. Schrader pays homage to Bresson's film in many of his, notably *American Gigolo* and *Light Sleeper*, where transgressors are redeemed and returned to a state of grace by the loyalty and sacrifice of a woman, while *Pickpocket* inspired the scene in *Taxi Driver* where Travis manufactures a sliding holster for his pistol that slaps the weapon into his hand.

Schrader, a mumbling young man of twenty-six, cigarette permanently smoking between his fingers, eyes obscured behind dark glasses, was at least as strange as any of the characters he wrote. After his first marriage broke up, he camped in the apartment of an ex-girlfriend when she was out of town, at other times in his car. Spare time was spent in porno theatres. 'I wrote it when I had fallen into a rather low point in my life,' he says of *Taxi Driver*. 'I was drifting, living in my car in LA. I started getting this pain in my stomach, and I went to a hospital and found I had an ulcer. At that point I realised I hadn't spoken to anyone in two or three weeks. I'd been floating in this sort of steel coffin through the city.

'Before I wrote the script, I reread *The Stranger* by Camus and *Nausea* by Sartre. It was a script that was written for the best of reasons, as self-therapy. The metaphor of the taxi cab occurred to me; a metaphor for a certain kind of male drifting loneliness. I just wrote two drafts of the script continually for ten days around February 1972. It jumped out of me like an animal.'

An outsider from the empty Midwest, a veteran with a shadowy war record in Vietnam, Travis Bickle materialised in Schrader's mind as he does in the film – with no baggage and no real history, only a sullen resentment that masks a fundamental psychosis. Like Schrader, who was born in Grand Rapids, Michigan, Travis is a product of the chilly American north. 'He seems to have wandered in from a land where it is always cold,' reads the character description, 'a country where the inhabitants seldom speak.' In another metaphor, Schrader compared Travis to a believer in some harsh rural Calvinist sect wandering through a Catholic cathedral.

Also like Schrader, Travis, when the story opens, is spending most of his time in a bleak New York hotel room, or watching pornography. A veteran of Vietnam, with an ugly scar across his back to prove it, he is no less psychically scarred, though his problem isn't simply a 'bad war'. Schrader makes him a borderline psychotic who has chosen New York as the stage for an act of glorious insanity – as he puts it in the screenplay, 'the psychopath's suicidal fantasy – his coming into glory'.

'New York is a place where you come to be lonely,' says Schrader. 'You can only be lonely in a crowded atmosphere.' Travis winds himself into a state of pathological alienation by objectifying the city, thus providing an excuse to destroy it. By choosing to drive all over New York, day and night (recalling De Niro's character in *Jennifer on my Mind* who 'wasn't yellow' and would 'go anywhere'), he ensures that he will meet the most detestable and worthless of New Yorkers.

Each time his better nature drives him towards a life-affirming act, Travis crushes the impulse. Talking always about improving his health, he eats nothing but starch and sugar: peach brandy on a bowl of cornflakes and white bread. Railing against drugs, he pops pills to stay awake, choking them down dry with a spasmodic toss of the head. Having persuaded Betsy, his sexual ideal, to go out with him, he takes her to a porno film, knowing it will disgust her.

Once the people around him have become as remote and faceless as the Viet Cong, Travis embarks on an orgy of slaughter, ostensibly to rescue an innocent (though she has no wish to be saved). In the final irony, his psychotic rampage turns him into a tabloid hero. Now, when Betsy gets into his cab in the last scene, he just chats, drifting in a Nirvana of calm – awaiting the next episode, inevitably more bloody than the previous one. Schrader went even further in the script, suggesting that Travis's fame made him sexually attractive to Betsy. 'Maybe I'll see you again sometime, huh?' she says in his first draft. But this went too far for Scorsese, who simply shows her standing on the kerb, watching, a little forlornly, as Travis drives away.

Plenty of people who read early versions of *Taxi Driver* admired it, but nobody believed any Hollywood studio would fund so nihilistic a project. This perception changed in 1973, when Warners bought the script for the Japanese thriller *The Yakuza*, written by Schrader and his brother Leonard. Dizzy with success, Schrader moved to Los Angeles and angled tirelessly for work, even looting the Rolodex of his publicist girlfriend for contacts. When she left him to work on George Lucas's *American Graffiti*, he begged her to come back – but only, she suspected, so he could score an introduction to Lucas.

Like everyone in Hollywood with a taste for violence, Schrader gravitated to the company of screenwriter John Milius, whose amiable ursine persona belied an obsession with weaponry and *machismo*. Milius was looking for a project to launch his career as a director, and *Taxi Driver* interested him. He inspired Schrader to incorporate more gun lore, showing Travis accumulating a private arsenal, and imitating the bizarre haircut of American Special Forces fighters who infiltrated Viet Cong tunnel complexes.

Brian De Palma also wanted to direct *Taxi Driver*, and brought together Scorsese, De Niro and Schrader at the new year party of Julia and Michael Phillips in Hollywood at the beginning of 1973. Julia Phillips had already read the second draft, with its Milius-inspired additions. 'After I read the script,' she says, 'I refused to be alone in the house with [Schrader]. He was following Milius around, and had bought his own .45, an act of romantic adulation.' She persuaded them to forget *Taxi Driver* and find projects that reflected their personal obsessions – voyeurism and Hitchcock for De Palma, and epic grandeur for Milius. It was good advice, leading De Palma to *Sisters* and Milius to *The Wind and the Lion*.

At the Oscars the following April, *The Sting*, produced by Tony Bill and the Phillipses, took Oscars for Best Film, Best Director, Best Original Screenplay, Best Art Direction, Best Adapted Score, Best Costumes and Best Editing. Suddenly Bill/

Phillips was the hottest outfit in town, and studios were ready to consider even its most outrageous projects – including *Taxi Driver*. But Schrader's concept was simply too weird for a Hollywood fixated on what Charles Schnee called in his script for *The Bad and the Beautiful* 'films that end with a kiss, and black ink on the books'. Nobody was quite ready to make a commitment.

For a year, the project kicked around Hollywood with no director attached. Scorsese, the obvious candidate, was making *Alice Doesn't Live Here Any More* and had no time to think about his next film. Knowing it was pointless to approach the likes of George Roy Hill, who'd directed *The Sting*, Julia Phillips offered *Taxi Driver* to second-string directors with counter-culture credentials. Irving Kershner and Lamont Johnson were considered. Some were interested if Schrader would recast the script as a love story, with Travis and Iris driving away at the end into a Midwest sunrise. Another offered a package with Jeff Bridges as Travis, directed by Robert Mulligan, who made the soft-centred *Summer of '42*. Schrader, whose contract with the Phillipses gave him final approval of all story and casting decisions, refused these approaches. He was not very keen on Scorsese either, until he saw *Mean Streets*. After that, he agreed to meet him. It was Schrader who suggested De Niro, and persuaded Scorsese to send him the script in Italy. 'And it turned out,' Schrader said, 'that Bob had a feeling for people like Travis.'

Novecento had started shooting around Parma in the spring of 1974, but De Niro had already been commuting between New York and Italy for months. Discreet and provincial, Parma, like most cities in northern Italy, had been comprehensively bombed by the Americans during World War II. Looking at the prosperity of the area, and the elegance of the people in its streets, one would scarcely believe that when the US Army arrived in 1945 many of its most beautiful buildings lay gutted and smoking.

To everyone who visits Parma, the overwhelming impression is of politeness and good behaviour. Most find it hard to credit that for more than a century this area, Emilia Romagna, was a byword for violence between aristocratic landowners and their farmworkers, to whose production of Parmesan cheese and Parma ham the region owed its prosperity.

Most locals prefer to forget that Benito Mussolini was born an *Emiliano*, and is buried in his native town of Predappio, not far from Parma. Some do remember such facts, however, and, what's worse, choose to remind the world of them. For most of 1974 and 1975, Bernardo Bertolucci, to the barely-suppressed fury of the locals, refought these century-old battles, this time for the cameras.

Bertolucci, then in his mid-thirties, was the son of the revered poet Attilio Bertolucci, who still lived in Parma. He had grown up in an atmosphere equally rich in poetry and politics. 'Emilia has traditionally been a very Red country,' he says. 'It was a strong Communist milieu and I was very close to the peasants, and that's why I was participating in their emotions, [listening] to their words; going with them to their demonstrations [in the forties and fifties,] and I lived a kind of split life. Half with the family of my father – my grandfather was a landowner – and half with the peasants.'

Having a poet as a father introduced Bertolucci early to the ambiguities of experience. 'When I was eight or nine,' he says, 'there was a poem that I read of my father's called "The White Rose". It is dedicated to my mother. It says, "You are like the white rose in the bottom of the garden. The last bees of the summer have visited the rose...". After reading the poem I would run out of the house, run to the bottom of the garden and there was the white rose. So I made no difference between the rose of the poem and the rose of the reality.'

To Bertolucci, 1900, the year after which he named his film, marked the beginning of the split between the political left and right that led inevitably to Mussolini's march on Rome in 1919, the resulting establishment of a Fascist state, and, argued the director, finally to World War II and Italy's defeat.

That defeat opens the film. As word spreads of the surrender, peasants on the Berlingheri estate turn from the harvest to hunt down their fleeing Fascist masters, in particular Attila, the sadistic farm manager, and his wife Regina. One of the peasant boys, desperate to be included, begs a rifle from a partisan and heads for the mansion, where, after carefully wiping the mud from his boots, he finds the head of the clan, grey, balding, stooped Alfredo Berlingheri, at breakfast, and levels the weapon at his chest.

Despite the presence of Depardieu and Sutherland, De Niro received top billing, and was expected to carry the film. 'It was hard,' he said. 'It's not my culture, so I spent a lot of time there before it was shot to get a sense of the place and the people and so on.' All the same, his role of Alfredo Berlingheri emerged from his characterisation of the middle-aged Vito Corleone. But where Vito was assertive, confident, and sufficiently violent to gut the old don who killed his mother, Alfredo was tentative, existing in the shadow of the peasant hero Olmo, played by Gerard Depardieu, and cowed by the swagger of Donald Sutherland's Fascist overseer Attila.

Over the years, Bertolucci's films had become increasingly an aspect of his Freudian psychoanalysis. In 1979's *La Luna*, he would explore his ambivalent feelings towards his mother in the story of incest between an opera singer and her teenage son. In *The Spider's Stratagem* (1970), a young man returning home from World War II encounters the Fascist sins of his father, while *Last Tango in Paris* (1972) would exorcise a fantasy that haunted Bertolucci for years, of consensual sex with a total stranger.

'What is very strange,' he mused, 'is that in many of my movies there is the murder of the father or the attempted murder of the father. There was a kind of natural living in the poetry in our daily life. And yet, with this wonderful father and mother I had to kill them all the time in all my movies. My father always tells me a simple thing, "This way you can kill me without going to jail." It's a movement inside me which still feeds my movies.'

This conflict inspired repeated rewrites of the *Novecento* screenplay, most of them the night before a scene was to be shot. The method drove away some actors even before filming began. Orson Welles had agreed to play Alfredo's father, but lumbered off the project, to be replaced by Burt Lancaster. Maria Schneider, Bertolucci's star from *Last Tango in Paris*, also fled, supposedly over 'artistic disagreements', but actually because of her heroin addiction; she didn't appear in another film for three years. Stefania Sandrelli, a star of *Il Conformista*, stepped into the role of Olmo's Communist common-law wife. Shortly after, she and De Niro were noted by the Roman *paparazzi* as regular companions, a relationship that appears to have been revived whenever De Niro was in the Italian capital.

Few Italian films proceed at a relaxed pace, but this one was a cockpit, with the three lead actors shouldering one another for a place in the limelight. Depardieu, five years younger than De Niro but playing his exact coeval, had been ten years in movies without making any name for himself outside France, where he was best known for the raunchy comedy *Les Valseuses*.

Because Depardieu spoke no English, Bertolucci threw out his idea of an English-language shoot and let everyone speak his or her own language, dubbing them later in English, Italian or French. Depardieu, painfully aware that he had been cast only to guarantee French release of the film, and discovering, too late, that his salary was only half De Niro's, adopted a combative tone, and the air on the set when the two men worked together seethed with male egos in conflict.

After hours, Depardieu partied mainly with Sutherland, who spoke French. The two men would fall to commiserating with one another over the things Bertolucci demanded of them. In one new scene, Attila, demonstrating how the *Fascisti* must deal with Communists, ties a cat to the wooden sign outside a barbershop showing a simpering, deferential manservant, and then runs at it, crushing the animal with his head. After numerous takes, Sutherland reeled off the set, dazed, and was still groggy when he and Depardieu went drinking in a Parma hotel that evening. They fell in with an American salesman, and Sutherland repeated the cat scene, this time with a mirrored pillar in the hotel lounge. Glass showered down, slashing his ear, and Depardieu, no stranger to open wounds after a wild childhood on the wrong side of the law, hauled him to the hospital and supervised the staff as they closed the cut with seventeen stitches.

De Niro didn't party. Not only was he reclusive by nature; he had to get up early each morning to be made up as the sixty-ish Alfredo. He had aged modestly but convincingly in *Godfather II*. But Bertolucci had his own agenda for Alfredo, part of which was the decision to make him not only resemble his own father, but to act like him as well.

De Niro bridled at the lapidary direction. 'The first few days with De Niro were a nightmare,' says Bertolucci, 'and I had to keep telling myself that what I felt about him when I first met him was so strong that I could not possibly be wrong. This was certainly true. You cannot judge him by the first few days. He is a very sensitive and probably neurotic person, so a director can be fooled. But if one has the patience, well, it's worth it.'

De Niro was no less guarded about his director. 'We had some problems in the beginning,' he conceded. 'As a person I liked him very much, but as a director he has another style that for me wasn't as good as it could have been.'

What problems? With De Niro, there was only ever really one. 'He told me what to do. The worst thing is a director that tells someone how to do something. You know, some directors like results, and they'll tell you, "You do this and go over and you smile." You say, "I've never been in this situation. What do you mean, I go over and smile?" They don't understand that you could do it in another way and that it would be better for you. Not only better for you, but it would give you more confidence and more joy. And you would know that they trust you and your choice. It might not be the way the director imagined it. But in the long run it will have the same effect. So that's the most important thing, because you can break somebody's spirit very easily.'

Though De Niro's stubborn spirit was well nigh unbreakable, it could be bent, and every day he became increasingly aware that his fellow stars were marginalising him. Sutherland, an accomplished scene-stealer, sneered and strutted so flamboyantly as Attila that one hardly had time to watch anyone else. Depardieu, hulking, intensely physical, with a habit of looking around from under lowered brows, like a young bull about to charge, oozed testosterone. By contrast, De Niro appeared callow, unsure, an effect emphasised by Alfredo's wan lines in the script.

De Niro felt the triviality of his role most painfully in scenes he shared with both the other men. The most telling of these came when, after having seen Attila, Alfredo and Olmo as boys on the estate, we meet them again for the first time as adults. It's 1918, and both Olmo and Alfredo have returned from the war, Olmo a private, Alfredo a dapper lieutenant. Both are chagrined to see Attila now supervising the estate, to which he has introduced all the latest technology. Strutting around a shuddering machine which separates and bags the wheat, supplanting the work of hundreds of peasants, Attila lords it over the two returning soldiers. Traditionally the peasants take their winter grain from the estate's stock, but Attila forbids them. Protesting, Alfredo plunges his sabre into a sack, a futile gesture. Olmo simply shoulders a bag and carries it into his mother's house, leaving Alfredo puzzled and unsure in the courtyard, sneered down upon by Attila, who has climbed to the top of the sacks and, legs apart, Fascist leather boots planted in the grain, challenges him to do something about it.

Alfredo can't. It's the peasant women who take matters into their own hands. Led by Olmo's lover Anita, they slash the sacks, snatch up handfuls of grain and fling them at Attila as to a chicken, mocking him with clucking noises like the self-important rooster he resembles. Skulking in the middle distance, Alfredo has no more dignity and importance than the farmyard dog.

Alfredo becomes a spectator at the lives of others. Falling in love with his cousin, the flamboyant Ada (Dominique Sanda), he trails in her wake as she blunders into a peasant dance and embarrasses everyone by pretending to be blind. Groping her way among the dancers, she snatches Olmo from Anita and kisses him hungrily.

Visiting Capri with Ada and his homosexual uncle Ottavio, Alfredo gingerly tries cocaine, then participates in an erotic *tableau vivant* for Ottavio's camera. As Ada dances, naked except for a diaphanous scarf, a servant brings news that Alfredo's father has died. Alfredo starts up from the couch where Ada reclines, near naked, and Ottavio's camera catches his terrified glance into the lens – the instant of the end of innocence. At Alfredo's subsequent wedding to Ada, Ottavio will steal the scene again with his gift, a pure white horse which responds, he whispers in Ada's ear, to the name Cocaine. And when, subsequently, Ada descends into alcoholism and Olmo emerges as the film's moral hero, De Niro felt himself pushed even further to the sidelines.

The most startling and, for De Niro, shaming scene in the film follows Olmo and Alfredo as, newly returned from the war, they take a forbidden excursion to Parma. 'What would my father say if he saw me with you!' Alfredo says to his friend – Bertolucci stoking the fires under his own Oedipal conflict.

They find a group of travelling acrobats performing in a court-yard, and Olmo remembers them from his childhood. Alfredo, however, is more interested in Neve, the pretty young girl who, oblivious of her heavy basket of wet washing, stops to stare at the show.

The two men follow her back to her room, and offer her money for sex. She accepts.

'See, I told you she was a whore,' Alfredo hisses.

'She just needs the money,' says Olmo. But he strips like his friend and joins him in the wide bed.

'Who goes first?' they ask.

'Both at once,' says Neve, played by Stefania Casini. Sliding in between them, she begins masturbating both men. Put off slightly by her matter-of-factness, Alfredo forces her to drink some wine, even though she protests that alcohol makes her 'go strange'. What she means soon becomes clear as she begins to spasm and foam at the mouth. Neve is an epileptic.

As he led them through take after take of this scene, all three performers became increasingly aware that Bertolucci was once again confronting, if not luxuriating in, one of his sexual fan-tasies. The slow crane shot over the foot of the bed to reveal Casini with De Niro's penis in one hand and Depardieu's in the other was startling in its frankness. If this was not pornography, it was close to it. (In fact, the scene would be cut from American versions of the film, and survive only in the rarely-seen European versions.)

Almost worse for De Niro, however, was the fact that in this scene Alfredo appeared once again as the weakling. As Olmo tries to help Neve, struggling to control the fits until her mother arrives, Alfredo just cowers in the corner. Later, he will run to his father and uncle to have them buy off a scandal.

While De Niro was working on *Novecento*, David Scott Milton, who wrote the play on which *Born to Win* was based, sent him what he calls 'a small script that I had written about a writer's relationship to his dying mother. He called me from Italy to thank me for having thought of him for the film. He told me how much he liked the script, but he had to do larger films now. He had moved up onto a different level from the De Palma films, *Born to Win* or even *Mean Streets*. He was on his way to becoming a major American film actor.'

It was increasingly clear to De Niro that, if he was to become a major American film actor, it would not be in *Novecento*. He confronted Bertolucci about the dwindling nature of his role, but Bertolucci had his own concerns. The sheer size of the film, which now looked like running more than five hours, had begun to terrify him. Bouts of hypochondria and depression forced him to shut down production for weeks. Sutherland, a demon at self-promotion, used this time productively. Hearing that Federico Fellini was planning a film of the life of Casanova, he took the opportunity of a visit to the set by the *maestro*, himself a *Romagnolo* from nearby Rimini, to propose himself for the part. A bunch of roses duly arrived at Fellini's office in Rome, along with a letter Fellini dismissed as 'almost a love note'. Nevertheless, after considering numerous better-qualified actors, including Marcello Mastroianni and Robert Redford, Fellini chose Sutherland to play the great seducer.

De Niro decided to follow Sutherland's lead and think about his next role. Travelling backwards and forwards to Italy gave him plenty of time to read, and he'd come across a book he liked – a biography by Peter Savage and Joseph Carter of the boxer Jake La Motta, called *Raging Bull*. 'It wasn't very well written,' De Niro says, 'but it had a lot of heart.' Visiting Scorsese on the set of *Alice Doesn't Live Here Any More*, he'd left a copy with him.

La Motta represented, in an almost concentrated form, the rage that was De Niro's true stock in trade as an actor. De Niro also responded to La Motta's frequent references to the physical transformation demanded of a boxer, particularly one with his habitual weight problem: in his career, he'd gained and lost a total of two tons. Once he stopped boxing, his body ballooned.

'I thought it would be interesting,' De Niro said, 'to see how someone could fall apart *graphically*, just by gaining this weight and getting totally out of shape.' It was just the sort of role De Niro relished – one where he could convey the truth of a character through physical transformation.

But for the moment the project most likely to find funding was *Taxi Driver*. And Travis Bickle too was someone to whom De Niro could instantly relate; someone fuelled by rage. De Niro was a bottle waiting to be filled, and Travis would fill it. 'Bobby only exists when he is in someone else's skin,' said Schrader.

CHAPTER TEN

Sleepless

Oh, I don't sleep. At night my heart cries blood. A fish swims all night in the black ocean – and this is how I am all night with one eye open. A mixed-up man like me crawls away to die alone. No woman should hold his head.

Clifford Odets, *I Can't Sleep* (1935)

As a first step in 'earning the right' to play Travis, De Niro needed to find the someone to mimic. On his first off-day from *Novecento*, he drove to a nearby US Army base, finagled a pass, and found his way to the mess. Within an hour he'd zeroed in on a group of young techs with the flat Midwest accents and junkyard-dog look he visualised for Travis. He struck up a sort of friendship with these kids. It took a few more visits to learn how they dressed, sat and stood, held a beer, lit a cigarette, drove a car. And what he had learned, he could reproduce.

In the lengthening periods of down-time on Bertolucci's film, De Niro returned to the United States, got a chauffeur's licence and drove a cab around New York. A couple of his fares recognised him. 'You're the actor, aren't you?' said one passenger. 'I guess regular work is hard to come by.' (The sympathy wasn't misplaced. Until well after the completion of *Godfather II*, De Niro still drew unemployment benefit between films.)

In December 1974, *Godfather II* briefly screened in New York to qualify it for the Academy Awards given the following March. Word began to circulate of De Niro's bravura performance. Now that Hollywood had got used to them, Scorsese, De Niro, Schrader and the Phillipses looked more bankable, and studios started to show interest in *Taxi Driver*. Finally David Begelman at Columbia green-lighted the project for a meagre budget of $1.3 million. Even with everyone working for minimum rates, it would hardly be possible to make it for so little, and in fact the film actually came in at just under twice that.

Shooting in New York posed many of the same problems as it had on *Mean Streets*, but Scorsese was glad not to have front-office supervisors breathing down his neck. This freedom, and the tight budget, encouraged him to follow his instincts in casting. As a result, the cast is peppered with people from the 'old neighbourhood'. Peter Boyle played another cabbie, the sage Wizard. Albert Brooks, a local stand-up comedian, was Tom, a campaign worker, a role Scorsese originally envisaged for Harvey Keitel, who chose instead the much smaller part of the pimp Sport. Keitel lived in Hell's Kitchen, one of New York's worst neighbourhoods, and had no shortage of raw material. The original of Sport lived just down the block. Scorsese also found a small role for Diahnne Abbott, unrecognisable as the sullen concession girl in a porn cinema.

De Niro took pistol lessons from the same expert who later taught Carrie Fisher not to flinch when she fired a ray gun in *Star Wars*, though what he mostly learned was how to flinch realistically when he tests his guns on a firing range. He haunted taxi garages and the all-night Belmore Cafeteria, a cabbie hangout, and taped some of the drivers' dialogue, though almost all the lines in the film are Schrader's.

Between Schrader writing the script and Scorsese starting to shoot it, the diaries of Arthur Bremer, who shot and permanently paralysed Alabama Governor George Wallace in 1972, were published. De Niro asked Schrader to read Bremer's malign ramblings into a tape recorder, and played them back repeatedly during the long periods he spent in his trailer during shooting – periods during which even Scorsese knew better than to disturb him.

Happily surrendering to the paranoia of the role, De Niro

periodically met with Schrader, always in obscure cafés where, fearing – he said – to be recognised, he would change tables three or four times. Seeing that De Niro wanted, essentially, to become him, at least as he had been while writing the script, Schrader gave him his own jeans and boots. Augmented with an old Air Cav jacket from Vietnam, they dictated the distinctive Bickle walk; pigeon-toed, bandy-legged, kicking forward slightly with each step, as if seeking to free his feet from the moral slime clogging the sidewalk.

Creating Bickle burned away any residue of the slouching, apologetic Alfredo of *Novecento*. Scorsese fed De Niro the oxygen of praise, encouraging him to push the character beyond even the wide territory delineated by Schrader. Whipcord-thin, every muscle defined as in an anatomical drawing, De Niro transcended flesh, becoming a creature of pure rage, a burning spirit out of William Blake. Like Charlie in *Mean Streets*, Travis holds his hand in the flame to prove the mastery of body by mind. Scorsese may have longed to torture himself in the same way, but lacked the necessary masochism. De Niro, however, was sufficiently in love with pain for both of them.

All the same, Scorsese insinuated himself before the camera. His reasons were complex. Agonising about his standing as a director, an anxiety fed by his asthma and the paranoia that came with his growing reliance on cocaine, he felt that, after the relatively lightweight *Alice Doesn't Live Here Anymore*, he needed to re-establish his credentials as the imp of the counter-culture. *Taxi Driver* became a manifesto announcing his Manichaean conviction, rooted in his Catholic guilt, that evil not only existed, but was infinitely seductive, and could only be exorcised by blood sacrifice.

Feeling his commitment earned him a role in the story, Scorsese appeared first – a gnomish figure coiled on a cornice in the background as the camera pans past – in the scene where Travis catches his first glimpse of Betsy. When, however, George Memmoli was hurt on another film and couldn't play the cuckolded husband who hires Travis to loiter outside the apartment where his wife is meeting her black lover, Scorsese needed no encouragement to take the role. The lines about putting a .44 into a woman's vagina and pulling the trigger are Schrader's, but the bile is Scorsese's, fed by De Niro's decision never to turn and meet the man's eyes. He watches him only in the mirror, objectified, like a specimen on a glass slide. Scorsese's all-too-evident mania made such an impression that he was offered the role of Charles Manson in the TV version of Steven Bugliosi's book *Helter Skelter*.

For Betsy, the campaign worker on whom Travis becomes fixated, Julia Phillips envisaged someone like Farrah Fawcett, a cool-shelf blonde. There are conflicting stories about how Cybill Shepherd got the part. Shepherd says Scorsese rang agent Sue Mengers and told her, 'I need a Cybill Shepherd type.' Mengers, who represented Shepherd, rose to the bait. 'Why not the real thing?' she demanded. Scorsese sent a screenplay to Shepherd, who reportedly threw it across the room – 'insulted', she said, 'to be offered such a nothing part'.

In Mengers' version, she touted the actress, who desperately needed a job, to Scorsese after the disasters of *Daisy Miller* and *At Long Last Love*. Scorsese was immediately interested.

Mengers excuses her manipulation as being in the best interests of Shepherd, who was 'so cold [i.e. unpopular with audiences] she had icicles forming on her body'. She also agreed to the meagre $35,000 Scorsese was offering. 'Cybill needed to work with a director with that cachet,' says the agent in justification.

Shepherd was due to appear in another Columbia production, Peter Bogdanovich's comedy of early film-making, *Nickelodeon*, but David Begelman, sharing Mengers' doubts about her drawing power, told Bogdanovich to cast someone else. When Shepherd protested, Begelman threatened not to release her for *Taxi Driver*. He couched it as a choice, but it was really an ultimatum.

Once he had her, Scorsese had second thoughts about Shepherd, who believes he used her to exercise his private sexual obsessions. In particular, she cites the sequence where Travis takes her to a porno movie. 'He shot it in a real porno movie house on 42nd street, late at night,' says Shepherd. 'I had to have bodyguards because of the crazies on the street. I'm overwhelmingly repulsed by pornography anyway, and for five or ten minutes I was sure, I *knew*, that asking me to make the picture was just another way of humiliating me.'

Here, as in other situations, De Niro imitated Scorsese. 'He treated Cybill like a pile of dogshit,' says one observer. Julia Phillips recalls seeing Scorsese's rushes of the scenes between De Niro and Shepherd. As the crew set up the shot, the two sat, silent, at the same table, ignoring one another, Shepherd fiddling with her hair, De Niro scowling – only to launch into playful sexual fencing when Scorsese called 'Action.'

Shepherd claims that De Niro made sexual advances to her, but that she refused him. After that, he missed no opportunity to mock her. When, during shoots in the heat, Shepherd cooled herself with a portable electric fan, De Niro sneered, as if she were acting like a princess rather than a serious performer. 'Bobby treated people badly if he decided they were not up to snuff,' noted one crew member.

A curdled view of women also emerged in Scorsese's casting of fourteen-year-old Jodie Foster as the prostitute Iris. He'd discovered Foster for *Alice Doesn't Live Here Anymore*, where she played a streetwise latchkey kid and petty thief ('Tucson is *weird*. Weird capital of the world, man'). But it was Schrader who found the original. Cruising the city, he spotted Billie Perkins, a street whore who seemed to him perfect for the part, and hired her for the night, taking her back to his suite at the Pierre Hotel (and, he insists, putting her to sleep on the couch). Then he told Scorsese's answering machine, 'I met Iris last night. Come and have breakfast with us.'

Scorsese modelled Iris on Perkins, who even has a small role as Iris's friend. Foster herself, trying to discuss the life of a teenage hooker, found the girl utterly ordinary. 'She was no use at all,' she said dismissively. 'She just talked in clichés.'

In any event, Iris was not a part Foster approached with enthusiasm. The hotpants, halter tops and wedge sandals horrified her to the point of tears, and when Scorsese inserted a new scene in which she dances with Sport to a Barry White-style song, then gives him a blow job, she refused even to mime the sex act. Instead, her older sister Connie stood in for her in this and other difficult moments.

Both scene and song were suggested by Keitel, who composed the latter, entitled 'I Love You Baby, Come to Me', in collaboration with the film's line producer. For weeks before shooting, Keitel and the pimp on whom he modelled Sport spent days at the Actors Studio, working up the character in a series of improvisations. Keitel then delivered the result to Scorsese wrapped in shiny psychobabble. 'There is great humanity in a pimp,' he pontificated. 'I don't mean humanity in the benevolent sense. I mean humanity in its suffering sense. They come out of a place of great need, usually of poverty, of broken homes, of never having opportunity.' That his model for the character of Sport was actually black didn't get a mention. In fact, in Schrader's first draft, all the pimps and whores had been African-American, but Julia Phillips persuaded him this might be thought racist.

While Keitel was all too easy to understand, Foster found De Niro puzzling and remote. Periodically during pre-production, he'd ring her and suggest they have coffee together. 'We would go by cab or subway to different diners all over New York,' she said. 'The Bronx. Spanish Harlem. We'd rehearse the scene over and over and over. I'd get bored with it. And then he would throw in something new. And he was right. If you are going to improvise, you have to know the scene so well that you're bored with it. Then you can riff with it.'

Scorsese crammed *Taxi Driver* with visual quotes. Many were from Jean-Luc Godard, including the close-up of Alka-Seltzer fizzing in a glass, lifted from *Two or Three Things I Know About Her*, and the pans between two people in conversation, the signature technique of *Le Mepris*. Others evoke the great New York still photographers. The terminal slaughter might have come from the portfolio of Arthur Fellig, aka 'Weegee the Famous', master of the flash shot of murder scenes. Travis's encounter with the Secret Service men at the rally of presidential candidate Charles Palantine recalls Robert Frank and Gary Winogrand, who often frame people off to one side, staring out of picture, or decapitate them, the better to draw attention to body language. Less impressively, the camera pans off Travis from time to time to gaze round a cluttered cab garage, or linger with affectless detachment on that cliché of Photography 101, the empty hallway.

An insistence on exact framing bedevilled the production. As Scorsese told critic David Ehrenstein, 'The big trouble came in the scene in the coffee shop when I put Cybill and Bob against the window, and you can see all of Columbus Circle – the buses, the lights of the city. It doesn't sound like much, but it's very important, because the city is a character in the film, and the scene really establishes that. It's basically a two-shot profile with a number of panning movements where the camera goes back and forth between the actors. Well, what happened was I was to take a shot of Cybill alone, and one of Bob alone. Half the frame would have been the window and what was just outside it, and the other half would have shown each of them. It was very hot and rainy that summer, with a lot of thunderstorms, and when I went back to get those shots I couldn't get them to match the ones we'd already taken. I had to wait for the weather to change. That took time, and time is money. The studio said, "Well, can't you cheat it? Can't you pan the camera over to the right and have her against a white wall?"' Needless to say, Scorsese refused. This, after all, was the director who would threaten to take his name off *Raging Bull* because the sound mix failed to render the words 'Cutty Sark' with the clarity he demanded.

For the film's climax, where Travis, a walking arsenal with a murderer's Mohawk haircut, fixed grin and glassy stare, invades Sport's house to 'rescue' Iris, Scorsese took over a condemned building at 89th Street and Columbus Avenue. The scenes were shot in sequence, so the cast and crew mounted the staircase each day past walls splattered with stage blood – a rerun in reverse of the slow track back down the stairs that ends the sequence.

Retarding the film's motion and periodically dropping frames, Scorsese and editor Marcia Lucas turned Travis's attack into the assault of a cyborg. Face plastic-pale, he stalks in eerie silence up the stairs, absorbing bullets and dispensing death. With everyone but Iris dead, he turns his guns on himself, but both are empty. Slumping to the couch, he grins at the arriving police, puts a bloodied finger to his temple, and three times mimes shooting himself in the head.

By the time they shot this, De Niro was so deep in the part that it seemed he might never emerge. The character of Travis etched itself permanently on his face. An inch-long slanting crease between the bridge of his nose and his right eye developed into a permanent feature. He also began to display what would become a trademark crooked grin that half-closed his right eye and pulled down that side of his mouth. Both remained after *Taxi Driver* – became, indeed, more prominent with time: elements, usually ill, of future characterisations.

The film's *tour de force* remained the 'Are you talkin' to me?' scene where, having armed himself, Travis rehearses confrontations in the mirror of his apartment. Schrader simply wrote, 'Travis talks to himself in the mirror.' De Niro improvised the rest – though with what materials nobody quite agrees. David Scott Milton points out that Stella Adler's students used an exercise incorporating versions of 'Are you talking to me?' Others mention that rocker Bruce Springsteen, slouching on stage in response to the shouts of his audience for an encore, would use the same phrase.

The real threat of the scene doesn't lie in the language, however, but in the fact that it's directed at the audience. For the first time in the film, we feel that Travis menaces not simply the manufactured characters of the story, but us. It is a bridge that briefly and disquietingly links cinema to life. If John Hinckley, the loner obsessed with Jodie Foster who, in her name, shot Ronald Reagan in 1981, was truly motivated by having seen *Taxi Driver*, this is the scene that tipped him towards murder.

Why is De Niro so convincing as Travis Bickle? Paul Schrader provided a clue when, some years after, he pointed out the Oedipean nature of the story. 'He decides to kill the father figure of the girl who rejected him, which is of course a reflection of his own father figure, and when he is thwarted by that he moves on to the pimp, the other father figure.' To someone as conflicted about his own parental model as De Niro, the situation had a painful relevance.

In his other films, Scorsese had used pre-recorded music that lingered in the collective unconscious of his characters, but all we see of Travis's taste in music is an anodyne dance number on the TV show *American Bandstand*. Quixotically, Scorsese invited a score from Bernard Herrmann, composer of Hollywood classics from *Citizen Kane* to *Marnie* and *Vertigo*. Irascible and perfectionist, Herrmann initially refused: 'I don't do things about cab drivers.' The script changed his mind, however. 'I like when he poured peach brandy on the cornflakes,' he mused. 'I like that. I'll do it.'

His music drew on the fruity rhetoric of forties *film noir*. Its sensual saxophone theme for Betsy is ruptured by an *accellerando* of military snare drums. Ominous tympani and jolting orchestral chords connote Travis's troubled state of mind with the bump of his cab over potholed asphalt. Seemingly anachronistic, the music proved exactly the element needed to lift *Taxi Driver* out of the gutter and into the rarefied atmosphere of fable.

It was helped by night-time shots of the taxi gliding along wet streets. Second-unit director David Nicholls filmed these, including the shot that ran under the credits and become one of the film's most famous, of the taxi emerging from steam like Leviathan from the deep.

Among the people who visited Scorsese and Lucas as they cut *Taxi Driver* at the old Astoria Studios on Long Island was Steven Spielberg. He was looking for actors to appear in *1941*, a gigantic World War II comedy about the panic that swept California immediately after Pearl Harbor when Japanese air armadas were rumoured to be *en route* to bomb Los Angeles. Spielberg had seen John Belushi on the TV show *Saturday Night Live*, where one of his routines involved a samurai baker who sliced cakes with a sword. Thinking he might play a small role as the skipper of a Japanese submarine, Spielberg met the comic and his friends at a restaurant called One Fifth Avenue.

'You want to see my Japanese submarine skipper?' Belushi asked. Upending a coat rack into a periscope, he scanned the room and yelled, 'Gveeet Yankeeee Shipping!' He stayed in character for the rest of the night, to the astonishment of Spielberg, who had never met anyone like him. Finally – and disastrously – Belushi would not simply have a role in *1941* but be its star.

Through Scorsese and Spielberg, De Niro and Belushi also became friends. They were near-neighbours in the Village, where Belushi also rented, on Morton Street, a soundproofed basement wired with giant amplifiers. Visitors to the pizza-box and candy-wrapper-littered space were treated to impromptu amateur rock performances by the usually-stoned Belushi. According to Bob Woodward in his biography of Belushi, he and De Niro took cocaine together around this time, and De Niro fell down, cutting himself badly enough to need stitches. The friendship continued, in New York and Hollywood, for years, until Belushi's death in 1982.

Even while he was shooting *Taxi Driver*, De Niro fielded new projects and cleared up old ones. Scorsese announced that he would direct De Niro in a film about shoplifters called *Booster*, but nothing more was heard of it. De Niro auditioned for the role of impresario Billy Rose in *Funny Lady* opposite Barbra Streisand, but saw the role go, once again, to James Caan.

He also returned to Rome to dub his *Novecento* role into English for the film's American release – which, it turned out, still lay two years in the future. He found Bertolucci distracted by the demands of his Italian and American financiers, both of which refused his first six-hour cut. 'I had re-edited, recut and redirected the movie in the editing suite until it conformed to acceptability by Paramount,' Bertolucci said. 'I could not let it go, but also I could not allow it simply to be massacred, sliced up like a piece of salami.'

Watching the 'American' cut, still more than four hours long, De Niro saw that, for all Bertolucci's brilliance, the subject had defeated him. In a voice performance that echoed his doubts,

De Niro didn't even attempt to recall the rhythms of Italian speech; rather, Alfredo talked like a well-bred American middle manager.

The impetus for this came from the project he was preparing early in 1975. Martin Scorsese recalls, 'Harry Ufland – who was my agent then as well as Bob's – came by the set one day while we were making *Taxi Driver*. Bob had a suit on. He was, between takes, checking out a suit for the wardrobe of *Last Tycoon*. Harry didn't recognise him. For twenty minutes Bob wasn't Travis Bickle any more. He had become Monroe Stahr. It was amazing.' Disconcertingly, De Niro, once he was finished shooting *Taxi Driver*, remained in the character of Stahr until the new film started shooting. At the 'wrap' party for *Taxi Driver*, he was an apparition in double-breasted evening jacket among the shabby boho crew.

The Last Tycoon, F. Scott Fitzgerald's final, uncompleted novel, was a story of Hollywood, inspired by the career of Irving Thalberg, MGM's production head during some of its greatest years. Thalberg, always in poor health, died at thirty-seven in 1936, of natural causes, but Fitzgerald, jaded with Hollywood, chose to show his hero as a creative genius destroyed by the east coast money-men who truly ran the movies. Critic Edmund Wilson, Fitzgerald's friend, gathered up the six chapters Fitzgerald completed before his death in 1940, combined them with his notes, and managed to create enough story for the book to be published; but the narrative had only a spasmodic coherence, and lacked a conclusion.

De Niro had never met anyone like the producer of *The Last Tycoon*. Sam Spiegel was one of the last old-fashioned piratical independents, with a face like a bad-tempered boxer, and a taste for dumb blondes and huge cigars. In forty years of film financing, he'd mastered the art of playing both ends against the middle. It got him jailed in the early 1930s in Britain, and resulted in his deportation to the US, where disguised – barely – as 'S.P. Eagle', he financed films like *On the Waterfront*. The gloss he won by producing *The Bridge on the River Kwai* and *Lawrence of Arabia* hadn't refined his streetfighter methods: 'If you woke up in a motel with a dead whore who'd been stabbed,' said Billy Wilder, 'who would you call? Sam Spiegel.'

Spiegel boasted – or complained – that he'd invested \$5.5 million in *Tycoon*. He'd persuaded Mike Nichols, then high from *The Graduate* and *Carnal Knowledge*, to direct. Both of Nichols' stars from those films, Dustin Hoffman and Jack Nicholson, were ready to play Stahr. This was enough to persuade Paramount to put up the money.

To script *Tycoon*, Spiegel hired English playwright Harold Pinter, whose screenplays for *The Servant*, *Accident* and *The Go-Between*, not to mention the film versions of his own plays, were masterpieces of compression. It was a nervous collaboration, since Pinter and Spiegel had locked horns in the past, over Nicholas Mosley's novel *Accident*, which Pinter was adapting. Fearful, in the words of Pinter's biographer Michael Billington, that the producer would 'want to leave his visible thumbprints over the finished film', Pinter and Mosley persuaded Spiegel to sell his rights in *Accident* to the more *au courant* Joseph Losey.

Pinter wrote slowly, and Dustin Hoffman, anxious to get on with his career, couldn't resist the role of Carl Bernstein in Alan Pakula's *All the President's Men*. While Nichols waited, he paired Nicholson with Warren Beatty in the comedy *The Fortune*, from a script by Elaine May.

At the Academy Awards in April 1975, De Niro was named Best Supporting Actor for *Godfather II*, in the face, most people agreed, of only modest competition. The other nominees were Fred Astaire, belatedly and sentimentally proposed for a feeble non-dancing role in *The Towering Inferno*, Jeff Bridges for *Thunderbolt and Lightfoot*, and two colleagues from *Godfather II*, Michael V. Gazzo and Lee Strasberg. Coppola, who took Best Picture, Best Director, Best Original Screenplay, Art Direction and Best Musical Score, also accepted the Oscar on behalf of De Niro, who stayed away.

Even when he did discuss the award with the press, he was hardly enthusiastic. 'Lots of people who win the award don't deserve it,' he told *Woman's Wear Daily*, 'so it makes you a little cynical about how much it means. Did it mean that much to me?

Well, I don't know. It changes your life. Like anything that will change your life, people react to it. I mean, it's not bad winning it.'

De Niro had other things on his mind. Diahnne Abbott was pressing him to legitimise their relationship, but friends counselled him that marriage to an African-American could impair his career. Plenty of stars slept with black women; none married them.

He was also experiencing problems with his next film. Pinter still hadn't 'licked' *The Last Tycoon*. Partway through writing it, he was seized with the idea for what would become *No Man's Land*, one of his most successful plays, and diverted much of his energy into that.

While they waited, Mike Nichols proposed that De Niro star in another project, 'Clark Gable Slept Here', an original screenplay by Neil Simon, Broadway's hottest comedy writer.

Simon's wife Jean had died in 1974, and he'd just married Marsha Mason, the actress appearing in his play *The Good Doctor*. He hoped that 'Clark Gable Slept Here', changed to *Bogart Slept Here* when Gable and his late wife Carole Lombard became the subject of a new film, *Gable and Lombard*, would launch Mason in movies. The main character, an actor with a loving wife – the Mason part – and two small kids, strikes it rich with a big movie role, and is transformed overnight into a teenage idol. Girls besiege him, and he has to decide whether to succumb, or stay with his family.

Part of the story took place in Hollywood's venerable Château Marmont Hotel, where, as the title suggests, many stars had slept, seldom alone. Publicity caricatures for the film showed De Niro walking down Sunset Boulevard against a background of the Château. It became his favourite hangout in Los Angeles. He moved there after his marriage broke up, and the hotel would figure in the later death of his friend John Belushi.

Despite Dustin Hoffman having been first choice for the role of the actor (he would be offered it again when the project fell apart), both Simon and Nichols denied that the piece was inspired by Hoffman's overnight success in *The Graduate* and subsequent divorce.

De Niro's reasons for accepting such a shopworn part were much like those for taking on Monroe Stahr; it was a character he'd never played before. The film was also a comedy, a form in which he'd never excelled. Admittedly, Nichols' last comedy, *The Fortune*, had flopped. But Nichols had won his reputation as one half of a hugely successful comedy improv team with Elaine May, had directed *The Graduate*, and, moreover, had just successfully fought off a Supreme Court obscenity charge over his film *Carnal Knowledge*, which managed to be both popular and profound about sexual relations. If anyone could unearth De Niro's well-buried vein of humour, surely it would be Nichols.

Not so evident during the pre-production honeymoon period were Nichols' doctrinaire manner, his unshakeable belief in the rightness of his comic vision, and the influence wielded over Simon by his new wife. Although, in June 1975, Nichols was still full of enthusiasm for the project and its Oscar-winning star, insisting that this was not 'just another wisecrack comedy', *Bogart Slept Here* ran into problems as soon as rehearsals began.

Having been bossed by Bertolucci, De Niro was in no mood to take the same from Nichols. Interviewing him for *Playboy* in 1989, Lawrence Grobel said, 'There's an eyewitness who said that during *Bogart Slept Here*, he saw you, Marsha Mason and Nichols in the studio commissary, having lunch. You were bent over your food as Nichols pointed his finger at you, telling you what comedy was. Mason supposedly kicked you under the table and whispered that you should show more respect to Nichols. You looked up, said you had to go, left the table, walked out the door, went to the airport and flew to New York.'

De Niro poured scorn on the anecdote, but it's incontrovertible that, after two weeks' shooting, he departed abruptly. The studio issued the customary statements about 'artistic disagreements', but Nichols was reported as saying, 'This man is undirectable,' and that De Niro 'simply wasn't funny'. Simon conceded, 'Robert De Niro is a very intense actor. He doesn't play joy very well.' Marsha Mason concurred.

Nichols tried various replacements, including Jack Nicholson, James Caan, Tony Lo Bianco – and Dustin Hoffman, who had to decline, since he was committed to make *Marathon Man*. Of all who auditioned, the one who appealed most to Mason and Simon was Richard Dreyfuss. A few years later, Simon would write *The Goodbye Girl* with Dreyfuss and Mason in mind. In effect the same story as *Bogart Slept Here*, but from the woman's point of view, it would describe a middle-aged actress with a child who arrives home from another disappointing audition to find her boyfriend has left for Hollywood, and rented part of their apartment to another actor. He also becomes her lover, but when the newcomer gets his chance at a movie career, she faces being abandoned again.

The role fitted Dreyfuss so well that it won him an Academy Award. But the experience of *Bogart Slept Here* profoundly depressed Nichols, who resigned from *The Last Tycoon*, returned to his first love, the theatre, and didn't direct another movie for five years. De Niro's take on the experience with Nichols was succinct. 'He fired me. They tried not to pay me. They did not succeed.'

Asked, many years later, by talk-show host Conan O'Brien if he enjoyed doing comedy, De Niro, though more than usually inarticulate, hinted at the reason for his difficulty with it. 'Well, I . . . I enjoy it,' he said, 'and it . . . it sometimes . . . it's not as . . . it's not as, like . . . it's not as intense maybe, serious in some ways and also, but . . . yet, if it's a comedy and it's over the character takes themselves . . . themselves seriously, well, then, you know, then it's funny. You can't be loose about that. But there's still . . . there's more of . . . like, more room to kind of kid around, fool around, a certain way of experimenting with things in . . . in the comedy, at this point for me, it seems.' Comedy, then, is attractive to him to the degree that it isn't comedy.

CHAPTER ELEVEN

If You Can Make it There . . .

Coke or smoke – check it out.

Street cry of New York dope-sellers, 1970s

Starring in *The Last Tycoon* should have signalled De Niro's arrival in the top rank of movie stars. That it didn't says something about the evolving Hollywood system, but also about De Niro himself.

Old Hollywood wasn't dead – just *playing* dead. Although young directors, performers and producers were giving the gerontocracy a headache, the rules of making movies hadn't really changed. One needed money to produce a picture, and, as banks would only lend to solid companies, even the hottest new talents had to take their project to a studio, which exacted a high price for its help.

The market hadn't changed much either. More young American males watched movies than anyone else. George Lucas and Steven Spielberg, whose films were popular with this group, could impose their conditions on the studios: quicker payment, higher percentages, a more generous share of the rights. But De Niro and Scorsese lacked that mass appeal. The problems of *Last Tycoon* and De Niro's subsequent film, *New York, New York*, showed he was a movie *actor*, not a movie *star* – a crucial distinction when it came to bankability.

*   *   *

To replace Mike Nichols on *Last Tycoon*, Sam Spiegel coaxed sixty-six-year-old Elia Kazan, who directed *On the Waterfront* for him two decades earlier, out of virtual retirement. 'Gadge' Kazan had abandoned film for fiction in the early sixties, and his last three films were all adaptations of his own novels.

Kazan did not return to Hollywood with rose petals strewn at his feet. He was deeply unpopular with many in the film community, both for his arrogance and because he had informed on fellow Communists during the witch-hunts of the fifties.

Spiegel still wanted Jack Nicholson for Stahr, or, failing him, Al Pacino. But without Nichols in charge, Nicholson wasn't interested. Pacino never even responded to Spiegel's feelers, and later admitted he didn't bother to read the script.

In their place, Kazan suggested De Niro – largely an instinctive choice. 'I knew little about Bobby,' he said. 'I was playing a hunch.' Spiegel rejected the proposal with contempt. De Niro was 'common', he said. But, with no other options in sight and Paramount pushing for a start date, he eventually acquiesced.

By 3 November, when shooting started, De Niro had read everything on and by Kazan. He brushed off criticism from liberal friends about the morality of working with a notorious turncoat. This, after all, was the director who first put Stanislavski to practical use on Broadway. Mutual admiration was the order of the day. De Niro so admired a Kazan monograph on directing that he had copies printed up, and presented them to friends.

Kazan was no less warm towards his star. In an interview for *Newsweek*, he compared him favourably with both Brando and James Dean. 'Dean represented the release of anger against the failure of parents to understand. Brando was happily arrogant, a free spirit. Dean was sad and sulky; you kept expecting him to cry. De Niro is a number of things, all at once. There are lots of different people in him. He finds release and fulfilment in becoming other people. Picture after picture, he gets deep into the thing. He's found his solution for living at a time like this: in work.'

Once they started filming, Kazan's admiration grew. 'He's the only actor I've ever known who called me up on Friday after we got through shooting, and said, "Let's work tomorrow and Sunday together." He's the hardest-working actor I've ever met and one of the best guys I've ever met in the business.'

Harold Pinter's script, when it finally arrived, alarmed Kazan. It viewed Fitzgerald's book entirely as a romance rather than a story about the movie business. Still in love with the memory of his dead movie-star wife, Minna Davis, Stahr almost canonises her, to the point of maintaining her dressing room as a shrine, and urging writers and directors to make all women in the stories they write for him 'perfect'.

Even after he falls for the mysterious Kathleen, who is her double, memories of Minna continue to haunt him. Kathleen, about to marry another man, also older than her but obviously more impressive than Stahr, treats him as a diversion. After having sex in his half-built beach house, she drops him, and Stahr, his dream of a second chance destroyed, perversely ruins his life and career, defying the New York office and brawling drunkenly with the representative of the Writers' Union who's come to negotiate.

Fitzgerald wrote the book during his relationship with the young, adoring Sheilah Graham, his mistress and protégée for the last months of his life. Nobody knew how he would have ended *Last Tycoon*, and Pinter didn't try to second-guess him, choosing instead to find solutions in other Fitzgerald books. Stahr, like Gatsby, is destroyed by 'living too long with the same dream'. His end demonstrates the truth of Fitzgerald's dictum, 'There are no second acts in American lives.'

Kazan found the script too talkative, and too little concerned with Stahr. The story of the last tycoon had become that of the last tycoon's girlfriend – about whom, frustratingly, we learn almost nothing. Once Kathleen's out of the story, the script tails off. Kazan complained there wasn't even a final scene, so he had to invent one, of Stahr walking off through the deserted studio.

'Kazan was after a sexually very explicit film,' recalled cast member Donald Pleasence, 'and Harold would never go for that.

He didn't want people writhing about the floor with no clothes on.'

Spiegel had promised Pinter that Kazan would shoot his script without changing a word. Kazan wrote to Pinter, pleading for rewrites. 'Pinter never replied, or commented on them,' said Kazan, 'and absolutely nothing was done to make it more interesting.' Later, he decided that Spiegel intercepted his letter before Pinter saw it. De Niro sided with Kazan. 'I frankly think that a script *should* be changed,' he said. 'You have to make the adjustments, or it becomes something rigid.'

But Spiegel, who was six years older than Kazan and who would also retire after this film, was determined to give *The Last Tycoon* the status befitting Fitzgerald and his own roster of masterpieces. He dictated a stately production, rooted in the tradition Irving Thalberg helped create. In sets so solid a tank couldn't dent them, beautiful people, costumed and made-up to within an inch of their lives, delivered the sort of lines that only people in Hollywood movies ever said. It was as if *Mean Streets* and *Taxi Driver* had never been made.

The Last Tycoon mixed established stars with newcomers – the antithesis of Scorsese's films, which were saturated with new people on both sides of the camera. A young Theresa Russell plays Cecilia Brady in a style wildly at odds with that of Robert Mitchum, playing her father. Peter Strauss has two scenes as young screenwriter Wylie, Cecilia's boyfriend – the vestiges of a much longer part.

Embarrassing as a Latin lover troubled by impotence, Tony Curtis preens and poses bare-chested in a scene opposite an equally improbable Jeanne Moreau playing the stock temperamental European actress. Donald Pleasence is clichéd British novelist Boxley, struggling to write for the movies, while Dana Andrews and Ray Milland linger in the shadows as fading director Red Ridingwood and front-office lawyer Fleischacker.

Jack Nicholson agreed to take the small role of the Writers' Union organiser Brimmer; his scene with De Niro is among the best in the film. Spiegel gave the role of Kathleen Moore to Ingrid Boulting, a moon-faced debutante with a voice plummy with

RIGHT: The 'real'
De Niro, c.1980.

BELOW: As Travis
Bickle, sociopathic
loner of *Taxi
Driver* (1976).

BELOW RIGHT:
After gaining forty
kilos to play the
ageing Jake La
Motta in *Raging
Bull* (1980).

LEFT: As gang boss Al Capone in *The Untouchables* (1987).

BELOW: Playing redneck killer Max Cady in *Cape Fear* (1991).

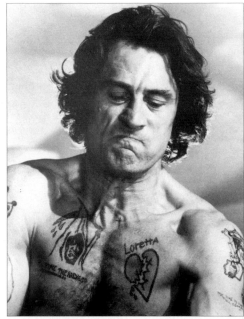

BELOW: As escaped convict Lustig in the modernised *Great Expectations* (1998).

DE NIRO'S TROUBLED
RELATIONSHIP WITH
HIS FATHER DREW
HIM TO ROLES AS A
FATHER FIGURE

RIGHT: De Niro with
Robert De Niro Sr.

LEFT: De Niro
with his adopted
stepdaughter Drena.

RIGHT: Travis Bickle
tries to develop a
relationship with
teenage prostitute
Iris (Jodie Foster) in
Taxi Driver.

RIGHT: As blacklisted screenwriter David Merrill with his son Paulie (Luke Edwards) in *Guilty by Suspicion* (1991).

ABOVE: Playing tyrannical father Dwight Hansen in *This Boy's Life* (1993).

RIGHT: As veteran Nick Wells in *The Score* (2001), instructing young thief Jack Teller (Edward Norton).

RIGHT: De Niro
with Liza Minnelli
and long-time
collaborator Martin
Scorsese on *New
York, New York*
(1977).

LEFT: De Niro
and Jane Fonda
with Martin Ritt
during the
filming of *Stanley
and Iris* (1990).

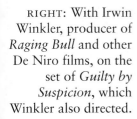

RIGHT: With Irwin
Winkler, producer of
Raging Bull and other
De Niro films, on the
set of *Guilty by
Suspicion*, which
Winkler also directed.

ABOVE: Elia Kazan directs De Niro and Ingrid Boulting on *The Last Tycoon* (1976).

BELOW: De Niro on the French location of *Ronin* (1998), with producer Frank Mancuso Jr (left) and director John Frankenheimer (right).

De Niro endured repeated beatings as Jake La Motta in *Raging Bull*.

ABOVE: To prepare for the role of cab driver Travis Bickle in *Taxi Driver*, De Niro drove a taxi in New York and haunted cafés where drivers hung out. Conversations recorded there became dialogue for characters like driver/philosopher Wizard (Peter Boyle).

BELOW: De Niro learned the saxophone – not very well – to play forties musician Jimmy Doyle in *New York, New York*.

BELOW: Rehearsing barefoot on the stones of the Amazon for the role of Rodrigo Mendoza in *The Mission* (1986).

elocution lessons who phoned him after hearing about the film at a London dinner party. 'I felt like working,' she later explained languidly, 'and I knew I could play Kathleen.' As 'Ingrid Brett' she'd cringed and flinched her way through a few British horror films, but this was to be her first – and, as it turned out, last – major screen role, since she too, like the film's producer and director, fled from the movies afterwards.

Kazan never cared for Boulting. It shows in the demure downward glances and doe-eyed stares that characterise her performance. Her dismal showing suggested to some people that she was Spiegel's mistress. This wasn't the case, though he did shove his actual eighteen-year-old 'protégée' into a bit part. 'Do me a favour,' Kazan murmured to Spiegel after her scene. 'Try to persuade her to give up acting' – a comment that didn't endear him to the producer.

Playing a stiff, repressed, short-back-and-sides Jewish film executive who seldom removed his jacket, let alone his tie, represented a considerable stretch for De Niro: that in itself was the appeal of the role, though his $200,000 fee, plus a percentage of the profits, also played a part. But he knew he stood little chance of getting inside a character whom even the author viewed from outside: the novel is narrated by the infatuated Cecilia, daughter of studio executive Pat Brady, and we see Stahr only through her eyes.

With no behavioural 'hooks' on which to hang the character, De Niro compromised by putting on a three-piece suit and walking up and down the corridors at Paramount, repeating to himself, 'All this belongs to me.' He sat in on preview screenings, and listened to directors, editors and executives wrangling over the look and sound of a movie. Leasing a modest three-bedroom house in Bel Air of the sort Stahr might have occupied, he moved in Diahnne, her daughter Drena, and Diahnne's cats; the animals had so lacerated the furnishings of the Beverly Hills Hotel that De Niro and the manager practically came to blows, and a lawsuit was threatened.

He slimmed down forty pounds, the better to fit into Stahr's double-breasted grey suits. He also submitted to a new, fuller haircut, with waves, and a more prominent nose. But nothing satisfied Spiegel. De Niro's request that the production pay the costs of his relocating to Hollywood, a conventional clause of every such contract, simply convinced him still further that the actor was only one step from the gutter: a 'petty larceny punk'.

'He still has that petty larceny look,' Spiegel told Kazan, 'especially when he smiles. He has no nobility.' He called De Niro 'wilful and arrogant, and spoiling fast', and threatened to replace him. 'It was in moments like this,' said Kazan, 'that I had to remind myself that this was the man who made *Lawrence of Arabia* – what courage! – and *The Bridge on the River Kwai*, and how, except for him, *On the Waterfront* might never have been made.' By the end of shooting in January 1976, Spiegel and Kazan were screaming at one another.

De Niro said Spiegel 'had good taste, and he was funny', but that he 'tried to finagle paying me what he said he would'. His description of their showdown is laconic enough to have been written by Pinter.

'In the make-up trailer one night when we were shooting, Sam came over and said, "Bobby . . ."'

'And I said, "Sam, you didn't do what you were supposed to do."

'"Well . . ." he said.

'And I just walked away from him.

'But I liked him.'

Kazan gave cameo roles to a couple of fellow teachers of drama – old cronies. Jeff Corey played Stahr's doctor and Peggy Feury one of the writers in the film's – and the book's – best scene, where Stahr, for Boxley's benefit, invents a movie story in his office, featuring a stove, a mysterious girl, a pair of black gloves and a nickel. When Boxley asks, 'What's the nickel for?' Feury gets to deliver the punch-line, 'The nickel is for the movies.'

A few images briefly bring *Last Tycoon* to life: a shot of Stahr threading his way through slumped workmen against what appears to be a bright blue sky, only to be revealed, as the camera tilts up, to be a painted backdrop; an afternoon assignation in an empty parking lot – a red and a black roadster, the cracked asphalt scattered with branches from the pepper trees, a sense of enervating heat and silence. These are all there is to suggest what *The Last Tycoon* might have been.

Once he got into the cutting room, Kazan started looking for reassurance. He rang his cameraman, Victor Kemper, and asked him, now that they were no longer employer and employee, to give his frank opinion of the film. Kemper never returned the call. Other members of the cast were hinting of their doubts about De Niro. 'I never thought he quite got to grips with the part,' said Donald Pleasence. Spiegel insisted on showing a first cut to David Lean, who left without making any comment. Later, Lean told Spiegel he thought De Niro didn't have the force to carry a major starring role.

'There you are,' Spiegel said triumphantly. 'I told you. He's just an East Side punk.'

Scorsese finished editing *Taxi Driver* while De Niro was still at work on *Tycoon*. In what seemed a portent for the superstitious director, Bernard Herrmann died on Christmas Eve 1975, just after finishing the score.

Drugs had been a motif of the *Taxi Driver* unit, and little changed during the editing process. Almost everyone was on something – cocaine, heroin, an entire pharmacopoeia of pills. In the cutting room, Scorsese washed down Quaaludes with Dom Perignon.

Dope skewed perception, impaired judgment. When an attractive redheaded freelance journalist named Julia Cameron turned up on the set to interview everyone for *Oui* magazine, she ended up sleeping with Scorsese. Sandy Weintraub exited in a fury, not before ripping the wipers off Scorsese's Lotus. Hardly had she gone than Scorsese asked Cameron to rewrite Palantine's political speeches and the conversation between the cabbies in the Belmore Cafeteria. On 30 December 1975 they were married – bizarrely, in her home town of Libertyville, Illinois.

Columbia hated *Taxi Driver*, and wanted to cut much of it, beginning with the violent conclusion. Scorsese called all his director friends to his house and went crazy, fantasising about aping Travis and massacring the Columbia brass. Resourcefully, Julia Cameron Scorsese took a work print to New York and showed it to Pauline Kael, who praised it in her *New Yorker* column, and offered to publish an open letter to David Begelman if that would help. News that the influential Kael liked the picture shook the executives, and they modified their demands. Finally, only one shot, of blood gushing from an exploded hand, was cut, and Scorsese agreed to moderate the amount of blood in that sequence by de-saturating the colour. John Huston had done this on *Moby Dick* and *Reflections in a Golden Eye*, imposing a hazy, painterly quality, and Scorsese had long wanted to experiment with the technique. To his glee, it gave the carnage a ghostly horror even more disquieting than the original.

De Niro was offered the part of folk singer Woody Guthrie in Hal Ashby's *Bound for Glory*, but turned it down. Richard Attenborough also wanted him for the film of Cornelius Ryan's account of the abortive Arnhem campaign, *A Bridge too Far*. He and the producers haggled, not over the fee, which, at $500,000 *a day*, was generous, but over the character. De Niro wanted to sit down with the director and discuss his role in detail. Attenborough, not strong on motivation at the best of times, had enough to do assembling the rest of his all-star cast and managing the film's enormous logistics. De Niro dropped out. Robert Redford got the role.

Success didn't modify the habits of De Niro's earlier frugal days. In Hollywood, he'd elected to rent, not buy, his house, and lease a car – both tax-deductible. He carried this image to the Cannes Festival when *Taxi Driver* was shown there in May 1976 (Bertolucci also previewed his cut of *Novecento*).

At the press conference after the screening, De Niro – who, like Scorsese and Keitel, spoke no French, and relied for translations on Jodie Foster, who'd graduated valedictorian of the Lycée Français de Los Angeles – explained how he'd hitch-hiked to

Cannes last time, and confided that he'd always imagined he'd spend his life travelling the same way.

French *scriboulards* responded to this refreshingly non-Hollywood attitude, and to Scorsese's obvious love of movies. American hacks were less happy, since De Niro and Scorsese hid at the luxurious Eden Roc Hotel on Cap d'Antibes, talking only to foreign press. Too many movies had been ruined by negative pre-publicity carried back like a virus from Cannes by Stateside pressmen anxious for a headline. Columbia also kept the American public as much in the dark as possible about the film. The sixty-second trailer then running in US cinemas showed only De Niro's face, while a rolling title reproduced reviews from earlier films. There was no actual footage from the film.

The reaction of everyone who saw *Taxi Driver* at Cannes was enthusiastic, with the exception of Tennessee Williams, who, as President of the Festival jury, made a widely-publicised attack on films of violence. Without mentioning *Taxi Driver*, he complained on behalf of the jury about 'films without hope, some of which reflected a violence seldom seen before. We are well aware that this violence and hopelessness reflect the image of our society. However, we fear that violence breeds violence, and that, instead of being a denunciation, it leads our society to the escalation of violence.'

This came oddly from a writer whose work encompassed cannibalism and rape, and who, moreover, had been a close friend of Robert De Niro Sr. Who knows what old scores were being settled? Williams' sentiments weren't shared by other members of the jury, however, and an excited Scorsese woke his mother in New York at 5 a.m. to announce that *Taxi Driver* had won the Palme d'Or.

After a publicity coup like this, Columbia pushed the film into immediate release. The night before it opened in New York, Scorsese hosted a dinner for most of the principals, at the end of which he told them, 'Whatever happens tomorrow, we *know* we've made a great film.'

But all were astonished, riding around town the next day, to find people queueing in their thousands. Better still, those standing patiently on the sidewalk at 10 a.m. weren't waiting for the 11 a.m. performance but for the one at 2 p.m., since the earlier screening was already sold out. Within a few months, the film had grossed $12.5 million, making it a major hit.

Not only were the reviews excellent, but the Palme d'Or turned out to be only the first of *Taxi Driver*'s awards. Jodie Foster won the Best Actress award of the British Academy. The Los Angeles Film Critics' Association and the New York Film Critics' Circle picked De Niro as the year's best actor. The National Society of Film Critics honoured De Niro and Foster, and named Scorsese the year's best director.

In April 1976, riding high on the success of *Taxi Driver*, De Niro married Diahnne Abbott at the Ethical Culture Center in New York. The small list of guests included Sally Kirkland, Julie Bovasso, Joseph Papp, Jay Cocks and Verna Fields, Barry Primus, John Hancock and Shelley Winters, Elia Kazan and Sam Spiegel, as well as Scorsese, Schrader and Keitel. 'It was a very strange selection of people,' Paul Schrader said. 'Everybody there was somebody who had helped Bobby become a different person.' A *better* person? 'Absolutely not – somebody *different*.'

Everyone skirted the question of colour. When a journalist raised it, Harvey Keitel professed astonishment that it should cross anybody's mind, least of all De Niro's. 'Are you kidding?' he said. 'If you asked Bobby that, he'd say something like, "Is Di black?"'

This was absurd. Abbott's very blackness was her appeal, and De Niro had obviously balanced his desire for so provocative a trophy against any professional threat posed by the marriage. Normally inarticulate, he had all the arguments at his fingertips when he discussed this question. While disclaiming any 'particular courage [in] marrying a girl who is not white', he insisted that it was no longer a professional impediment. 'Ten years ago, maybe, this marriage couldn't have happened. But the studios don't work like that any more, and I don't expect any trouble. I don't think about it at all. No one has said anything to me and if they thought about it they certainly didn't say it. Even if they did I wouldn't listen to them.'

Yet he listened sufficiently well to be able to cite two cases in which the studios had censured artists who entered mixed marriages. Lennie Hayton was fired as musical director of MGM for marrying Lena Horne, and Columbia warned off Sammy Davis Jr when he tried to marry Kim Novak (he later married white actress Mai Britt anyway). De Niro could also have mentioned that the Phillipses thought colour enough of an issue to transform all *Taxi Driver*'s villains from black to white only a year before.

To coincide with the wedding, Robert Sr published, at his own expense, a book of poetry called *A Fashionable Watering Place*. The printing was limited to a hundred copies and illustrated with his own Matisse-like sketches. A note after the contents page pointed out tersely, 'These poems are by Robert De Niro, the painter, not to be confused with Robert De Niro, the actor, his son.'

De Niro and Abbott honeymooned in Rome. He did some additional dubbing for *Novecento*, which was opening at the New York Film Festival. While in Rome, Abbott became pregnant – in the Raphael Hotel. Once their son was born in January 1977, they would name him Raphael. 'Just as well they weren't staying at the Hilton,' said Shelley Winters sourly when she heard the news.

The couple moved into an apartment on Barrow Street, in the Village, but within a year were looking for a new one. Abbott, now a celebrity by marriage, if a second-level one, had become friendly with Andy Warhol, who featured her on the cover of his magazine *Interview*. In August 1977, he wrote in his diary about a dinner with Abbott and his partner Bob Colacello, during which Colacello quizzed her about being black. 'And then,' wrote Warhol, 'he got it down to what did it feel like to be coloured and in bed with Bobby De Niro. Then I think she must have slipped Bob some coke – he went into the bathroom and came back a zombie.'

After this, Abbott invited them back to Barrow Street. 'She had clothes all over; she was buying lots and lots of clothes.

They're looking for a new apartment and I suggested Park Avenue, but she said they have an image to protect. She served Dom Perignon, showed us baby pictures.'

Scorsese was enjoying Hollywood. Doors once barred to him now swung invitingly open. During the arguments over *Taxi Driver*, United Artists and MGM had each offered to buy the film from Columbia and release it themselves. Both had made enough money with the controversial *Midnight Cowboy* and *Last Tango in Paris* to show that even X-rated material had a large market. Now they listened incredulously as the man who'd filmed corridors running with blood and men with hands blown off pitched them what sounded like . . . well, a Cinemascope Technicolor stereo showbiz musical, with Robert De Niro playing tenor sax.

Scorsese had read in a newspaper that Irwin Winkler planned to make a film called *New York, New York* about the days of the big swing bands during and just after World War II. Impulsively, he rang his agent Harry Ulfland and said, 'Hey, can I do that?'

Winkler's career had not prospered since *The Gang that Couldn't Shoot Straight*, but by sheer persistence he and his partner Robert Chartoff had shepherded half a dozen films to the screen, and, more impressively, survived their subsequent failure. These included the student revolution movie *The Strawberry Statement* and Peter Bogdanovich's *Nickelodeon*. They'd recently taken a chance on a low-budget boxing film written by and starring an unknown actor named Sylvester Stallone, but Winkler had no way of knowing, when he started negotiating with Scorsese, that *Rocky* and not *New York, New York* would make him rich.

Producers incredulous that Scorsese and De Niro wanted to make a musical should not have been surprised. Though both New Hollywood and the *nouvelle vague* revolted against what the French called *le cinéma de papa*, they were mainly aggrieved that it refused to admit them. Once they'd broken down the door, they started to make the kind of films papa used to make, since those were the ones on which they'd grown up. Scorsese respected John Cassavetes, but he *loved* the musicals of Vincente Minnelli. (And hadn't even Jean-Luc Godard made his own musical, in *Une Femme est une femme*?)

Not that *New York, New York* was really a musical. It belonged to an equally venerable form, the backstage melodrama. Michael Powell and Emeric Pressburger's 1948 ballet story *The Red Shoes*, and Vincente Minnelli's *The Bad and the Beautiful* (1952) had been childhood favourites of Scorsese. He even modelled himself on the ruthless producers in both films who succeeded by inspiring love and fear in equal quantities among the people they created. 'I wanted to create an aura of being a nasty old bastard who's got this violent nature,' he told *Rolling Stone*. He always kept a couple of 'breakaway' chairs around the office which he could smash to kindling against the wall when he needed to dramatise his bad temper.

The debt of *New York, New York* to George Cukor's *A Star is Born* (1954) was obvious. Scorsese even discussed the film with Cukor a few times before he started shooting. Each begins with a twenty-minute set-piece, with crowds, dancing, music, and all the major characters introduced. Each tells the story of a talented man declining while his protégée flourishes. In each a mediocre but sensitive piano player remains the heroine's confidant and friend throughout.

De Niro pursuing Lisa Minnelli after their first meeting, discovering where she lives, keeping her up all night and almost losing her a new job, parallels James Mason's first meeting with Minnelli's real-life mother Judy Garland. Lionel Stander, who played the gruff but loveable press agent in William Wellman's 1937 version of *A Star is Born*, plays the gruff but lovable agent in *New York, New York*. Scorsese also shot his equivalent of Garland's song 'The Man that Got Away' in Minnelli's performance of 'Around and Around', where a recording studio becomes a kind of stage, melodramatically spotlit. Each film features a twenty-minute song-and-dance extravaganza, supposedly extracted from the female star's first Hollywood film, in which she summarises her career. And in each case, that scene would become a centre of controversy.

De Niro wasn't sure about playing sax player Jimmy Doyle. For one thing, he had no musical training. Nor was it a role that required much in the way of transformation. He would rather have made the film of the Jake La Motta biography, *Raging Bull*. No less uncertain both of De Niro's drawing power as a romantic lead and his ability to make a convincing sax player, United Artists suggested Barbra Streisand to star, opposite her ex-boyfriend Ryan O'Neal – who couldn't play the sax either, but was a bigger box-office name.

Scorsese countered by offering the part of singer Francine Evans to Liza Minnelli. There was a wonderful symmetry to the idea: for your first musical, who better to star than the daughter of Judy Garland and Vincente Minnelli? The suggestion didn't enchant MGM quite as much. A famous loose cannon, plagued by health problems and a drug habit that would see her in the Betty Ford Clinic two years later, Minnelli, though married to Jack Haley Jr, son of the Tin Man from *The Wizard of Oz*, was also carrying on an affair with dancer Mikhail Baryshnikov – with the full knowledge of Haley, who would divorce her in 1979 for infidelity.

But, reasoned the studio bean-counters, she *had* won the Best Actress Oscar for *Cabaret*. And De Niro *had* got an Oscar for *Godfather II*. And Scorsese's new film, *Taxi Driver*, looked like it might sweep the board at the Oscars. Once John Kander and Fred Ebb, who'd written *Cabaret*, agreed to create new songs for the film, UA decided to put up the money.

They might have hesitated had they heard about Scorsese's first meeting with Minnelli.

'It's going to be a great pleasure to make this film,' she said, 'particularly with James Caan.'

Scorsese put her straight about the casting, and screened *Mean Streets* for her.

'De Niro – was he the one who always wore the suit?' she asked afterwards.

'No, that was Harvey Keitel. Bobby is the guy in the hat.'

'Oh . . . right . . .'

*   *   *

Irwin Winkler already owned a script for *New York, New York* by first-time scenarist Earl Mac Rauch, but Scorsese's old writing partner Mardik Martin, now under contract to Chartoff and Winkler, had rewritten it. Much was changed, including the ending; in Rauch's version, the De Niro character leaves jazz and becomes a record producer, specialising in rhythm and blues – historically a valid progression.

When blame was being doled out for the failure of *New York, New York*, Scorsese, Martin and others would cite Rauch's screenplay as the culprit, but people who have read it speak of an expert and fully realised piece of work; and in truth, the blame for what happened to *New York, New York* is not hard to place.

Though Scorsese called the film his 'valentine to the musical', he also hoped to 'redefine the genre'. To that end, he decided to improvise most of the dialogue and action. It was as classic a case of overreaching as Peter Bogdanovich's decision to record the cast of his 1975 musical *At Long Last Love* live, with a real orchestra, rather than later, and to playback, even if that meant them dancing through Manhattan, singing to the sound of a hidden band heard on earpieces. In both cases, the result was catastrophic.

De Niro meanwhile had United Artists pay for the most expensive tenor saxophone on the market and started learning how to use it. Mostly he saw the film as just another acting job. Musical ability didn't enter into it, and indeed he seems to have little natural talent. After the film he bought his own alto sax, easier to handle than the hefty tenor, but soon admitted that he no longer bothered even to try playing it.

Georgie Auld, a fifty-eight-year-old veteran of the band scene, coached De Niro. The career of Canadian-born Auld almost paralleled that of the film's Jimmy Doyle. He too began as a sideman for the big bands of the thirties, playing tenor and alto with Bunny Berrigan, Benny Goodman and Artie Shaw, and backing singers like Billie Holliday. In the forties, he converted to 'bop', and in 1943 formed a distinctive but unsuccessful small orchestra playing in that *avant garde* style. He also, like Doyle in the film, opened a club – the Troubadour, on New York's 52nd Street.

De Niro worked hard to master the music. Arriving at his Brentwood house early in 1977, *New York Times* journalist Susan Braudy heard 'an unsteady saxophone howl the last bars of "Misty" in the cool evening air'. Initially, De Niro's dedication impressed Auld. 'He has a talent for grasping things like nobody I've ever seen,' he said. 'I couldn't believe he could do that great. He must have listened to the records seven thousand times.' Soon, however, he began to wilt in the face of the actor's relentless seriousness and monosyllabic manner. 'He's about as much fun as the clap,' he said. 'I called him "Mumbles". He reminded me of Benny Goodman when I worked with Benny.'

Auld felt he finally became a 'slave' of De Niro. 'We thought he was going to climb in bed with us with the horn,' complained his wife Diane. And practice didn't in this case make perfect. 'He had the externals, but not the inside stuff,' said Auld. 'That was a robot up there.' Though De Niro mimed playing in the finished film, it's Auld we hear.

New York, New York started shooting in June 1976 on what was supposed to be an eighteen-week schedule. Budgeted at $2.5 million, it doubled, then tripled that figure. Like Francis Ford Coppola six years later on his disastrous *One from the Heart*, Scorsese soon came to realise that the classic Hollywood musical depended on the classic Hollywood factory system. With stars, crew and musicians on staff, and the films turned out on an assembly line, mostly on existing sets, they could be made economically. Produced from scratch, they were doomed to lose money. He started to cut corners, including scrapping a plan to shoot at the Waldorf-Astoria Hotel in New York, and used a Pasadena hotel instead. Too late.

In the beginning, Scorsese rehearsed De Niro and Minnelli in the script for a couple of hours a day, but soon decided it would need something more radical to 'remake' the musical form. Throwing away the script except as a guide, he spent the day improvising scenes, recording every minute on videotape. He then took the tape home, and condensed the scenes into dialogue.

Loyally, Minnelli, to whom improvisation didn't come naturally, told a *Rolling Stone* reporter that the lines Scorsese chose were 'the most natural, the best, the gems that he considers, like, the inside of a diamond. And from five hours, it's suddenly like two pages. But it's all there; all the beats are there.' If the actress seemed partial, it was probably because, in another venerable tradition of Hollywood, she was now sleeping with the director.

Scorsese started shooting with the set-piece that opens the film, the celebration in New York on the night the Japanese surrendered. The first shot is evocative – a shirt fluttering out of a hotel window to land on a confetti-strewn sidewalk. A few moments later, Jimmy Doyle emerges in his first civilian clothes for years. A strutting wiseguy in a gaudy Aloha shirt, hair slicked down, jaws chewing rhythmically, he heads for the gigantic Rainbow Room, where the bored-looking band of Tommy Dorsey is playing Glenn Miller's 'Pennsylvania 6–5000' and other swing hits, culminating in a version of 'Opus One' which, because of the necessities of the plot, goes on for twelve minutes.

Over the next twenty minutes, most of it improvised, Doyle 'works the room', waving to the stolid Dorsey, obviously an ex-employer, linking up with his army buddies, but also trying to pick up women, always with the same patter. Only Francine Evans (Minnelli), also recently demobilised, resists him, which simply drives him to greater effort.

Ingmar Bergman and Bernardo Bertolucci would visit the set during this scene, but its most prestigious visitor was the first – Vincente Minnelli himself, coaxed in by the MGM publicity machine to give his blessing. Watching the crew sweating over an elaborate camera set-up, Minnelli said, 'You know, this used to happen constantly. I did a movie once called *Meet me in St Louis*, and there was a scene where we had to turn out some lights . . .'

Scorsese knew every frame of it: Judy Garland and Tom Drake go through the house after a party, turning down all the gaslights . . .

'Why, yes,' said Minnelli, taken aback at his encyclopaedic recall. 'That scene took three days to set up . . .'

Scorsese's grin wilted a little.

'. . . and four minutes to shoot.'

Looking around the giant set jammed with jiving extras and sweating bandsmen, Scorsese knew it would take a lot more than four minutes to get this on film. Finally, they shot for weeks, and the first cut of the scene lasted one hour. Some celebrity extras didn't last the distance. Producer Dawn Steel, Scorsese's old girlfriend from his first days in Hollywood, was fitted out with a dazzling forties evening gown and full make-up, but after sitting around all day without a foot of film shot, simply left.

Wastage was enormous. Costume designer Theodora van Runkle says, 'People still tell horror stories about the filming of *New York, New York*. We would get our first call at 7 a.m. and often they wouldn't get their first shot until after dark. The crew were treated like peasants . . . totally ignored. Meanwhile, Marty and Liza would be closeted in her trailer. Going over the script, presumably.'

The lesson that extravagance seldom pays off was hammered home by the film's intended climax, 'Happy Endings', a twelve-minute musical number, supposedly a scene in Francine's first movie role.

She plays a cinema usherette who, watching movies night after night, dreams of a showbiz career. Shining her torch on her face like a spotlight, she sings:

> Happy endings, far as I can see
> Are only for the stars
> Not in the stars
> For me.

Bankrolled by a wealthy patron who just happens to wander into the cinema, she sees her wish come true, only to wake and find he was a dream. She despairs – until the same patron walks in for real.

Scorsese created a massive set for the number, with a cinema audience and prancing chorus girls. For the patron, he persuaded Broadway star Larry Kert, who created the role of Tony in *West Side Story*, to dance in his first major movie. The MC of the show was played by Jack Haley Sr, Minnelli's then-father-in-law.

It took weeks to shoot the twelve-minute sequence, and at one time or another every director on the lot came by to watch. In August, after nine weeks' shooting, the film should have been half finished. It was nowhere near that: Scorsese would actually shoot for another fourteen weeks. Part of the delay was attributable to him having taken time off to shoot and edit a documentary about the last performance of Bob Dylan's old backing group, The Band, led by Robbie Robertson, a friend and confidant of Scorsese. While he was editing *New York, New York*, he was also cutting this film, eventually released as *The Last Waltz*.

Despite delays, however, Scorsese insisted on honouring his promise to screen forty minutes of *New York, New York* for the crew and some friends. He and editor Irving Lerner worked thirty-six hours non-stop to prepare the material. It included the opening VJ-Day sequence, the 'Happy Endings' number, and some of the more stylish homages to the old musicals, including a scene where, pausing on an elevated railway at night, Doyle looks down on a sailor and his girl dancing a Gene Kelly-style adagio under a streetlight.

A celebrity audience, including Vincente Minnelli and George Cukor, applauded furiously. Some wept. Heading to the commissary for the party that followed, they ran into a hollow-eyed and spaced-out Scorsese, flanked by his wife, ex-wife, and aides. 'After a night's worth of screaming,' wrote the *Rolling Stone* reporter, 'and bleached with sad resignation, he faced society. He looked like a Christian heading for the chopping block.'

That everyone said they loved it didn't help. These were friends. The public wasn't likely to be so kind.

New York, New York was shot on the same sound stages as many of MGM's classic musicals, including Stage 29, where Vincente Minnelli filmed *An American in Paris* in 1951. Liza

Minnelli had her mother's old dressing room, which boasted a chandelier, more red roses than a hothouse, along with pinned-up telegrams, make-up, portraits of her, posters, empty bottles and the remains of half-eaten meals – all the paraphernalia, in short, of the classic Hollywood star's hangout.

De Niro, by contrast, gloomed in monastic seclusion, appropriately near Greta Garbo's old dressing room. One visitor described his facilities as 'spare, trimmed only with a clock mounted on petrified wood, a record player, a few swing-band albums and a radio playing the news'. All the usual framed posters and portraits had been removed; De Niro didn't want any other images to distract him from the character that now preoccupied him – fighter Jake La Motta. He spent hours shadow-boxing.

Old Hollywood pervaded the studios. Sydney Guilaroff cut Liza's hair, as he'd also cut her mother's. When Barry Primus needed a suit appropriate to a professional musician of the forties, Wardrobe found him one that John Garfield had worn, and the grips and script girls told stories about working on *Touch of Evil* and *High Sierra*. And also, as in Garland's time, when uppers and downers sharpened the performance and helped one sleep afterwards, drugs, particularly cocaine, were omnipresent.

As a favour to De Niro, Scorsese wrote in a jazz club scene where Diahnne Abbott croons an assured if uncharismatic version of 'Honeysuckle Rose'. Other friends, and wives of friends, played small roles. Gravel-voiced and amiable, Georgie Auld impressed Scorsese so much that he cast him as band leader Frankie Harte. But in an event that cast a pall over the unit, editor Irving Lerner died of a heart attack on Christmas Eve 1976, a reminder of Bernard Herrmann's demise the year before at just the same time of year.

In January, Diahnne gave birth to Raphael. After thinking about building a new home in the LA suburb of Brentwood, De Niro bought a modern but, in the words of the *New York Times*' Susan Braudy, 'forbiddingly secluded' house there – which, all the same, boasted swimming pools, a guest house, a sauna, extensive gardens, and views of both the city and the Pacific. Leaving the rented Bel Air house, they had to contend with another claim over Abbott's cats – this time a bill for $10,000 from the landlord for 'soiled and clawed rugs, draperies and furniture'.

De Niro seldom socialised in Los Angeles, to the frustration of Abbott, who'd got to like the fast lane in New York. When they did go out, he vacillated between hovering defensively around her and dialling out of the conversation. On one occasion, he made his boredom clear by curling up under the table at the Beverly Hills Hotel and going to sleep.

At home, he made even fewer concessions to sociability, welcoming their infrequent guests in his habitual off-duty uniform of loose flannel shirt and baggy corduroys. The visitors were always old friends from New York – Scorsese, Peter Boyle, Brian De Palma, Barry Primus, plus wives – and the ambience anything but glamorous. Invited to Christmas dinner, Boyle took the opportunity to drop his pants and 'moon' the turkey.

'When Robert De Niro is the host of a party,' wrote Susan Braudy, 'it has no centre, no focal point. All night long he will listen to his guests, nod his head, grin, and occasionally say in his familiar husky voice, "Yeah guys, hey, hey guys, hey, that's too much." He is an onlooker, a member of the crowd.'

Others found his detachment sinister. Kathi McGinnis, who played Ellen Flannery in *New York, New York*, speculated, 'I think he's hiding something he thinks may be too weird. I mean, he's protecting himself with all that silence. There's some part of him he can't show, because he's afraid it's insane. Maybe it's only egomania, maybe not.'

On 19 March 1977 the Academy awarded the Oscars for the previous year's films. *Taxi Driver*, though nominated for Best Picture, Best Actor (De Niro), Best Supporting Actress (Foster) and Best Original Score (Herrmann, in the second posthumous nomination of the night), won none of them. The popular winner was *Rocky*, with *All the President's Men* and *Bound for Glory* scooping most of the rest. De Niro, who of all those involved in *Taxi Driver* looked to have the best chance, lost to a dead man: Peter Finch campaigned so vigorously for his role as the crazy newsman in *Network* that he died of a heart attack a few days before the ceremony. After that, the sentiment of every voter was on his side.

In practice, what De Niro and Scorsese lost with *Taxi Driver*, they picked up by association with Chartoff and Winkler, whose *Rocky* had won Best Film, Best Director and Best Editing, making them the hottest producers in Hollywood. The failure to cede even one Oscar to *Taxi Driver* stung Scorsese, but at least he was working on a new film. And what else mattered?

After shooting the VJ-Day sequence on *New York, New York*, Scorsese threw out both Rauch's and Martin's screenplays. The scene following, where De Niro, having failed to seduce Minnelli, follows her to her hotel, then embarks on a long and embarrassing routine in which he pretends to be a wounded veteran with a stiff leg, was entirely improvised, as was the rest of the film.

In this new climate, everybody felt free to suggest new lines, and even entire scenes. Georgie Auld claimed to have invented 95 per cent of De Niro's dialogue – obviously an exaggeration, though he did provide lines for the scenes opposite real musicians.

Liza Minnelli recalled, 'It got to the point where everybody was running around with these little tape recorders saying, "What was that? Say that, that!" It was incredible! Incredible! I think back and I don't know how any of us survived it. The energy level that went on was just incredible, and my own energy level isn't exactly zilch as you know. This is the only movie I can remember making where I can't remember ever sitting down. It was like a whirlwind.'

Fearful that people would question his professionalism, Scorsese jumped in to contradict her. 'The movie wasn't written on tape recorders,' he insisted. 'Everything's naturally structured and worked on. We would structure the ideas we put into the tape recorders.'

But in July 1977, Julia Cameron Scorsese, partying in New York with Andy Warhol (who noted in his diary that 'she was walking kind of drunkenly on blue high heels and her pupils were dilated'), spilled the beans. Warhol wrote in his diary, 'Julia told me how they do things on Marty's movies – they rehearse the people, do videotapes, then Julia picks out the best things and they have the people redo them that way on camera later in the shooting. She said they change the plot and twist it during the shooting.'

For some sequences, improvisation worked – like an audition for Dick Miller's club-owner where De Niro as Doyle, typically thorny, is ready to walk out over an imagined slight when Minnelli rescues the gig by starting to sing 'You Brought a New Kind of Love to Me' *a capella*, inspiring Doyle to join in. Unfortunately, but typical of the film, Scorsese, to show that Doyle hasn't changed, inserts an almost identical scene later in the story when Doyle tries to launch his own band and, once again, Francine steps in to charm the backers.

Under pressure, De Niro and Scorsese became an even tighter team than usual. Other actors complained that nobody could get near the director. 'Bobby hogs Marty on the set,' said one. 'Marty gives Bobby anything he wants. And what Bobby wants is constant attention – constant talk about his character.'

Their inventions mirrored the reality around them. With his stabs of temper and abrupt attacks of sentiment, Doyle resembled Scorsese, while Francine, marginalised and alienated after the birth of her son, reflected many aspects of Julia Scorsese, jealous at her husband's affair with his star.

Lacking opportunities to exercise his capacity for rage in the part of Doyle, De Niro redirected it into manic humour. When a train starts pulling out of a snowy station without him, he tries to hold it back, only to be pushed slowly along the platform. Dragging Francine out into the snow to marry her, he smashes a glass panel in the justice of the peace's door, then lies down behind the taxi and urges it to back over his head. 'When you get that kind of input,' said Scorsese, 'you can't say, "No more ideas, I'm sorry, stop the ideas." So we shot the scene; we covered ourselves with the master shot so that we could cut the scene without Bobby putting his head under the wheel of the car, because we were concerned about the elements of farce, you know, farce turning into drama.'

But exactly that metamorphosis was taking place in what

started as a celebration of the frothiest of Hollywood genres. Watching De Niro and Minnelli brawl in a taxi, pummelling and scratching, no punches pulled, one crew-member murmured incredulously, '*This* is his tribute to the Hollywood musical?'

CHAPTER TWELVE

Going for a Soldier

My role in this film is the best performance I have ever given.

Robert De Niro of *The Deer Hunter* (in a comment he later denied having made)

Following his success as the police chief in Steven Spielberg's *Jaws*, Roy Scheider spent most of 1976 commuting between New York and Managua as one of the stars of *Sorcerer*, William Friedkin's remake of the 1953 Henri-Georges Clouzot thriller *The Wages of Fear*, about four fugitives hiding out in South America who try to buy their tickets home by ferrying nitroglycerine to an oil-well fire.

The bulk of the shooting took place in Nicaragua, where Scheider met Michael Cimino, shooting one of the TV commercials from which he made a living between features. He was so successful at these that he could drive a Rolls-Royce and live in some luxury in New York, actually inside the United Nations building.

Scheider knew Cimino from his Oscar-winning *Thunderbolt and Lightfoot*. A Yale graduate with a degree in art, Cimino possessed a baroque sensibility that thrived on excess. Soft-spoken, stocky, with a round head and prominent nose that made him resemble, from the shoulders up, a Roman emperor, he concentrated on his work to a degree that Scheider found rare in Hollywood – particularly after a year working with the febrile Friedkin.

Cimino showed Scheider a draft screenplay for a film about Vietnam, *The Deer Hunter*. Its source was 'The Man Who Came to Play', an original script by little-known screenwriter Louis Garfinkle and Quinn Redeker, an actor whose credits included *The Three Stooges Meet Hercules* and *Spider Boy, or the Maddest Story Ever Told*.

What the man 'came to play' was Russian roulette, and Cimino liked the idea well enough to ask Deric Washburn, his co-writer on the science fiction film *Silent Running*, to incorporate this suicidal game into a story about the Vietnam war. Redeker and Garfinkle didn't contribute to the Cimino/Washburn screenplay, and even Washburn's name was absent from most early drafts of *The Deer Hunter*. It took a Writers' Guild of America arbitration to impose a joint credit, Redeker, Garfinkle, Washburn and Cimino for original story, and Washburn for the screenplay.

The new story anatomised the war's effect on three young steelworkers from Pennsylvania, called up in 1968. Despite his claims for its veracity, Cimino admitted he meant the film to be about Vietnam only in the most general sense. 'It could be any war,' he said. 'The film is really about the nature of courage and friendship. Even the landscape is surreal. And time is compressed. In trying to compress the experience of the war into a film, even as long as this one, I had to deal with it in a non-literal way.'

Cimino's back-pedalling was justified. While claiming an intimacy with the kind of steel towns in which his characters lived, he later admitted his acquaintance was limited to having been best man at a Russian Orthodox wedding of the sort that opens the film. He also withdrew his claim that he had been 'attached to a Green Beret medical unit' in Vietnam.

The real roots of *The Deer Hunter*, at least for the sequences set in Pennsylvania, lie in *The Best Years of Our Lives*, William Wyler's 1946 film of veterans returning home after World War II, which was adapted in turn from the book-length poem *Victory for Me* by Mackinlay Kantor. In both films, three servicemen face difficulties in readjusting to a world changed by war. The main characters of each hang out in a bar, and congregate around its piano-playing owner. In each, one veteran is an amputee. Both films also include an adulterous love affair, and a long sequence of a white wedding.

As for *The Deer Hunter*'s combat sequences, these relate only tangentially to Vietnam. The film's Viet Cong villains could just as easily be Apaches or Mexicans, and the setting a dozen remote locations around the world. What the war episodes of Cimino's story most resemble is James Dickey's novel *Deliverance* and the film John Boorman made from it. Both share the same plot: a group of friends from the city are menaced by homicidal locals during a trip into the wilderness.

No vet would recognise Cimino's war. The three heroes, all white and from the same town, somehow contrive to be posted to the same unit, even though two are lowly 'grunts' while the third is a member of the elite Green Berets. Except for two girls dancing lethargically in a club supposedly in Saigon (shot in Thailand), there's little sense of the omnipresent sex and drugs that accompanied 'R & R', nor the rock 'n' roll that provided the war with its anthems. Instead, as the film's theme, Cimino commissioned a sentimental and Italianate 'Cavatina for Guitar and Orchestra' from British composer Stanley Meyers.

Above all, the motif of Russian roulette, with money bet on the outcome, was particularly suspect. Nobody could recall the game being played by either side in Vietnam. There were vague rumours of it being employed as a torture, though by Americans, not Vietnamese.

In Nicaragua, Cimino offered Scheider the role of Michael Vronsky, *The Deer Hunter*'s moral hero, guardian of an almost mystical tradition of nature, friendship and the hunt. In an early scene with overtones of Germany's 'mountain films' of the early thirties, so beloved of the Nazis, as well as fables like that of the magic 'free shot', on which Carl Maria Von Weber based his opera *Der Freischütz*, the three friends head up into the wilderness. Michael, priding himself on only needing one shot to kill his prey, holds up a round from his rifle and tells his companions with heavy significance, 'This . . . this is *this*.' Cimino filmed most of these sequences in the relatively undramatic Appalachians, but later sent a crew to Lake Chelan in the Cascade Mountains of Washington state to film their jagged peaks, more consistent with his vision of a purer, cleaner world above the tree line.

Scheider jumped at the part, particularly since, in this early version of the story, it was Michael who stayed on in Vietnam, becoming addicted to Russian roulette, and his unworldly friend Nick who returned at the fall of Saigon in an attempt to rescue him. Whoever played Michael would be on screen almost every moment of the film.

'We worked on it for months,' Scheider recalls. 'I grew the beard and everything.' Meanwhile, his agent negotiated with Universal, which had him under contract. The studio refused to let him make *The Deer Hunter*. They preferred that he repeat his role as the Amity police chief for *Jaws II*. 'Because I was a nobody!' explodes Scheider, bitter to this day. Ironically, *The Deer Hunter*, initially funded by the British company EMI, would be distributed by Universal.

EMI, rich on the sale of medical technology, was spending some of its profits in the movie market, exploiting a loophole which offered a quick profit to Americans who invested in European projects. EMI's Barry Spikings and Michael Deeley offered Cimino $7.5 million to make *The Deer Hunter*, confident some American company would provide 'end money'.

It was Deeley who suggested De Niro to play Michael. His dark Italian look, Deeley reasoned, might appeal more to European audiences than the blue-eyed, clean-cut Clint Eastwood, Robert Redford or Ryan O'Neal.

Cimino sent De Niro the screenplay. 'It had a picture of a guy with a deer tied over the hood of a white Cadillac,' De Niro says, 'with steel mills in the background. It was such a great shot.' The photograph was almost the most substantial element of the screenplay, many sequences of which were only sketched. Episodes that occupied thirty minutes on screen were simply hinted at: ('Scene 22. They dance').

This simplicity appealed to De Niro, who still shied away from cerebral roles. The film's central section, set in Vietnam, also offered scope for the fury which was his stock in trade. He had few convictions about Vietnam, since the war hadn't impinged on him personally. As Orson Welles reflects in *The Third Man* during his speech on the Prater Wheel, how much we care about people depends on how close they are. From the top of the wheel, looking down on human beings who seem as insignificant as ants, we'd have little compunction in snuffing out one, a dozen, or a hundred. It's only face to face that we begin to have qualms.

'I thought that the war was wrong,' De Niro said, 'but what bothered me was that people who went to war became victims of it; they were used for the whims of others. I don't think the policy-makers had the smarts. I didn't respect their decisions, or what they were doing.' Not profound political thinking, but consistent with De Niro's character – self-involved, sentimental, concerned mainly with finding the keys that admitted him to the character he's decided to play.

He would still have preferred the Jake La Motta project, now carrying the working title 'Prizefighter', but it had become stuck in a thicket of second thoughts. Some people felt the subject might be more palatable to potential backers if it was first performed as a play, so Mardik Martin was busy adapting it for the stage.

De Niro had just read an advance copy of William Goldman's novel *Magic*, about a psychopathic ventriloquist whose disturbed personality communicates through his dummy. Goldman already had a screenplay ready to go, and De Niro was attracted to such a flamboyant role. Steven Spielberg was interested in directing the film, but De Niro couldn't see himself becoming part of Spielberg's comic-book world. Instead, he took the project to Roman Polanski, who was then in Los Angeles. They met in December 1977, and De Niro left the book with him.

For the Christmas issue of French *Vogue Hommes*, Polanski had shot a photo-essay about young girls in Hollywood. A few days after he and De Niro met, police arrested him on a charge of having sex with an under-age girl, and giving her drugs. By January 1978 he was in Chino prison, and De Niro had committed finally to *The Deer Hunter*.

EMI published ads based on the screenplay's cover photo;

now De Niro, rifle in hand, joined the deer on the car. He felt comfortable with the production from the moment Cimino started casting out of New York, selecting young performers without Hollywood reputations. John Savage, cast as Michael's friend Steve, had appeared mainly on TV, and the actor chosen for Nick, Christopher Walken, though almost exactly De Niro's age, and well-known around New York, had done mostly supporting roles, relying, 'like Blanche Dubois', he joked, on 'the kindness of strangers' for anything more interesting. George Dzundza was almost unknown, and Chuck Aspergen, who played Axel, was a real steelworker, spotted by Cimino during a research trip.

Periodically during the filming of *Deer Hunter*, De Niro returned to New York. He found Scorsese's personal life in chaos. Struggling with cocaine and a blood infection, the director drew closer to the equally febrile Liza Minnelli, his affair with whom was an open secret. He had agreed to direct her on Broadway in a musical by Kander and Ebb, *The Act*, but dropped out because of bad health, giving the job to Gower Champion. There were public arguments with Minnelli, often about her continuing relationship with Mikhail Baryshnikov. Sometimes these took place in front of their spouses, the hapless Jack Haley and Julia Cameron Scorsese, now pregnant.

In January 1978, the producers took a look at Scorsese's first cut of *New York, New York*. Everyone felt the production numbers dwarfed the human story. Producer Irwin Winkler was among them. 'We wanted to tell a story about the relationship between two people,' he said. 'It was not proper if we went off on a tangent for twelve minutes. We had a choice between, really, a marvellous entertainment and a story about people. And we decided to tell a story about people.' He instructed a furious and distraught Scorsese to cut an hour.

A few days later, the doorbell rang at the home of designer Halston. As Andy Warhol recounted in his diaries, 'It was Liza in a hat pulled down so nobody would recognise her, and she said to Halston, "Give me every drug you've got." So he gave her a bottle of coke, a few sticks of marijuana, a Valium, four Quaaludes, and they were all wrapped in a tiny box, and then a little figure in a white hat came up on the stoop and kissed Halston, and it was Marty Scorsese, he'd been hiding around the corner, and then he and Liza went off to have their affair on all the drugs.'

In April, Scorsese recalled some cast and crew for reshoots. Sequences were truncated or dropped altogether. These included a big production number of the forties hit 'South America, Take it Away', and almost all the songs by Mary Kay Place, who played the singer who replaces Minnelli with Doyle's band: a critic friend of Scorsese hinted they would 'ruin the picture'.

Scorsese also cut most of 'Happy Endings', which went from twelve minutes to three. Winkler claimed the number only cost $350,000 anyway, but other sources suggested a figure closer to $1.2 million.

Without 'Happy Endings', the film lacked a climax. Scorsese showed the butchered version to critic friends, asking for suggestions. One was so horrified that he fled without giving an opinion. Finally, Scorsese decided to close on Kander and Ebb's title number, 'New York, New York', which now became the film's theme. In the story, Doyle composes it as a jazz tune, but Minnelli adapts it as a show-stopper. Shortly after, he delivered a version of 152 minutes – total cost $8.7 million.

Losing the musical numbers had the undesired effect of throwing the personal story into relief. Not everyone found this agreeable. Francine now spent most of the film either cringing or smiling through tears. At the same time, De Niro's Jimmy emerged as, by turns, manic and vicious. Why, one critic at the preliminary press conference asked, should the audience feel sympathy for such an 'unrepenting jerk'?

'I think he's an artist,' said Winkler. 'Not everybody in life that you meet is a Miss Goody Two-Shoes.'

Liza Minnelli tried to put a cheerful face on the experience of making the film, pretending that even improvisation had all been a lark: 'Part of the fun of doing the film, was, well, a lot of these things that occur, I didn't know about it. Bobby and Marty would say, "Well, we're just going to . . . well . . ." and I'd say, "Well, *what*?" and they'd say, "Wait. You'll see . . ."'

Scorsese, with his narrowed eyes and quick, snake-like smile, moved hurriedly to neutralise even this hint of a lack of direction: 'You *did* know, at first,' he corrected her. 'But after the first two days, see, it was moving, so after that, we were full of surprises.'

But the surprises all favoured De Niro's character. Minnelli got his leavings: domestic arguments, scenes in which she conciliates between Doyle and disaffected backers or band members, or tearful soliloquies as the abandoned wife.

It escaped nobody that Scorsese and De Niro, when they spoke of the project, gave the impression they made it all between them. Phrases like 'Bobby and I discussed this,' or 'Bobby and I talked about the scene,' or 'Marty and I talked about this,' peppered their interviews. One journalist remarked, 'Minnelli seemed always to be the last to find out what was going to happen when the camera rolled. Add to that the fact that De Niro's performance in the film is a virtual circus of horrors that seems bent on upstaging Minnelli, and that the character she plays is tolerant to the point of saintliness of De Niro's tantrums and rages, and it becomes ironic that producer Winkler proclaimed *fortissimo* early in the press conference, "This is one of the greatest feminist films ever made."'

Another writer asked the makers how they thought *New York, New York* would go down with audiences.

'Who knows what any public will feel?' Scorsese replied bleakly. If he hadn't intuited the answer before the press conference, he was in no doubt by the end.

Other films were being made about Vietnam at the same time as *The Deer Hunter*, but movies like Coppola's *Apocalypse Now* dealt with an elite of Special Forces officers and a clandestine conflict remote from the reality of the war. Washburne's people were working class, inarticulate, and sincere. Cimino called them 'ordinary people, who go through a crisis and come out of it to continue their lives'.

Admittedly, Hal Ashby's *Coming Home*, *Deer Hunter*'s main

competitor, took place mostly in a Veterans' Administration Hospital among paraplegic victims of the war, but while it overlapped part of *Deer Hunter*, the story stressed reconciliation, repatriation and romance – elements far from Cimino's vision.

'That's what I liked about the script,' De Niro said. 'I liked the characters. I liked that they didn't say much, that there wasn't anything that was condescending or patronising toward them.' He embarked on his usual period of research – 'earning the right' to play Michael. He and Cimino travelled 150,000 miles during the making of the film, a large part of it scouting locations before production started. This search, and other problems, including negotiations with a newly-established political regime in Thailand, delayed the shoot for three months.

'I spent a lot of time in Mingo Junction and Steubenville, Ohio, soaking up the environment,' De Niro said. 'I talked to the millworkers, drank and ate with them, played pool. No one recognised me as being an actor during that time. Friends just introduced me as "Bob", and I went from there.'

He exchanged his New York driving licence for a Pennsylvania one, and started to drive a car with Pennsylvania plates. He also got a Pennsylvania gun licence, though most of the filming took place in Clairton, on the Monongahela River, just over the border in Ohio, where a lone steel mill remained open. Clairton's population, shrinking with the steel business, was down to thirteen thousand when the *Deer Hunter* unit moved in. That sense of social decay suffused the film.

Other than De Niro, the best-known performer in *Deer Hunter* was John Cazale, who had played Fredo in *Godfather II* and a desperate candidate for transsexual surgery in Sidney Lumet's *Dog Day Afternoon*. Cazale did few films, preferring the stage, and hadn't worked in movies for three years. De Niro suggested him for Stan, the arrogant, violent womaniser who knocks his girlfriend unconscious on the dance floor, and prefers to stay at home while his friends go to war. Once he was cast, Cazale proposed his girlfriend Meryl Streep for the small part of Nick's girl Linda. Streep hadn't then done her first major film role, in Fred Zinnemann's *Julia*. De Niro and casting director Cis

Corman saw her in a Chekhov play at the Lincoln Center, and a made-for-TV film about hockey called *The Deadliest Season*, on the strength of which they put her in *The Deer Hunter*.

But Cazale's routine insurance medical on the eve of shooting revealed that he was suffering from terminal bone cancer. The day before he began filming, Cimino received a panic call from EMI.

'Shooting had already been delayed,' says Cimino, 'and both John and Meryl wondered if it would ever work out for them. I bluntly told the company we were going to start shooting the movie, and they responded by saying that, unless I got rid of John, they would shut down the picture. The only alternative, they said, was to write another script which excluded John's character completely. I said, "Go ahead and shut the picture down," and slammed down the phone.'

Cimino compromised by re-arranging the schedule to film Cazale's part first. Rather than going to Thailand for the Vietnam sequences during the American summer of 1977, and returning to film the hunting scenes in autumn, he reversed the order. As a result, when De Niro and his companions climbed into the supposedly icy mountains for their deer hunt, it was high summer. The 'autumn foliage' was faked, and they were streaming sweat under their lumberjack shirts and padded jackets. During the final scene of the film, shot in the real bar used throughout as a set, the temperature hit 105 degrees. The crew stripped down to their underwear, and the actors cooled off between takes in the walk-in refrigerator. Cazale survived this and other strains of the production, but *The Deer Hunter* would be his last film. He died on 12 March 1978.

De Niro recognised some of Scorsese's mania in Cimino, though it was the relentless obsession of the stalker rather than Scorsese's chair-smashing fury. Even more than Scorsese, Cimino perceived the world in terms of despair. The chill of the steel towns, sunk in perpetual dank blue-grey twilight, would recur in *Heaven's Gate* and *Year of the Dragon*.

The Deer Hunter's first image established the film's sense of imminent doom. An ugly tanker truck, exhaust spouting sparks, thunders down the hill at nightfall into Clairton. Racing ahead of it, often almost under its wheels, are the heroes in a beat-up example of that most potent symbol of American excess and arrogance, the 1959 '61 Series' Cadillac convertible, with its saurian shape and shark-like tailfins.

The mood is intensified by the scenes that follow, of Michael and his friends, robed like demons, channelling molten steel. De Niro couldn't persuade a company to let him work a shift in a steel mill. Cimino finally shot the scene in the Cleveland mill of US Steel, but only after EMI bought an additional $5 million in insurance should something go wrong when De Niro, Cazale, Savage, Walken and Aspergen tapped the blast furnace.

Making commercials had honed Cimino's ability to fill the frame. His was a panoramic vision, in which men crept about under an uncaring sky. The Clairton scenes hark back to nineteenth-century allegorical painters like Caspar David Friedrich, and even the interiors hint at a mystic dimension. As the newly-married Nick and Linda drink a loving cup at the wedding celebration, a few drops of wine fall on Linda's dress, hinting at the blood to come. And the Green Beret who turns up in the bar during the party, but refuses the revellers' invitation to join them in a drink, simply snarling, 'Fuck it,' could not be any more ominous a spectre had he been a skeleton with a scythe.

De Niro is in his element in these scenes, a moody presence, bearded and monosyllabic, reserved in the midst of the drunken groping on the dance floor, shooting pained glances at Linda as she clings to her lover. When, at the end of the wedding, he runs naked through the town, collapsing on the school basketball court, we sense a flight back to childhood and innocence; Stan hints that Michael may even be a virgin. The next day, the man of action, once again in charge of himself, he leads the hunt into the mountains, and drops a stag with a single shot. As he will prove in Vietnam, Michael is happiest with a gun in his hand.

Cimino's signature is the shock cut, and *The Deer Hunter* has one of his best. One moment, the men relax after the hunt in John's bar, listening to him play the piano. In the next, they're in a burning Vietnam village, with Michael, now a Green Beret, blasting a Viet Cong soldier with a flamethrower. An instant later, he, Nick and Steve have been captured and imprisoned with a few other men in bamboo 'tiger cages', half immersed in the river. Periodically they're taken out and forced to play Russian roulette as the Cong bet on the outcome.

Nick regards these events with a moony lack of affect which will intensify as the film goes on, until he's able to play Russian roulette night after night in the clubs of Saigon and remain at least partly sane. Steve, by contrast, becomes hysterical, and can be calmed only by Michael with a litany of profanity and consolation.

Once all three are gathered around the table with the gun, Michael dares the Vietnamese to put not one but three bullets into the cylinder. While their leader looks understandably suspicious, the men betting on the game, preferring the shortened odds, goad him into it. Michael and Nick survive long enough for Michael to empty the three full chambers into their captors, and escape.

Because of the change in schedule brought on by Cazale's illness, *Deer Hunter*'s Thai sequences were shot at the height of the monsoon season. Flooded out of Bangkok, the unit moved to north central Thailand and the famous River Kwai. Factions hostile to the 1976 military takeover of the country were camped on the Burmese border, only 150 kilometres away, but producer John Peverall on his earlier research trips had established good relations with the new regime, and the unit could sleep peacefully, with one Royal Thai military policeman standing guard for every three Americans. Even so, graft and extortion were facts of life in that corner of the world, and Cimino thought it wise to ship all film, unprocessed, direct to the US rather than risk what UA executive Steven Bach called 'mishaps (civilian or political)'. This drove up costs enormously.

The tiger-cage scene and its aftermath gave De Niro all the opportunities he could have hoped for to indulge in physical acting. The rats and insects were real, the rain and the river chilling. As in *Taxi Driver*, he doesn't so much act his emotions

as embody them. A steely presence in the gloom of the cage,
Michael sustains his friends by sheer effort of will. Skin tight
to his flesh, flesh shrunk onto the bones, he will do anything to
survive. Thus might a trapped animal gnaw off its own leg to
escape.

Cimino drove the actors to the limit of their endurance, both
in the water and during the Russian roulette sequences. It's
impossible not to watch De Niro as, grinning fixedly, he curses
his friends, his captors, the war, forcing himself to put the gun
to his head. To feed his frenzy, Cimino told Walken to spit in
De Niro's face – something De Niro wasn't expecting, as is clear
from his reaction. For his part, De Niro was instructed to slap
Walken and Savage, and not to pull his punches.

De Niro is reticent about the effort needed to do these scenes.
'It's very hard to sustain that kind of intensity. I mean, we were
really slapping each other; you sort of get worked up into a
frenzy. It's a very difficult thing to do. It took a long time.'

To tone down Walken, not the world's most subtle performer,
De Niro told him, 'Do everything you're doing, take as much
time, just play the whole scene in your head. Don't talk.' Walken
understood what De Niro meant. Thinking his dialogue rather
than saying it made Nick seem vaguely distracted, his mind elsewhere. 'That was a great direction,' Walken recalled. 'You don't
have to say everything – *think* it. I'd love to make a silent movie
[. . .] a serious silent movie.'

Did De Niro realise that no evidence existed of Russian roulette being played in Vietnam? He says he argued with Cimino
about it, but that the director overruled him. It's hard to believe,
however, that he pressed very vehemently for a change. For one
thing, the game provided him, and the film, with his best scenes.
Also, Russian roulette is the ruling metaphor, a clumsy but
potent representation of American foreign policy in Asia – moral
and physical suicide for dubious gain. Without it, there is no
film.

And of course actors like De Niro are not concerned with
reality – what *really* happened – but rather with authenticity –
if it *had* happened, would it have looked like this? De Niro as

Michael Vronsky and De Niro as Frankenstein's monster are the same man.

The three friends escape downriver into a rocky ravine, where a helicopter attempts to rescue them from a bridge. Clint Eastwood's old stunt double and regular stunt co-ordinator, Buddy van Horn, handled the scene, but his helicopter pilot was nervous about descending into the narrow defile, particularly since the camera of Vilmos Zsigmond was so close that stunt doubles couldn't be used.

Fifteen takes were needed to get the shot. During one of them, as the helicopter rose, the skids to which the three actors were clinging snagged the cables supporting the bridge. Fearing that the helicopter might crash, with them underneath, De Niro and the others let go, dropping into the water. Their fears were real. A few years later, a helicopter would crash onto actor Vic Morrow and two Vietnamese children during the shooting of *The Twilight Zone: The Movie*, killing all three.

In the story, the fall from the helicopter separates Nick from his friends, and badly injures Steve. Michael carries him through the jungle to a road clogged with refugees. Halting a North Vietnamese jeep, he drapes Steve over the hood, as he draped the deer he killed.

Nick stays behind in Saigon, drifting into its underworld as the South slides into anarchy. Unable to forget his experience of playing Russian roulette, he gravitates towards the game, sending his winnings anonymously to Steve, who's lying in a veterans' hospital, having lost both legs.

Back home in Clairton, Michael can't re-adjust. 'I feel a lot of distance,' he confesses to Linda. 'I feel far away.' He still hunts with his friends, but this time he fires over the deer's head. Out of a sense of duty, and in the hope of resolving his guilt at being, as he thinks, the sole survivor of the three who went to war, he returns to Saigon on the eve of its fall in 1975, and finds Nick, now a drug addict, recreating his experience as a prisoner by playing Russian roulette while frantic gamblers bet on the outcome. Michael communicates with his numbed friend the only way he can – face to face across the table, passing the revolver between them. Just as Nick begins to swim up from the pool of forgetfulness, his luck runs out. What would have been his last shot kills him. As in the hunt, one shot makes all the difference.

Nick's death proves the key to reconciliation for his friends. Steve, who wouldn't leave the hospital for any other reason, agrees to return home for the funeral. Afterwards, the surviving friends meet to reflect on what the war has cost them. Spontaneously, they sing 'God Bless America'.

In September, De Niro was in New York, where Martin Scorsese had been hospitalised. When his marriage collapsed after *New York, New York*, Scorsese had moved into the Hollywood home of The Band's Robbie Robertson, and embarked on an even more self-destroying life than before.

With producer Tom Luddy, the German director Wim Wenders, two Czech directors and Isabella Rossellini, his girlfriend of the time, and later wife, Scorsese had spent a hallucinating weekend in Las Vegas, at the end of which he collapsed, apparently the victim of bad cocaine which reacted disastrously with his asthma medication.

'I couldn't function,' he said later. 'I didn't know what was happening to me. Basically, I was dying. I was bleeding internally all over, and I didn't know it. My eyes were bleeding, my hands, everything except my brain and my liver. I was coughing up blood, there was blood all over the place. It was like a nightmare. I made it back to New York, they put me in bed, and the next thing I knew I was in the emergency ward at the New York Hospital. The doctors took care of me for ten days.' His weight, normally around seventy kilos, dropped to forty-nine.

Scorsese had never entirely committed to the La Motta project. The script reflected this. 'It was like *Rashomon*,' he said of Mardik Martin's version. 'He got twenty-five different versions of the story because all the characters are still alive [i.e. active in the story]. And I still hadn't made up my mind about directing the picture.'

Robbie Robertson could see that denial played some part in Scorsese's desire to destroy himself. 'Let's get off the fence with this thing,' he told him. 'Are you passionate about this? Do you have to do this movie? Because if you don't have to do it, don't do it. Can you go on with your life without doing this?'

Over the Labor Day weekend, De Niro came to visit Scorsese in hospital. In deference to his status, he'd been given a suite previously occupied by the Shah of Iran. They discussed the latest draft of Martin's much-rewritten script.

De Niro told Scorsese it was time to get serious – both about the film and his life. 'What's the matter with you, Marty?' he demanded. 'Don't you wanna live to see if your daughter is going to grow up and get married? Are you going to be one of those flash-in-the-pan directors who does a few good movies and it's over for them?'

Ultimately, Scorsese decided the chalice would not pass from him. He must make *Raging Bull*.

He said as much to De Niro, who told him, 'Go and see Isabella when you get out of hospital, spend a few days in Rome and relax. When you come back, we can work on the script together, if you like.'

Scorsese's relief at having finally taken the decision is reflected in the closing sequence of the film. After the grim story of Jake La Motta's fall has reached its ambiguous end, Scorsese superimposes a quote from the Bible, John 9:13–26:

> They brought to the Pharisees the man who had been blind.
>
> 'Give glory to God,' they said. 'We know this man is a sinner.'
>
> He replied, 'Whether he is a sinner or not, I don't know. One thing I do know. I was blind but now I see.'

CHAPTER THIRTEEN

Jake

Bob wanted to make this film. Not me. I don't understand anything about boxing. For me, it's like a physical game of chess.

Martin Scorsese, *Cahiers du cinema*, March 1996

For most of the fall of 1978, editing continued on *The Deer Hunter* at Universal in Los Angeles. Cimino prowled the corridors, ready to 'kidnap' the film if anyone tried to cut it without his permission. The producers would have preferred a running time close to two hours, but Cimino insisted that, as promoter Allan Carr would put it later, 'At three hours, it's a masterpiece but at two a flop,' and the studio, as much gripped as Cimino himself with the illusion of his genius, gave in.

While *The Deer Hunter* inched towards completion, Irwin Winkler and Robert Chartoff brought *Raging Bull* to United Artists.

On one level, this story of many levels was the biography of a boxer, though a boxer beside whom Rocky Balboa was a Girl Scout. Born in the Bronx in 1922, Jake La Motta, christened 'The Bronx Bull' because of his brute indifference to attack, learned to fight in jail while serving a term for robbery. In 106 fights he was never knocked out – less because of his boxing skill than a masochistic ability to absorb punishment. After a suspension over throwing a fight, he returned to the ring in 1949, won and defended the world middleweight championship, but lost it in

1951 to 'Sugar' Ray Robinson, the most gifted boxer of his time. 'I fought Sugar Ray so many times it's a wonder I don't have diabetes,' La Motta said. (It would have been a better joke if he could have said 'licked Sugar Ray', but he beat Robinson only once.)

La Motta retired in 1951, and thereafter went downhill. Bankrupt, divorced, and imprisoned for pimping under-age girls in his Miami bar, he survived by doing a rueful stage act in strip clubs that poked fun at his roller-coaster career. In 1970 an autobiography, *Raging Bull*, compiled with an old Bronx pal, Pete Petrella, writing as 'Peter Savage', revived his memory among a public that had largely forgotten him.

Sex, and in particular sexual jealousy, powered La Motta's success. Before a fight, Vicky, the second of his three wives, whom he married at sixteen, would visit him in his dressing room, wearing a sheer nightgown under her clothes, and excite him to erection. Instead of ejaculating, however, he would douse his genitals in ice water, believing the conserved sexual energy helped him beat his opponents to pulp.

Frustratingly for his wives, boxing dissipated La Motta's sex urge. Instead of pleasuring them, he repeatedly beat them up, often on the pretext that they were sleeping with other men – behaviour that drove away his brother Joey, who served a vital function in mediating between him and the organised crime figures who ran boxing.

La Motta's book contained numerous scenes of sex, violence, verbal obscenity, and an overall tone of existential despair. Mardik Martin, who was under contract to Winkler, had tried to turn it into a screenplay to please Scorsese, but had no sympathy with the material, much of which he suspected was invented.

Initially at least, Scorsese liked Martin's take on the story. Reflecting journalist Pete Hamill's vision of boxing in the forties and fifties as 'the great dark prince of sports', it depicted boxers as gladiators, battling to the death for the pleasure of wealthy patrons who crowded close to the ring, perversely delighted when blood splashed over their jewels and furs.

Inspired, Scorsese started to insert material from his own life.

His grandfather had believed he would live as long as the fig tree in his garden, and duly died with it. Martin attached details like this to the life of La Motta's father, knowing as he did so that they had no place in this story.

De Niro didn't hide his dissatisfaction with these changes to what he regarded as his personal project. 'What is this?' he demanded when Martin handed him the first draft. 'What's going on here? This is not the picture we agreed on.'

'I was really trying to please Marty,' Martin says. 'I had another job at the time, also, and I'll never forget Irwin Winkler coming to me and saying, "You're going to go crazy. Let's have someone else do it." I said, "Thank God."'

In the autumn of 1978, Paul Schrader was directing *Hardcore*, about a Calvinist businessman tracking his runaway daughter through the world of porn movies. He was surprised when De Niro asked to see him; they were not close friends, and Bobby seldom dropped in on anyone just for the pleasure of it. De Niro showed him Martin's script, and asked him to rewrite it. Schrader agreed to do a polish, and Martin, glad to be rid of this unhappy project, willingly relinquished all his notes and research. Once Schrader read them, however, he knew he'd have to start from scratch.

He, De Niro and Scorsese met for dinner at Musso and Frank's, an old-fashioned Hollywood restaurant the wood-panelled booths of which had seen half a century of dirty deals. Scorsese resented De Niro taking charge of the project, but reluctantly agreed to Schrader rewriting the script.

Editing *Hardcore* by day, Schrader began work by night, mostly at Nickodell's, a bar on Melrose Avenue, near the Paramount studios. In those days, he preferred to write while drunk. 'When you're sober, your critical faculties start to get in the way,' he said, 'but when you're drunk you get grandiose and emotional, and start to go with the flow.' Most of his ideas were scribbled down on bar napkins.

Schrader was struck by the character of Jake's brother Joey, who didn't appear in Martin's script. The brothers started out as boxers together, but Joey, smarter and more social, quit to manage Jake. 'The only thing Jake was good at was taking a beating,' says Schrader. 'He wasn't a terrific boxer but he could take a beating, and meanwhile Joey was off managing and getting all the girls. So injecting that sibling relationship into the script made it a financeable film.'

Schrader made other changes, softening an incident in which La Motta, furious about an overcooked steak, beat his wife sense-less and kicked her in the stomach, causing her to miscarry. In Schrader's script, he knocks her unconscious, while in the finished film he simply shoves her into the bedroom and closes the door.

Schrader didn't cut extensive nude scenes with two women, including the sixteen-year-old Vicky, and a sequence where, locked in solitary confinement in a Florida jail, Jake tries to masturbate. Unable to ejaculate, he pounds the wall with his fists, shouting repeatedly, 'I am not an animal.' Not unexpectedly for someone working on a film about the porn world, Schrader wanted the audience to share the pin-ups and scraps of old movies that passed through Jake's mind.

UA welcomed Schrader's new version. 'I found this revision vastly superior to the previous two versions of *Raging Bull*,' wrote studio reader Geoffrey Grode in an internal report dated 14 November 1978. 'It is still a story of several cycles of triumph and degradation, but the storyline is cleaner and clearer, less concerned with macho rituals and aberrant sexuality. Subplots that were introduced but never developed in the last version (e.g. La Motta's hatred for his father) have been eliminated.'

At Thanksgiving 1978, two weeks after they read this report, UA executives Steven Bach and David Field, in town for the first screenings of *The Deer Hunter*, met Scorsese and Irwin Winkler at Scorsese's austere East 57th Street apartment.

The executives were taken aback to find De Niro also there. Bach remembers him as 'a dark, wiry, silent presence in jeans and bare feet' who emerged unexpectedly from the depths of the apartment. His presence unnerved them. This wasn't the usual wardrobe of movie stars, nor the demeanour of an actor meeting executives who had the power to green-light the project or axe it. He just sat on the couch, 'silent and watchful' in Bach's words, taking no part in the discussion.

Bach and Field voiced their doubts about the script. (Describing this meeting in his book *Final Cut*, Bach confuses parts of it with earlier discussions, because some scenes of which he complains had already been removed by Schrader.)

'We have a real question whether this story can ever be made as a movie any audience will want to see, whatever the rating,' Field said.

'Why?' Scorsese asked.

'It's this man,' Field said. 'I don't know who wants to see a movie that begins with a man so angry, so . . . choked with rage, that because his pregnant wife burns the steak, he slugs her to the kitchen floor and then kicks her in the abdomen until she aborts. Violence may be part of this man's life, demons of rage may be fucking up his head, but why should anyone stick around for the second reel? Can any writer make him more than what he seems to be in the scripts we've seen?'

'Which is what?' Scorsese asked.

'A cockroach,' Field replied.

De Niro spoke for the first time – his voice 'calm and even and resolute', according to Bach.

'He is not a cockroach,' he said. Then he repeated it.

The firestorm over *The Deer Hunter* was not long arriving. Convinced that the film would bomb without skilful pre-publicity, Universal hired publicist and manager Allan Carr, whose triumphs included making the minimally-talented Ann-Margret a star, and turning the film *Grease* into a hit.

'I knew I wouldn't like [*The Deer Hunter*],' Carr said. 'It's about two things I don't care about – Vietnam and poor people – directed by this guy Cimino who I remember directing Ann-Margret in Canada Dry ads five years ago. Three hours of Pittsburgh steelworkers. After lunch at my hangout, Ma Maison, I went to see the film for friendship reasons. By the middle of the movie, I was crying so hard I had to go to the men's room to put cold water on my face.'

Carr scrapped Universal's scheduled autumn release and set up one-week screenings in New York and Los Angeles for early December 1978. These made the film eligible for Academy Awards nomination while keeping it tantalisingly out of reach of most people.

Even though audiences in New York were limited to five hundred per showing, news soon spread of something nasty but impressive on its way. Hardly had the first screenings ended than the left was railing against the depiction of the Viet Cong as snake-eyed sadists gambling with the lives of American servicemen. For the next two years, starting with the Oscars in April 1979, any showing of *The Deer Hunter* anywhere in the world was likely to produce protest, pickets and walkouts – exactly the reaction for which Carr had hoped.

Taking his cue from Carr, Cimino claimed in interviews that, at screenings everywhere, even men who hadn't fought in Vietnam were stumbling, sobbing, to the rest room, sometimes leaning on the arms of friends, but returning, having collected themselves, to watch the rest of the film. In reality, far more watchers stayed seated to revel in the film's violence and, particularly when De Niro blasted his captors, roar their approval.

The fuss was enough to guarantee *The Deer Hunter* robust representation in the Academy Award nominations. It was nominated for Best Film, De Niro for Best Actor, Cimino for Best Director, Walken for Best Supporting Actor, Streep for Best Supporting Actress, with nominations also for Original Screenplay, Cinematography, Sound and Editing. Its main competition, ironically, was *Coming Home*, another film about Vietnam vets, set in a hospital for paraplegics. Hal Ashby's film was also nominated for Best Film, Best Director and Best Original Screenplay, while its stars Jane Fonda, Jon Voight and Bruce Dern received nominations as well. Fonda's attacks on Cimino's film promised a noisy confrontation on Oscar night.

Elsewhere, De Niro had more personal concerns. In March, he and Diahnne agreed to separate. The news didn't become public until July, but the split was widely rumoured for months before.

News of the separation surprised nobody. Both had spent most of the marriage in different worlds, physically and intellectually. When he worked on a film, De Niro lived in character. He was seldom at home, but, even when he was, Abbott had to contend with the moods of Jimmy Doyle and the remote misogyny of Michael Vronsky. She preferred to spend her time in New York, hobnobbing, none too successfully, with the Warhol set, in the hope of creating some sort of career as a singer and actress. At the time, a starring role in *The Josephine Baker Story* was rumoured to be in prospect, but nothing came of it.

De Niro probably never had high hopes for the marriage, though his later comments juxtapose naïve optimism and resignation. 'Neither Di nor I would have ever signed the papers knowing there might be all sorts of hard times ahead of us,' he said. 'You can struggle together as man and woman, but when you become man and wife the contract creates obligations.'

The obligations which troubled De Niro, inevitably, were towards his son, Raphael. 'We wanted to have children,' he said. 'We wouldn't have gone ahead and had them without marrying because eventually it places an undue moral burden on them.'

People who knew De Niro noted how closely his marriage paralleled that of his parents. Both couples remained together for about two years. Both marriages produced a son. Once separated, the couples didn't divorce for some time. Raphael continued to spend time with his father as Bobby had spent time with his, and the estranged parents came together for family occasions and holidays.

When he wasn't in their Barrow Street brownstone in New York, De Niro made his Los Angeles base at the Château Marmont Hotel. Built in 1927, the Marmont, old-fashioned, nondescript, even threatening on the hill above Sunset, accessible only by a narrow, half-hidden switchback street, enjoyed a reputation for discreet bohemianism. Columbia's legendary tyrant Harry Cohn told his young studs of the fifties like William Holden and Glenn Ford, 'If you must get in trouble, do it at the Château Marmont.'

De Niro discovered the Marmont when he first came to Hollywood. The promotion of the abortive *Bogart Slept Here* featured him walking along Sunset in front of the hotel. Like many of Hollywood's most reclusive stars before him, he enjoyed the anonymity of its gloomy corridors and panelled rooms, and of the bungalows scattered through the wooded grounds. John Belushi in particular appreciated their seclusion. (Bellhops still respectfully indicate Bungalow 3, where the comedian 'checked out' in 1982.)

Though De Niro partied with Belushi in his bungalow when the comedian was in town, he preferred to live in one of its two penthouses, which he rented for two years after the break-up with Abbott. It was a Hollywood choice. Elizabeth Taylor had brought Montgomery Clift there to recuperate from his 1956 car accident. A decade before, it had been occupied by Howard Hughes, who kept a telescope permanently focused on the girls in the swimming pool below.

Separation from Abbott loosened De Niro's reserve, particularly when it came to women. On the set of *Deer Hunter*, Meryl Streep was among the first actresses to glimpse the new and more sensual Bobby. 'When you look into his eyes,' she said, 'it's like looking into the fathomless deep. In my scenes with him, I felt the unreality of the set and the cameras and all those things that want to interfere. Bobby's eyes were like – oh! I just felt enveloped in their gaze. Huge emotions right under the surface.'

The effect escalated once De Niro started research on his role in *Raging Bull*. La Motta's divorced second wife, Vicki, lived in Florida with her daughter Stephanie. De Niro visited them repeatedly, going over their life with the boxer, and watching old home movies, which Scorsese recreated for the film.

At fifty, Vicki La Motta remained attractive, and found herself drawn to the actor, particularly as he had come increasingly to resemble her ex-husband. 'Bobby was so much like Jake that I just wanted to go to bed with him,' she confessed. 'How could I not? An affair seemed the most normal thing to do. But Bob wanted things to be businesslike. I should have just attacked him or something.'

Had she done so, De Niro might not have struggled for long.

Even before he and Abbott split, he'd started an intimate relationship with New York African-American model and caterer Doris 'Toukie' Smith. As tall as Abbott and eleven years De Niro's junior, Smith had a penchant for crimson dresses, and in those days dyed her hair blonde, creating a spectacular effect. De Niro continued, however, to cruise for women, particularly in Los Angeles, partying at Hugh Hefner's Playboy Mansion and at the high-security On the Rox club on Sunset Boulevard.

After the Thanksgiving meeting with Bach and Field, Scorsese and De Niro retreated to the Caribbean island resort of St Martin to rewrite *Raging Bull*. Schrader did no further work on the project. 'I would not have done this on my own,' he says, 'and I don't think Marty would have, either, but it was Bob's passion.' On the day filming began, he would wire Scorsese and De Niro, 'Jake did it his way, I did it my way, now you do it your way.'

Six months after the Thanksgiving meeting, the new screenplay for *Raging Bull* was submitted to UA. 'The script was unaccompanied by any request for writer payment,' said Steven Bach, 'and no credit arbitration was ever requested from the Writers' Guild. The picture would bear the names of the first two writers and no others. But the title page that covered the draft of *Raging Bull* that made Jake La Motta human said, in small type, tucked modestly in the lower-right-hand corner, "RdN". "MS" didn't even claim that.'

Whatever work De Niro did on Schrader's script, the changes weren't as fundamental as Bach suggests; most appear in Schrader's (signed) script, which UA had seen before the Thanksgiving meeting.

Schrader had already minimised the character of La Motta's father, a sullen presence who spoke only Sicilian, and infuriated the brothers by selling up the tenement building they'd bought to support him through his retirement, returning to Sicily with the proceeds. De Niro and Scorsese eliminated him altogether.

They reduced the presence of organised crime to two people, Joey's friend Salvy, and Tommy Como, a local *capo* who speaks for the Mob. They also dropped some incidents from the Schrader version that made La Motta seem trivial and self-interested rather than a pure force of nature. These included his ducking the draft by pretending to have been made deaf in the ring, and his custom of being injected in both hands with morphine before a fight.

The theme of *Raging Bull* had always been frustrated sexuality and sexual jealousy, but the revisions made this more overt. Even the gangsters exist mainly as objects of Jake's paranoid delusion that Vicky is promiscuous. By omitting the heterosexual eroticism of earlier scripts, the new version directed *Raging Bull* in the somewhat unexpected direction of homoeroticism. Scorsese and De Niro sexualised, indeed homo-sexualised, the violence of *Raging Bull*. Both men had recently left wives who, like La Motta's women, accused them of emotional and physical neglect. Since then, they had pursued casual sex with women who meant little or nothing to them. De Niro's memories of his father's homosexuality might well have played a part. But whoever was responsible, the concept largely accounted for the film's success.

Schrader had already noted a 'kind of hidden sexual bond between [Jake and Joey]. The sexuality of the siblings expresses itself by Jake being convinced that his brother has cheated him.' In the finished film, boxing is shown throughout as homoerotic and sado-masochistic. The first time Jake seduces Vicki, the most prominent image in the bedroom is a double portrait of the brothers squaring off against one another. La Motta complains often that he has 'women's hands', too small to give the impact he needs to move up to heavyweight and fight the real champions, like Joe Louis.

De Niro and Scorsese rewrote La Motta's fight with Tony Janiro, showing Jake driven to a jealous frenzy by a casual comment from Vicky that the boxer is handsome. Now he sadistically smashes the young man's face, and struts back to a neutral corner with a sideways glance of triumph at Vicky, who lowers her head. Watching from ringside, Tommy Como comments, 'Well, he ain't good lookin' any more.' Later, it's mentioned with glee that Jake's attack moved Janiro's nose from one side of his face to the other.

The same lasciviousness permeates all the boxing scenes, which decelerate periodically into slow motion, the better to show gouts of blood spurting from ruptured flesh – the only ejaculations Scorsese and De Niro permit La Motta.

De Niro and Scorsese emphasised the homoeroticism and sado-masochism of the ring, but scoured sex from everything else. Vicki doesn't appear naked, but is dressed with Victorian *pudeur* throughout, and while we see Jake dump a jug of ice water into his shorts, we don't see a penis. Also missing were the scenes of Jake trying to masturbate in jail. De Niro replaced the latter with something he'd seen La Motta do. During their discussions at the Sherry Netherland in New York, the boxer pounded his head against the wall. In the film, De Niro does the same, beating the wall with head and fists, shouting, 'Why? Why? Why?'

The final script drops a distracting character in Pete Petrella, Jake's only friend (and co-writer of the book *Raging Bull*), and emphasises that of Joey. It's now his brother who becomes the target of Jake's jealous rage. In a key sequence, Jake accuses him of sleeping with Vicky, then storms into his house in his under-wear and beats him brutally in front of his family.

Jake makes two attempts at a reconciliation with Joey, both failures. In the first, he sits silent in a telephone booth, unable to frame the words of apology. The second takes place when Jake is on the skids. Spotting Joey in the street, he follows him, calling for him to stop. Joey plods stolidly to his car, and though Jake embraces him awkwardly, it's obvious that the rift is unbridgeable. Jake ends the film alone, doing his nightclub act, reciting texts about fighters in defeat: Brando in *On the Water-front*, 'Man Mountain' in Rod Serling's *Requiem for a Heavy-weight*, Shakespeare's Richard III.

The new script was sufficiently different to convince UA that they might barely make a profit on the film. (They didn't: it cost about $10 million and earned back about $6 million.) 'It was still brutal and violent and profane,' Bach said of the revised screenplay. 'It was still a serious commercial gamble. But the darkness Jake La Motta inhabited was that not of an insect but of a man lost in the mysteries and pain of his own violent nature.'

Though the rewrite, by removing most of the cheap elements of La Motta's character, played a part in persuading UA to green-light the film, the growing acclaim for *The Deer Hunter* and De Niro weighed more heavily. Cimino's film proved the audience would accept the pornography of violence more readily than that of sex, and that De Niro, like Lon Chaney before him, was 'The Man of a Thousand Faces' whom the public preferred to see punish himself in such masochistic roles. More heavily still, how-ever, weighed the success of *Rocky*, to which Chartoff and Winkler owned the rights. Faced with the prospect of losing one guaranteed money-maker of a boxing picture, UA agreed reluctantly to fund another which they suspected would flop.

As well as working with La Motta and his family, De Niro hunted for unfamiliar faces to play supporting roles. On late-night TV he saw *The Death Collector*, a low-budget 1975 crime story which presaged *Goodfellas* and *Casino*, but was shot in the cheap style of *Mean Streets*. Playing a young career criminal who becomes an 'enforcer' for the Mob's loan-shark operations, Joe Pesci struck De Niro as someone who could play the role of La Motta's brother.

Born in the same year as De Niro, the diminutive Pesci was a singer in childhood, when he appeared regularly on the TV variety show *Startime Kids*. Like De Niro, he dropped out of high school, in his case in a failed attempt to become a lounge vocalist, then played guitar with the rock group Joey Dee and the Starliters. After a few roles in low-budget movies, he'd started managing an Italian restaurant in New Jersey, with no thought of returning to show business. When the call came from De Niro and Scorsese, he hadn't made a film in eight years. 'I don't want to go back to acting unless I get a part that proves I'm good,' he said. De Niro explained about Joey: 'It's a good role; not a great role.' Pesci took it anyway, and earned an Academy Award nomination.

Dozens of actresses, getting wind of the part of Jake's second wife, Vicky, had already thrown their hats into the ring, and some much more. To the embarrassment of everyone, Jodie Foster's mother, hearing that the role called for Vicky to appear in a swimsuit, sent Scorsese pictures of her daughter in a bikini.

On his trip to Florida to see La Motta's ex-wife, De Niro met his daughter Stephanie, who, at twenty-eight, strikingly re-sembled her mother as a girl. They talked about her playing Vicky in the film, but De Niro decided against it. 'He couldn't cope with being married in the film to someone he thought of as his daughter,' said Stephanie, who would become the first of the La Motta clan to have a grudge against the film of *Raging Bull*, charging, 'Robert De Niro has made my father look like a drunken wife-beater' – not far from the reality depicted in La Motta's own book. Deborah La Motta, Jake's third wife, suing him for divorce, claimed that De Niro's almost continual presence in their life for two years contributed to the collapse of her marriage.

Joe Pesci suggested Cathy Moriarty for the role of Vicky. He'd first seen her picture flashed on the wall of a New Jersey disco, and been struck by her seventeen-year-old blonde good looks. Once she'd visited his restaurant a few times, he found she also possessed a seductively husky voice, and a confident sexuality beyond her years. She had never heard of De Niro, but the moment they saw her, Scorsese and De Niro knew she was ideal, though the Screen Actors Guild took some convincing. Cis Corman finally laid ten photographs of Vicky La Motta on the desk of the SAG executive, next to ten of Moriarty, and said, 'See?' His objections evaporated.

De Niro would never be satisfied simply to 'pad up' to play the bloated La Motta of the sixties. This would not 'earn the right' to play the character. Rather, as soon as he'd finished shooting the boxing scenes, he proposed to add the fifteen pounds he'd lost getting into shape to play the young Jake, and thirty or forty more besides. It was a feat both of will and endurance, and De Niro recognised that, at thirty-six, he was close to the age where he would not be able to achieve it. 'I don't have more than two years during which I can do that to my body,' he told Scorsese. 'We have to make this film now.'

De Niro already knew both the La Motta brothers, and had

started taking boxing lessons from Jake at the famous Gramercy Gym, as well as perfecting his Bronx accent. For weeks on end, he and Jake sparred under the supervision of Sly Stallone's trainer from the *Rocky* films. 'I guess in the first six months we boxed a thousand rounds, a half-hour straight every day,' said La Motta. The boxer regarded the film as the ultimate vindication of a life of violence, and was a strict critic of De Niro's performance. 'Keep ya head up,' he yelled. 'Ya gotta keep ya head up. Whaddya want people to think – that I was some kinda jerk?'

So brutal had La Motta been in his day that sparring partners wore body protectors as well as face masks, and even in retirement he could hit hard. 'Bobby wouldn't train unless we wore headgear and mouthpieces, because he knew he was starting to get through my defences,' he said. 'We both ended up with black eyes, and my upper teeth caps were busted.' UA paid $4000 to repair La Motta's dental work, though De Niro said later that the most damage he inflicted was to break one of La Motta's teeth, while the 'thousand rounds' were more like half that number.

De Niro's body was thickening with all the exercise, helped by a high-protein diet. Make-up built up his nose, and his hair was darkened and curled. Once he was proficient in the ring, De Niro, whom La Motta, with typical hyperbole, said he'd rate among the twenty top middleweights in the world, sparred through three real fights in a Brooklyn boxing ring. Spieled by the ring announcer as 'a young La Motta', he outpointed his opponents in two of the three.

Though he continued to loathe boxing, Scorsese went to these fights and many more. Details he saw there, like blood dripping from the ropes, would find their way into the film. He also watched De Niro sparring in the 14th Street gym, though sometimes the obvious punishment his friend was taking caused him to turn his head away. On one such occasion, De Niro climbed out of the ring.

'Are you watching?' he asked.

'Yes, yes . . .' Scorsese said.

'I'm doing this for you, you know,' De Niro said, and climbed back through the ropes.

De Niro was thoroughly into the character of La Motta when the Academy Awards were presented on 9 April 1979. He dithered about attending the ceremony, and initially asked if he could sit backstage rather than in the auditorium, where his reactions at winning or losing would not be paraded before the TV audience. The show's producer, Jack Haley Jr, refused. (The humiliations Haley had endured during the production of *New York, New York* would not have inclined him to stretch a point for any of that film's stars.)

In the event, it was just as well De Niro didn't attend. Pro-Vietnam protesters picketed the Dorothy Chandler Pavilion, and De Niro lost the Oscar for Best Actor to Jon Voight for *Coming Home*, while *Deer Hunter*'s most vociferous critic Jane Fonda took the award for Best Actress. However, the rest of the night belonged to *The Deer Hunter*, which won Best Picture, Director, Screenplay, Sound and Editing. Accepting his award, Cimino said, 'Especially I embrace Robert De Niro for his dedication and for his great dignity of heart'. With these wins, *The Deer Hunter* was well on the way to its eventual $27.4 million gross.

Immediately after the Oscars, Scorsese and De Niro shot the first scenes of *Raging Bull*, a boxing match, filmed in a Los Angeles warehouse standing in for New York's Madison Square Garden.

Since, unlike the *Rocky* films, *Raging Bull* would never appeal to a mass market, Scorsese decided to film in black and white. La Motta provided a clue to this approach at the beginning of his book: 'Now sometimes at night when I think back,' he wrote, 'I feel like I'm looking at an old black and white movie of myself. Why it should be in black and white I don't know, but it is. Not a good movie, either, with gaps in it, a string of poorly lit sequences, some of them with no beginning and some with no end.'

Schrader had picked up on this already, suggesting that, when Jake tries to masturbate in his cell, we should see scraps of old black-and-white porno films. Scorsese said later that he hoped, in using black and white, to recreate the look of old newsreels and newspapers, and the flash shots of Weegee, which he'd already evoked in the conclusion of *Taxi Driver*. But he also remembered how, in *Taxi Driver*'s climax, Michael Chapman, who would also act as lighting cameraman on *Raging Bull*, de-saturated the colour to tone down the effect of blood. Since *Raging Bull* intended, literally, to pull no punches, becoming the most consistently bloody big-budget American film to that time, monochrome promised to make the result less nauseating.

Knowing he would have to work close to the fights in order to capture De Niro's performance, Scorsese decided to shoot all of them with one camera from inside the ring. Until *Raging Bull*, the benchmark in boxing sequences had been Robert Rossen's 1947 *Body and Soul*, shot on roller skates with a hand-held camera by cinematographer James Wong Howe. Scorsese also put Michael Chapman in the ring with the fighters, and had him take the role of the opponent, backing away from the boxers as they advanced with the look of killers in their eyes. Taking a leaf from the book of dance instructors like Arthur Murray, Chapman, Scorsese and De Niro plotted the movements like dance routines, with diagrams of feet, and arrows showing the direction of movement. Rather than lose his momentum, De Niro placed a punchbag in a 'neutral' corner, and worked on it between takes.

Filming like this took time, the five-week schedule for the fight scenes swelling to ten. Patience was never Scorsese's virtue. He'd retire to his caravan, put on an album by The Clash, listen for a while, then burst out, yelling, 'It's more than one side of The Clash, Michael. What are you doing?' A little while later, he was smashing chairs against the wall – to the alarm of the Teamster transport captain, who was responsible for any damage.

Chapman's care mostly protected the actors and their doubles from accidental injury, though in a scene where Jake spars with Joey, De Niro broke one of Pesci's ribs, despite the heavy body padding he wore. Pesci took just as much of a psychological battering in the dialogue scenes with De Niro, where the star employed all his technique to jolt other members of the cast out of rote performances. Playing the key scene with Pesci, in which he accuses him of sleeping with Vicky, De Niro didn't feel he was getting enough indignation from Joey's denials. Taking a leaf out of Cimino's direction in *Deer Hunter* that Christopher Walken spit in his face, he suddenly demanded of Pesci, 'Did you fuck your mother?' Pesci's startled reaction is proof that the technique works.

Once the boxing sequences were shot, production was halted and the crew kept on salary while De Niro took off for Europe on a four-month eating binge. Always an enthusiast for Italian cooking, he ate his way through the great restaurants of Italy and France. 'It was very easy,' he explained later. 'I just had to get up at 6.30 in the morning and eat breakfast at seven in order to digest my food to eat lunch at twelve or one in order to digest my food to eat a nice dinner at seven at night. So it was three square meals a day, that's all. You know, pancakes, beer, milk.'

In the break, Scorsese married Isabella Rossellini. They honeymooned in Japan, where he experienced an anxiety attack in the Shinkasen 'bullet train', which had to let him off when he became convinced he was having a heart attack. A phlegmatic Japanese doctor had him breathe into a paper bag, which solved the problem in a few minutes.

By the time De Niro got back to the US, he'd ballooned from 145 pounds to 215. The last two weeks of shooting were a trial. He couldn't tie his shoelaces or bend, had sore feet, high blood pressure, and experienced trouble breathing. His voice descended to a husky murmur. Drowsing in the make-up chair, he now snored noisily. His adopted stepdaughter Drena regarded him with disbelief, even distaste, and tried to keep him from meeting her friends.

The make-up artists provided him with the thickened features of an old pug, eyebrows ridged with scar tissue, nose swollen and misshapen, with a bulging growth spreading under the skin below his left eye. As Scorsese said, De Niro's performance lifted *Raging Bull* out of the ruck of the sports story. 'To call *Raging Bull* a boxing picture is ridiculous,' he said curtly. 'It's sports, but it's something to do with living. Jake La Motta takes on aspects of everybody.' It was the peak of De Niro's career as a transformative actor, though it must have crossed his mind, as it crossed those of his colleagues, that it would be a performance almost impossible to top.

CHAPTER FOURTEEN

A Harp with Class

Introibo ad altare Dei. Ad Deum qui laetificat juventutem meam.

(I will go unto the altar of God. To God who giveth joy to my youth.)

First words of the Catholic Mass

Delays in production pushed *Raging Bull* into 1979, making it ineligible for the Oscars presented in April 1980, so Scorsese had no incentive to hurry with his post-production. Robbie Robertson agreed to be music producer, the start of a new career for the rocker, who would also do Scorsese's *The King of Comedy* and *The Color of Money*. In the end, however, little modern music found its way into the film. Instead, Scorsese celebrated his and La Motta's shared Sicilian heritage with extracts from the operas of Pietro Mascagni, which Coppola would also use in *The Godfather III*. Scorsese later rated the opening, where La Motta dances in slow motion in a smoke-wreathed ring to the stately romanticism of *Cavaliera Rusticana*, as his favourite sequence in all his films.

Few films are as exciting to listen to as *Raging Bull*. Evoking the tunnel hearing of the athlete high on endorphins, the mix isolates the clink of ice cubes in the bucket where Jake soaks his battered hand, the murmured advice of the seconds, the muted roar of the crowd, the half-heard announcements over the public address system, the crackle of an old-fashioned flashbulb imploding – matched often in the film to the crunch of leather on flesh.

These effects were created and edited by Frank Warner, who did the sound effects for *Taxi Driver* and Spielberg's *Close Encounters of the Third Kind*. 'None of the sound was pre-planned,' he said, 'but I knew I wanted it to be from Jake's standpoint. What does a punch sound like in his ears? How would he hear the crowd? I figured, OK, it was going to take about seven weeks to mix the picture, but it took sixteen more weeks!' Among the sounds employed to duplicate the effect of a punch on the person receiving it were rifle shots, and a blade crunching through the shell of a watermelon. The sources of many more were never revealed; Walker burned his tapes rather than reveal his secrets.

In the middle of post-production, Winkler complained that Scorsese was mixing the film 'inch by inch'. 'That's the way it's going to be done,' grated the director. At the last moment, with a deadline looming, he requested a remix of one reel because the name of the whisky 'Cutty Sark' wasn't sufficiently clear in a restaurant scene. When Winkler protested, Scorsese said, 'If you don't let me change it, I'll take my name off the film.' He wouldn't relinquish the print until four days before the film's opening.

The inactivity that followed *Raging Bull* left De Niro feeling depressed, as the gaps between films increasingly did. 'Every character I play takes a great deal out of me,' he confessed, 'and afterwards there is a sense of loss and let-down until I start digging into the next one.' When someone suggested that he must be glad of a rest after playing La Motta, he said moodily, 'What am I going to do with myself?' Friends would have helped him out of his depression, particularly those like Meryl Streep, whom he'd helped get over the death of John Cazale, but nobody knew of it. 'Bob has always been very loyal to me, during a really hard time in my life,' said Streep, 'and I feel I can count on him. But deeply, I don't know him. He is a very kind of unto-himself person, too.'

To add to De Niro's gloom, the Cannon group of Yoram Globus and Menahem Golan resurrected *Sam's Song*, the unfinished short in which he'd appeared in 1969. Behind the penumbrous pseudonym 'John Shade', John Broderick, a line producer who'd directed *Six Pack Annie* and *Bad Georgia Road*, cheap features for the drive-in market, added a framing story to Jordan Leondopoulos's film, maximising De Niro's role as Sammy Nicoletti, the young film-maker who gets into trouble partying with the fast set on a Long Island weekend.

The new version, called variously *The Swap* and *Line of Fire*, begins with Nicoletti murdered in his cutting room, having filmed, as it turns out, the indiscretion of an ambitious politico. Years later, his gangster brother Vito (Anthony Charnota, sometimes credited as 'John Medici') gets out of jail and, after a visit to Sammy's grave to swear vengeance, starts to track down the killers.

Since nobody who'd acted in *Sam's Song* cared to play themselves twelve years on in *The Swap*, Broderick cast people with only the vaguest resemblance to the originals, which confers on the film an increasingly surrealist air, not helped by the poster copy: 'He's Tough. He's Cool. He's Murder on Women . . . and they're Death on Him!'

De Niro found it harder than he'd expected to lose the lard accumulated to play La Motta. And, now that the pressure was off, he wasn't trying too hard. 'It doesn't interfere with my sex life,' he said defiantly. 'Some women never give a look unless they find out whom I am, but believe it or not, some liked me fat – thought I was a big teddy bear.'

Proof of his ability to find women was provided by Helena Springs, who worked as a back-up vocalist for performers like Bob Dylan and Barbra Streisand. Springs was driving her car down Santa Monica Boulevard when De Niro, wearing a loud Hawaiian shirt, pulled up next to her in his open sports car. He continued to stop next to her at each traffic light until she gave him her phone number.

The pick-up developed into a classic showbiz liaison. Springs was often on the road, and De Niro, even when he was in town, usually immersed himself so completely in the character he played that he might as well have been in another country.

De Niro enjoyed the difference in status between himself and his lover. 'You are Shelley Winters to my Montgomery Clift,' he told Springs, who preened – not knowing movies well enough to realise that Clift's wealthy love in *A Place in the Sun* isn't Winters but Elizabeth Taylor: Winters plays the dumb factory girl whom he impregnates, then contemplates murdering. According to Springs, De Niro always spoke of Toukie Smith as 'my girlfriend', and fretted that news of his Los Angeles mistress might get back to New York. Some years later, the real-life romance developed a melodramatic twist similar to Theodore Dreiser's novel *An American Tragedy*, on which *A Place in the Sun* was based, when Springs also became pregnant, and De Niro found himself, like the book's hero, in court.

In February 1980, De Niro visited Rome to promote *Raging Bull*, and revived his relationship with Stefania Sandrelli, one of his co-stars from *Novecento*. Now divorced, Sandrelli wasn't nervous about being seen with De Niro. He even brought her to New York, where they were spotted holding hands. The *NY Daily News* reported him 'altogether smitten'.

Around the same time, CBS producer David Burke paused on a morning walk through TriBeCa to watch workmen hoisting a number of living trees two metres tall towards a loft eleven floors above Hudson Street.

'What's going on?' he asked.

'That actor Robert De Niro's moving in,' one of the workmen told him.

1981 marked De Niro's definitive move back to the east coast. When the Hudson Street building was turned into a condo, De Niro bought his apartment for $875,000. Over the next two years, teams of carpenters turned the loft with its views in all four directions into one of the most luxurious in downtown Manhattan. The transformation cost $3 million, including $200,000 on the carpentry alone, which included an atrium and entranceway in red oak, a master bedroom panelled in cedar with a redwood skylight, a private gym and bathroom in teak, and a kitchen in butternut.

The trees, trucked across country, flourished. De Niro found a tree frog in one of them. Later, it became the hero of a children's book, *Cesar's Amazing Journey*, written by De Niro's co-producer Jane Rosenthal, with Craig Hatkoff. According to the synopsis, 'When he and his tree are uprooted and shipped to New York City, Cesar the tree frog sees the sights while looking for a new home with the help of a hipster spider, B. Cider.'

For two years, cabinetmaker Bill Russell worked almost exclusively on the De Niro residence. His final project was a cabinet eight metres long and two metres high to house state-of-the-art video and sound playing and recording equipment. But when he submitted the bill for his final payment of $15,000, De Niro refused to pay, accusing Russell of having been 'greedy' and failing to 'fully install' the cabinets.

'It came out of the blue,' Russell said of the dispute. He attributed it to De Niro's ego. 'I treated him just like another customer, and he found that difficult, because he's used to people kissing his butt.' In September 1983, the Manhattan Supreme Court ordered De Niro to pay Russell the $15,000, plus $5000 legal costs, with interest.

De Niro gravitated back to the people he'd known in his earlier days in New York, including the Warhol set. Soon after he arrived back, he hinted to director Paul Morrissey that he might find him the money to make *Trash II*, which he was then writing – the first sign that De Niro contemplated producing films as well as acting in them.

'I was intent on doing something that was more serious,' he said later. 'I thought, "If I'm going to do it, I better do it now, because there's going to be a point where I'm not going to have the energy or the desire." I didn't want it to be thought of as a vanity thing, which was the way people were going to think about it, anyway. "OK, fine, it doesn't matter," I thought. "I'm just going to do what I'm going to do." I wasn't sure how or where it was going to go, but I knew it was going to go in some direction.' That direction was Tribeca Films and the Tribeca Film Center, which De Niro would open in 1989.

The decision to base his life in New York once again was reflected in his friendships with people like John Belushi, and Robin Williams, the ex-stand-up comedian who'd won a short-lived reputation in the TV series *Mork and Mindy*. Williams wouldn't make his film debut until 1980 in Robert Altman's misconceived *Popeye*, but he was already part of the Warhol group, where De Niro met him.

Along with Belushi, who adulated De Niro, calling him 'Bobby D', Williams was a foundation member of a gradually accumulating De Niro 'circle' that included friends from the old neighbourhood like Clem Caserta, for whom De Niro found a cameo role in almost all his films.

Another was Sammy Cahn, lyricist of everything from the pot-boiler 'Three Coins in the Fountain' to the elegiac 'I Should Care'. Short, cocky, a natural raconteur, Cahn went on Broadway in 1974 with a one-man show about his career, in which he toured the world for the next twenty years. To De Niro, Cahn represented exactly the unpretentious talent of the New York musical theatre, and they became close friends. De Niro would dedicate his first film as director to his own father and to Cahn, both of whom died in the year of its release, 1993.

Returning to New York also allowed De Niro to repair his relationship with his father, who had flourished modestly during the seventies. That he would never become wealthy from painting, nor amass a major reputation, mattered as little to Robert Sr at fifty-eight as it had at eighteen. 'I'd run into him at gallery openings two or three times every season,' says Greenwich Village bookseller Mashall Clements, 'and we would embrace and talk for a few moments, but never again had a real conversation. When I would introduce him to whichever friend was with me on these occasions, they would inevitably ask whether he was related to the actor, and he would say that, yes, he was his father. He seemed pleased by compliments on his son's talent and quietly proud of his success, although I have heard that relations were quite strained between them during Bob Jr's adolescence and teenage years.'

Becoming better known had made Robert Sr marginally more social, and he turned up occasionally for parties, sometimes with Virginia, the last vestiges of whose student radicalism had been eradicated by success in business. Her tendency towards conformity, which Anaïs Nin had noticed thirty years before, when Virginia had told her primly, 'I'm not interested in the unfamiliar. I like the familiar,' had hardened.

Mashall Clements remembers her as 'rather quiet; more a listener than a participant in the spirited and sometimes heated discussions of painting that were dominated by Nell [Blaine], Bob De Niro [Sr] and Leland Bell – all three quite passionate arguers. Bob was even carrying on the arguments with Lee Bell after Bell's death [in 1991]. At the memorial gathering for him at the New School, for example, Bob got up to speak and began with, "I didn't write anything down. I thought I'd just talk about things I remembered. But I don't remember much. Well, the arguments. I mean . . . Arp!!!" (Lee was pro, Bob, con.)'

When his father did agree to sell his paintings, De Niro bought them, often as gifts for friends like Francis Ford Coppola. Robert Cordier, who'd relocated to Paris as a stage producer and writer, saw Bobby occasionally, and remembers him as preoccupied with his father, and his father's reputation. 'A lot of times people that get big, who are good at what they do, have a revenge to take about what happened to their dad. His father was important to him, and his father was not recognised, and I think Bob got serious thinking, "I owe him one." I think becoming famous was very important to him to pay back his father. That has a lot to do with his drive. I think that has a lot to do with Bob's will to succeed. His father is not in the books, he's not rated. [This made] Bob very serious – dedicated.'

Word of De Niro's performance in *Raging Bull* had spread, and the number of screenplays landing on the doorstep of his new agent Harry Ufland skyrocketed. Most were of little interest, though De Niro did discuss *Continental Divide*, a Howard

Hawks-ian comedy by newcomer Lawrence Kasdan in which a Chicago journalist on the run has an affair with a reclusive ornithologist in a remote hut in the Rockies. Once he dropped out, the male role would go, after months of haggling, to Belushi. De Niro's readiness to contemplate any role, the less like him the better, led to his name being attached to some bizarre projects. In August 1981 it was announced that he was considering playing British serial murderer Peter Sutcliffe, the so-called 'Yorkshire Ripper'. Unfortunately the film's 'producer' turned out to be Michael 'Rocky' Ryan, a notorious hoaxer of the tabloid press, though it was intriguing to imagine De Niro's version of a Northern accent.

Many of the films on which De Niro worked during the eighties can be traced back to Ufland (who, not surprisingly, eventually left the talent business to become a producer). Not only did he represent many of De Niro's closest professional colleagues – Scorsese, Jodie Foster and Harvey Keitel – as well as directors Martin Brest, Ridley and Tony Scott and Adrian Lyne, plus Continental stars Marcello Mastroianni and Catherine Deneuve; he had the instinct for bringing together two apparently antipathetic personalities who would strike creative sparks from one another. Through Ufland De Niro met the American artist Terry Gilliam, who, after making his reputation in Britain as one of the *Monty Python* team, had become a director of distinctive fantasies, one of which, *Time Bandits*, was a major box office success.

Ufland also introduced De Niro to Arnon Milchan, a tanned, fast-talking, hyperactive and flamboyant Israeli of his own age who had the best of all qualifications for producing movies: he was already rich. After graduating from both the London School of Economics and the University of Geneva, he stepped into the family business, a conglomerate of more than twenty companies involved in everything from aerospace to agribusiness. Independent producer Elliott Kastner lured him into international movie finance in 1977 by taking him to dinner with Elizabeth Taylor – the start of a highly active, if erratic, career as producer during which Milchan would finance two of De Niro's most interesting films.

De Niro agreed to do another film for Chartoff and Winkler. In retrospect, it was a role he should have avoided, but fatigue and a lack of direction played their part in the choice. He also needed the money, both to pay for his new apartment and to invest in more property – the beginning of what would become the preoccupation of his middle age.

True Confessions started life as a novel by Californian writer John Gregory Dunne, husband of novelist Joan Didion, with whom he collaborated on the screenplay. Irish by descent, Dunne mined the culture of Irish-American Catholics. This tight-knit society of what he called 'Harps' shared a suspicion of outsiders that encouraged a Mafia-like loyalty which accommodated every vice. Harps could as easily be property developers as priests, nuns as whores. The film begins with a priest found dead in a brothel and ends with the Catholic Layman of the Year implicated in a sex murder.

Inspired by the unsolved 1947 'Black Dahlia' slaying, in which the mutilated body of a young woman was found in a Los Angeles suburb, Dunne wove an intricate tale of ambitious Monsignor Desmond Spellacy, being groomed for bishop, who becomes involved in a killing under investigation by his brother Tom, an LAPD detective. The clash between their rival value systems echoes that of the Catholic community at large, where mobster-turned-property-developer Jack Amsterdam is given a lucrative contract to build diocesan schools. The investigation destroys Des's career, though it may also have saved his soul by removing him from Church politics and exiling him to a desert diocese reserved for pariahs.

Chartoff and Winkler owned the screenplay, and were eager to film it as proof that, in making *Rocky*, they hadn't abandoned their liberal principles. After the trials of playing Jake La Motta, De Niro too relished the prospect of a role with some intellectual substance, but, moreover, one which demanded nothing in the way of transformation except in a few scenes where he had to look like a priest in his sixties, worn out with ministering to a parish in the Californian desert.

He still went through the tortuous experience of learning large portions of the Catholic Mass in Latin, and studying with Father Henry Fehren, who rated him 'the most authentic priest ever seen on the screen'. As usual, De Niro absorbed the character's physical habits, even to dressing as a priest at home, and practising saying Mass on the altar of a real church. For the sequence set in the Mojave, he had Father Fehren compile a few pages of meditation on the moral and metaphorical significance of the desert as the ageing Spellacy might have perceived it.

The director was Ulu Grosbard, a Belgian who'd worked his way into features via Broadway and stints as assistant to Sidney Lumet and Elia Kazan. De Niro knew Grosbard from the days of *The Wedding Party* – he'd been one of the directors scheduled to contribute a segment when that project had been a *film à sketches* – and since then they'd met in Greenwich Village, where both lived.

Appropriate to someone who'd trained as a diamond cutter, Grosbard was a meticulous worker who rehearsed his casts extensively. This suited both De Niro and his *True Confessions* co-star Robert Duvall, as did the director's liking for improvisation. Neither De Niro nor Duvall was deterred by the fact that Grosbard's last film, a cumbersomely titled Dustin Hoffman comedy, *Who is Harry Kellerman and why is he Saying those Terrible Things About Me?*, had flopped everywhere.

True Confessions was an ensemble film. De Niro and Duvall had equal screen time. Meaty roles also went to De Niro's old friend Charles Durning as Jack Amsterdam and to Grosbard's wife Rose Gregorio as a madam. Nobody seemed much concerned with the labyrinthine plot ('We do reveal who killed the girl,' Grosbard said, 'but it doesn't really matter'), but this took a back seat anyway to the intricacies of Church politics.

The slow pace gave De Niro no opportunities for the explosions of rage that lit up other performances. Instead, he seemed languid, moving slowly and speaking in a low, monotonous voice. The effect was emphasised by his lingering flab: columnist Rex Reed wrote bitchily of him 'whispering piously through his stoic double chins'.

De Niro and the screenwriters spent a lot of time going over the script. 'De Niro wanted his lines pared to the minimum,' says John Gregory Dunne. 'His only specific request was that we write him a scene without a single word of dialogue. He offered no suggestions, and we wrote a sequence that began with an exterior shot of De Niro removing his golf clubs from the trunk of his car, then travelled with him across the large manicured lawn of the archepiscopal estate, moved with him inside the ornately-appointed residence he shared with the cardinal of the diocese, and followed him up the staircase and down a corridor to his small bedroom, sparsely furnished with a chair, bureau, crucifix, and bed, on which was a package of laundry. De Niro took off his shoes, put on his slippers, and at the cut was staring into space. The sequence took two minutes and twenty seconds of screen time, and made the character more explicable than dialogue could ever have done.'

Not everybody agreed. *Time* magazine's reviewer Richard Corliss commented that 'characters who should percolate with rage simply simmer . . . De Niro's big scene has him hanging up vestments.' In the *New Yorker*, Pauline Kael dismissed Grosbard as 'a serious director who lacks a film sense. He simply has no feeling for the vital energies that propel a movie.' She also suggested that 'something has gone wrong with Robert De Niro's acting. In *The Godfather II*, he was so intense that he looked in danger of imploding. Now, in *True Confessions*, when he's quiet and almost expressionless, there's no intensity – there's nothing. He could be a potato, except that he's thoroughly absorbed in the process of doing nothing. It may be that De Niro took up an intellectual puzzle in 1976 on the set of *The Last Tycoon*. How do you act without doing anything? In *True Confessions*, he's carried it so far that he's not in the movie.'

None of this influenced De Niro, who would work with Grosbard again a few years later on *Falling in Love*. Meanwhile *True Confessions*, which cost $12 million to make, returned only a meagre $5.9 million at the box office.

Before it was released, however, *Raging Bull* hit the theatres, putting into the shade everything else De Niro had ever done. Even the hostile reviews acknowledged his physical achievement.

When the Oscar nominations were announced in February 1981, the film was proposed for Best Picture, Scorsese for Best Director, Michael Chapman for Cinematography, the sound team for its mix, Thelma Schoonmaker for editing, and De Niro, Pesci and Moriarty for their acting.

Following the American release of *Raging Bull*, Scorsese and De Niro went on the road in Europe with the film. *True Confessions* opened in November 1981 in Britain, where it was a solid critical and box office success. Some magazines and newspapers would rate it among the best of the year, though it never turned a profit.

In England, De Niro shied at the probing style of TV interviewers like Michael Parkinson. He and Scorsese were furious when the censorious Rank organisation refused to screen *Raging Bull* because of its profanity. The Grade organisation picked it up, but not before some testy exchanges between film-makers and executives. The gala premiere, which De Niro and Scorsese were in London to attend, was cancelled.

In Rome, De Niro ran into Harvey Keitel, and the two went on the town, pursued by *paparazzi*, who'd perfected a technique of goading their prey with their intrusiveness, then snapping them as they rounded on the cameramen. Hoping to do the same with De Niro and Keitel, one photographer made a fake call to the police, claiming he'd spotted two well-known terrorists, and giving them the number of De Niro's car. The actors were held for ninety minutes before someone recognised them. 'These guys will do anything to get a picture,' De Niro told the papers angrily. 'I'd like to get some of them inside a ring.'

De Niro was mainly in Rome to talk to Sergio Leone, the spaghetti-western director who had finally found the money to make the gangster epic he had had in preparation since 1967 – before *Bonnie and Clyde* created the vogue. In fact, Leone claimed Warren Beatty had stolen his idea. 'One night, I told him the story of my film: an old Jewish gangster remembers his crazy youth of the years from 1920 to 1933. It was a chance to make a fresco of the Prohibition years with the actors of that period – James Cagney, Glenn Ford, Henry Fonda, George Raft.

Eight months later, he released *Bonnie and Clyde*. After that, there was *The Godfather I* and *II*. It became very difficult to film anything original about that period.'

Leone spoke only a little English, but over seven hours, in two sessions, speaking through an interpreter, he described the whole film to De Niro. 'He told the story almost shot by shot,' De Niro recalled, 'with the flashbacks, and it was beautiful. I said, "This is something I'd like to be part of."'

Ironically for an Italian, the film Leone proposed was about New York's Jewish gangsters, no less influential than the Sicilians and Italians in organising crime in the United States. He had spent two years buying the rights to *The Hoods*, a book by Harry Grey II, a career criminal who had spent large parts of his life in Sing Sing. He'd hired Norman Mailer to write a screenplay which Leone claimed he never delivered. The two men were in court over it.

The Hoods told the story of four street kids from the Lower East Side of New York who became rich as gangsters during Prohibition. Noodles the Shiv, Big Maxie, Cockeye Hymie and Patsy the Gonif didn't differ too much from the characters in *The Godfather* except in being Jewish, and as much interested in sex as violence. The ethnic background of his characters didn't concern Leone much. The book would be the pretext for a film which, like his *Once Upon a Time in the West*, would celebrate the American genre movies he admired by dignifying them with an epic treatment.

Except for a few scenes on the Lower East Side, under the piers of Brooklyn Bridge, and a couple in Florida, Leone proposed to shoot the whole film in Italy, on enormous sets recreating New York from the twenties to the sixties. It would have an international cast. De Niro agreed to appear in what many recognised could be a rerun of the disaster of *Novecento*. Bad as it would be for De Niro, however, it would have worse effects on Leone, who never directed another film.

The Oscars were scheduled to be handed out on 30 March, but other events were to dominate the news that month.

On 5 March, De Niro was at the Château Marmont in Holly-wood, staying as usual in one of its two penthouses. John Belushi, in town to talk up his next project, a comedy about the wine business called 'Noble Rot', had created a sort of clubhouse in Bungalow 3, in the grounds. Robin Williams, also in town and about to start a sixty-city tour of stand-up clubs, had just done a 1.30 a.m. stint at the Comedy Store on Sunset Boulevard, and drove to On the Rox, one of the group's favourite hangouts. Finding it closed, he called De Niro, who told him to come round and meet Belushi in his bungalow.

They arrived to find Belushi with Cathy Smith, a woman who hung around the fringe of the music and film industries, some-times singing back-up, but mostly 'fixing' things for stars – some-times sex but more often dope. Neither Williams nor De Niro liked Smith, whom they'd met before at On the Rox and other clubs, and they didn't stay long. Belushi didn't seem to want them to. Already stoned, he was working to his own self-destructive agenda: his projects included a film about punk rock in which he would actually be injected with a real heroin dose.

Williams and De Niro snorted coke with Belushi, but left the bungalow about 3 a.m. A little later, Smith, at Belushi's request, injected him with a 'speedball' – cocaine and heroin mixed. It killed him. He was declared dead at one o'clock the following afternoon. Shocked, De Niro retreated to his penthouse and spent days with the shades drawn, watching old videos of *Saturday Night Live*. One friend described his manner as 'scary, but very controlled'.

When disaster strikes, Hollywood looks after its own. Only Cathy Smith knew that De Niro and Williams had visited Belushi that night, and, at least for the moment, she wasn't available to be interviewed; friends had spirited her away to her native Canada.

In any event, Belushi's death was put in the shade by events that took place later that month. At 2 p.m. on 30 March, Presi-dent Ronald Reagan was climbing into a limo in Washington DC when twenty-five-year-old drifter John Hinckley Jr stepped forward and fired a number of shots from a .22 pistol. One hit

Reagan in the chest. Doctors successfully removed the bullet from his lung, but his press secretary James Brady was permanently invalided by a head wound.

In deference, the Academy delayed the Oscar ceremony for twenty-four hours, but, consoled by the ancient wisdom that The Show Must Go On, presented them on 31 March.

Thelma Schoonmaker won an award for her editing of *Raging Bull*, but not the sound team, while Pesci and Moriarty were also out of the money, audiences preferring Timothy Hutton in *Ordinary People* and Mary Steenburgen in *Melvin and Howard*. The same impulse towards the lightly amusing and everyday also defeated Scorsese, who watched Robert Redford climb on stage to take the Oscar for his first effort as a director, the anodyne *Ordinary People*, which also won Best Picture.

There was no doubt, however, that De Niro had Best Actor locked up, even against the competition of another transformative *tour de force* by John Hurt in *The Elephant Man*.

Aware that he was the front-runner, De Niro attended the ceremony, accompanied by Diahnne Abbott. Jake La Motta was there too, though not his brother Joey, who, in what was almost a family tradition by now, disliked the film, and was suing Chartoff and Winkler over his portrayal.

Oscar ceremony producer Howard W. Koch and Jack Valenti, Motion Picture Academy of Arts and Sciences head and Hollywood's ambassador to the White House, fought a vain holding action against the flood of scandal that threatened to overwhelm the event, but real life crowded in everywhere. Nervous about more violence, the security staff admitted Scorsese, De Niro, their wives, and their agent Harry Ufland into the Dorothy Chandler Pavilion before anyone else. While they waited to be seated, De Niro asked about the green ribbon worn by ABC-TV page Thomas Rogers. When he explained it was a symbol of solidarity with the African-American community of Atlanta, Georgia, then terrified by a serial murderer, De Niro asked if he could wear it. Thomas pinned it to his lapel.

Once the ceremony began, Dan Aykroyd, though he'd promised Koch not to do so, couldn't resist reminding the world of Belushi's death. Presenting the Oscar for Special Effects, he referred to his long-time *Saturday Night Live* and film partner as 'something of a special effect himself'.

De Niro duly won the Best Actor Oscar, which was presented by Sally Field. His flustered speech began, 'I'm a little nervous. I'm sorry. I forgot my lines so the director wrote them down.' He thanked 'Vicky La Motta and all the other wives, Joey La Motta, even though he's suing us . . .'. This drew nervous laughter – lawsuits were too common in Hollywood to be a source of amusement. 'I want to thank my mother and father for having me,' he went on, 'and my grandmothers and grandfathers for having them', after which he hailed 'everyone else involved in the film, and I hope that I can share this with anyone that it means anything to and the rest of the world and especially with all the terrible things that are happening . . .'. Without needing to be too specific about what these might be, he ended with, 'I love everyone.'

Heading back to his seat clutching his statuette, De Niro had to be steered by Field to the backstage area where all recipients faced the press. It was here that he discovered that John Hinckley had told police he shot Reagan in the hopes of impressing Jodie Foster. He'd stalked her for many months, sending her letters and even having some brief telephone conversations with her at her college, but the obsession began with *Taxi Driver*, which he'd seen repeatedly.

Inevitably, the first questioner asked De Niro what he thought of Hinckley's confession. Utterly unprepared, he could only stammer, 'Well . . . it's a different thing . . . That's a loaded question, first of all. I don't want to be asked that. I can't express it now . . . It's a terrible thing . . . but the connection . . . I have no idea . . . It's an assumption . . . I don't know . . .'. He began a crablike retreat towards the door. 'I thank you. I said what I had to say when I accepted the award, and you all look very nice. Thank you . . .' Pursued by more shouted questions and camera flashes, he disappeared towards Ma Maison and the *Raging Bull* party, where he passed on the news of Hinckley's claim to an alarmed Scorsese.

The following day, De Niro was still off-balance. He made a date with Helena Springs at her house, arriving there depressed and trembling. Seeing the degree to which he relied on her for consolation and comfort, Springs began to hope for a more permanent relationship, even to plan for it. But a few days later De Niro left for New York, and the romance once again went into cold storage.

By coincidence, when Hinckley shot Reagan, Scorsese and De Niro were in the last stages of preparing a film about obsessed fans who inflict violence on the subjects of their admiration.

As with *Raging Bull*, De Niro and not Scorsese wanted to make *The King of Comedy*, the script by film critic Paul D. Zimmermann that he'd bought ten years before. Scorsese would have preferred his pet project, a film of Nikos Kazantkazis's *The Last Temptation of Christ*, with De Niro playing a controversial revisionist version of the Messiah, prey to human lusts and doubts. He now had the rights to the novel, and Paul Schrader was working on the script. Paramount would finance it, with Winkler producing.

But De Niro refused. Not only did he lack Scorsese's deep-seated religious guilts; he had no ambition to play any character not part of his own world, though Scorsese's proposal would plant the seed of his one period role, in *The Mission*. Instead, he told Scorsese, he wanted to make a comedy.

Comedy represented the ultimate pitfall to both Scorsese and De Niro, as it did to all the film-makers of New Hollywood. Steven Spielberg's World War II farce *1941* had fallen flat on its face. George Lucas found some laughs in *American Graffiti*, but the film's overall tone was bitter. Any humour in Spielberg's *Raiders of the Lost Ark* belonged to Lawrence Kasdan, the screenwriter who was emerging, along with Paul Schrader, as the laureate of the new generation of American film-makers.

It rankled with De Niro that his one attempt at comedy, *Bogart Slept Here*, had ended in disaster. Mike Nichols, a true king of comedy, regarded him as simply not funny. To De Niro, such an attack was a powerful incentive to try again. If he could play

Jake La Motta, he reasoned, surely he could tell a joke. Seasoned comics could have told him that taking a punch in the face was nothing compared to delivering a one-liner, but the praise for *Raging Bull* drowned them out.

Scorsese still felt exhausted from the effort of working on the earlier film, but there were good reasons to think seriously about *King of Comedy*, among them a threatened strike by the Directors' Guild of America, which would freeze all production. Once again, Harry Ufland (who has a small role in the film) was instrumental in persuading Arnon Milchan to produce. Milchan found companies were ready to fund Zimmermann's script because it could be shot in New York, away from Hollywood's studios, frantically completing films ahead of the deadline, and with a relatively small cast and nothing like the resources demanded by *Raging Bull*.

In fact, since the story was set in the world of television, Scorsese suggested they film it in that style – old-fashioned framing, almost square, largely empty sets furnished in primary colours, a flat lighting style; a reaction, in short, to the critics who'd said admiringly of some recent Scorsese films that the images were so beautiful you could have framed them and put them on the wall.

But his usual photographer Michael Chapman disliked this idea, and declined the project. Instead, it would be shot by Fred Schuler, just making his name as a lighting cameraman after having operated the camera on *Taxi Driver*, *The Last Waltz* and *The Deer Hunter*.

Zimmermann had been inspired ten years before to write *The King of Comedy* after seeing a TV programme in which commentator David Susskind interviewed autograph-hunters about their systematic stalking of stars. 'I was fascinated by the intimacy with which autograph-hunters spoke of these people they didn't really know,' Zimmermann said. 'Like, "Barbra's very tough to work with." Which means, Barbra Streisand told them to shove it up their ass.'

Zimmermann graphed the rise and fall of one such obsessive, a relentlessly likeable office messenger named Rupert Pupkin who's obsessed with Jerry Langford, host of the country's biggest late-night talk show. The basement of the Brooklyn home Rupert shares with his mother contains a mock-up of Langford's set, complete with life-size cut-outs of Langford and the sort of all-purpose celebrity who haunted such shows – in this case Liza Minnelli. In this setting Rupert acts out imaginary scenarios in which, having become as big a star as Langford, he modestly accepts his praise for his comic writing, and lets himself be talked into taking over his show while Langford takes a break. A chance encounter with Langford allows Rupert to send him a tape of his comedy act. When it's rejected, Rupert, helped by rich but ditzy fellow obsessive Masha, kidnaps Langford, ransoming him in return for a spot on the show.

In the light of the Hinckley shooting, Zimmermann's script looked prescient. In the decade since he wrote it, celebrity magazines like *People* and such TV gossip merchants as Rona Barrett had proliferated, swelling the number of people who felt symbiotically attached to their favourite stars, studying them compulsively. These people re-interpreted Andy Warhol's comment that 'In the future, everybody will be famous for fifteen minutes' to mean that everybody was *entitled* to their quarter-hour of fame. Television, voracious for new subjects and sensations, catered to that belief with fly-on-the-wall 'reality' documentaries and talk shows like those of Geraldo Rivera, which encouraged people to parade their sexual and social oddities in public.

Programmes like *Catch a Rising Star* broadcast performances from the hundreds of stand-up comedy clubs proliferating around the country, and implied that one could walk into such clubs unknown, and come out famous. But most people, when they did get their chance in front of the camera, proved to be woefully untalented.

Zimmermann's script ended with Rupert appearing on Langford's show, introduced as 'the kidnapping king of comedy', and giving a performance which, as far as he's concerned, has the audience in stitches. It's never clear whether or not he really does appear, however, and we never see the audience. Would they have laughed at such an awkward comic as Pupkin, with his clumsy hand gestures and sometimes tasteless material? Maybe

the whole TV appearance is just another basement solo performance. Perhaps there was never any kidnapping either.

At this point, De Niro parted company with the script. He
wanted *The King of Comedy* to be a success story, culminating
in Rupert being revealed as a talented comic. Zimmermann acquiesced. De Niro and Scorsese went away to Long Island to work
on revisions.

De Niro spent time around stand-up clubs, and incorporated
elements of Robin Williams and John Belushi in the role of Pupkin, but his real models were the wannabes who hovered at the
stage doors of TV stations or flocked to memorabilia fairs and
shops like New York's Movie Star News to buy publicity stills
and posters of the stars.

These people were never 'off'. Their clothes were costumes,
their lifestyle a twenty-four-hour-a-day performance. To find
Rupert's 'look', De Niro walked down Broadway, checking the
windows of the *schlock* men's outfitters. One displayed a dummy
dressed in a polkadot jacket, blue shirt, red tie, blue trousers
with white belt, and white shoes. De Niro bought the whole
ensemble, and made it the basis of his wardrobe in the film. To
emphasise the theatrical effect, he lengthened his hair, which was
cut in a style calculated to look like a wig, and grew a moustache.
As critic Mark Morris would write in Britain's *Guardian*, 'It was
the moustache that told you everything you needed to know.
The moment you saw the thing on Rupert Pupkin's upper lip,
you knew he was a man who thought he was funny but wasn't.
More than that, he was convinced of what a tragedy it would
be if the world was robbed of his comic gifts.'

Rupert's foils are Masha, the wealthy fruitcake who aids in the
kidnap, and Langford himself. Zimmermann imagined Masha as
weepily sentimental, the sort of person who might knit sweaters
for Langford, send him fudge, or a card on his birthday. De Niro
proposed Meryl Streep for the part, and she discussed it with
Scorsese, but they decided mutually that Masha should be someone more unstable, even dangerously so.

Sandra Bernhard was one of the rare female comics on the
stand-up circuit. Emphasising her height, scratchy voice, kinky

hair, blubbery lips and equine overbite, she embodied the Man-hattanite with Attitude. Once he cast her, Scorsese rewrote the script to make Masha predatory, hysteric, teetering on the edge of breakdown.

In the film's opening scene, she throws herself into Langford's car as he leaves the studio. Langford bolts back to the sidewalk, and the credits run over a freeze frame of her hands, pressed from the inside against the car window – Scorsese reminding us that, even when a fan breaks into the private life of a celebrity, he or she remains isolated from them by the sense of difference that makes them fans in the first place.

Johnny Carson still refused to take on the role of Langford. His earlier essays into movies had been disastrous, proving, to his satisfaction anyway, that his deadpan charm worked only on TV. Scorsese considered Orson Welles and Frank Sinatra, then Sinatra's crony Dean Martin – which led to the unexpected choice of Martin's old comic partner Jerry Lewis.

Utterly against type, Lewis plays Langford as monosyllabic, fastidious, misogynistic – a loner of almost Noël Coward *froid-eur*. The inspiration wasn't Carson but Milton Berle, TV's first comedian, who'd survived half a century in radio and TV by liquidating potential rivals, often when they least expected it: singer Julius La Rosa didn't know he'd been purged until Berle announced it on camera. Lewis catches the slight jerkiness of Berle's manner, his dark suits and, above all, the expressionless stares that intimidated even the most recalcitrant audience into a laugh.

Langford lives alone in an austere New York apartment, fur-nished so sparsely that one's reminded of Jacques Tati's *Mon Oncle* or Antonioni's *L'Eclisse* or *La Notte*, where bleakness of decor suggested spiritual aridity. Coming home, he pauses by a TV set to watch pickpocket Richard Widmark rifle the handbag of prostitute Jean Peters on a crowded subway train in Sam Fuller's callous 1953 *Pickup on South Street* – a film about exploi-tation, manipulation and deceit. Then he eats a solitary dinner at an empty table, back turned to a bird's-eye view of Manhattan.

Langford is more king than comic. In a key scene, he leaves

the studio and strolls the few blocks to his apartment. At every corner, people greet him, as he expects – this isn't a walk but a royal progress. Construction workers shout down from high on a building site, and an old woman talking on a public telephone hails him like a friend. When, however, he refuses to say a few words to the ailing relative she's calling, she screams after him, 'You should get cancer!'

As usual with any Scorsese/De Niro film, familiar faces packed the cast. Their real-life agent Harry Ufland plays Langford's agent, and the producer of the *Tonight Show*, Fred de Cordova, appears as his manager. Scorsese has a small role as a TV director contending with guest star Tony Randall, worried about his lines, and his mother appears as the disembodied voice of Mrs Pupkin, bawling down the basement stairs. Mardik Martin plays the man in the bar who, after Rupert's triumphal TV appearance, says blearily, 'Hey, that guy who just left was the same one who was just on TV,' while the second patron, Dan Johnson, was the long-time cook for the crew. He died during production, and the film is dedicated to him.

De Niro cast Diahnne Abbott as Rita, the ex-high-school queen, now bartender, whom Rupert desperately wants to impress. Her first line, 'Don't I know you?', coaxed a smirk of recognition from those aware of their personal history, but Abbott's role was all downhill from there. A better performer would have made the relationship poignant, as the lonely and disappointed Rita responds to the well-meaning and romantic Rupert by admitting him to her bed, and going along with his fantasy friendship with Langford. But Abbott isn't up to it. There's as little electricity between them on screen as there was off. Instead, De Niro makes her Dulcinea to his Don Quixote, the ignorant serving wench on whom he drapes all the trappings of the romantic heroine.

Staying, as usual, in character throughout the film, De Niro disconcerted Jerry Lewis, who took the more traditional Hollywood view that one removed the costume when one went home at night. He even invited De Niro to dinner, only to have his co-star snap, 'I wanna blow your head off. So how can we have dinner?' Lewis wasn't impressed. 'De Niro has obviously never heard Noël Coward's advice to actors – that their job was to say the lines and not bump into the furniture,' he said. 'He just could not forget the part at the end of the day's work.'

De Niro also used his favourite technique of interjecting a shocking line to jolt a fellow actor out of his rote performance. In Lewis's case, he leaned over and made an anti-Semitic remark just before they started a scene. Lewis's surprise and anger showed – just as De Niro had hoped. He also asked if he could wear one of Lewis's watches, telling him it would 'transfer some of his humour'. In fact, it made Lewis feel that someone was taking over his life, as Rupert does in the film.

With the downbeat ending looming, both Scorsese and De Niro had second thoughts. Maybe audiences wouldn't understand the ambiguous conclusion, which may or may not take place in the mind of Rupert, no longer able to separate reality from fantasy. Hurriedly, Scorsese improvised a new finish, in which Rupert wows Langford's audience with his stand-up routine, goes to jail for the kidnap but is freed after two years, writes a best-selling memoir, and becomes the true king of comedy he's always hoped to be. 'Better to be king for a night than a *schmuck* for a lifetime,' he says glibly, articulating the philosophy that will make the public love him.

Nervous about the directors' strike, producer Arnon Milchan pushed the start date of the $19 million project forward from July to June. Shooting on the streets of New York, never fun, was made less so by blazing heat. Whether because of that, the effort of trying to play comedy, the problems of his private life, or a sensitivity to the critics of *True Confessions* who said he no longer appeared to be acting, De Niro gave a performance of painfully strained intensity. Without the crutch of physical trans-formation or heavy make-up, he's forced to transform himself while performing, as if he can make himself charming or funny simply by an effort of will.

Mannerisms appeared which were to become a fixture of his style. Trying to project sincerity, he expended such effort that one expected sweat to bead on his brow. He wrinkled his forehead, squeezed his eyes half-shut, tilted his head, rocked it from side to side, and gestured expansively with both hands – nowhere more so than in his stand-up routine, which looked more like semaphore than choreography. None of it was convincing. *Raging Bull* would be the apotheosis of De Niro's career as an actor. Though he would occasionally hit the high of former times, *The King of Comedy* was evidence of an inexorable decline.

CHAPTER FIFTEEN

The Epic that Never Was

I'm here for the ... um ... er ... um ... experience.

De Niro at the Cannes Film Festival, 1983

Since nobody had connected De Niro to Belushi or suspected his presence in Bungalow 3 on the fatal night, he continued to live at the Château Marmont during the pre-production of *Once Upon a Time in America*. He also bought a Rolls-Royce.

De Niro's car may have changed, but not his naïve approach to women. Casting director Barbara Johnson arrived at the Marmont for a meeting with *King of Comedy* producer Arnon Milchan, and was taken aback when a man began to circle her as she waited in the lobby. 'He followed me everywhere. I did not realise who he was at the time. He had a beautiful smile, warm eyes. But I actually wasn't too comfortable with this strange man. I hurried up, went to my meeting. Once out, there he was again. Same routine, until I finally got into my small VW and left. He waved from the garden area, and only then did I realise who had been trying to pick me up.'

Even had De Niro managed to pick up Johnson, he'd have had little time to enjoy the relationship. A few weeks after the death of Belushi, the Los Angeles District Attorney empanelled a grand jury. Cathy Smith, who'd fled to Canada, accepted $15,000 from the tabloid *National Enquirer* for her story, which revealed that De Niro and Williams visited Bungalow 3 that night.

De Niro may not have fled to Italy to start work with Sergio

Leone on *Once Upon a Time in America*, but he certainly did not delay his departure, so by the time the news broke he was in Rome, where he would stay for almost a year. When the grand jury required his testimony, he gave it by phone.

To complicate his life still further, Helena Springs had just had a baby, Nina Nadeja. De Niro was not the father, but Springs clearly thought he was, or at least persuaded him of the fact. According to her, De Niro at first tried to force her to have an abortion. 'He seemed to know what to do,' she said. 'He gave me a prescription of herbs. When that didn't handle it, he became upset and went berserk for five days.' She also recited a litany of what she claimed were acrimonious exchanges with a drunken De Niro, who told her bluntly, she said, 'Your job is to fuck me between planes.'

Such callousness hardly squared with De Niro's generosity towards Springs and the child. He gave Springs $50,000, and had a room in her apartment redecorated as a nursery. Even more doubt was cast on her version of events when DNA testing ten years later revealed that De Niro was not Nina's father.

In both his private life and the films he chose to make, De Niro, in part because of his complex relationship with his own father, was increasingly preoccupied with the balance we strike between self-interest and responsibility for others. In *Once Upon a Time in America*, *The Deer Hunter*, *Taxi Driver*, *The Mission*, *Brazil*, *Jacknife*, *Goodfellas*, *Mad Dog and Glory*, *Sleepers* and his first film as director, *A Bronx Tale*, he would play people who assume responsibility for others, and suffer, even die, for it, while in *Awakenings* and *Flawless* he's the victim of a physical disaster restored to partial life by a person who is himself an outcast – in the case of *Flawless* a flamboyant homosexual.

In private, De Niro worked for various charities, including serving on the board of the AIDS-oriented Smith Family Foundation, set up by Toukie Smith after the death from AIDS of her brother, fashion designer Willie, in 1987. He meticulously remembered birthdays and anniversaries, always sending gifts and cards. He could be kind and thoughtful to strangers – more often, some would have said, than to those close to him. His relationship to his stepdaughter Drena was as warm as that with his son Raphael, if not warmer. But he chose not to live with her mother, or anyone else, and when he next conceived children, it would be through a surrogate mother.

When De Niro met British actor Bob Hoskins on the set of Francis Ford Coppola's *The Cotton Club* and heard that Hoskins' wife and daughter had already returned to England, leaving him alone in New York at Christmas time, he invited him to spend the holidays with him and his grandmother in Syracuse. In the end, shooting finished in time for Hoskins to return home, but the two men continued their friendship in London.

It is perhaps understandable that De Niro was attracted to the character of 'Noodles' Aaronson in *Once Upon a Time in America*. Noodles tries, unsuccessfully, to save his friends, sees them, as he believes, all dead, and is exiled for thirty years to an icy world where his only solace lies in opium. In De Niro's mind, the gate of intimacy, like that of Dante's inferno, is surmounted with the warning, 'Abandon hope all ye who enter here.'

Sergio Leone embodied the contradictory character of the Italian cinema. Though he'd made his name with violent westerns, he longed to create epics that combined the vision of John Ford with the sentiment and melodrama of D.W. Griffith. *Once Upon a Time in the West* (1969) had a beautiful but helpless heiress, a villain of unregenerate evil and a rock-jawed and laconic hero, all filmed in Ford's favourite Monument Valley settings, while, as usual, an Ennio Morricone score propelled the action and emphasised Leone's romantic yearnings.

'He was very insecure,' said Leone's screenwriter and friend Sergio Donati. 'That insecureness became more apparent as he became more and more successful. I remember telling him many times, "Sergio, why do you always want bigger and bigger pictures? This is dangerous. Why don't we make small thrillers?" I think he would have been a very successful director for thrillers. His dream model was David Lean. He dreamed of making the remake of *Gone with the Wind*.'

In the ten years he'd spent trying to make *Once Upon a Time in America*, Leone's vision of the film had changed. At first, he imagined three different teams of actors, with the men in old age played by various veteran stars with gangster-movie credentials. When De Niro insisted that he could play a man at both thirty and sixty, Leone, aware that James Cagney, Glenn Ford, George Raft, Jean Gabin and Henry Fonda (his villain from *Once Upon a Time in the West*) were now either dead or uninterested in the project, accepted the argument.

Once Upon a Time in America was another Arnon Milchan production. He persuaded Warner Brothers and Alan Ladd Jr's company to put up $10 million, a third of the budget, including De Niro's fee of $3 million – the largest of his career – and managed to borrow the rest.

Nobody could accuse Leone of not starting the film as he meant to go on. The opening half-hour is enigmatic and obscure. In an unidentified time and place – actually New York's Lower East Side in 1933 – an insistently ringing telephone rouses David 'Noodles' Aaronson (De Niro) as he lies stupefied in an opium den. As the phone shrills twenty-five times, slowly and ominously, like a tocsin announcing a death, the owners hustle him out the back door, one step ahead of the killers whom we've already seen murder Noodles' girlfriend (Darlanne Fleugel) and beat his friend Joey (Burt Young) almost to death.

Who Noodles is and why these people are hunting him won't be explained for a good hour. Instead, Leone flashes backwards and forwards through his life. At one moment Noodles is a street kid scuffling to survive with his friends Max, Cockeye and Hymie, and going to jail on their behalf after knifing a cop. The next, it's 1968, and a grey-haired Noodles has returned to Manhattan from exile in Buffalo, in upper New York state. In between, we see him as a rich gangster in the thirties, besotted with his childhood sweetheart Deborah but so accustomed to achieving his ends by violence that he rapes her the moment she gives him a kiss.

When Noodles falls, it's through the same contradictory fusion of affection and violence. Having become rich on selling booze,

Max proposes that the partners rob the Federal Reserve Bank. Convinced it will be a disaster, Noodles informs on his friends, hoping to save them, but instead they are mown down by police, and Max's body is burned beyond recognition. A traumatised Noodles flees to Buffalo, changes his name and becomes an opium addict.

In fact Max survives, and retires with his wealth to a luxurious estate, building a tomb in a nearby cemetery for all the friends – including Noodles, whom he summons thirty years later for a final reckoning. Neither can kill the other, however, and in a comically literal final scene, Max climbs into the maw of an automated garbage truck, consigning himself to the trash heap of history.

As its story slowly unrolled, *Once Upon a Time in America* acquired the erotic insubstantiality of an opium dream. Sexually discreet in his other films, Leone invested all his repressed eroticism in the lives of these cocky young gangsters and their women. As kids, the boys spy on local beauties like Fat Moe's sister Peggy, and the silent, watchful Deborah, who grow up to be, respectively, a Rabelaisian fatso (Amy Ryder) and a prim actress (Elizabeth McGovern). They are joined by Carol (Tuesday Weld), a nymphomaniac who insists that the gang round off the robbery of her diamond-merchant employers by screwing her over her desk. Cockeye needs no encouragement, but when she turns up later as a whore in a high-class brothel she demands a 'short-arm parade' to identify her assailant.

Leone meant the relationship between Noodles and Max to reflect the lifelong friendship of Meyer Lansky, organised crime's most cunning financier and strategist, and Benny 'Bugsy' Siegel, who conceived Las Vegas and started to build the gambling city in the desert, only to be executed by his partners, worried over the cost. Lansky was still alive, though ailing, and De Niro tried to meet him, with the help of Jerry Blavatt, a Philadelphia DJ. Blavatt put the request to a hood named Nicodemo 'Little Nicky' Scarfo, but the meeting never took place.

Offered his choice of roles, De Niro took Noodles, though, on paper, Max is the more interesting. He has all the best scenes, like that in the brothel, not to mention the *coup de théâtre* of the revelation that he survived the massacre in which his friends died. But Noodles embodies selfless suffering, while also offering opportunities for physical transformation, twin temptations De Niro couldn't resist.

Playing Max marked the beginning of a successful career for the young James Woods. He called working with De Niro 'one of great experiences of my life, because he is, I think, one of the greatest actors in the history of cinema. And he is a wonderful guy personally. Very devoted to the work and to his friends. A very loyal man. And we became friends, and have been friends ever since.

'I remember at the time when we did the old-age sequence where we were supposed to be in our late sixties, and Bob had this wonderful idea. He said, "You know, you're playing the very successful guy at the end, and I'm the guy down and out. Do you ever see those successful guys who've had surgery and they have brand new caps for teeth?" They always show older guys with kind of grey, yellow teeth and he said, "It would be great if you had brand new caps." And it was very expensive to have done, and the studio didn't want to pay for it or something, and Bob actually paid for it out of his own pocket because he thought it would be great for my character.

'Bob is one of those people who has a barometer for the truth of a scene. I mean, he just can't act if the scene isn't right. He just isn't able. He just sort of says, "Oh, this feels false." He just doesn't know how to do it. And if the scene is right in the way it's set up and conceived and written and the acting is going pretty well in rehearsals, he just flourishes. He's a natural. And it's not like he puts his foot down or something, he's just not very good at doing – he just isn't capable of doing bad acting. He's just not capable of it. And he's just a natural when everything's right.'

Except for scenes under the Brooklyn Bridge and some winter cityscapes, shot in Montreal, Leone filmed the whole of *Once Upon a Time in America* in Italy. Set designer Carlo Simi built an entire block of the Lower East Side in Rome, basing it on photographs of the early 1900s, the building frontages with their signs in Hebrew, Chinese, Italian and English showing how successive waves of immigrants washed over this area, each leaving it, a little more dilapidated, for the next arrivals.

People raised in a place can take it for granted, but for the outsider every wall can be a background and every door an invitation to drama. The strength and the weakness of *Once Upon a Time in America* is Leone's willingness to stand and stare at America, as the first explorers had done, 'face to face for the last time in history', as Scott Fitzgerald put it, 'with something commensurate to his capacity for wonder'. Characters move against the New York backdrop as those in *Once Upon a Time in the West* had moved against the background of Utah, the walls of the East Side tenements dwarfing them as the pinnacles of Monument Valley dwarfed Claudia Cardinale, Henry Fonda and Charles Bronson in the earlier film.

But the more detailed the reconstruction, the less we believe Leone's New York, an effect intensified by Tonino delli Colli's burnished photography and the plaintive Morricone score, made even more poignant by the breathy shrilling of pan-pipe virtuoso Georgy Zamphir, if not by the incongruous inclusion of the Lennon/McCartney song 'Yesterday'. Pauline Kael would call the film 'a compendium of kitsch, but kitsch aestheticised by someone who loves it and sees it as the poetry of the masses'.

De Niro had the usual problems working with an assertive foreign director, but with fewer fights than he had had with Bertolucci, in part because Leone was in poor health, and lacked stamina.

On one occasion, De Niro arrived on the set to find Leone absent and the crew waiting for directions on how to set up a shot. He took charge, dictating the placement of the camera and directing the short scene.

Even when Leone was present, he breached etiquette by questioning the director's staging in front of the crew. Leone kept his temper and explained his thinking. De Niro finally agreed that it would work that way.

'I'm glad you think so,' Leone said evenly, 'since I am, after all, the director.'

De Niro conceded later that he argued with Leone. 'I'd sometimes say to him, "Show me how you would do it,"' he said.

But, pressed to explain the differences between working with Leone and other directors, De Niro took refuge in his own increasingly incoherent personal lexicon. 'If you hit the moment right, then you get the language in a very organic way from the director. When he did that, I'd say, "OK, I've got it. You're not giving me the performance but I see the way you did it." After that, I had a way to do it.'

People working with De Niro learned not to rely on verbal communication. If anything, he used language as a screen. When he said something, he could even mean the opposite. Art Linson, who produced *The Untouchables*, recalls their discussion of the clothes created by Giorgio Armani for the first actor cast as Al Capone, Bob Hoskins.

'How is everything going?' Linson asked after De Niro tried on his costumes from the $500,000 wardrobe.

'Great, just great.'

'So, what do you think about the clothes?'

'Good, very good,' De Niro said.

'How good?'

'Nice . . . The people here, they are very nice.'

Sensing a subtext, Linson pressed. 'Yeah, they're swell . . . What about the clothes?'

'I like them,' said De Niro amiably. 'They're good, they're interesting.'

'So, let me see if I'm hearing you correctly,' Linson said. 'You have given this a lot of thought, and you have come to the conclusion that you hate the wardrobe. You would like me to start over and have it completely redesigned by the time you get back from Italy, under your supervision.'

'Exactly,' De Niro said.

Experience with the *paparazzi* made De Niro cautious about spending his leisure time in Rome during the shooting of *Once Upon a Time in America*. In breaks, he went incognito to London or Paris, where he met old friends like Barry Primus and Robert Cordier, and stayed as a house-guest of Roman Polanski.

Even in Paris, he appeared little in public, and when he did, remained as reserved and enigmatic as ever. Director John Sturges, who met him at Cannes, said admiringly, 'He comes into the room like a snake – but what presence!' Another person who remembers him from Paris recalls 'sitting in the apartment of the late black American fashion designer Patrick Kelly, when he was newly arrived there and rather struggling himself. He was good pals with the model Toukie Smith, who was always hanging out there, too. I was sketching something and looked up and suddenly *he* had materialised. Very much in character, stone-silent, furtive, unapproachable (even in a small room in a private apartment), looking quickly about and missing nothing. And gone just as fast.'

Leone's first cut of *Once Upon a Time in America* ran over four hours. People who saw it, particularly Milchan and his backers from Warner Brothers, were baffled. The kaleidoscopic construction juxtaposed scenes set thirty years apart, with nothing to link them but a chance remark, a sound, or a memory.

De Niro was convincing as both the young and the ageing Noodles, but Deborah, having become a stage star (she's playing Cleopatra on Broadway), still looks, three decades later, almost exactly as she did when Noodles, now a grey-haired man in his sixties, raped her. As for the apparently dead Max, he has become 'Christopher Bailey', a wealthy political 'fixer'. For reasons best known to himself he decides, thirty-five years after his faked death, to renew contact with Noodles. Summoning him to New York, Max plants a series of clues that lead Noodles to his Long Island estate and a belated showdown. Leone takes a perverse delight in complicating the search, cutting back and forth between the 1920s and the 1960s, so that a left-luggage locker can at one time contain a suitcase filled with money, at another a pile of old newspapers. Finally, a letter about the sale of cemetery plots leads Noodles to the vault where all his friends, including, he believes, Max, are interred.

The American distributors understood none of this, nor the

conclusion where Max, after the showdown with Noodles, apparently commits suicide by climbing into the compactor of a garbage truck, while Noodles returns to Buffalo and the *fumerie*. They demanded cuts, changes, and, above all, a shorter version. Leone refused. The stage was set for a battle between artistic vision and commercial pragmatism that would last for years, and result in the end of Leone's career, and his death.

The King of Comedy went on release on 11 March 1983, when De Niro was just completing *Once Upon a Time in America*. Critics greeted it with respect, if not enthusiasm, but the public shunned it, making the film Scorsese's worst financial failure: of its $19 million cost, it recouped only $1.2 million.

It was shown out of competition at Cannes in May. De Niro reluctantly turned up with Jerry Lewis and screenwriter Paul Zimmermann, though none gave the impression of much liking the film. Zimmermann said sourly, 'It's like having a baby that looks like Martin Scorsese.'

De Niro had returned from Italy to an American film industry even more preoccupied than before with trivia, sensation and the pursuit of an audience which became younger every year. Most of his fellow actors were struggling for work. Dustin Hoffman made *Kramer vs Kramer* in 1979 and *Tootsie* in 1982 (the latter, significantly, a film about an unemployable actor), then worked on stage until *Rain Man* in 1988 – a film which, arguably, would never have been made without his hot young co-star Tom Cruise.

Al Pacino, on average, made a film every two years. Between the disaster of *Revolution* in 1985 and the revival of his career with *Sea of Love* in 1989, he was totally absent from the screen. Harvey Keitel and Christopher Walken, no longer regarded as leading men, were resigned to character parts in increasingly trashy productions. Director Alan Rudolph summed up the situation pessimistically. 'You're looking at historically the shallowest period of American film history in forty or fifty years,' he said. 'Because they discovered the *Jaws* phenomenon – that one movie can make more money than all the others combined. In the eighties, the villains were the film-makers. The ones who mattered picked your pocket. The film-makers who bought into the idea of trying to be honest and pursue truth were swimming upstream.'

De Niro didn't have the energy to fight the current. *Once Upon a Time in America* had worn him out. He was also enmeshed in negotiations over a divorce from Diahnne Abbott, who was making another attempt at a screen career by appearing in John Cassavetes' *Love Streams*. The haggling continued through 1984, and ended in the summer, when Abbott announced from Havana, where *Love Streams* was screening at a film festival, that she and De Niro had reached a 'reasonable' settlement and that relations between them were 'pleasant and friendly'.

Looking around for a project he could do without too much effort, De Niro found *Falling in Love*. 'I was tired,' he said. 'This script came along. It was a nice story, set here in New York. I thought I could concentrate on things other than what I usually concentrate on – make-up or whatever. I don't always have to do high-risk parts. I thought it was something different to anything I had done before and for that reason alone it seemed like a good idea to do it.'

Falling in Love was an original screenplay by playwright Michael Cristofer, who'd created a splash four years earlier with *The Shadow Box*, a play about terminally ill patients in an experimental retreat which won the Pulitzer Prize and a Tony Award. When Paul Newman directed and appeared in a 1980 version for TV, it won a Golden Globe Award, and was nominated for an Emmy.

The undramatic story of two married New Yorkers in early middle age who, totally by chance, fall in love, *Falling in Love* lacked the intensity of *The Shadow Box*. Rather it echoed *Brief Encounter* (based on Noël Coward's play *Still Life*), but without that film's poignancy. Infidelity in Coward's world was close to a crime, whereas bourgeois New Yorkers usually dismissed it with a shrug.

Like Coward's couple, Cristofer's lovers have the train in common. Both take the commuter shuttle from Westchester to Manhattan. They literally bump into each other in a 5th Avenue bookshop, accidentally pick up each other's Christmas presents, meet again a few times, fall in love but never go to bed, agree to split up rather than leave their partners, but leave them anyway, and, at the end, bump into one another once more.

Though De Niro was hardly likely to find hidden depths in his character, Frank Raftis, a construction engineer, he insisted that playing him 'only *appeared* to be easier. You always have to worry. You always have to concentrate. It's just more deceptive when you are working on the surface. I did some research on being a construction foreman. But that didn't make the role any easier. He's still not me.'

To some people involved in the film, it seemed that all this research was just De Niro marking out his turf. Visiting one building site, he noticed that the foreman had a portable phone – not standard issue in those days. The production manager was directed to acquire an identical telephone, even though it didn't appear in the film.

De Niro suggested Meryl Streep to play Molly, the woman he loves. With thoughts of her success in *Kramer vs Kramer* – Paramount would promote *Falling in Love*, unsuccessfully, as 'the *Kramer vs Kramer* of 1984' – the studio put up $12 million, most of it paid to the stars, though a good deal also went on expensive and probably unnecessary scene-setting. When Frank and Molly kiss for the first time at Grand Central Station at rush hour, the crowd were all extras who had to be funnelled through the enormous space repeatedly for a day and a night. The production also took over Saks 5th Avenue department store for two days, redecorating it for the Christmas shopping scene.

Together, Streep and De Niro spent hours going over the screenplay, looking for ways to animate the characters. As Molly, a designer who's given up her career to look after her husband, and who has a caring relationship with her terminally ill father, Streep had a little more to work with, but De Niro's Frank, apparently happily married and with two young sons, is a cipher.

Ulu Grosbard directed, despite the box-office flop of *True Confessions*. The film, he claimed, would show 'a new De Niro. Nobody has ever seen this De Niro before. He's funny. He's tender.' Harvey Keitel got the role of Frank's womanising friend Ed, a sounding board for his doubts.

Streep knew De Niro well enough to tell him he must lose the ten kilos of flab still remaining from *Raging Bull*. A friend sent him to the Sports Training Institute, where Chris Meade specialised in getting models and actors into shape. This was Manhattan health care at its glitziest – clients included Kevin Kline and Bianca Jagger. When Meade's assistant, Dan Harvey, an ex-model and college wrestler, wrote a book, *Working out for Men*, it was launched at the fashionable Studio 54 disco.

De Niro didn't want to work out at the Institute, so Harvey became his personal trainer. 'The first time we tested him,' says Harvey, 'his body fat was 19.92. Almost 20 per cent of his body was fat. His resting pulse was seventy-two. Blood pressure was about normal. His aerobic capacity, his oxygen consumption, was very low – only twenty-seven millilitres of oxygen was being pumped through the blood to the muscles. Fifteen weeks later, his body fat content came down from 19.92 to nine. His resting pulse from seventy-two to fifty-six and his aerobic capacity went from twenty-seven millilitres of oxygen to eighty-nine, which is phenomenal. The lady who tested him had never seen anything like it, so much improvement in such a short period of time. He had to be working out an hour a day just to drop his resting pulse from seventy-two to fifty-six. He was ready for *Falling in Love*.'

Falling in Love started shooting in April 1984. Throughout production, De Niro was involved, reluctantly, in the promotion of *Once Upon a Time in America*. After battling with Warners for more than a year, Sergio Leone collapsed with a heart attack. He had already removed half a dozen sequences, reducing the running time from 260 minutes to 225. Warners previewed this version in Boston in February. An audience accustomed to *Jaws* and *E.T.* couldn't make any sense of it, and didn't feel like trying – which the studio took as a pretext to make their own shorter and more 'logical' cut.

Warners' editors reduced the running time to 143 minutes,

and battered the complex flashback structure into a chronological one, beginning with the four friends as street kids and ending with the suicide of Max (who doesn't climb into a garbage truck, but shoots himself). Symptomatic of the new simplified structure, the phone in the opium den no longer rings twenty-five times, but only once. Leone called this version 'barbarously massacred'.

In May, De Niro went to Cannes for the premiere of the four-hour version. At the subsequent press conference he was attacked by American women in the audience, incensed at the protracted rapes of Elizabeth McGovern and Tuesday Weld in the film. 'It is blatant, gratuitous violence,' one of them shouted. 'As a woman, I feel deeply embarrassed to have witnessed it. I feel totally demoralised.' To De Niro, it was like a replay of the Oscar-night furore over John Hinckley. Pulling his white baseball cap down over his eyes, he dived into his car and was driven to the Eden Roc at Cap d'Antibes. After that, he said and did almost nothing in public to defend the film, which, for all the critical raves, earned only a little over $5 million at the box office.

Despite the feminists, most critics who saw *Once Upon a Time in America* at Cannes admired it. At other festivals and special screenings, it accumulated a reputation as a flawed fusion of poetic sensibility and epic vision. Leone began planning for his next film, *The 900 Days*, an even more lavish production about the battle of Stalingrad – in which, he announced, De Niro had agreed to star. But he died in 1989, and the film was never made.

Once Upon a Time in America became a rallying point for European *cinéastes* concerned at the increasing international power of American studios. For Leone, the film would be both his monument, and a gravestone of sorts for the ambitions of European film-makers in the world market. As he recognised in his films, if not in his business dealings, the future belonged to America. Unfortunately, they had no idea what to do with it.

CHAPTER SIXTEEN

The South American Picture

Brady: *What about the South American picture?*
Stahr: *We're going ahead with that.*
Brady: *With the same budget?*
Stahr: *Yes.*
Brady: *It's out of proportion.*
Popolos: *With that budget, you got no chance.*
Stahr: *It's a quality picture . . .*

The Last Tycoon. Screenplay by Harold Pinter, from F. Scott
Fitzgerald's novel

When *Falling in Love* was released on 21 November 1984, and
proved another flop, making back only $5.7 million, De Niro
found himself with the dubious distinction of being – after, perhaps, Marlon Brando – the most respected and sought-after
screen actor in the world, but at the same time among the least
successful. He hadn't made a profitable film since *Taxi Driver*,
and wouldn't do so for some years. As David Puttnam would
point out in the middle of shooting *The Mission*, if that film
earned the combined grosses of De Niro's last five films, it would
still lose money. That De Niro and Brando remained in demand
reflected the contradictory values of a Hollywood preoccupied
with profit but also smarting about its lack of status.

Hollywood in the eighties had its tearaways, but most movie
people went to bed early, and usually alone. The cokeheads of

the seventies had been replaced by a less flamboyant generation for whom movie-making itself was turn-on enough. Steven Spielberg and George Lucas had no major vices, nor the imagination to develop any. The shock of Woody Allen's dalliance with Soon-Yi Previn lay not in any ethical dimension but in the idea that he would even *want* to.

This community of high-school dropouts held artistic excellence in guilty respect, regarding certain performers and filmmakers as one step down from deity. And the more contempt these legends showed for the business, the more New Hollywood ran after them. It was an old story. When Alexander Korda went bankrupt in the forties, he took large amounts of investors' money with him. Shortly after, he moved into a luxurious apartment on the floor below one man who'd lost a fortune.

'What happens when they meet on the stairs?' someone asked.

'Oh,' explained a friend, 'the man is always hoping Alex will invite him to dinner.'

Nothing had changed in two generations. Warners continued to finance Stanley Kubrick for years as he developed films they knew would never make money. And any producer who could deliver Brando, De Niro, Dustin Hoffman or Jack Nicholson was almost certain to find funding, even if the stars' salaries killed any hope of the film making a profit.

Brando had long understood this power, and used it on Hollywood's lawyers and accountants with the capriciousness of a cheerleader tantalising the high-school football team. De Niro was less experienced, but by the mid-eighties had surpassed the fat man on Mulholland Drive. Brando might be demanding, but De Niro, everyone agreed, was *impossible*.

'He's gotten difficult,' admitted John Hancock, who directed De Niro in *Bang the Drum Slowly*. 'He's was very easy then. He was just a real sweetheart. But not any more.'

Hancock blamed celebrity for the change. 'Everybody competes to get your limo, and provide you with a gym to exercise in, and get you women. It rots your spirit – that's one thing. Also, he's played all these very dark roles. Jake La Motta, *The Godfather*. He works very deeply, and I think that's had some impact on his world view. He and Marty have a kind of white–dark view of nature. It's been deepened and aggravated by working so much.'

During the mid-eighties, Hancock, with De Niro, developed a screenplay about a theatre group formed inside San Quentin by convict Rick Clutchy. 'Bob was going to play the story of a man who was condemned to death in the electric chair,' says Robert Cordier, a friend of both De Niro and Clutchy. 'Rick Clutchy went to prison. He started learning acting in prison, and he wrote Samuel Beckett, and Sam Beckett wrote back, and came to America to see Rick in prison. And Beckett started a thing to get Rick out of prison, and this guy was going to the electric chair, and Beckett got him out.

'Rick wrote a play called *Cage*, and Bob was going to play the lead. Clutchy came to Paris and we became friends, because he had asked me to do his play in Paris. And he talked to me a lot about Bob, saying Bob was fantastic, and that it was fantastic that Bob was going to play his life.

'Rick inherited a lot of money from Beckett when he died, and when he came back a second time, I said, "How is it going with De Niro?" and he said, "Bob is a fucking bastard! He's really impossible. It's gone to his head." I thought that was strange, because he had never struck me that way, but he said, "No, he's a real son-of-a-bitch."'

John Hancock called the new version of Clutchy's play *Weeds*. 'We really wrote *Weeds* for [De Niro],' he says. 'He wanted to do it, and set up a deal at MGM. He and I flew all over the country, visiting different prison drama groups for about six months. I found that it was like dealing with Jake La Motta. "This is how it has to be." He had gotten so successful that he had in his contract approval of every prop, approval of every music cue, approval of every cast member. So, what does the director do?' In the end, De Niro backed out. Nick Nolte starred in Hancock's 1987 film of *Weeds*, which was not a big success.

Despite the failure of *The King of Comedy* and *Once Upon a Time in America*, De Niro still trusted Arnon Milchan. Perhaps the producer's disastrous career bolstered his apparent probity: manifestly, here was someone who was not in it for the money.

Consistent with this theory, Milchan invested in a film being directed by American ex-*Monty Python* animator Terry Gilliam. During a hallucinating few days at the 1983 Cannes Festival, Milchan and Gilliam bamboozled Fox and Universal into splitting the $15 million budget of what the studios thought was another surrealist comedy in the style of his highly commercial 1981 *Time Bandits*. In fact Gilliam, with help from Tom Stoppard, had confected a sour, dystopic fantasy of an over-regulated, over-populated Britain with a crumbling technological infrastructure – the condition of Bulgaria, extrapolated into the future, and extended to cover all of Europe.

The idea came to Gilliam in the Welsh mining town of Port Talbot, when he heard Ry Cooder's version of the song 'Maria Elena', and mused on the incongruity. 'I had an image of somebody sitting on a beach, a beach blackened by coal dust, somebody just sitting there in the evening with a radio and that haunting song coming over the airwaves – escapist, romantic sounds suggesting that somewhere out there, far from the conveyor belts and ugly steel towers, is a green and wonderful world.'

Kurosawa's *Rashomon*, Bergman's *Wild Strawberries* and Fellini's *8½* made their stylistic contribution to the screenplay, which Gilliam jokingly called '1984½' or summarised as 'Kafka meets Capra'. Its actual title, however, after the forties song that replaced 'Marie Elena' as a symbol of everything free, exotic and utterly lost to this society, was *Brazil*.

Having interviewed numerous young actors and actresses for the main roles, including Tom Cruise and Madonna, Gilliam instead chose his old friend Jonathan Pryce to play the bedevilled and finally doomed bureaucrat Sam, and newcomer Kim Griest the truckdriver girl he loves. Milchan, nervous about the lack of a big name, offered De Niro his choice of parts to play a cameo role. De Niro chose Jack Lint, a sinister civil servant who hounds Sam to his death; but that was reserved for Michael Palin from the old *Python* group. Reluctantly, De Niro accepted the much smaller part of Harry Tuttle, terrorist plumber.

RIGHT: The role that first drew attention to De Niro – dying baseball player Bruce Pearson in *Bang the Drum Slowly* (1973), with Michael Moriarty (centre) as his friend Henry Wiggen and Vincent Gardenia as team manager 'Dutch' Schnell.

LEFT: De Niro upstaged by the charismatic young Gerard Depardieu in Bernardo Bertolucci's *Novecento* (1976).

RIGHT: Betsy (Cybill Shepherd) storms away from Travis Bickle after he has taken her to a porno film in *Taxi Driver*.

LEFT: De Niro's most compelling role, as the psychopath Travis Bickle sledding doggedly through the moral filth of New York in *Taxi Driver*.

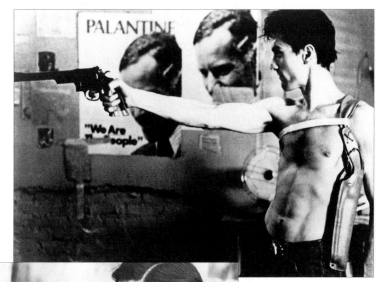

RIGHT: 'Are you talkin' to *me*?' Travis Bickle practises for the assassination of presidential candidate Charles Palantine in *Taxi Driver*.

LEFT: De Niro as Jimmy Doyle in *New York, New York*.

RIGHT: Just one bullet. Michael Cimino's *The Deer Hunter* (1978) gave De Niro one of his most memorable roles as steelworker and crack shot Michael Vronsky.

BELOW: De Niro as gunman 'Noodles' Aaronson with girlfriend Darlanne Fluegel in Sergio Leone's confused, much-mutilated *Once Upon a Time in America* (1984).

ABOVE: A killer reborn. Ex-slave trader and mercenary Rodrigo Mendoza gains absolution for the murder of his brother by helping Jesuit missionary Father Gabriel (Jeremy Irons) to convert Amazonian Indians in *The Mission*.

LEFT: De Niro as troubled bounty hunter Jack Walsh in *Midnight Run* (1988), another failed attempt to make him a comedy star.

ABOVE: De Niro and Sean Penn as escaped convicts in the remake of *We're no Angels* (1989).

RIGHT: *Stanley and Iris* traduced Pat Barker's novel *Union Street*, turning illiterate factory-worker Stanley Cox into a genius inventor.

ABOVE: As screenwriter David Merrill, based on real-life blacklistee Abraham Polonsky, De Niro shouts defiance of the House Committee on Un-American Activities in *Guilty by Suspicion*.

LEFT: De Niro in the 1992 *Mad Dog and Glory* as mild-mannered forensic photographer Wayne Dobie, ironically named 'Mad Dog'.

ABOVE: Baseball fan Gil Renard in *The Fan*
(1996), ready to kill to aid the career of his
favourite player.

BELOW: De Niro as undercover CIA man
Sam, posing as a mercenary in *Ronin*.

ABOVE: De Niro in one of his most
engaging roles, as political 'fixer'
Conrad Brean, with helper Anne Heche
in *Wag the Dog* (1997).

ABOVE: 'You're good!' De Niro as gang boss Paul Vitti praises nervous psychiatrist Ben Sobol (Billy Crystal) in *Analyze This* (1999).

BELOW: Arguably the nadir of De Niro's career, playing cartoon character Fearless Leader in *The Adventures of Rocky and Bullwinkle* (2000), which his company also produced. Jason Alexander and Rene Russo are henchpersons Boris and Natacha.

Tuttle is a commando repairman who intercepts calls to Central Services about collapsing air conditioning and dysfunctional ovens, abseils down the outside of apartment buildings, bursts through the window in balaclava and combat boots, and fixes the fault before disappearing into the darkness again. His pragmatism and independence are the ultimate affront to a world obsessed with forms and regulations. Fittingly, he's trapped not by human beings but a cloud of wind-blown papers, a metaphor for the bureaucracy. They envelop him, and when they disperse he's no longer there.

Initially, Gilliam and his crew were delighted that De Niro was going to be in the film. Gilliam brushed off his requests to discuss the character of Tuttle, telling him, 'Bobby, you *are* that man. You're a hero to all of us, and you don't have to complicate it – just *be*.'

But De Niro was in the business of complication. 'He kept flying to London,' says Gilliam, 'and spent months arguing over every piece of costume and every prop. He was going to brain surgeons he knew in New York and watching operations, because I'd said that the character, though a plumber, was like a surgeon.'

The crew built a mock-up of the set, where De Niro could practise. His military fatigues, boots and all the tools had to be manufactured specially. He decided Tuttle should wear thick glasses, and these had to be made up.

'When it came to shooting, it was just the same,' Gilliam recalls. 'I had him on the set for a week in advance so that he could get used to the crew. But apparently he was up all night before his first day's shooting, wearing his costume, and he arrived on the set really nervous.'

Pryce and the other actors needed only two or three takes for their scenes, but De Niro was taking twenty-five or thirty, and still forgetting his lines. In the end, his scenes occupied not one week but two, and even then he left many cutaways unfilmed when he returned to the US. The hands seen manipulating the tools in Tuttle's scenes belong to Gilliam.

Unaware of the effect he'd had on the crew, or perhaps unconcerned about it, De Niro assured Gilliam warmly that he'd had a wonderful time and would work with him again any time he wanted. 'We were all in awe of De Niro,' says Gilliam, summing up the experience, 'then we shifted round 180 degrees and wanted to kill him.'

De Niro had his reasons for wanting to be in London as much as possible. He'd just found a new woman, a heavy-breasted young model of Caribbean extraction named Gillian de Terville. In the official version of their meeting, De Niro saw her posed bare-breasted on Page 3 of the *Sun* tabloid newspaper, and got her phone number from a friend. Out of the blue, he rang her at her parents' home in suburban Sydenham and asked for a date. This developed into an eighteen-month transatlantic affair.

With de Terville on his arm, he turned up at the London disco Tramp for dinner with Christopher Walken and Joan Collins, but was just as happy, she said, sitting on the couch with her family in their home, watching TV. Periodically, he brought her to New York for a weekend in his TriBeCa loft, now impressively furnished, including a giant bed fitted with all manner of electronics built into the headboard, from which they could turn on almost every appliance in the house.

So discreet were the couple that the London press didn't spot the affair until it was over, and de Terville spilled the beans in November 1985 to the same tabloid that had published the topless pictures which caught De Niro's eye. De Niro would follow almost the same scenario a decade later, dating London-based black model Charmaine Sinclair after having seen her pictures in a magazine, but in that case the romance would become public, and end in the courts.

Being in London led to some embarrassing moments for De Niro, since Helena Springs had moved there in July 1984 to marry recording executive Anthony Lisandrello. Nina, whom she continued to claim was De Niro's child, was now two years old. De Niro and Springs sometimes turned up at the same nightclub, only to ignore one another. De Niro also went backstage at an Elton John concert where Springs was singing back-up, leading to yet another frosty encounter in the private bar.

De Niro's regular companion continued to be Toukie Smith, who apparently regarded his dalliances with equanimity. In New York she had her own apartment, and her own party-catering business, as well as her modelling. When De Niro was in New York, it was she who accompanied him to the few public events he could be persuaded to attend. Like Diahnne Abbott, Smith had ambitions to act, in which she expected De Niro to help her. She also wanted a family, ideally with him as father. With his highly-developed sense of responsibility, however, and with one potential paternity suit hanging over his head, De Niro was cautious about any entanglement.

That caution made him vulnerable to plausible women who managed to find his phone number. One of these was Whitney Walton, a social worker from the American South who was able to coax many Hollywood stars onto the phone during a ten-year period, convincing them she was a glamorous model named Miranda. Warren Beatty, Quincy Jones, Billy Joel, Buck Henry and De Niro were among her 'conquests', none of whom ever met her in person, but who carried on a number of long and steamy telephone conversations. Her story became public when journalist Bryan Burrough wrote it up in the December 1999 issue of *Vanity Fair*, later turning it into a screenplay. MGM promptly bought the script, which has been announced as a possible future Tribeca production, with De Niro directing and/or starring.

While he was in London, De Niro also met director Roland Joffe and producer David Puttnam, who, with Italian producer Fernando Ghia, were assembling a film about the catastrophic impact of the Spanish and Portuguese on the Indians of South America during the eighteenth century.

Originally called 'Guarani', after the tribe massacred in the battle for territory, the project dated back to the sixties, when Ghia had seen a play by Frederick Hochwalder called *The Holy Experiment*, dealing with the attempts by a small group of Jesuit missionaries to convert the Guarani, most of whom lived on a barely accessible plateau on the border of modern-day Paraguay and Brazil.

The Guarani tied the first missionaries to crosses and floated them over the Iguassu Falls that plunged hundreds of metres to the Parana River. But they had an extraordinary ear for music, and once the Jesuits sent in men who could play rather than simply preach, the tribe was converted. Soon they could sing or play any music they heard, and were manufacturing instruments for the orchestras of Europe.

The tranquillity and productivity couldn't last. Spain opposed slavery, but the Treaty of Madrid in 1750 ceded that corner of its South American colonies to Portugal, which did not. No longer protected, the Jesuit missions were destroyed by the Portuguese landowners, and the Indians enslaved.

Ghia commissioned a screenplay from Robert Bolt, scenarist of *Lawrence of Arabia* and *Doctor Zhivago*. Bolt created two characters to represent the opposite points of view: devout Jesuit Brother Gabriel, and Rodrigo Mendoza, a slaver and brawler who, having killed his brother in a jealous duel over a woman, becomes filled with remorse and takes refuge with the Jesuits. Gabriel challenges him to face his crime and devise a penance commensurate with his guilt. The next thing we see, Mendoza has joined the monks on a climb to the plateau of the Guarani. Though unarmed himself, he's dragging a net filled with armour and weapons, which his penance apparently demands he must haul to the top of the falls. Having redeemed himself, Mendoza joins the Jesuits, becoming Gabriel's friend and helper. However, when the Portuguese begin burning the missions and enslaving the natives, and the Church, for political reasons, orders the Jesuits not to resist, he leads the Guarani in a last-ditch stand.

Puttnam had produced the Oscar-winning *Chariots of Fire* in 1981, and Joffe had just finished *The Killing Fields*, a harrowing story of a journalist and his local colleague involved in the Cambodian genocide of Pol Pot – credentials solid enough to impress De Niro. He also liked the role of Mendoza, a character who, like many of those De Niro played, assumed responsibility for the weak. It also demanded considerable physical effort.

During successive visits to London for *Brazil*, Puttnam and De Niro cautiously circled one another. Puttnam told him about conditions along the Argentina/Paraguay border. Not only would the film have to be shot in those jungles, but the actors playing the missionaries would have to scale the cliffs with the roaring falls at their elbow. In De Niro's case, he would do so in bare feet, and dragging a net full of armour. With news of De Niro's thirty takes on *Brazil* all over town, Puttnam warned him that he couldn't behave like that on *The Mission*.

'I understand your problem,' De Niro told him, 'and I will never delay your picture.'

Puttnam pressed harder. 'I'm also not totally convinced that you are right for the picture.'

Startled, De Niro said, 'Nobody has ever said that to me before, David. I'm an actor, and my feeling is that I'm right for anything that I really sincerely feel that I can do.'

In the end, Puttnam and Joffe agreed that De Niro would bring more to the film than they risked losing. A deal was struck with Harry Ufland under which he received $1.5 million and 13 per cent of the net receipts, plus 'expenses'. However, as a back-up, burly young Irish actor Liam Neeson was signed for the small role of Brother John Fielding. If De Niro caused problems or hurt himself, Neeson, reasoned Puttnam, could take over. (He apparently wasn't aware that the high-strung Neeson suffered from anxiety-derived intestinal problems and had already had extensive gastric surgery.)

De Niro grew a thick beard, moustache and long hair, and learned to ride a horse. With Puttnam, he visited Argentina and the Colombian city of Cartagena, where many of the exteriors would be filmed. This was cocaine country, with kidnappings and killings daily events. De Niro would need round-the-clock bodyguards.

De Niro also invited Robert Bolt and his companion Sarah Miles to dinner to discuss the film. Since a stroke had partly paralysed Bolt and made speaking difficult, such a meeting was a considerable physical trial for him. According to Bolt's biographer, Adrian Turner, De Niro spent the meal 'absorbing every single thought Robert had about the story and the character of Mendoza. De Niro was like a sponge, and when there was nothing left within Robert to soak up, he sat silently and allowed Robert the privilege of paying the bill, even though Robert and Sarah were supposedly his guests. De Niro's self-absorption – if not downright meanness – made Sarah angry for a week.'

In April 1985, De Niro agreed to submit to an on-stage discussion at London's National Film Theatre as part of a series sponsored by the *Guardian* newspaper. He declined air fares and an appearance fee, but at the same time refused to let the event be televised or to permit the showing of scenes from the unsuccessful *Falling in Love*. He and Martin Scorsese arrived unexpectedly with members of Scorsese's favourite band, The Clash, for whom seats had to be found in a sold-out auditorium. Having been pursued by autograph hounds from his hotel and ambushed in the NFT's green room by a fan who managed to snap his picture before escaping, De Niro became so nervous that he couldn't bear to watch the montage of clips that preceded his appearance.

The interview itself was unrevealing. Asked about his childhood, De Niro said evenly, 'That's not something I can talk about in front of four hundred people.' Every probe by film critic Chris Auty was turned back with a bland generalisation or a blank refusal to answer. Fortunately Scorsese spontaneously started fielding questions from his seat in the audience, enlivening an otherwise inert event. People who'd imagined De Niro was simply reticent now began to wonder if he really had anything to say in the first place.

De Niro's involvement in *The Mission* threw the project off-balance. On the simplest level, it lifted the budget to $23 million, which made the backers nervous, and put more pressure on Joffe, Puttnam and Ghia to cut costs. Jeremy Irons had already agreed to play Gabriel for a modest salary. Now Puttnam scaled down the role of Mendoza's brother Felipe, which went to the little-known Aidan Quinn, and gave the part of Carlotta, the young widow over whom the brothers fight, to Joffe's girlfriend Cherie Lunghi.

Cardinal Altimirano, the Vatican investigator, had the film's second-longest role, as well as the best dialogue, including a literate voice-over as he dictates his findings for the record. Joffe cast the Irish actor Ray McAnally, whose rich brogue gave Bolt's lines all the shading and depth the writer could have asked for. The fact remains, however, that the role needed a Brando or an Anthony Quinn to instil a little Hollywood bombast.

Shooting began in July. As usual, De Niro gave himself 100 per cent physically to the role. David Puttnam's wife Patsy, visiting the location and climbing the scaffolding at the top of the falls with producer Iain Smith, looked down to see 'a ragged, bearded figure on the rocks below, running and jumping around in his bare feet'.

'Who on earth's that?'

'It's Bobby De Niro,' Smith explained. 'He's got to do that in the scene tomorrow.'

Looking at the jagged rocks, Patsy Puttnam said, 'But his *feet*!'

Smith, who knew De Niro's methods by then, just said, 'I know.'

The great pleasure of *Lawrence* and *Zhivago* had been their compressed one-liners, and the charged conversations between powerful men, where each phrase was like the clash of steel on steel. But De Niro, used to improvising his lines, wasn't comfortable with Bolt's formal language. In place of intensity, he gave brow-wrinkling and eye-rolling, mutters and glares. He had been right all along in his aversion to period parts – he simply could not play them. But to have discovered this fact in so public and expensive a fashion was cold comfort.

When he did try a Bolt line, the effect was often ludicrous, and in general he remained Bobby from the Big Apple throughout. As Paul Attanasio wrote in the *Washington Post*, 'While Bolt has suggested a complex psychology for Mendoza, a man whose desire for heaven never quite transcends his own violent nature, De Niro doesn't play it. In the last five years, he's become curiously inert, and *The Mission* features his most sombre and withdrawn performance yet. He's about as expressive as a church icon, and his contemporary acting approach and New York accent are comically inapt, particularly when Bolt has him delivering lines like, "So *me* you do not love." You keep expecting to find him in the eighteenth century's first pool hall.'

This would be the verdict of history on *The Mission*, and De Niro's part in it. A role that needed *gravitas*, anguish and exaltation was played flatly and without presence, in a style out of character with the period. Film editor Jim Clark despaired of giving it coherence. 'With De Niro,' he said, 'you don't cut him – you *mine* him. You have to seek out the performance because it varies so.'

When his part in the film finished in the fall of 1985, De Niro said goodbye to Puttnam and Ghia with the same warmth he'd shown Terry Gilliam. If they ever wanted to work with him again . . . . Hardly had he left, however, than Puttnam found himself dealing with a backlog of 'special expenses' run up by De Niro. He'd budgeted these at around $80,000, but they actually came to two and a half times that, including air fares, special fencing lessons, telephone calls, and a physiotherapist. Three weeks later, Ufland submitted yet another claim. Puttnam gritted his teeth, and paid.

On his return to New York, De Niro found himself once again entangled with Helena Springs Lisandrello. In the autumn of 1986, about the time *The Mission* went on release in the United States, a mutual friend told De Niro that Springs wanted to see him again, and for him to meet her daughter Nina. Springs came to the loft on Hudson Street, where, she claims, she spent the night with De Niro. The next day, he accompanied her to the apartment of *New York, New York* actor Barry Primus and his wife Julie to meet Nina.

Accounts vary of what happened next. Springs said De Niro was 'very sweet' with Nina, bought her ice cream, told Springs he'd like to spend more time with her, and that they could 'work something out' on the question of patrimony and their own relationship, even though he remained committed to Toukie Smith.

De Niro insists he felt 'embarrassed and uncomfortable' with the little girl, but was 'curious' to see if she resembled him (and relieved when she did not). After the meeting, Springs and Nina returned to London, and though Springs tried from time to time to extract money from De Niro for nursery school fees, she claims he never replied.

CHAPTER SEVENTEEN

Falling Angel

At some point in the late eighties Robert De Niro became boring. 'He did Midnight Run, *for God's sakes, and* Jacknife,' *a producer said to me with disgust. 'He started doing package pictures for the money.' Then De Niro started doing interviews, finally, when he bought his studio in TriBeCa – and that was the moment the mystique started to fade.*

Paul Rosenfield, *The Club Rules: Power, Money, Sex and Fear – How it Works in Hollywood*

Brazil wouldn't open in the US until December 1985, and *The Mission,* which De Niro hoped might be a *succès d'estime* on the scale of *Raging Bull,* not until November 1986. In the meantime, he put his career into low gear, doing cameos, character roles, and even a play.

Asked at the National Film Theatre if he'd ever return to theatre, he'd said, 'I haven't been on the stage in ten years. I like doing films, and just don't get the time.' He did admit, however, that he was 'looking for plays'.

Once De Niro returned to New York, Joseph Papp, pioneer of low-cost theatre in New York with his Shakespeare in the Park series and his Public Theater in downtown Manhattan, offered him the role of an illiterate Cuban drug dealer raising a teenage son in Reinaldo Povod's *Cuba and his Teddy Bear.*

Creating Broadway silk purses from off-Broadway sows' ears was a Papp speciality. His big hit was *A Chorus Line*; his alumni included Meryl Streep and Kevin Kline. Twenty-six years old, Povod was the son of a Puerto Rican mother and a Cuban/Russian father, and had impressed Papp sufficiently to be made resident playwright at his Public Theater.

Both Povod and De Niro grew up in downtown Manhattan: *Cuba and his Teddy Bear* takes place in an apartment on 13th Street. Both their fathers placed themselves outside conventional society: Povod's characters were mainly street hustlers, dope dealers and minor criminals – the kind of people De Niro saw every day as a kid. Once Povod, who would be dead six years later, told De Niro that he'd been on drugs himself, had watched him as a child filming *Taxi Driver*, and written *Cuba* with him in mind, the star was sold. He agreed to play the role for eight weeks at Equity scale. Ralph Macchio, hoping to put *The Karate Kid* and its sequels behind him, took the part of Teddy, a sixteen-year-old with ambitions to write, but with a drug problem for which his father's only solution is to suggest the boy get high at home, where he can keep an eye on him. Burt Young from *Once Upon a Time in America* shared top billing.

Once word spread of De Niro live on stage, the box office was swamped. Scalpers made a fortune. When all the seats were sold, Papp took a hall across the street, and charged $7 a head to watch on closed-circuit TV. Finally, he persuaded De Niro to move the play to the Longacre Theater, where it ran from 16 July until 21 September – De Niro's first and, so far, only appearance on Broadway.

Though *Cuba* won the Oppenheimer/*Newsday* Award as Best Broadway Play and De Niro the *Theatre World* Award, Povod was no Eugene O'Neill. Not that this mattered to the crowds. Pupkins all, they flocked in to see De Niro in the flesh, and most left with a new respect for his sheer physical presence. At the play's most dramatic moment, when a dealer offered his son drugs, De Niro took the 185-pound man by the shirt, lifted him off his feet and slammed him against the wall. 'I can't tell you how long he held him,' said Irwin Winkler. 'There is no way you can hold up 185 pounds against a wall like that. It was just the force of the actor doing that. It was remarkable.'

Along with Dustin Hoffman's Broadway *Death of a Salesman*, *Cuba and his Teddy Bear* prefigured a new star-driven Broadway, where few serious dramas found a stage unless a movie 'name' was attached. In the thirties, Hollywood stars would do a season in Ibsen at the Pasadena Playhouse when they wanted to tread the boards again. Now they came to Broadway, tackling roles for which their untrained voices and lack of stage technique made them miserably ill-equipped. New York became accustomed to oddities like TV star Kelsey Grammer as a ludicrous Macbeth and a three-week production of *Waiting for Godot*, hammed up by Robin Williams and Steve Martin. Seeing his play turned into stand-up *shtick*, Beckett must have groaned in his grave.

De Niro was lucky in the mid-eighties to encounter David Mamet. Mamet gave him the eloquence denied him by birth. His words, though De Niro didn't always do them justice, would be the most memorable he delivered on screen over the next decade – perhaps during his whole career.

Mamet and De Niro were never friends, and seldom met, Mamet preferring a remote cabin in New England. His ability to write for De Niro was rooted in their shared misanthropy.

When producer Art Linson approached him to script a film version of *The Untouchables*, the playwright had just won the Pulitzer Prize for *Glengarry Glen Ross*, about a group of real-estate salesman. Linson's track record was erratic, veering between low-budget successes like *Car Wash*, prestige pictures like *Melvin and Howard* and such oddities as *Where the Buffalo Roam*, in which Bill Murray played gonzo journalist Hunter S. Thompson, and which Linson also directed.

With Mamet, Linson laid his meagre cards on the table. 'Dave,' he said, 'don't you think that the best career move for somebody who has just won the Pulitzer Prize would be to adapt an old television series like *The Untouchables* for a *shitload* of money?'

'Yes, I think so,' said Mamet.

The Untouchables had run from 1959 to 1963 on ABC-TV, with Robert Stack playing agent Eliot Ness, who leads his 'untouchable', i.e. unbribable, agents against Al Capone. The stories were fiction, but the juxtaposition of a lock-jawed Stack as Ness and Neville Brand as a flamboyant Capone won millions of viewers.

For the movie, Linson cast Kevin Costner as Ness and, as Capone, the portly Bob Hoskins – to whom he frankly confessed that he was hoping to get a bigger name, in which case Hoskins would be out. Brian De Palma was directing, which, given his past history with De Niro, suggested immediately who that name might be.

The need for someone like De Niro became more pressing when a survey of American teenage males, the primary audience of *The Untouchables*, revealed that almost none had seen the original series or heard of Eliot Ness, but that all recognised the name of Al Capone.

Cuba and his Teddy Bear was still running when Linson, through his agent, approached De Niro to play Capone. De Niro read Mamet's script, asked questions, asked more questions, met De Palma, to whom he addressed even more questions, and said he'd let them know as soon as he'd finished his next project, a small role as Satan in Alan Parker's *Angel Heart*.

Filming William Hjortsberg's 1978 novel *Falling Angel* was an old project from an odd source. In this modestly conventional occult thriller, Lucifer, hiding behind the all-too-penetrable alias of Lou Cyphre, hires gumshoe Harry Angel to track down a swing-band singer named Johnny Favorite. After a traipse through private insane asylums, and the homes (and beds) of voodoo devotees and psychics, most of whom he later finds murdered, Angel discovers that he himself is Favorite. Years ago, he sold his soul to the devil in return for fame, attempted to evade the debt by switching his body with that of a young soldier, then had psychic Margaret Kreusmark erase all memory, just as he erased the memory that all the murdered witnesses to his former life were killed by him. At the conclusion, Angel's lover, voodoo priestess Epiphany Proudfoot, is found tied to his bed with his army dogtags, and shot to death through her vagina with his gun. In Cyphre's little joke, the electric chair will inaugurate Angel's eternal damnation.

Despite the story's pulp fiction elements, Hjortsberg belonged to the Montana group of serious novelists that coalesced around Richard Brautigan and Thomas McGuane (both of whom contributed warm endorsements to the novel's dustwrapper). A grant from the National Endowment for the Arts supported him while he wrote the book, which appeared from prestigious publisher Harcourt Brace Jovanovich, with a flashy gold cover of a gun-toting Byzantine angel stalking a demon with a knife through Manhattan.

Impressed by Hjortsberg's credentials, various people optioned the novel, including Robert Redford, but it was independent producer Elliott Kastner who, according to British director Alan Parker, 'dropped the book on my table one lunchtime at Pinewood Studios early in '85'.

When he graduated from TV commercials, Parker had announced he wanted to try his hand at every movie genre, and, as he later remarked, 'this novel embraced not one but two'. Just finishing his version of William Wharton's novel *Birdy*, Parker had already done the musicals *Bugsy Malone* and *Fame*, but remained best known for *Midnight Express*, about the survival in a Turkish prison and eventual escape of American dope smuggler Billy Hayes. *Midnight Express* was dark, erotic and violent – all qualities Parker inculcated into his attempt to combine the horror and detective genres, *Angel Heart*, as *Falling Angel* was puzzlingly renamed.

Kastner and Parker found money from Andrew Vajna and Mario Kassar, who were rich on the proceeds of *Rambo* and its sequels. Part of the price of their involvement was at least one major star. 'I had a secret desire to ask Robert De Niro,' Parker confessed, 'but in those early days couldn't pluck up the courage.' Kastner sent him the script, however, and De Niro liked it well enough to ring Parker and ask which role he was being offered, Angel or Cyphre. Parker told him, 'Either.' However, since Angel needed to play nude love scenes with Epiphany Proudfoot while blood gushed from the ceiling and spattered their bodies, that option was discarded early.

Nothing more was heard from De Niro, so Parker offered the role of Angel to Mickey Rourke, who accepted it with enthusiasm. Controversially, Epiphany Proudfoot was played, in her first movie role, by eighteen-year-old Lisa Bonet, Bill Cosby's daughter in the long-running sitcom *The Cosby Show*. Her nude scenes with Rourke launched her into the limelight, and just as quickly out of it. *The Cosby Show* fired her. She didn't make another film until 1993, and little after that.

By the end of 1985, De Niro was still considering the Cyphre role. In November, he and Parker had another long discussion. After that, nothing for months, during which he, with Christopher Walken and Treatt Williams, attended the International Festival of New Latin American Cinema in Havana. Cuban director Tomas Guittierrez Alea approached him to play Prospero in an international version of Shakespeare's *The Tempest*. De Niro told *Variety* that the film was 'a definite possibility. It just depends on the project. If the director and person are right, it goes beyond countries. It could be anything. But it would be good to do it here. The primary thing is the piece itself.'

De Niro also received Nicholas Kazan's screenplay for *At Close Range*, which young director James Foley was about to direct. The lead role was a career criminal, head of a highly successful mob which stole farm machinery, who periodically returns to his home in rural Pennsylvania where his abandoned wife and mother look after a son who's inherited some of his father's sociopathic ways and runs his own small gang. Desperate for his father's affection, the son persuades his father to use him and his followers in his thefts, only to discover that he's ready to sacrifice them, and him, for his own ends.

It was reported that the producers wanted De Niro to play the son – a real feat of transformation for a man in his forties, not to mention a step down in terms of billing. De Niro turned down the film on the pretext that it was 'too dark'. Christopher Walken was cast as the father and Sean Penn as the son in what turned out to be a highly effective and significant study of parental neglect and betrayal.

In December, *Brazil* opened in the US to puzzled but generally appreciative reviews. Arnon Milchan persuaded De Niro to appear with Terry Gilliam on TV, promoting the film. The two men did the rounds of morning talk shows, culminating in one hosted by Maria Shriver. At first the tone was amiable, but Shriver's query, 'I heard you're having trouble with the studio,' brought an instant reaction from Gilliam.

'I don't have a problem with the studio,' he said. 'I've got a problem with one man. His name is Sid Sheinberg, and he looks like this' – and Gilliam, to De Niro's astonishment, pulled out an 8 x 10 glossy of the production boss of Universal, and flourished it in front of the camera.

In February 1986, De Niro resumed contact with Alan Parker. 'Once again,' wrote the director in his journal, 'I had a three-hour meeting with De Niro at his apartment, where he questioned every dot and comma of the script. He is a very intelligent man and on every film agonises over saying yes . . . I said goodbye to him, leaving him with a folder of information on the world's greatest villains, from Rasputin to Himmler.'

On 9 March they met again, this time at the Harlem mission where Harry Angel first encounters Louis Cyphre. 'We sat alone in the seedy old Elks room,' says Parker, 'reading through the script, with Bob feeling out the part he'd be playing, the chair he'd be sitting in, and sniffing the air that he'd breathe. Afterwards, we had a drink in a Harlem bar he knew well. He ordered two Margaritas. I drank them both. He still hadn't said yes.'

On 17 March, only two weeks before the start of primary photography, De Niro rang at 8 a.m. to say he was 'of a mind to do the film', which was his way of saying 'Yes.'

Parker's crew hurriedly accumulated a wardrobe. All De Niro's clothes, painstakingly chosen as always, and laundered repeatedly to give them a look of lived-in comfort, came from Rome. De Niro augmented each outfit with a silver-topped cane, chosen from a collection of more than twenty, some of which he'd found in a specialised boutique in Paris during a Christmas holiday. (It took a special phone call from Parker to persuade him not to buy the store's entire stock.)

As usual, De Niro took his costumes home and wore them in the weeks leading up to shooting, to the disquiet of his friends. He also agreed to be fitted with a selection of false fingernails, which appeared to grow longer in each scene, and with contact lenses that made his eyes appear yellow. His hair, still long from *The Mission*, was kept in a bun, and only revealed in the final scene.

While everyone else had to travel to the film's uncomfortable and inconvenient locations, like New Orleans, De Niro's scenes were shot in New York. 'I never even saw him,' says Charlotte Rampling, who played Margaret Kreusmark. The first rehearsals with Rourke took place in the Harlem mission where Parker and De Niro had first read through the script. 'As we began, it was akin to a couple of prize-fighters testing one another, rather than an acting rehearsal,' said Parker. 'Slowly, they circled one another. An ad-libbed jab, a wisecrack clinch. Bob was cool, meticulous, charming and generous, but had us all under control. Mickey was disarming and ingenuous, but at all times gave as good as he took. As the "referee" onlooker, it was, for me, electric to watch.' To make sure he missed none of this high-priced talent, Parker shot the scene with two cameras.

All primary colours were leached out of the costumes and settings, leaving only ochre, browns and greys. The brooding tone and Parker's flair for melodramatic effects prefigured the baroque horror films of the nineties like David Fincher's *Se7en*, though few appreciated them at the time, least of all the American and British censors, who shortened some of the bloody sex scenes. The film would come into its own in the nineties, when a 'director's cut' restored them.

De Niro liked *Angel Heart* well enough, and respected Parker, but felt the script unravelled at the end. And, in truth, the final image, of a freight elevator descending interminably, presumably into hell, belonged in a thirties Broadway revival of *Faust*. Cyphre, likewise, is a comic-book Satan. The role demanded little of De Niro but to smile sardonically in a variety of shadowed locations, hands folded on his cane to display his lengthening nails, and bounce one-liners off a deadpan Rourke ('"Mephistopheles" is such a mouthful in Manhattan').

The Mission won the Palme d'Or at Cannes in May 1986, the first American-funded film to do so in thirteen years, but a pall was cast over the festival by the fact that American planes had just bombed Libya, killing the daughter of President Gadaffi. Reprisals were expected, and most stars, including De Niro, stayed away.

Warner Bros delayed the film's US release until November 1986, in order to bring it as close to the Oscars as possible. The strategy was successful, and *The Mission* garnered nominations as Best Picture, Best Director for Joffe, as well as Cinematography, Set Decoration, Original Score, Editing and Costume Design. But in a strong year, with no clear winners, Academy members spread their votes thinly. *Platoon*, *Aliens*, *Hannah and her Sisters* and *A Room With a View* all scored, while *The Mission* was fobbed off with an Oscar for Chris Menges' scenic photography. Morricone's music, destined to become among the most recognised of all film scores, lost to Bertrand Tavernier's *Round Midnight*, the music of which was mainly improvised jazz.

Without the impetus of serious Oscar wins, *The Mission* only grossed $17.3 million – almost the same as *Angel Heart* – which meant that both films lost money, continuing De Niro's persistent losing streak.

By the time De Niro finished *Angel Heart*, Brian De Palma was ready to start shooting *The Untouchables* in Chicago. But still De Niro wouldn't commit, and continued to ponder other offers. Knowing his taste for and skill in transformation, studios sent him any story in which the main character had to become unrecognisable. In John Godey's novel *The Three Worlds of Johnny Handsome*, a gangster with a disfiguring birth defect is transformed by surgery, but can't escape his roots. Another novel, William Kennedy's *Ironweed*, about two alcoholic drifters trying to survive the winter of 1937, had the advantage of Meryl Streep as co-star.

Also on offer were two projects from Penny Marshall. After years as an actress in TV sitcoms like *Laverne and Shirley*, Marshall had directed one film, *Jumping Jack Flash*, a comedy with Whoopi Goldberg which made a modest profit. Now, two years later, she was offering two very different films.

Awakenings had its improbable source in a series of case studies compiled in the late sixties by the neurologist Oliver Sacks about the effects of the drug L-Dopa (dopamine) on twenty patients suffering from the disease *enchephalitis lethargica*. Most were survivors of an epidemic of this obscure 'sleepy sickness' which swept Europe in 1919, and had been in coma ever since. The drug returned many of them to full intelligence and mobility, only, in most cases, tragically to let them slip back irretrievably into coma after a few months.

Sacks published his book in 1973. Over the next decade it was adapted into a documentary film, a radio drama, and various plays, including Harold Pinter's *A Kind of Alaska*. In 1979, two screenwriters, Walter Parkes and Larry Lasker, approached Sacks to film his story. Fox got interested in the project, then turned it down, and the script joined the thousands that circulated sluggishly from slush pile to studio slush pile, which is where Marshall found it while looking for a film to follow *Jumping Jack Flash*.

Awakenings had a personal relevance to Marshall, since her mother suffered from Alzheimer's Disease, and had degenerated into a vegetative state. She coaxed Columbia to buy the project from Fox, and commissioned a new screenplay from Steven Zaillian, who'd written *The Falcon and the Snowman* and would adapt Thomas Keneally's novel *Schindler's Ark* into *Schindler's List* for Steven Spielberg.

Marshall's second project was *Big*, a screenplay by Gary Ross and Spielberg's sister Anne. Another transformation film, it dealt with a boy who wishes to be 'big' and wakes up an adult, but with the fears, preoccupations, and, more usefully, the enthusiasms of a child – which, when he gets a job in a toy company, make him its most valuable executive.

Both films appealed to De Niro, but he could see that, given Marshall's background in comedy, she would make a better job of *Big*. And comedy remained, for De Niro, the great unscaleable peak. It had beaten him twice already, but maybe three times was the charm. He turned down *The Three Worlds of Johnny Handsome*, which would be made by Walter Hill, badly, in 1989 as *Johnny Handsome*, with Mickey Rourke in the lead, and also *Ironweed*, in which Jack Nicholson would star opposite Streep, but continued to negotiate on *Big*.

Columbia offered him $3 million to star. De Niro wanted $6 million, and negotiations broke down. While money was assumed to be the sticking point, rumours circulated that Columbia preferred a younger actor with more teenage appeal. This story rankled with De Niro, who was still sensitive in 1990 when British film critic Barry Norman raised it during a television interview. He gave an evasive answer on camera, but, once it was turned off, snarled at Norman, 'You had to get that one in, didn't you?'

The two men argued, and De Niro gave his version of the *Big* negotiations. In Norman's words, 'The producers had approached him to do the role, he had been interested and he had agreed to do it. Then they started talking about where and when and how much money he would be paid and he walked away. Within a few days of him walking away from the whole enterprise the story started spreading that he had asked for the job and they had told him to go away.'

Columbia chose Tom Hanks for *Big*. At twenty-nine, he was more resilient than De Niro. He also cost a lot less. More would be heard of *Awakenings*, but for the moment, De Niro's most promising project was *The Untouchables*.

While De Niro and Columbia haggled over *Big*, the executive in charge of *The Untouchables*, the notoriously demanding and pessimistic Ned Tanen, had been urging Linson and De Palma to stop thinking about De Niro and his $2 million-plus price tag, and learn to love the low-cost Bob Hoskins. Linson hired Giorgio Armani to create a half-million-dollar wardrobe for Hoskins, but, just in case De Niro changed his mind, scheduled Capone's scenes for the end of shooting.

Technically, De Niro was too old for Capone as well: the gangster's reign ended when he was only thirty-two. But Mamet's script won him over. So much did De Niro admire Mamet that he debated appearing in a film version of *Glengarry Glen Ross*, playing Shelley Levine, the ageing salesman who, feeling himself slipping, struggles frantically for new clients. Al Pacino would have appeared opposite him as new-broom Ricky Roma. The project didn't take off, and it would be five years before Mamet's play reached the screen, with Jack Lemmon as Levine.

'I've always wanted to play Al Capone,' De Niro said. 'I've never seen it done the way I think it should be done. Capone wasn't just pure evil. He had to be a politician, an administrator, he had to have something going for him other than fear. He must have had a certain crazy charm.'

The film's best scene was dashed off during one of Mamet's rare and usually acrimonious visits to Linson's office. Challenged to fatten Capone's part, he sat down at the desk of Linson's secretary and wrote the lines that became the most famous in the film.

Capone is entertaining his henchmen at supper after a performance of *I Pagliacci*. In impeccable evening dress, he circles the table and delivers a kind of homily.

'Life goes on,' he says with a grin.

Laughter from the guests.

'A man becomes pre-eminent, he's expected to have enthusiasms.' He pauses reflectively. 'Enthusiasms . . . enthusiasms . . . What are they? What draws my admiration? What is that which gives me joy?'

He produces a baseball bat.

'Baseball!'

Laughter.

'A man. A man stands alone at the plate. This is the time for . . . what?' A pause. '*Individual achievement*.'

Everyone murmurs agreement, and continues to do so as he circles the table.

'There, he stands alone. But in the field, what? *Part of a team*. Looks. Throws. Catches. Hustles. Part of one big team. Bats himself the livelong day. Babe Ruth. Ty Cobb. And so on.'

More laughter.

'If his team don't field, what is he? You follow me? *No one*.'

By this time, Capone has placed himself behind a plump and contented lieutenant, who, drawing on a good cigar, nods at everything his boss says.

'Sunny day,' Capone continues, 'the stands are fulla fans, what does he have to say? "I'm going out there for myself. But . . . I get nowhere unless the team wins."'

As everyone laughs sycophantically, Capone swings the bat hard against the unsuspecting henchman's head. There is a sound like a watermelon crunching, repeated as he smashes down again and again. The rest of the gang flinch away, and the man's blood oozes darkly across the white linen tablecloth.

De Niro could play this kind of scene better than anyone else. 'Part of me was very upset as I was doing it,' he admitted later. 'But there's also a black humour and irony in the way David Mamet wrote it.' He was less effective in the scenes where Capone and Ness confronted one another – probably because, in real life, the two men never met, and the Untouchables in fact had little to do with Capone's downfall, which was engineered by accountant Frank Wilson, whose unravelling of Capone's financial machinations cleared the way for his conviction of tax evasion charges.

In Mamet, De Niro found for the first time a writer who could articulate those thoughts which, until then, he'd been able to communicate only by facial semaphore. Capone's limping syntax, the unfinished sentences and unattached words, mirrored exactly his own faltering diction. De Niro's incoherent response to the questions posed at the Oscars about John Hinckley could have been from a Mamet play. Not only that, but Mamet, in the brief Capone scenes, also tapped the rage that drove De Niro's best performances.

De Niro was so impressed by the script that he offered to defer $1 million of his salary to play Capone. Even then, Ned Tanen remained doubtful. To win him over, Linson led the executive round the lavish sets on which De Palma would shoot the film.

'Ned, think of it,' he murmured. 'When Bob De Niro kills somebody with a baseball bat, with Brian directing, it will never be forgotten.'

No doubt recalling that he'd called *American Graffiti* 'unreleasable' and turned down *Star Wars*, Tanen acquiesced.

Three months remained before they reached the Capone scenes. This was just as well, since, even after Tanen agreed, De Niro didn't commit unconditionally until the very last moment.

Linson decided it was time they met: until then, they'd communicated only through agents. De Palma called Linson to his room one night at 11 p.m. De Niro was sitting on the couch, 'eyeing me', as Linson wrote later, 'with the same quiet dismissiveness one would expect him to give a producer whose name drew a total blank'.

Linson wasn't too impressed either. 'Dressed in khakis, old Topsiders, and a short-sleeved shirt, Bob looked frail and small. He was so unassuming, I thought he might disappear. If De Palma's introduction had not confirmed that this was Robert De Niro, I would've asked for some verification. Perhaps a passport would have helped to explain how this unimposing figure was planning to chill Eliot Ness to the marrow. He didn't look like he could tear paper.'

Hoskins accepted $200,000 to drop out, and De Niro plunged into his customary intensive research, beginning with a trip to Italy to gain ten or fifteen kilos. He saw every movie which depicted Capone, and read hundreds of clippings. The Armani wardrobe was completely redesigned, De Niro adding silk underwear from Sulka, which also supplied Capone. He shaved his hairline to give the impression of baldness, and also the hair over the temples, to widen his face. To add to the effect, De Palma would always shoot him from a low angle. Physically, Hoskins was almost a double for the gang boss, but De Niro *lived* the role.

*   *   *

In 1987, De Niro changed agents. Long-time representative Harry Ufland closed his agency to become a producer with ex-studio head Joe Roth. De Niro, with many other Ufland clients, went to Creative Artists Agency, then run by the hottest agent in Hollywood, Mike Ovitz.

De Niro's career, financially at least, was in decline. Stars like Bruce Willis, Sylvester Stallone and Arnold Schwarzenegger might not get his reviews, but their pay packets doubled and tripled his price of $2–3 million, and climbed higher every year. Soon, $20–30 million would be the norm for the biggest box-office draws.

Ovitz began his showbiz career as a guide on the Universal Studios Tour, and learned the business with veterans like Marty Baum, who'd started as an agent, then become producer of films like *Cabaret* and *They Shoot Horses, Don't They?*. One of Ovitz's first acts at CAA was to make Baum a partner. It was Baum who suggested going after De Niro by offering to represent Diahnne Abbott. The stratagem worked, and soon both Abbott and De Niro were in the CAA fold.

Ovitz ran CAA like a studio, dreaming up vehicles, cramming his clients into them, and launching them at the majors. As an inaugural film for De Niro, he suggested the action comedy *Midnight Run*, written by another new CAA client, George Gallo. Ovitz convinced De Niro it would revive his career, and admit him to the well-paid company of Bruce, Sly and Arnie. '*Midnight Run* I thought might lighten the image I've had of heavy dramatic pieces, you know,' De Niro told a press conference after the film was released. 'Everyone thinks that all I have is this dark side. I am a bit sick of always being taken seriously' – strange talk from an actor who used to believe that only by suffering could one 'earn the right' to take on another personality.

Gallo had just participated in one CAA package, *Wise Guys*, directed by Brian De Palma, with Joe Piscopo and Danny De Vito, and had no illusions: this was film-making to supermarket principles. 'De Palma was a CAA client,' said Gallo, 'and that was when CAA was like the Mafia. They would just plug their guys in. Brian said he wanted to do a comedy, Joe was CAA,

Danny was CAA, Brian was CAA and so was [producer] Aaron [Russo]. And at the time so was I.'

Midnight Run was scarcely distinguishable from fifty other Hollywood films, from *Silver Streak* to *Busting* and *The Odd Couple*. Two bickering male protagonists, one a chain-smoking slob, the other a fastidious pedant, flee across America from a glowering gang boss with the usual complement of comic henchmen. Also in pursuit are some exasperated law enforcement officers under a choleric boss, and a couple of venal independents determined to frustrate the heroes. Even the title sounded generic, and would later be recycled both for film sequels and a TV series.

De Niro would be Jack Walsh, bounty hunter for a bail bondsman. An honest ex-cop, hounded out of Chicago by gang boss Jimmy Serrano (Dennis Farina), he agrees to locate defaulting accountant Jonathan Mardukas, who's stolen $15 million and given it to charity. Pursued by Serrano and the FBI, Walsh plays a game of wits with Mardukas as he tries to get him from New York to Los Angeles before the bond runs out. In the process they become friends, and Walsh sets Mardukas free when they reach California.

Ovitz took the package to Ned Tanen at Paramount. It included Gallo's screenplay, De Niro as Walsh and Martin Brest of *Beverly Hills Cop* fame as director. Tanen offered $20 million, but as Brest complicated the story, adding helicopter and car chases, and the budget climbed to $31 million, he blew cool. For that kind of money, he said, he needed more elements. Maybe Mardukas could be rewritten to attract Dustin Hoffman – or, since the film had no romantic interest, a female star like Cher, then hot following the success of *Moonstruck*.

Neither Hoffman nor Cher was interested. 'We were spending an awful lot of time trying to find the right person to play the other part,' De Niro said. 'It had to match up. Casting is like 90 per cent of it to me. If you get the right people, you're OK.'

Robin Williams, not then the big name he would soon become, was eager to play Mardukas, and offered to audition for the role, an astonishing concession even for a rising star, but Brest and De Niro refused. Although Williams was now off cocaine, he remained unpredictable, and he could easily take over a film with his improvised stream-of-consciousness dialogue.

They settled on Charles Grodin. Almost ten years older than De Niro, he'd been around for decades without rising above the general ruck. Skilled in deadpan and the incredulous stare, with a petulant lower lip that protruded at moments of stress, Grodin would prove an ideal foil for De Niro, though Tanen wasn't convinced, and put *Midnight Run* into turnaround, for sale to anyone who would reimburse Paramount for the money spent. Ovitz persuaded Universal to pick it up.

De Niro shmoozed with a couple of real bounty hunters and went on a cautious raid with a police team, the members of which demanded he wear enough body armour to stop a missile. However, the true authentic details are his methods of speedily picking a lock (scenes cut by the nervous British censor) and of tracking a fugitive through credit card and telephone records.

In most respects, Walsh is a one-size-fits-all tough-guy, untidy, unshaven, violent and profane. 'You're a fuckin' criminal,' he rages at Mardukas in a typical speech, 'and you deserve to go where you're goin' and I'm gonna take you there. I hear any more shit outta you I'm gonna fuckin' bust your head, and I'm gonna put you back in that fuckin' hole, and I'm gonna stick your head in a fuckin' toilet bowl and I'm gonna make it stay there.'

Critics of *Midnight Run* invented a drinking game associated with the film. The rules were: '1. Drink whenever the word "Fuck" is said. (This will average just over once a minute over the course of the two-hour movie.) 2. Drink whenever anyone calls Jonathan Mardukas "The Duke". 3. Drink whenever a gun/weapon is fired. 4. Drink twice any time Mardukas visibly annoys Jack Walsh.' They might have added: '5. Drink whenever someone lights up a cigarette.' Tobacco is a motif of the film. Everyone, but particularly De Niro and rival bounty hunter John Ashton, smokes furiously. There are running gags about stolen cigarettes, and plot points that turn on matchbooks.

To humanise Walsh, Gallo introduced a sub-plot in which the fugitives visit Walsh's ex-wife to borrow money, precipitating a morose reunion with his teenage daughter. After this, Mardukas becomes a combination pal and confessor, feeding Walsh advice on health, investment strategy and emotional well-being, while at the same time angling to be released. Grodin, an accomplished comedy technician, handles these scenes expertly. He's just as good conning a dumb bar owner out of some money by pretending to be an FBI agent investigating counterfeiting.

> MARDUKAS: What's the name of this establishment?
> RED: Red's Corner Bar.
> MARDUKAS: Are you Red?
> RED: Yes.
> MARDUKAS (looking at Red's brown hair): Do you dye your hair?
> RED: No.
>   [Pause]
> MARDUKAS: Why do they call you Red?
> RED: It's short for 'Redwood'. My last name's Wood.
> MARDUKAS: What's your first name?
> RED: Bill.

In this scene, as in many others, Grodin makes the running; De Niro just hangs about. *Midnight Run* was a cruel lesson in the truth of what Mike Nichols had said at the time of *Bogart Slept Here* – he simply wasn't funny. Following *Midnight Run*, De Niro would content himself with playing the straight man – not funny himself, but able to provide a foil for someone who is. It was a function he'd fulfil opposite Billy Crystal in *Analyze This* and Dustin Hoffman in *Wag the Dog* – Laurel to their Hardy, Abbott to their Costello.

Shooting *Midnight Run* was no picnic. Brest was such a demanding director that, halfway through shooting, his entire camera crew, his first assistant and a number of other crew members quit. 'Generally my instincts about who I'm compatible with are pretty good,' Brest said. 'This time, I made a mistake.'

Among the scenes interpolated into Gallo's screenplay was one in which De Niro leaps into foaming rapids and is rescued by

Grodin. In the dead of winter, all the white water in the United States was freezing, so Brest moved the unit to New Zealand. De Niro went with them, and did part of the stunt himself – less out of machismo than the demands of the script. The two men have to haggle before Grodin extends a branch to pull De Niro from the water – something a stuntman could hardly have done, since both are in medium close-shot.

After shooting *Midnight Run*, De Niro went on the road with *The Untouchables*, promoting it at European festivals in the summer of 1987.

At Deauville in France, actor Lou Diamond Phillips, claiming he had always wanted to meet the star but lacked the nerve, borrowed a bellhop's uniform and served De Niro champagne in his suite. Confronting him later in the hotel bar, he boasted of his coup. De Niro grinned and pushed a $5 bill into his hand – supposedly a tip, and a subtle putdown to the brash young actor.

In September, De Niro agreed to be on the jury at the Moscow Festival. A showcase for *glasnost*, it was showing a number of films suppressed under the old regime, including *The Deer Hunter*. Also at the festival was British director David Jones, who'd had some success with *84 Charing Cross Road*. He hoped to film another play, Stephen Metcalfe's *Strange Snow*, with a Vietnam theme that recalled *The Deer Hunter*. De Niro brought the screenplay back with him to New York.

Now that both his stepdaughter Drena and son Raphael were teenagers, De Niro included both in his social life. He escorted Drena to a tribute to Vincente Minnelli at the Museum of Modern Art, and invited both Raphael and Diahnne Abbott to the cast party for *Cuba and his Teddy Bear*, after which his ex-wife left with friends while De Niro took his thirteen-year-old son back to the TriBeCa loft for the night. Parental influence evidently wasn't enough, however, since in December 1991 Raphael would be arrested for spray-painting graffiti on a subway train.

A housemaid in Barranquilla, Colombia, who'd worked as an

extra on *The Mission* and given birth to a child in 1986, claimed a year later that De Niro was the father. He denied this vehemently, and no suit was ever filed.

Closer to home, Helena Springs continued to demand he recognise the paternity of her daughter, and provide for her. On one visit, she claimed, De Niro told the little girl, 'I'm your daddy. Give me a kiss,' and that he and the child spent the afternoon together. She also said he contributed to her upkeep, though when asked for evidence of this she explained that he always gave her the money in untraceable cash.

De Niro's relationship with Toukie Smith remained warm but distant. She continued to turn up at the public events he attended, but never on his arm, almost always arriving by herself, and leaving alone. At the post-preview party for *Midnight Run* at the Greene Street Café in New York, she seemed happy to cede the limelight to more flamboyant celebrities like Liza Minnelli, Debbie Harry, Brooke Shields – and, unexpectedly, De Niro's father, defiantly bohemian in crumpled linen suit and Borsalino hat.

Still ambitious to act, Smith pressed De Niro to help out. Through his friendship with casting director Bonnie Timmerman, she got her a small role in two episodes, 78 and 79, of the failing TV series *Miami Vice*, opposite another non-acting actress, English singer Sheena Easton. The network gave the first episode, *Love at First Sight*, a big push, running it in sweeps week of January 1988, when pollsters assess the popularity of new shows, but the series was too tired to be revived with celebrity cameos – even by more attractive ones than these – and Toukie's career never took off. Between 1985 and July 1990, she also played a small continuing role in NBC's all-black sitcom *227*.

Also in 1988, Smith became pregnant, but miscarried. Their relationship continued, although De Niro continued to pursue other partners, but in his customarily naïve style. Sometimes his choices were stars, like the singer Whitney Houston. Ostensibly he wanted her to star opposite him in a remake of the 1955 Doris Day/James Cagney melodrama *Love Me or Leave Me*, based on the relationship between twenties singer Ruth Etting and her gangster lover, Marty 'The Gimp' Snider.

John Gregory Dunne and Joan Didion had updated *A Star is Born* to the world of rock and made a fortune, so there was some merit in the idea of a version of *Love Me or Leave Me* relocated to the movie business, with De Niro as the limping lower-class Snider opposite someone like Houston.

Houston didn't care for the script, however, with its 'kept women and corrupt film-makers', as she put it, and sent it back, but De Niro kept calling. Her parents, with whom she lived, advised her not to get involved with a man who, besides being white, was almost twice her age. Record executive Clive Davis echoed this advice. For a young black singer such a relationship would be 'career suicide'.

De Niro deluged Houston with flowers, and gifts that included a teddy bear with diamond earrings. 'Yeah, he was sweatin' me,' she acknowledged, but claimed that her mother returned all his gifts. Once someone leaked details of his interest in her to the press, De Niro recoiled. With his well-publicised dislike of personal publicity he was a favourite target of *paparazzi*, which made him even more cautious about being spotted in public with any woman, particularly one of the kind he was known to find sexually attractive.

One photojournalist admitted to ABC-TV's *Turning Point* programme that, having bluffed his way into a private party by pretending to be its 'official' photographer, he shot De Niro with Sean Penn and Toukie Smith, then sent his pictures to a number of magazines with a story that De Niro lost his temper with Penn when he made advances to Smith.

'Any of it true?' asked the interviewer.

'Absolutely not,' said the photographer, laughing.

Given this situation, De Niro was cautious when he tried to meet wannabe starlet Tatiana Thumbtzen. A long-legged African-American, she achieved brief celebrity as the girl Michael Jackson pursued in the video for his 1987 song 'Bad'. When jobs didn't appear, Thumbtzen, who had signed a long-term contract with the Jackson organisation in order to get into the video, took a job checking coats at the China Club in Los Angeles. The club's owner, Danny Fried, told her that De Niro had seen her photograph in his office, and asked to meet her – an improbable story, since Martin Scorsese directed the 'Bad' video and would have known just where to find her.

Thumbtzen arrived at the club the following night for her assignation with de Niro, bringing a girlfriend for moral support, since someone had warned her that the star was 'a player' who wouldn't be shy about trying to rush her into bed. The two women waited for half an hour, wondering why De Niro hadn't turned up, until the friend, looking around the club, spotted him drinking incognito with a friend at another table.

Thumbtzen introduced herself, but De Niro, she said, 'acted as though he had no idea who I was, as though I were some anonymous fan coming over to him'. Bearing out the theory that the story of De Niro seeing her picture in the manager's office was fabricated, he also seemed, she said, 'to have no idea who Danny, the manager, was'.

As soon as Thumbtzen sat down, De Niro announced that he and his friend had to leave, but that he would give her a call.

'You don't even have my number,' she protested.

'Oh, don't worry,' De Niro said smugly, 'I've got your number.'

A few days later, De Niro took Thumbtzen to lunch in a secluded restaurant. Wearing 'goofy-looking' reading glasses, he went unrecognised. Since he seemed genuinely interested in her career, she mentioned the contract she'd signed with Michael Jackson.

After their second date, a Japanese lunch, De Niro rang her from a bungalow in the grounds of the Beverly Hills Hotel late at night and asked her to come over. It was almost midnight when Thumbtzen arrived, with her contract.

'He took it, looked it over a bit, and threw it on the couch,' she said. 'Then, all of a sudden, he turned into an octopus. His arms were everywhere.'

The rest of her description has an element of farce. Telling her that he was 'changing into something more comfortable', De Niro, she said, emerged from the bedroom in an elaborate robe, which he suddenly threw open.

'There he was, naked, flashing me,' said Thumbtzen. 'He hopped up on the bed and jumped up and down, giggling like a little boy.'

'This is ridiculous,' she said. 'Please call a cab.'

When he made no move to do so, she said, 'What would you do if there was a fire in this hotel right now?'

'Well, I guess I'd run out of here,' De Niro said.

'Wow,' said Thumbtzen, 'then everyone would say, "There goes De Niro; what a little weenie!"'

This gibe was enough. De Niro called her a cab. Some time later, they went on a last date, to see *Pretty Woman*. But the relationship ended there. 'He made me feel like a piece of raw meat,' Thumbtzen said, 'or a trophy for his collection.'

CHAPTER EIGHTEEN

The Man Upstairs

If you're a producer, all you've got is the credit and some plaques on the wall. They don't know what you do.

Stanley Motss (Dustin Hoffman) in *Wag the Dog*. Script by David Mamet and Hilary Henken, from Larry Beinhart's novel *American Hero*

While De Niro commuted between coasts, projects were developing elsewhere that would bring him back to New York, and for good.

One was *Awakenings*. In September 1987, while De Niro was in Moscow, Steven Zaillian delivered his rewritten screenplay to Penny Marshall. He had cut back the story to the relationship between Sacks and the patient he called 'Leonard L', whose recovery and subsequent decline showed dopamine's effects at their most striking. The story now focused on 'Dr Malcolm Sayer' and his star patient, 'Leonard Lowe'. In Act One, Sayer fights against bureaucracy to use the new drug. Act Two – Leonard Lowe emerges from decades of coma to become a warm and lively human being, with a budding romance. Act Three – the disease takes hold again, and Lowe sinks back into coma with a whispered 'Learn from me,' leaving Sayer to be consoled by his nurse, with whom he walks off hand in hand at the close.

Critics would charge that Sacks' collection of case histories had been transformed into a 'Disease of the Week' movie of the sort that infested network TV. Whether it traduced the original or not, Zaillian's version proved the key to 'licking' *Awakenings*. The story of an ailing person who rallies under a new stimulus and enjoys a period of delirious gratification, only to sicken and die, was as old as *Camille*. Cliff Robertson won a Best Actor Academy Award in 1968 for *Charly*, playing a retarded man briefly transformed into a genius by experimental therapy.

Marshall, who was still shooting *Big*, sent Zaillian's script to Sacks. After years of comparative obscurity, the neurologist felt overwhelmed by attention. As well as the Marshall project, his book had been turned into a stage play by the Chicago City Lit company, and he was also advising Dustin Hoffman on his role as the autistic Raymond in the forthcoming *Rain Man*.

Elsewhere in New York, Martin Scorsese was also preparing a project that would involve De Niro.

Two decades of wire-taps and revelations by informers had stripped the Mafia of its glamour. Coppola's vision of Mafia dons as modern-day Borgias whose doings had the stateliness of opera was gone, replaced by one of organised criminals as acutely *dis*organised – an agglomeration of thieves and psychopaths, paying lip-service to an antiquated code of honour while preying remorselessly on one another. Some of their shenanigans made *The Gang that Couldn't Shoot Straight* look like documentary realism.

In 1985, Scorsese, shooting *The Color of Money* in Chicago, read an extract in *New York* magazine from Nicholas Pileggi's book *Wise Guys*, subtitled *Life in a Mafia Family*, and based on the confessions of a gangster named Henry Hill, who'd informed on his friends and colleagues in 1980 in return for amnesty and a new identity under the Witness Protection Program.

When Scorsese rang Pileggi to tell him he wanted to film Hill's story, Pileggi, a fan of his films, gave him *carte blanche*, and for more than a year worked with him on the script of what would become *GoodFellas*: the title 'Wiseguys' had already been used by Brian De Palma, as well as for *Wiseguy*, a TV series with Ken Wahl and Dennis Farina.

Irwin Winkler read the *New York* extract at the same time as

Scorsese, and rang Mike Ovitz, who was handling the book. From there, it was a short step to a Winkler/Scorsese/De Niro/Pileggi package. However, when CAA approached studios for funding, almost all shied away from the project. All had memories of Scorsese's *The Last Temptation of Christ*, with its scandal and, worse in their eyes, poor box office. Warner Bros eventually made an offer, but it was contingent on Scorsese attracting a major star.

Scorsese asked De Niro, who agreed, subject to seeing the script and choosing a character. In the meantime, he had other things on his mind. He was going into the production business.

Traditionally, when directors or performers weary of Hollywood or feel excluded from it, they set up shop in a more congenial location, and coax, bribe or bully others into joining them. De Niro was no exception.

In 1989, the Martinson Coffee Building, a turn-of-the-century eight-storey red-brick-and-limestone warehouse on the corner of Greenwich and Franklin, just a few blocks from De Niro's loft on Hudson Street, was up for sale. With property developer Paul Wallace and Stuart Lane, stage producer of *La Cage aux folles* and other Broadway hits, De Niro took a 50 per cent stake in the company that raised the $7.2 million to buy it and spend that much again on turning it into the Tribeca Film Center.

Friends said De Niro hoped to re-establish the 'lively New York film-making scene of the sixties', but those with longer memories knew such a scene had never existed. Alone among film-makers, Woody Allen had established himself in Manhattan – something which, as an actor/writer/director, he was uniquely qualified to do.

De Niro simply didn't like Hollywood, and was prepared to put his career on the line to get out of it. He admitted that Hollywood encouraged the best work. 'You just come up with ideas when you're around people,' he said. 'I always tell people I work with, if you just spend time together, an hour or so, you're bound to come up with something.' But for the moment he didn't feel he could work in Los Angeles any longer. If they wanted him, they would have to come east.

The transformation of the Martinson Building indicated how De Niro wished to be perceived. The architect, Chinese émigré Lo-Yi Chan, had none of the flamboyance of I.M. Pei. He'd converted buildings at Harvard and Columbia University, and followed the same discreet tone in TriBeCa. 'He is the ultimate New Yorker,' Chan said of De Niro, 'and he wanted the building to be very New York. No Hollywood veneer. He just wanted a place he could walk into and have a great meal and make good movies.'

To pay for his new project, De Niro needed work, and took what he could get. During 1988, he starred in three features, and turned down many more, including the role of Sal, the pizza-shop owner who becomes the focus of racist riots in Spike Lee's *Do the Right Thing* – a part that went to Danny Aiello. Though all the films he did make were flops, his fees refilled his depleted coffers.

MGM's *Stanley and Iris* began life as *Union Street*, a 1982 novel by British writer Pat Barker. Barker's setting was northern England, and her characters seven working-class women living lives of drudgery and despair in an unnamed town where only an ailing steelworks and a cake factory offer work. Abortion, random violence, mental illness and suicide are commonplace. An old woman hangs herself rather than surrender to a heartless welfare system. Husbands routinely beat up their wives and brutalise their children. In the midst of this misery, the lumbering Iris King is both an answer and part of the problem. She does her best to console the despairing and protect the weak, but too often her overbearing manner leads to disaster, as when she pushes her sixteen-year-old daughter into a back-street abortion.

The director of *Stanley and Iris*, Martin Ritt, was blacklisted in the fifties for his left-wing politics, an experience that became the subject of his film *The Front*. He'd also directed the well-regarded 1979 *Norma Rae*, which won an Oscar for Sally Field's union organiser, as well as for Ritt's long-time husband-and-wife screenwriters, Irving Ravetch and Harriet Frank.

Ravetch and Frank also wrote the script that became *Stanley and Iris*, though well into production it was still known as 'Union

Street'. The project proved unlucky for all concerned: Ritt died a few months after the film was released, and Ravetch and Frank never got another screen credit.

Ritt threw out almost all of Barker's book, retaining only the idea of a woman in early middle age who helps people out, and the setting, a small town where many people work in a cake factory. Now, however, all the characters are Americans, and the town is Laurel, Connecticut – Norman Rockwell country. Barker's realism went the way of her setting and characters, replaced by a sermon on the social and personal consequences of illiteracy – an element barely present in her novel. The story also acquired a new character, Stanley, a mild-mannered worker in the cake factory canteen who happens to be illiterate.

Jane Fonda was Ritt's first choice to play Iris. She'd recently warned her agents, William Morris, that she wasn't happy with the star vehicles they were sending her, and wanted more challenging material. Seeing his chance, Ovitz lured her in the direction of CAA by promising her 'Union Street' plus De Niro and Ritt.

De Niro's motives were less high-minded than usual. He just wanted a 'go' project with a big paycheque. He didn't tax himself with delving into Stanley's character; a researcher interviewed some illiterates, and he watched her videotapes.

As played by Fonda, Iris is a widow of eight months still mourning for her husband, but forced to work in the cake factory to support her needy relatives. She meets Stanley when he saves her purse from being stolen, and after he's fired for his illiteracy, indirectly because of her – he can't read the label on the jar of aspirin asked for by his boss to cure Fonda's headache – she feels morally obliged to teach him how to read. 'Feelgood' elements were poured over the story like hot fudge sauce. Stanley, jobless, must put his aged father into a home, the excuse for a torrent of sentiment as the old man has to abandon his cosy middle-European home for the bleakness of an institution, where he dies.

Hollywood in the eighties strove to show people with physical and mental impairments not as handicapped but 'different'.

Dustin Hoffman's autistic Raymond in *Rain Man* was a mathematical genius with a flair for blackjack, while Randa Haines' *Children of a Lesser God*, based on Mark Medoff's play, suggested that deafness sharpened the other senses, and that sign language was as expressive as spoken speech. Thus, illiterate Stanley becomes a secret inventor, tinkering up gadgets in his home workshop; learning to read turns him almost overnight into an entrepreneur potentially worth millions.

'*Stanley and Iris* was a joke,' Pat Barker said, 'in the sense that my heroine – a fifteen-stone Middlesbrough housewife – was played by Jane Fonda, a woman who is famous for being slim. At the time, a lot of journalists expected me to say I was angry, but in fact I wasn't. My film agent, after watching the movie, said, "We-ell, that's Hollywood!" I can't think of a better comment.'

Stung by the accusations of mugging that would be levelled at him for *We're no Angels*, De Niro acted Stanley in a reticent, hesitant style that he would use again in *Mad Dog and Glory*. Wearing thick-rimmed spectacles, and with his hair darkened and trimmed in a shaggy crewcut with a widow's peak, he played on the variations implicit in the image of an illiterate genius, appearing at one moment stupid, at another watchful and contemplative.

This, finally, is the major fault of the characterisation. Could someone so smart have never learned to read? And surely, in forty years, he would have worked out strategies to deal with the problem of medicine-bottle labels ('I've forgotten my glasses. Can you tell me if these are aspirin?'). Stanley's problem would have made more sense had he been dyslexic rather than illiterate. But dyslexia is less curable, even by Jane Fonda.

Ritt shot most of the film in Westbury, Connecticut, with some locations in Toronto. Filming through August 1988 was complicated by Fonda's much-publicised, and still-remembered, anti-Vietnam stance. Veterans' groups picketed the production in Westbury, and were not entirely placated when 'Hanoi Jane' offered to hold a fund-raising event for victims of Agent Orange. Both Fonda and De Niro turned up for the 'Evening of Stars' at an amusement park near Westbury and posed for Polaroid pictures with their fans at $15 a time. Overall, the event raised $10,000.

After swearing he would never make another *Godfather* film, Francis Coppola announced he would direct *Godfather III*, bringing the story up to date, and embroiling the Corleone family in the scandal that had just engulfed the Vatican bank. At the conclusion, Michael Corleone is dead, and the new *capo di tutti capi* is Vincent, illegitimate son of Santino/Sonny.

Various young actors tried for this role, including Val Kilmer, Coppola's nephew Nicolas Cage, Charlie Sheen, Billy Zane and the final incumbent, Andy Garcia, but De Niro surprised Coppola, and indeed everyone, by suggesting he could play Vincent – who, according to Mario Puzo's original novel, was born around 1948, making him approximately De Niro's age. But Coppola, though he claimed to be updating the story to the present day, in fact only took it as far as the sixties, showing Vincent in his early twenties. De Niro still felt it worthwhile to fly to Coppola's California estate in the Napa Valley and read for the role, leaving the director with a conundrum – which, fortunately for him, events would solve.

In June 1988, Penny Marshall's *Big* opened to spectacular business, quickly running up grosses of $100 million. Overnight, Tom Hanks was a star and Marshall a hot director. The following October, she met Oliver Sacks for the first time at the Mount Carmel hospital to talk about *Awakenings*. They discussed who might play Leonard Lowe and Dr Sayer – a role which, as Sacks put it, 'bore some relation – but only some relation – to myself'. De Niro's name wasn't mentioned, but Marshall already had him in mind.

Two months later, United Artists released *Rain Man* to enormous acclaim. When Marshall suggested to Columbia that they might film *Awakenings*, perhaps starring De Niro, they needed little convincing.

De Niro followed *Stanley and Iris* with *Strange Snow*, based on the play English director David Jones had shown him in Moscow.

English producers put up part of the money, but the film, renamed *Jacknife*, would never have attracted even its meagre budget of $10 million had De Niro not offered to star as the eponymous main character. Even then, they had to shoot in Montreal in order to avoid high studio costs, and benefit from the Canadian government's underwriting of local production.

The producers of *Jacknife* hoped De Niro's presence would remind audiences of *The Deer Hunter*. In case it didn't, the poster line nudged their memory – 'Three Buddies in Vietnam. Two Survived. Only One is Really Alive'.

The 'really alive' survivor is Joseph Megessey, called 'Jacknife' in 'Nam, because that's what he once did to the rigs he drove as a long-distance trucker. Now a motor mechanic simply known as 'Megs', he turns up in a small Connecticut town to visit his platoon partner Dave Flanagan (Ed Harris), who's been hitting the bottle since the war ended. He and Dave weren't even particularly close. 'He was not my friend,' Dave tells his long-suffering schoolteacher sister Martha (Kathy Baker), with whom he shares a house, 'just a guy I was in the war with.'

A couple of flashbacks to 'Nam explain that neither Dave, the nervous one, nor the crazy Jacknife believed they would survive more than a few months, but that Bobby, the smart one, was expected to emerge with a medal and a commission. It's Bobby who dies, however, while both Dave and Jacknife make it through, though each is scarred emotionally. For both, it proves harder to survive the peace than the war, and the once irresponsible Megs finds peace and stability in helping out those in worse shape than himself. While his pretext for coming to Connecticut is a promise, long forgotten by Dave, to go fishing together on the first day of the trout season, he is in fact on an errand of mercy.

As the story develops, the war takes a back seat to the growing romance between Megs and Martha. Some of their dialogue has the guarded quality De Niro does well. 'Do your girlfriends come over and cook for you?' she asks over their first dinner out. 'Is that, like, a real question,' he responds, 'or are you just jerking my chain?' When Martha has to supervise the Prom at her school,

Megs shears his flowing mane, trims back his luxuriant facial hair to a moustache and turns up in rented white tux, with flowers and gifts, as her date. Thereafter, the two of them begin to coax Dave back to the sort of peace they've found.

Before *Jacknife* was even released, De Niro had taken on another film role, also in Canada, though this time in Vancouver, the west-coast city that was attracting more and more runaway American productions with its attractively wooded if often chilly locations.

We're no Angels was a project he'd nursed along for years, ever since he saw the 1955 comedy of which this was a remake. That in itself was odd, since De Niro loathed Humphrey Bogart, whose role he would play. The dislike was so deep-rooted that, when the film was released, Paramount's publicity staff ordered journalists not to bring up Bogart's name, since De Niro would refuse to answer questions about him: 'Mr De Niro doesn't like to speak ill of anyone, living or dead,' they explained.

Despite this drawback, De Niro had suggested to Art Linson that, after the success of *The Untouchables*, a version of *We're no Angels* written by David Mamet and starring himself might maintain their creative momentum. With the Capone film making healthy profits, Linson had no trouble raising the $20 million budget from Paramount. Thereafter, however, the project never faltered on the road to disaster. In retrospect, De Niro's decisions about *We're no Angels* foreshadowed his future as a producer, a job for which he showed little aptitude, since the combination that had worked so well on *The Untouchables* failed catastrophically.

The 1955 *We're no Angels* was a genial comedy/romance, directed by Michael Curtiz with his customary professionalism. In the French penal colony of Devil's Island, three of the more domesticated murderers stroll out through the front gate and hide in the store of Leo G. Carroll until they can stow away on the next supply ship from France. Played by Bogart, Peter Ustinov and Aldo Ray, the trio become indispensable to the incompetent shopkeeper and his family. When Carroll's cousin, Basil Rathbone, arrives from France to go over the books, they dispose of him, and act as Cupid to Rathbone's son and Carroll's daughter.

Mamet found nothing to like in the original, and changed everything. Instead of tropical Cayenne, the story takes place on the chilly border between the US and Canada in the mid-thirties. The three convicts become well-meaning Ned, his dumb pal Jim, and the brutal Bobby, who disappears early on, and only turns up as a *deus ex machina* at the end. Far from ambling out of the front gate of a prison that looks more like a holiday camp, the three bolt from a nightmare facility where sadistic guards impose the will of a relentless warden, intent on trying out the still-unperfected electric chair on a richly deserving Bobby.

The shopkeeper has disappeared. Instead, Jim and Ned exchange clothes with a couple of priests, and are mistaken for theologians by the monastic community of a small border town where a weeping statue of the Madonna has attracted attention. With Bobby skulking in the woods and the warden guarding the bridge that offers the only escape route to Canada, Jim and Ned are forced to carry on their imposture.

Plot and setting were grim, and became grimmer when Irish director Neil Jordan took over the project. Used to writing his own screenplays, Jordan didn't care for Mamet's. His direction exacerbated the dankness and chill, the brutality of the jail and the sourness of the locals.

Linson and his star also dictated much of the casting, normally the director's prerogative. Ray McAnally, in what would be his last role, glowered effectively as the warden, and Demi Moore did what she could with Molly, a disgraced single mother to whom Ned takes a shine. De Niro played Ned, and gave the role of Jim to his friend Sean Penn, lately in the news, and in prison, for attacking pressmen following his divorce from the singer Madonna.

That a competent comic team could get laughs with this sort of story would be proved a few years later when Robbie Coltrane and Eric Idle played similar roles in *Nuns on the Run* and Whoopi Goldberg in the *Sister Act* films. Woody Allen also proved with his 1985 *The Purple Rose of Cairo* that Depression realism could cohabit with comedy. But *We're no Angels* offered squalor without humour, and the unfunny spectacle of two straight men look-ing for a comic. Penn played Jim as sullen and stupid, while De Niro, as always when out of his depth, mugged, sneered and grimaced – a performance described by the *Los Angeles Times* as 'four or five comic glowers, and variations on wary, disguised hostility'.

Work continued on the Tribeca Center. Living just round the corner, De Niro was ideally placed to keep an eye on the recon-struction. On Super Bowl Sunday, he located the workers taking a break in a local bar to watch the game on TV, and rousted them out and back to work.

The more complex demolition work had to be done on Sun-days, when streets were clear, and incensed locals posted signs complaining of the noise. Dust filtered into the streets, and the rats that had long lived in the cellars emerged into the sunlight. Locals christened them 'Robertos'. One irate neighbour killed a few dozen with a baseball bat and laid the corpses at De Niro's door.

The ground floor was becoming the Tribeca Bar and Grill, with furnishings from the defunct Manhattan club Maxwell's Plum, and paintings on the walls by Robert De Niro Sr. A sev-enty-seat mixing theatre for recording film soundtracks occupied the second floor. Distributors Miramax bought the third, and, in an intra-company deal, De Niro purchased the top four floors for Tribeca Productions. Various friends rented space on the fourth floor at rates ranging from $1500 to $5000 a month. De Niro was so anxious to find tenants that he'd stop acquaintances on the street and pitch the merits of this new space.

The bar and grill attracted many more celebrity investors than did the office space. Going into the food business was an eighties showbiz fad, though high-water marks of earlier enthusiasms could be seen on fading frontages around Manhattan, where personalities as miscellaneous as Joe Louis and Rodney Danger-field had tried and failed to make it as bar and café owners. Truly successful actor entrepreneurs like Fred MacMurray and Fess Parker bought real estate and kept their names off it, but the 'Me' Decade of the seventies offered too many temptations, particularly to entertainment personalities. Elements of show and performance were more in evidence in a restaurant than in, say, a shopping mall. And investing in food had a certain ironic appropriateness to the decade when cinemas began to earn more from selling Coke and popcorn than from the movies they screened.

Steven Spielberg and Francis Ford Coppola invested in one or more cafés, a group of stars led by Bruce Willis and Sylvester Stallone put their names to the ill-fated Planet Hollywood chain, and Mikhail Baryshnikov, Bill Murray, Sean Penn and Christopher Walken all became partners in De Niro's Tribeca Bar and Grill. Madonna received a guided tour as well, but decided not to invest. Barbra Streisand was ready to sign until she found that, under New York law, anybody selling alcohol had to be fingerprinted. She refused to accept this threat to her civil liberties.

To run the restaurant, De Niro went into partnership with Drew Nieporent, who'd opened the successful Montrachet in 1985, and had once been a waiter at Maxwell's Plum. Massive, genial, bearded, as devoted to ostentatious outfits as any Oriental potentate, Nieporent nudged De Niro away from the Hollywood prime-rib-and-Zinfandel image. It wasn't always easy. While making *Jacknife*, De Niro had eaten at Stelle in Toronto, which served an exotic Thai-Italian cuisine. He flew the whole New York kitchen staff to Canada for a demonstration. The chef put on a spectacular show of his methods, but Nieporent, while applauding his expertise, murmured to De Niro, 'This isn't us.'

Undeterred, De Niro flew in chef Nobuyuki Matsuhisa from Nobu, the restaurant named for him in Los Angeles, to advise on a possible sushi bar. De Niro had been introduced to Nobu four years earlier by Roland Joffe, and always thought of him as the ideal chef for the Tribeca Grill. Matsuhisa spoke almost no English, but this didn't deter De Niro or Nieporent. Matsuhisa didn't contribute to the Tribeca Bar and Grill, but in 1994 De Niro and Nieporent opened Nobu in New York, with Matsuhisa as chef.

*   *   *

Penny Marshall started serious discussions with De Niro about *Awakenings* early in 1989. It was the worst time for him to think about new projects. Renovation estimates for the Center had proved too low, with the restaurant alone devouring $3 million. Though twenty-three people had signed up as partners, contributing a total of $2.8 million, that still wasn't enough. New investors had to be found, and it wasn't until July that De Niro felt sufficiently committed to meet Oliver Sacks.

Marshall offered De Niro the choice of Lowe or Sayer. He chose the former. Not that the decision could have been hard to make. Leonard was the kind of transformative role in which he excelled. Even better, the film would be made in New York. As an added sweetener, Columbia offered to install the production office in the Center.

De Niro also got a say in casting. He suggested Shelley Winters to play Leonard's gentle and attentive mother. Winters, however, had lost none of her self-importance, and when she began dictating terms, Marshall replaced her with the mouse-like Ruth Hudson. He was luckier in offering the role of Sayer/Sacks to Robin Williams, whose *Dead Poets' Society* had been released in June, proving that he could carry a non-comic role and do so without ad-libbing. Williams read the screenplay on a transcontinental flight, and, he said, wept so copiously the cabin staff thought he was ill.

De Niro visited Mount Carmel repeatedly to quiz Sacks. He learned that Zaillian's script had little to do with reality. The experiments with L-Dopa didn't always work, and when they did, its effects were unpredictable. Some of Sacks' patients recovered completely, others not at all, while many retained some residual symptoms.

With his intelligence and Harvard education, Leonard L. hadn't been a typical L-Dopa patient. Though paralysed except for very slight movement in his right hand, he'd been able to communicate through a Ouija board even before the L-Dopa treatment, and had carried on long conversations with Sacks and his nurses by that method. A tireless reader (providing someone turned the pages for him), he wrote long and intelligent book reviews for the hospital newspaper.

Once the L-Dopa took hold, however, Leonard's delight quickly gave way to what Sacks called 'painful, unsatisfiable appetites and desires'. He developed messianic delusions, and announced in his diary, 'I have Risen. I am still Rising. From the Ashes of Defeat to the Glory of Greatness. *Now* I Must Go Out and Speak to the World.' He bombarded newspapers and even the White House with letters, and begged Sacks to set up a lecture tour for him.

At the other end of the spectrum, he became obsessed with sex. In the first flush of recovery, he'd kissed the flowers in the garden and doted charmingly on the nurses. Soon, however, he was masturbating repeatedly, often in public, and harassing any woman who came within reach. 'Mr L. passed from a gentle amorousness,' wrote Sacks, 'to an enraged and thwarted eroto-mania. [. . .] He asked me if I could arrange for various nurses and nursing aides to "service" him at night, and suggested – as an alternative – that a brothel service be set up to meet the needs and the hungers of DOPA-charged patients.'

Some younger victims of the sleeping disease survived in a London clinic, and in August 1989 De Niro flew there with Sacks to meet them. 'He spent many hours talking with these patients,' Sacks wrote, 'and taping them (he always liked to make research tapes which he could study at length). This was the first time I had actually seen him with patients, and I was impressed and moved at his powers of observation and empathy . . . He ap-proached them as an artist and actor, as someone determined to make an accurate portrait, determined to *become* an accurate portrait.' De Niro also discovered Ed Weinberger, a vigorous venture capitalist struck down by Parkinson's Disease at forty, who began to design new and radically innovative pieces of furni-ture. Playing Leonard, De Niro mimicked Weinberger's symp-toms with what Weinberger called 'uncanny precision'.

Once De Niro became absorbed in his research, he shut Sacks out. 'Bob is very intelligent,' says Sacks, 'but he doesn't feel like talking much. He often says, "Shut up, let me feel it." This happened with one patient who is a very articulate, rather verbose Parkinsonian who said, "I have this freezing. I have seven different forms of freezing, let me enumerate." And he started to count, and Bob said, "No, I'll stay the weekend." And in fact he spent the next thirty-six hours non-stop with this man, observing all seven forms of freezing and observing him awake and asleep, alone and with others.'

Awakenings was shot through Christmas and New Year of 1989/90, using the same state mental hospital in Brooklyn where Milos Forman had filmed *One Flew Over the Cuckoo's Nest* in 1975. Public health being low on the priority of government spending, the hospital was in the middle of a gang-war zone, with gunfire heard most nights, and actors were ferried to and from the location under tight security. A surreal element was added when patients, who watched inordinate amounts of TV, hailed both Williams and Marshall by their names as sitcom characters – 'Hey, Mork,' and 'Hey, Laverne.'

Immersed in his role, De Niro lived the part, becoming just one more shuffling, dead-eyed inhabitant of the prison-like institution. Around the cast and crew, the life of the hospital went on, a regime of medication, incarceration, desperation. Sometimes the sound of screaming and shouting filtered into the soundtrack. However, none of this appears in the completed film.

Williams and De Niro knew at first hand something of what the real patients were going through. Both actors were prone to a cycle of elation and depression, and had experienced the paranoia induced by cocaine. Sometimes, role and real life intersected, and people were hurt. On *Awakenings* it was De Niro, whose nose was broken in a scuffle with Williams. In the official version, Williams/Sayer, struggling to subdue De Niro/Leonard in one of his manic fits, swung an elbow too vigorously, and smashed De Niro's nose. De Niro ordered the cameraman to keep on filming, and finished the scene before he got treatment. Rumours flew that the two men had really fought, but both denied it.

The Hollywood mill rounded off all the sharp edges of Sacks' case histories. A Randy Newman score of Copland-esque folksiness emphasises the essential good nature of even the film's ritual 'heavy', the hospital superintendent, yet another thankless role for John Heard, who would repeat it in Marshall's *Big*. The staff, not malevolent but simply unaware, rally handsomely once they realise that Sayer is on the right track, even handing over their paycheques to buy more L-Dopa.

The hospital assumes a sunny aspect which belies the stories of howling inmates and sirens in the night; that Anton Furst, the designer, would go on to the baroque splendours of *Batman* is nowhere evident in these spacious, well-polished interiors. He shows his hand only once. Sayer consults Max Von Sydow, who first identified the source of the malady in the early 1920s, and the old doctor screens 16mm films of his experiments in which white-robed victims lurch, stare and freeze in grotesque poses – a few truly Gothic Tim Burton-ish minutes.

Williams as the uncombed, nervous Sayer is the star of *Awakenings*. De Niro receives first billing for what is essentially a character performance, if a particularly flamboyant one, which extracts the maximum effect from Leonard's stares, tics and spasms. He might have done much with the real Leonard's mania and priapism, but neither is allowed to show itself, so Leonard, during the twenty minutes of screen time he spends in remission, is simply dull.

Before the Center was fully converted, De Niro consulted Scorsese on someone to become head of Tribeca Productions. He recommended Jane Rosenthal, who'd worked at Warner Bros and Disney, and been the executive in charge of *The Color of Money*, his 1986 sequel to *The Hustler*. Scorsese joined Tribeca in 1988, with initial responsibility to create a 'slate' of future productions.

Awakenings had just finished principal photography on 24 January 1990 when Tribeca Productions unveiled its slate. Rosenthal had compiled what looked like a respectable list, though anybody who knew the business saw it was stronger on optimism and promise than solid investment.

Most of the projects were 'in association' with Hollywood studios, sometimes jointly with other independents like Robert Redford's Wildwood Productions or the faltering mini-major Tri-Star, which agreed to pay $1 million a year towards the overheads of the Center in return for first refusal of their productions. TriStar collapsed shortly afterwards, however, and the majors would only come good on their promised investment in projects once Tribeca had developed a screenplay and coaxed a director and cast to commit.

Old pals figured prominently, as they did in the tenancy of the Tribeca Center – though, significantly, Martin Scorsese was not represented in either case, preferring to maintain his own down-town Manhattan headquarters. George Gallo had written an untitled comedy that was under consideration at TriStar. Another comedy, 'The Battling Spumonti Brothers', promised to pair De Niro and Danny De Vito, one of whom would probably direct it. Dustin Hoffman was also scheduled to star with De Niro in 'Gold Lust', an original screenplay by Robert Collector and Dana Olsen. Arnon Milchan would produce a feature by documentarist Bill Couturie, for whose Oscar-winning *Dear America: Letters Home from Vietnam* De Niro recorded part of the commentary. 'Stolen Flower' was a drama about a child kidnapped by a South American porn ring. Chris Menges, cameraman on *The Mission*, was down to direct 'Thunderhearts', about an FBI agent, played by Val Kilmer, sent to infiltrate a conspiracy of Native Americans, who finds he's part Indian himself.

Tribeca also proposed a series of short dramas for cable TV, and a number of cheap – i.e. under $5 million – features, mostly from first-time directors. They included an adaptation of William Least Heat Moon's narrative of travelling the backroads of America, *Blue Highways*. Joan Tewksbury would direct her own screenplay of the book, with an improbable Cheech Marin, formerly of the dope-crazed comedy double-act Cheech and Chong, in the lead.

Top of the list, however, was *Mistress*, a black comedy about the movie business that would mark the directorial debut of De Niro's old friend Barry Primus. Years before, as Primus struggled to find money, De Niro told him, 'If no one else does it by the time I start my company, I'll do it.'

These promissory notes were falling due, now that De Niro had hung out his shingle as a producer. He'd told actor Chazz

Palminteri something similar when he saw *Tales of the Bronx*, his one-man show about growing up in a mob neighbourhood. A number of producers wanted to film it, and bidding had risen to $1 million. Palminteri refused all of them, since none would allow him to star.

'Bob looked me in the eye,' Palminteri says. 'I'll never forget it. It was at the Bel Air Hotel, and he said, "If you make it with me, I will make it right." He said "*fucking* right", if you really want to quote him. He said, "You will be in it. I will protect you. You will write the screenplay."'

To do it 'right', De Niro felt he had to direct the film himself. As Jean Renoir said, everyone has only one story, and this was De Niro's – an older person takes responsibility for a younger and/or weaker one. In this case, a local mob kingpin 'adopts' the son of a Bronx bus-driver who has refused to inform on him to the police. Father and surrogate battle over the boy as he grows up. The story resonated with De Niro's own experience with his father, and their clash over his involvement, however peripheral, with the gangs of Greenwich Village.

But not every studio was eager to fund a first-time director, even if it was De Niro. *The Untouchables* had grossed $76 million and *Midnight Run* $38 million, but the worthy but dull *Jacknife* lost all but $2.2 million of its $10 million investment, and *We're no Angels* grossed a little over half its $20 million cost. The studios' hesitation was an omen for the future of Tribeca, which the Los Angeles-centred film industry would always regard as an upstart.

CHAPTER NINETEEN

A Made Man

> *I refuse to answer on the grounds that it may tend to incriminate me.*
>
> Conventional plea of witnesses standing on their rights under the Fifth Amendment to the Constitution of the United States of America

As soon as he finished *Awakenings,* De Niro went on to *Good-Fellas.* The *Godfather* films had given a falsely glamorous picture of organised crime in America, and *GoodFellas* did no less. In five drafts of their screenplay, written over a period of five months, Nicholas Pileggi and Scorsese transformed Henry Hill into a kind of American hero.

The real Hill was no hero. From his school days, he was involved with the Brooklyn Mafia family of a gangster named Paul Vario, whose protégé he became. Vario even arranged to terrorise the local mailman out of delivering letters from the School Board detailing Hill's truancy. For thirty years, Hill stole and extorted in Vario's service until, hooked on cocaine and involved in an increasingly retributive feud which had already killed off many of his partners in a major theft, he informed in return for anonymity for himself and his family.

When Pileggi met him in 1980, he was in the Nassau County Jail, facing a life sentence for his involvement in a massive narcotics conspiracy. 'The federal prosecutors were asking him about his role in the $6 million Lufthansa German airlines robbery, the largest successful cash robbery in American history. The New York City Police were in line behind the Feds to ask him about the ten murders that followed the Lufthansa heist. The Justice Department wanted to talk to him about his connection with a murder that also involved Michele Sidona, the convicted Italian financier. The Organised Crime Strike Force wanted to know about the Boston College basketball players he had bribed in a point-shaving scheme. Treasury agents were looking for the crate of automatic weapons and Claymore mines he had stolen from a Connecticut armoury. The Brooklyn District Attorney's office wanted information about a body they had found in a refrigerator truck which was frozen so stiff that it needed two days to thaw before the medical examiner could perform an autopsy.'

Hill was just a guy of average intelligence and literacy who happened to be an unrepentant career criminal – 'a mechanic', in Pileggi's words, 'who – literally – knew where the bodies were buried'. This appealed to Pileggi, who, as he confessed in his book, 'had gotten bored with the egomaniacal ravings of illiterate hoods masquerading as benevolent Godfathers'.

Scorsese too enjoyed Hill's contrast with Coppola's larger-than-life characters. *GoodFellas* inaugurated a trilogy of crime films in which he depicted the criminal world as far less monolithic than in the *Godfather* films, and more subject to the general rules of life in the United States. *GoodFellas*, *Casino* and *Gangs of New York* would have none of the darkness or operatic solemnity of Coppola and Leone. The first two at least would be shot less like *Once Upon a Time in America* than a Rock Hudson/Doris Day romance of the sixties, with pastel decor, a rock/pop score, and, at the core of the narrative, the story of three friends making it in the world of organised crime.

Ten years earlier, De Niro might have played Hill himself. Both were children of an Italian father and an Irish mother, and they had been born within a few months of one another. But Scorsese saw Hill as a mirror image of the young, upwardly mobile professionals of the sixties, a yuppie with a gun and a noseful of cocaine. Resigned to a lesser role, De Niro suggested that Scorsese talk to the little-known Ray Liotta, having seen him in a tiny role as Melanie Griffith's off-the-wall boyfriend in Jonathan Demme's *Something Wild*. Liotta's boyish brashness struck just the right note. Read by Liotta as a cheerful voice-over, Hill's recital of his criminal exploits made the whole business sound like a lark. 'As far back as I can remember,' he says at the start of the film, 'I wanted to be a gangster. To me, being a gangster was like being President of the United States.'

De Niro agreed – during a five-sentence conversation, Scorsese says – to play one of the two older musketeers to Hill's d'Artagnan. His character, James Conway, was based on Jimmy 'The Gent' Burke, who educated Hill and became his mentor and confederate until they fell out over the division of the Lufthansa spoils. Knowing that Conway was planning to have him murdered, as he'd murdered almost all the other members of the robbery gang, was Hill's primary motivation to turn informer.

And yet Burke had an innocent charm. 'To watch Jimmy Burke tear through the cartons of a newly hijacked trailer was to watch a greedy child at Christmas,' wrote Pileggi. 'He would rip into the first few stolen crates until his passion to possess and touch each of the stolen items abated. When Jimmy was unloading a truck, there was almost a beatific contentedness glowing on his sweat-drenched face.'

The third partner was more sinister. Plainly psychopathic, Tommy DeSimone would kill even close friends over some trivial betrayal. Pileggi never physically describes DeSimone, who was in real life 180cm tall, but Scorsese always saw his character, Tommy DeVito, as the diminutive and compact Joe Pesci. With the casting of Pesci came DeVito's characterisation as a little man, always alert for a slight, and ready to avenge it with a homicidal attack. In one of the film's most disturbing scenes, he picks up on a casual remark by his friend Hill that he's 'funny'.

'Do you think I'm "funny"?' DeVito says, expressionless.

Having seen him kill someone in a bar over just such a chance remark, and shoot a waiter with even less reason, we know the conversation could end in murder. Then, just as abruptly as it began, DeVito reveals with a grin that he's just joking – this time.

A continuing theme of *GoodFellas* is whether or not a gangster is 'made', i.e. part of a Mafia 'family'. Hill is barred because of his half-Irish parentage. Nor does DeVito qualify, though he still hankers after the honour. His final error is to kill a 'made' man during one of his rages. Members of the victim's 'family' tell DeVito they are going to admit him. He's so pleased that he doesn't realise he's being driven to his death.

The killing of DeVito gives De Niro one of his best scenes in the film. In Pileggi's account, Conway received the news on a public telephone, which he put down so hard that the booth shook. De Niro goes further, slamming the phone hard and repeatedly until it shatters – the actor's familiar rage kicking in, with its usual electric effect.

In general, however, Burke is a supporting role. Liotta and Pesci have the most flamboyant scenes, in particular the opening, where Hill introduces us to his world by showing how he impressed his new girlfriend – and, eventually, wife – by taking her to the Copacabana nightclub. Arriving through the kitchen, he leads her, and us, along corridors and into the crowded club, where a table appears miraculously as Hill keeps up a running commentary on the various Damon Runyon-esque criminals also present that night.

Pesci, oozing menace like sweat, gives the film's central performance, which rightly won him the Best Supporting Actor Oscar the following year. By comparison, De Niro's characterisation of Burke, an elder statesman with slicked-back greying hair, makes little impression. The film's publicists tried to raise its profile by claiming that Conway, then in jail, rang De Niro to say how well he'd played him, but De Niro denies they ever spoke.

The mob, however, knew very well how they were depicted on screen. Henry Hill told Scorsese that, years before, gang boss Tony Vario, who never left his house, was physically dragged to the cinema by his friends to see *Mean Streets*.

De Niro's scenes were shot in a relatively short period, and

Scorsese was able to have *GoodFellas* ready for release in September 1990, ahead of *Awakenings*, which opened briefly in December in order to qualify for the Academy Awards. The sentimental audience at which it was aimed wept quarts at Leonard's emergence from catatonia, and gallons as he returned to the dark, murmuring, 'L-l-learn from me.' Critics were less susceptible, particularly De Niro's *bête noire*, Pauline Kael, who trashed both main performances, calling Dr Sayer 'another of Robin Williams's benevolent-eunuch roles', and noting of De Niro, 'It's in the quiet moments that he's particularly bad.' The film took $52 million, however, going some way to restoring De Niro's commercial standing.

For the rest of 1990, De Niro divided his time between supervising the completion of the Tribeca Center and working on two more films, neither of them among his greatest work.

After many years as a producer, Irwin Winkler decided to break out as a director, and announced he was making a film about the Hollywood blacklist.

Guilty by Suspicion began life as an original screenplay by Abraham Polonsky, adapted from his novel *A Season of Fear*. Polonsky was a legend of the anti-Communist blacklist. An uncompromising socialist, he co-wrote the cynical boxing film *Body and Soul* in 1947 and co-wrote and directed *Force of Evil* in 1949, a meditation on the corruption endemic in modern life as symbolised by the all-pervasive 'numbers' racket, an illegal lottery controlled by the gangs.

Named as a Communist in the early fifties, Polonsky refused to inform on fellow believers, and left for Europe. In 1956 he wrote *A Season of Fear*, a novel about the blacklist in which the victim is a civil engineer with the Los Angeles Department of Water and Power. He returned to America in the sixties and in 1985 adapted the book into a screenplay, a copy of which found its way to Irwin Winkler. Between 1985 and 1989, Polonsky developed it for Winkler, then fell out with him and abandoned the script, which Winkler rewrote.

The new version, retitled 'Fear no Evil', then 'Dark Shadow', and finally *Guilty by Suspicion*, focused not on a civil engineer but on David Merrill, a successful movie writer/director for Twentieth Century-Fox's Darryl Zanuck. Merrill has been working in Europe for two years, following the collapse of his marriage. Arriving back in Los Angeles, he is initially amused to hear that a colleague has named him as a Communist in his testimony to the House Committee on Un-American Activities; his entire flirtation with left-wing politics consisted of attending a couple of Party meetings in the thirties.

At first, Merrill can't believe such charges are taken seriously. Then he finds he can't get work. Both Zanuck and his attorney urge him to inform. He's asked to return a $50,000 advance, his best friend begs to be allowed to name him in his testimony, and a fellow director, Joe Lesser, pauses on his way out of the country to warn him that things will get worse. He is even fired off the only film he can get, a cheap five-day western. Only his ex-wife offers practical help. Called before the Committee at last, he refuses to inform, saving his honour, if not his career.

De Niro says he read the screenplay, which he assumed Winkler had written alone, as a favour, and only offered to play Merrill after he'd become involved with the characters. Scorsese came on board to play Joe Lesser, the director based on Joseph Losey, who found work in England and France after being blacklisted. Another blacklistee, producer/director/actor Sam Wanamaker, played Merrill's lawyer. Annette Bening was Merrill's compassionate ex-wife.

Winkler retained Joan LaCour Scott, widow of blacklisted producer Adrian Scott, as 'technical advisor'. 'Abraham Polonsky took his name off the script after they mangled it,' says Scott. 'The rewritten script as first shown to me was credited to Irwin Winkler, who went on to be credited as the writer *and* producer *and* director – not a good idea. De Niro and Annette Bening co-starred in the movie, which not even De Niro could save.'

In truth, De Niro wasn't trying too hard. A new curly hair-do and some fifties suits were the extent of his characterisation, which friends felt came close to his off-screen persona: polite, reserved, ordinary.

De Niro disclaimed any knowledge of or feelings about the blacklist, except to say he 'wondered how he would have reacted in those circumstances'. Nobody appears to have explained the gestation of the script or Polonsky's involvement in it, nor would one expect De Niro to have taken much interest if they had. The little political activity to which he put his name has always been motivated by friendship, not conviction. He would campaign behind the scenes for Bill Clinton during the Monica Lewinsky scandal, and appear on stage, along with Scorsese, escorting the ageing Elia Kazan – who *had* informed on others to the House Committee – when he received his honorary Academy Award in 1999. (Asked what *he* thought about Kazan being thus honoured, Abraham Polonsky said, 'I'll be watching, hoping someone shoots him.')

In 1990, De Niro took up with a new woman, British fashion model Naomi Campbell. Just turned twenty, the 175cm Campbell had been discovered at fifteen while shopping in London's Covent Garden market. Since then, her slouching walk and pouting glare had become fixtures of international catwalks, while the tabloids chronicled her explosive temper and restless ambition to be something other than a high-priced clothes horse. In 1988, she became the first black woman to appear on the cover of American *Vogue*. To De Niro, she seemed the most desirable of trophies, while Campbell, with her hopes of stardom in other fields, looked on De Niro with interest.

For some time, their romance remained clandestine, De Niro preferring not to impair his relationship with Toukie Smith. They met in secluded locations like the island of Saint-Barthélemy, in the Caribbean, though anonymity eluded them even there. The couple were dancing at the Lafayette Club when a woman snapped a picture. De Niro demanded her camera. When she claimed she was only photographing her family, he said, 'If that photo ever gets published I'll find out who you are.'

Campbell would have preferred more publicity, not less, and resented sharing De Niro with Smith. When he spent a night with Toukie, Campbell, according to rumour, phoned in a false alarm of a fire in his apartment. Sooner or later, Campbell, not known for reticence, was certain to let the cat out of the bag – as she did, with dramatic results for De Niro and Smith, in 1992.

Backdraft was another potboiler – almost literally so, since the subject was the fire service. Director Ron Howard was under no illusions about De Niro's reason for accepting the role of fire investigator Don Rimgale. 'De Niro was paying off the buildings that he bought in New York, so occasionally he would have to look around and take a job,' says Howard.

Rimgale was far from the centre of Gregory Widen's screen-play, which dealt with dynastic conflicts between two generations of Chicago firefighters, the MacCaffreys. Kurt Russell played Stephen, the heroic fireman whose father had died in the service. William Baldwin was Brian, his younger brother, more anxious to get laid than burned. The conflict between loyalty to tradition, family and the team vs private life and individual achievement is catalysed by a series of sophisticated arson attacks. How these are engineered is explained to Brian by Rimgale, a tough old snoop with the burns to prove it.

Rimgale all but disappears after the film's first half-hour, though De Niro does have one memorable scene, not surprisingly played against another old pro, Donald Sutherland as arsonist Ronald Bartel. Concerned to keep Bartel off the streets, Rimgale turns up at his parole hearing. Insinuatingly probing, he prizes off the scab of contrition the firestarter has so carefully created to fool the board, revealing the festering psychosis underneath.

De Niro's asking price, even for a small role like this, was now $7 million, which Howard and producer Brian Grazer were happy to pay. 'I'm sure this was a money job for him,' says Howard, 'and we were thrilled to have him. No one was forcing him to do anything. He could have phoned it in if he had wanted to. But he came down for a week of rehearsals and research and he requested an additional week at no extra compensation because he thought he was learning something.'

In Chicago, De Niro visited burned-out buildings and sat in on the autopsy of a fire victim. He also spent time with three investigators, one of them the man on whom Rimgale was based. 'I slowly saw him build the character in front of me,' says Howard. 'He took one guy's posture, another guy's phrasing, and a bit of another guy's attitude. He was just drawing from all of them. He doesn't do accents or things unless the part calls for it. He's just Robert De Niro – but he isn't really. There's something about him which is just a little different each time.'

In September, *GoodFellas* opened to the best reviews either Scorsese or De Niro had enjoyed for years. It also grossed $46.38 million in the US domestic market, a respectable success, though not a hit – the film remained too raw for the teenage market. Scorsese and De Niro had an inkling of the possible public reaction when they previewed the film in the Los Angeles suburb of Sherman Oaks. 'People got so angry that they stormed out of the theatre,' says Scorsese. 'They thought it was an outrage that I'd made these people so attractive.' Vincent Canby in the *New York Times* called it 'evilly entertaining'.

GoodFellas even took a little criticism from organised crime. Lawyer Bruce Cutler, attorney for New York crime boss John Gotti, New York's 'Teflon Don', so named because nothing ever stuck to him, called the film 'a government propaganda movie. It makes a hero out of paid government witnesses, pokes fun at everybody in the movie, trivialises terrible acts of violence.' At the same time, Cutler acknowledged that Gotti hadn't actually seen the film. 'He is too intelligent to waste his time to see nonsensical movies like that.' Ironically, a few years later, De Niro would make Gotti and his downfall the subject of a Tribeca production.

GoodFellas was a solid enough success to put Scorsese's career back on track. In December, *Awakenings* came out. Again, the reviews were hearteningly unanimous. Even so, it made only a little more at the box office than *GoodFellas*.

The apparent anomaly of a performer who was at once among the most sought-after in the business and the least profitable was elucidated by *Backdraft* producer Brian Grazer. 'Everybody wants Robert De Niro. He hasn't had many hits, but he represents quality and integrity and you want to be associated with that. Also, if you're a producer who actually cares about movies and really likes telling stories, and loves film, then you want to be able to say, "I worked with Robert de Niro." You want to be able to say that to your kids, or your friends, or even to yourself in the mirror. It's kind of nice. He's a piece of film history and having him in your movie is like a hallmark, a seal of approval if you like.'

Grazer also noted the effect of De Niro's presence on other performers. 'They feel they are working with one of the great actors, so it elevates their performances. It also helps in marketing the movie for a producer. If we didn't have De Niro, then the other three or four star names wouldn't have added up quite as much.'

When the Academy Award nominations were announced early in 1991, they reflected De Niro's ambiguous standing in the film industry. Both *Awakenings* and *GoodFellas* were nominated as Best Picture. De Niro was nominated as Best Actor for *Awakenings*; Joe Pesci as Best Supporting Actor, Lorraine Bracco as Best Supporting Actress and Scorsese as Best Director for *GoodFellas*; *Awakenings* for Best Screenplay; and *GoodFellas* for Best Editing. In terms of numbers, however, the lion's share of nominations went to the directorial debut of actor Kevin Costner, the frontier drama *Dances with Wolves*.

In March, before the Oscars were announced, De Niro's career was celebrated in one of the tributes often accorded to people whom the industry feels have been unlucky either at the box office or in the Academy Awards. If an honorary Oscar isn't appropriate, they are honoured by one of the quasi-official film bodies, like the American Film Institute, the Directors' Guild of America, or, as in De Niro's case, the American Museum of the Moving Image.

Taking place at the Waldorf-Astoria in New York, the event, uneasily pitched between celebration and 'roast', had more than artistic significance. The AMMI, after seeking a home in Los Angeles for decades, had taken over the old Astoria film studios in Queens. The studios themselves were sold off to a developer, with one building retained as a museum. It opened in 1988, and needed friends in the film business. Honouring De Niro, a key player on the New York film scene, was no more than prudent.

De Niro turned up in person for the ceremony, in deference to the presence of New York Mayor David Dinkins and John Kennedy Jr. Guests included plenty of old friends, like Elia Kazan, Christopher Walken, Sean Penn, Aidan Quinn, Jeremy Irons, Joe Pesci, Harvey Keitel and Martin Scorsese.

How seldom De Niro attended such events was underlined by Charles Grodin in his speech. Joking about how often he stood in for De Niro at award functions, he said, 'I received the D.W. Griffith Award this week, for Best Actor – for Bob! Tonight I'm here – for Bob! Tomorrow I'm flying to Anaheim to accept another award – for Bob!'

De Niro managed a joke to start his speech. 'I consider myself too young for these kind of tributes. They should be given to guys like Al Pacino or Dustin Hoffman.' After this, his comments were more personal, and more sombre. Harking back to his lack of education, he called the event 'the prom I never went to and the graduation I never had'. He paid tribute to his parents, in particular his father, whom he called 'a painter who wished his work would end up in a museum', then ended, puzzlingly, 'I feel the same way not just about my films but about the things from my films.'

Listeners thought he meant the ideas that his films represented, but De Niro was referring to his accumulated props and costumes, which he'd continued to hoard, and which now needed an entire apartment to house. He'd pledged to deposit the collection with the Museum, though they wouldn't take delivery for another eight years, by which time it would total 2,600 costumes and five hundred props and items of make-up. Making the most of its De Niro connection, the Museum incorporated him into its karaoke exhibit where visitors can mime to famous movie lines. Six-year-old girls snarl 'Are you talkin' to me?' as Travis Bickle draws his gun on himself in the mirror.

When the Academy Awards were announced, the only winner from either *GoodFellas* or *Awakenings* was Joe Pesci – being honoured, most people felt, as much for his slapstick performance as a bumbling burglar in *Home Alone* as for *GoodFellas*. De Niro attended the ceremony, and even appeared on stage to introduce a clip from *Dances with Wolves*, reading the text tonelessly from a Teleprompter. MC Billy Crystal remarked deadpan, 'Mr De Niro gained seventy-five pounds to do that introduction.'

Though *Dances with Wolves* was the night's big winner, the Best Actor award went, unexpectedly, to Jeremy Irons for his performance as Claus von Bulow in *Reversal of Fortune*. Once again, De Niro emerged as one of the most respected but lowest paid and least honoured stars in the business.

Warners had held off releasing *Guilty by Suspicion*, to take advantage of any publicity fall-out should De Niro win the Best Actor Oscar. Lacking any such impetus, the film grossed a modest $9.4 million. In May, *Backdraft* grossed $77 million, evidence, if it were needed, that the teenage male audience wanted hairy-chested drama with action oozing from every pore.

Robert Mitchum had long been the hero of the new generation of actors in the 'American style'. His sleepy, snake-like stare and ambling walk, the rumbling voice and effortless way with a cigarette, gun or woman, were imitated, with varying degrees of expertise, by thousands of ambitious male leads, and admired by directors, who wondered how to capture the easy menace he exhibited in films like Jacques Tourneur's 1947 *Out of the Past* or Jack Lee Thompson's 1962 *Cape Fear*.

Cape Fear derived from a 1957 novel, *The Executioners*, by John D. MacDonald, one of the first writers to make his reputation with the cheap original paperback crime novels that started appearing in the late forties.

MacDonald wrote about a lawyer, Sam Bowden, who, posted to Australia during World War II, gave evidence against an American soldier, Sergeant Max Cady, accused of a brutal rape. Fourteen years later, Cady turns up in Bowden's home town in the South, where he's an unambitious attorney with a wife and three kids. Cady's mere presence is a threat, but Bowden can't do anything, since he's broken no law. As Cady's menace becomes more palpable, Bowden contemplates taking the law into his own hands. In the end, he and a policeman friend set up their remote home as a trap. Cady breaks in and kills the cop, but is shot dead.

J. Lee Thompson's 1962 film starred Gregory Peck as Bowden and Robert Mitchum as Cady. Screenwriter James Webb, who wrote the screenplay on commission from Alfred Hitchcock, initially supposed to direct it, widened the scope of MacDonald's novel from simple vigilantism, emphasising the element of sexual threat. Instead of MacDonald's Cady – 'about five nine, wide and thickset . . . more than half bald and deeply tanned, and he looks as though you couldn't hurt him with an axe' – theirs is an ambling six-footer with a good ol' boy manner and a taste for big cigars. He feels he was wrongly convicted, which in his eyes gives him the right to rape someone without penalty. He chooses Bowden's teenage daughter. Webb set the story in North Carolina so that he could use the name of a local beauty spot, Cape Fear.

Played by Robert Mitchum, Cady became at once menace and sex object. Bowden's wife and daughter are as much fascinated as terrified by him, and Bowden feels that not only his safety but his masculinity is threatened. Giving the role of Bowden to Gregory Peck, a symbol of integrity, further complicated the reaction of the audience, who were invited to reassess the hero of *To Kill a Mockingbird* as someone who would set a trap for a potential killer, with his wife and daughter as bait.

Cape Fear became a benchmark for the directors of New Hollywood. In particular Steven Spielberg wanted to film his own version of it (though surely no director was less well-suited psychologically to do so) and in the late eighties commissioned a screenplay from Wesley Strick. Strick admits he 'consciously styled it a bit for Steven Spielberg's sensibilities. There were a lot of "movie movie" moments, and some cute touches of Americana. It was a bit antiseptic.'

Among the independent producers De Niro and Jane Rosenthal approached to enter into joint ventures with Tribeca was Spielberg, whose production company Amblin remained a separate entity within Universal. Of the projects they discussed, the one which attracted De Niro most was *Cape Fear*, so Spielberg and Strick came to New York to talk it over.

'He seemed interested,' Strick said of De Niro, 'though he hadn't really committed. He got Marty Scorsese involved. He and Steven together sort of twisted Marty's arm – relentlessly, from what I gather.'

De Niro staged a reading of the script for a few friends, including Scorsese, who was finally convinced, mostly by Spielberg, who suggested a new version of *Cape Fear* could inaugurate a long-term contract for Scorsese at Universal.

Once he took on the project, a joint venture with his company Cappa Films, Amblin and Tribeca, Scorsese told Strick to weed out the feelgood moments inserted in the script for Spielberg, in particular one where Bowden and his family enjoy a sing-song round the piano. Spielberg, his commercial instincts offended, asked only that all the Bowdens remain alive at the climax – Hollywood would forgive much, but not the lack of a happy ending. 'You can have anything up to that point,' he told them. Strick and Scorsese took him at his word. Their *Cape Fear* would be at once a tribute to the gaudy pulp tradition from which it sprang and a moral updating, bringing it into line with nineties sensibilities.

The new script piled on several new layers of plot. Bowden, played by Nick Nolte, is no innocent country lawyer but an ex-public defender who represented the then-illiterate Cady in his trial for rape and battery. Repelled by the crime, Bowden 'buried' a report showing that the victim was promiscuous, which would have shortened Cady's sentence. Cady went to prison for fourteen years, where he learned to read, studied law, and discovered how he'd been railroaded. Released, he returns to town a tattooed, cigar-chomping, Bible-quoting psychopath with an intimate knowledge of the law, and his eye not only on Bowden's unsatisfied wife (Jessica Lange) and fourteen-year-old daughter (Juliette Lewis), but the flirtatious law clerk (Ileanna Douglas) with whom Bowden is contemplating an affair.

In a mounting spiral of violence, Cady poisons the Bowdens'

dog, rapes and batters the law clerk, demolishes the three thugs Bowden hires to drive him out of town, goads Bowden into threatening him and has him accused of assault, then follows the family to their houseboat, moored at Cape Fear, where he kills their maid and a private detective, and almost disposes of the Bowdens, who finally come together as a family to kill him.

The film was a conscious homage to Hitchcock, for whom the first version had originally been written. De Niro admitted, 'We spent a lot less time reconsidering the *Cape Fear* film from 1962 than we did watching many of the old Hitchcock classics, which were truly our inspiration here.'

Scorsese emphasised the resemblance to the original by recycling Bernard Herrmann's score. Elmer Bernstein, who adapted and re-recorded the music, was just one of the old pros recruited to give the film a sense of sixties movie values. In many shots, the sky is optically tinted orange or an ominous purple to recall the artificiality of classic Technicolor. Fireworks fill the sky, as in Hitchcock's 1955 *To Catch a Thief*, and the scene where Bowden spots Cady watching him and his family from the other side of the street during a 4th of July parade was inspired by *Strangers on a Train* (1951), where the heads of people watching Farley Granger play tennis turn metronomically to follow the ball, while that of his nemesis Robert Walker remains fixed on him.

Hitchcock designer Henry Bumstead did the decor, and the cameraman was Freddie Francis, veteran of numerous British horror films. At its best, the film has all the menace of their best work. At its worst, it's a collation of cheap horror-film effects, an anthology of bang and flash, with shock cuts, slamming doors, over-recorded sound and random violence. Frequently, Scorsese over-reaches himself, and the homage to Hitchcock becomes more like one to Brian De Palma's Hitch pastiches. The visual trick where the background figure of Bowden's maid turns out to be Cady wearing her clothes could have come from De Palma's *Dressed to Kill*.

The acting saves *Cape Fear*. Cameos went to Mitchum and

Peck, and to Martin Balsam, who had also been in the first version. Jessica Lange is provocative as Lee, Bowden's unfulfilled wife, and Juliette Lewis, though an indifferent actress, is good casting as Danielle, the hoydenish daughter with a marijuana habit, drawn inexorably to the sexuality of Cady's evil.

But De Niro's performance as Cady dominates the film, as much a thing of bang, flash and shock as the movie itself. No villainy is omitted; if a spoonful is good, the whole bottle is better. Tattooed with Bible texts and symbolic representations of retribution like scales, bolts of lightning and, somewhat incongruously, a clown with a smoking pistol, Cady is also, from the evidence of the books in his cell, both a Nazi *and* an admirer of Josef Stalin, not to mention a bodybuilding masochist and serial rapist.

Attacked and wounded, he spouts religious cant like blood. Reeling round a parking lot after being beaten by three hired thugs, and beating them in return, he raves with frightening confidence, 'I am like God, and God like me. I am as large as God. He is as small as I. He cannot above me, nor I beneath Him be'; then, like any autodidact, he pedantically credits his source: 'Selatius, seventeenth century.' At such times, he genuinely does seem more than human.

As Hal Hinson wrote in the *Washington Post*, 'Cady isn't merely a psychopath, he's a Nietzschean superman, the cruel, killing hand of justice meting out a stern, remorseless form of punishment. Every movement, every narrowing of his eyes, is a threat. Pulling his face into obscene, leering grins, he gives Cady a kind of goofy suavity, especially in the long, mesmerisingly languid scene in which he sweet-talks Danielle into his confidence.'

Scorsese stages this scene with sinister glee, setting it in a high-school theatre, with Cady sitting in the doorway of a cottage appropriate to a production of *Hansel and Gretel*. After telling Danielle he's from 'the Black Forest', he gives her a hit on his marijuana cigarette, an oral intimacy that intensifies as he kisses her, and puts his thumb into her mouth. She sucks it with pleasure, and we're in no doubt that, if he chose, she would willingly do the same to his penis.

The part of Danielle was written for a conventionally innocent teenager, but Lewis, though only seventeen herself, recognised its possibilities, and worked with Scorsese and De Niro in rehearsal to raise its erotic temperature. 'It was great because Marty allowed me to really create something,' she says. 'On the first day of shooting I thought, "OK, this is why I'm in this business."'

The film's three elements, erotic, comic and religious, fuse at the climax, where, having captured the Bowdens on their boat, Cady extracts from Bowden an admission that he railroaded him into jail. Bawling verbatim extracts from the legal code and the law on lawyers' responsibility, he's a manic parody of the legal system – even more so when he characterises their situation as 'just a couple of lawyers discussing a case'.

Scraps of autobiography fall from Cady as he lurches in pursuit of the Bowdens. He can't enjoy sexual gratification unless he beats and debases his partner – a legacy, it's hinted, of the repeated anal rape he suffered in prison. His assault on Lori Davis begins with handcuffing her hands behind her back. Then he bites a chunk out of her face, beats her up, breaking her arm, and submits her to forms of penetration so terrible that she can't bear to enumerate them in court, and flees town.

His mother belonged to a fundamentalist sect in the North Carolina hills. 'Granddaddy used to handle snakes in church,' he says. 'Granny drank strychnine. I guess you could say I had a leg up, genetically speaking.' At the moment of his death, neck-deep in the swirling river with his leg chained to a fragment of the Bowdens' wrecked houseboat, he begins to babble in tongues.

Strick's screenplay shrewdly builds up Cady's manic motives for assailing Bowden and his family. He's not only revenging himself but redeeming Bowden by 'teaching him something about loss', as he says in his initial threat. His attacks aren't random. Rather, he systematically robs Bowden of everything he values, in the hope that he will confess his sin and be forgiven. Each act of violence is justified by a biblical quotation.

It had been some time since he had worked hard enough to 'earn the right' to play a character, but Max Cady is a classic

De Niro creation. To master the accent, he studied tapes made with actual prisoners from the same region as Cady. Rumours circulated that he paid $5000 to have his teeth look bad for the role, then had to pay even more to restore them. If so, the work doesn't show. Physically, he made few concessions to the role, except to step up his exercise regime to develop the necessary muscles, slick back his hair, and develop a taste for massive cigars. Yet Cady is De Niro's masterpiece of transformation. Most of the change, however, takes place inside – the De Niro that's new to us is the maniac grinning out from behind the familiar face.

Unfortunately, the performance is too big for the film. It belongs, as many critics remarked, not in a thriller but a horror movie. Cady has the inexorable stride and unopposable strength of the Mummy, and the protean menace of Freddy Krueger from the *Nightmare on Elm Street* films. Burned and beaten, he surges back tirelessly, even, at one point, clinging under the Bowdens' car as they flee to Cape Fear. Eventually, the character becomes ludicrous in his malevolence and imperviousness to assault – Frankenstein's monster with a Southern accent, an aloha shirt and a cigar.

CHAPTER TWENTY

Rabbit in a Maze

The whole thing is for younger people who are sexy and youthful.

De Niro on acting, *New York Times*, 1993

1991 inaugurated a decade which would not only be De Niro's busiest professionally, but also his most frustrating. Film after film earned hostile reviews and/or mediocre returns. His personal life too would veer from clandestine to catastrophic, with the actor in and out of court and the tabloids.

The successful release of *Cape Fear* in November should have been a good omen, but it was followed almost immediately by his son Raphael's arrest for spraying graffiti on two subway train carriages. In March 1992, both De Niro and Juliette Lewis were nominated for Golden Globes and Oscars for their work in *Cape Fear*, but neither won.

Meanwhile, Irwin Winkler, hopeful of improving on *Guilty by Suspicion*, raised money from the Italian Penta group to direct another project with a McCarthy-ist connection.

When American director Jules Dassin relocated to London in 1949 after his own blacklisting, he resourcefully transposed the *film noir* world of dark, wet streets and desperate men to the English capital and made *Night and the City*. Hollywood writer Jo Eisinger adapted the novel by Gerald Kersh, who wrote about the underside of British society with cynical authority.

Richard Widmark and Gene Tierney were imported to star as

small-time hustler Harry Fabian and his devoted but despairing mistress Mary. Fabian survives by steering punters to Soho clip-joints, while having an affair on the side with the wife of club-owner Francis L. Sullivan. But then he stumbles on a potential source of cash – professional wrestling, featuring Gregorius, an ageing star who also happens to be the father of gang boss Herbert Lom. Confident that Lom's loyalty to his father will protect him, Fabian sponsors a world-class bout, only to have Gregorius die of a stroke. Abandoned by everyone, Fabian is crushed like a roach by Sullivan and Lom.

At a French festival where Winkler was showing *Guilty by Suspicion*, a critic suggested remaking the film. Richard Price, Scorsese's scenarist on *The Color of Money*, updated the Eisinger/Kersh story and shifted its setting to New York. Fabian became an ambulance-chasing personal-injury lawyer, wrestling was changed to boxing, and the Lom character metamorphoses into entrepreneur 'Boom Boom' Grossman, whose ex-pug brother Al Fabian befriends. When Al dies, Fabian's enemies, as in the first film, destroy him.

Winkler reunited the team of De Niro and Jessica Lange from *Cape Fear*, with Lange as Helen, wife of Fabian's best friend Phil, owner of the bar where he hangs out. The equivalent character in Dassin's film, played as a floozy by Googie Withers, wants her own place and tries to manipulate Fabian into finding the money and getting the necessary licence. But in Winkler's film Helen is also Fabian's girl, the character originally played by Gene Tierney. We're invited to see her as venal and loving at the same time – a trick Lange can't pull off.

Even surrounded by old pros like Cliff Gorman as Phil, Jack Warden as Al Grossman and Alan King as Boom Boom, De Niro couldn't bring Fabian to life. He fell back on gestures and tics from other roles, in particular Rupert Pupkin. Grinning, dodging and weaving, Fabian resembles the boxers he recruits for his bouts, even to the extent of delivering a speech reminiscent of Brando's 'I coulda been a contender' aria from *On the Waterfront*. Deciding that Fabian's movements should have an element of dance, Winkler put a tiny radio receiver in De Niro's ear and repeatedly fed him Chris Montez's song 'Let's Dance' – a disastrous idea, soon abandoned.

With Stella Adler, De Niro had learned the Method trick of basing a character on an animal. Fabian, he decided, was 'a chicken, but with its head cut off. Or a rabbit darting through a maze, literally running amok. He's not a party animal, he's a city animal.' Method gurus hooted at the misuse of the technique, not to mention the mixed metaphors, while others wondered where De Niro, raised in Greenwich Village, had ever seen a decapitated chicken.

Immediately after *Night and the City*, De Niro went into the first true Tribeca Productions film. Technically, that honour belonged to *Thunderheart*, which had been on the initial Tribeca slate, but the project was sold to Columbia, to be directed by Michael Apted. De Niro and Tribeca received credit, but had nothing to do with the production.

Mistress was another matter. Directed by De Niro's friend Barry Primus, it had been nursed along for a decade by Primus and his collaborator John Lawton, who incorporated into the plot all their experiences of trying to raise money in Hollywood. Primus even directed a short film, *Final Stage*, to demonstrate his ability behind the camera.

De Niro believed sufficiently in his friend to show the screenplay to other producers over the years, though none wanted to invest money in a satire about Hollywood, a notoriously chancy genre. Once Tribeca was up and running, however, De Niro decided to find funds for it, and to take a role as well.

Mistress is exactly the kind of debut film one expects from a small company. Resolutely non-Hollywood, indeed anti-Hollywood, with no major stars except De Niro, no overt romantic interest, no violence, but high literary content and a weary cynicism about its subject, it announced defiantly that its producers would make their own way. In short, it was a calamity, not only itself doomed to fail, but foreshadowing the failure of Tribeca in general.

Critics almost groaned at the opening credits, a pan over a

modern oil painting to flaccid music by Galt MacDermot, one of the composers of *Hair*. Even worse, the first shot shows director/screenwriter Marvin Landisman (Robert Wuhl) watching a 16mm print – not even a videocassette – of Jean Renoir's *La Grande illusion*, a gesture redolent of the fifties. Within a few minutes, De Niro and Tribeca had nailed their counter-cultural colours to the masthead.

The story that unreels is funny enough, but jaded in its view of everyone involved in the movie business, even its putative hero Landisman. A failed director clinging to the fringes of Hollywood, he supports himself making astrology videos for public-service TV. When Jack Roth (Martin Landau), a broken-down producer desperate for a project, unearths one of his screenplays, Landisman is still enough of a believer to go along with him, even though his potential money-men only want roles for their girlfriends.

In the end, there are three backers, gambler Carmine (Danny Aiello), retired clock merchant George (Eli Wallach) and racquet-ball club entrepreneur Wright (De Niro). All of them want their girls in the film, and all in the starring role. On the side, Carmine and Wright are both sleeping with one of the women, black actress Beverley (Sheryl Lee Ralph), while the young screenwriter also takes up with George's girl.

On top of this, Landisman has his own hidden agenda, extending back seven years to when his second feature was aborted after his star (Christopher Walken, even more moon-struck than usual) committed suicide on camera. By making the new film, which, not coincidentally, concerns an artist committing suicide rather than compromise his principles, he hopes to exorcise the ghosts of that disaster, and move on. Inevitably, the project collapses in a blizzard of recriminations.

De Niro contributes a brisk but shallow characterisation as Evan Wright, the globetrotting Armani-clad businessman whose pragmatism blows away the fantasies of Roth and Landisman like cobwebs in an icy draught. He's researched every detail of their miserable lives, and, over lunch, catalogues their bankruptcies, poverty and general failure. It's less the details that chill them than the way Wright ignores etiquette and discusses their dismal histories in public. On their incredulous faces one can see written, 'But this is *Hollywood*. You don't *do* that!'

Wright also spots Roth's clumsy attempts at a swindle with amused contempt. 'I use the same trick in my own contracts,' he says, 'but I thought I was doing business with a better thief than this.'

All the more unlikely, then, that Wright would be so easily wound round the little finger of the assertive Beverley. When he attempts to thwart her, she murmurs, with ominous seductiveness, 'I'll make you regret it – and you know I can.' Wright's response is to hover indecisively around her, too vain to give in and too besotted to leave. A good director might have known how to extract this performance from De Niro, but Primus had no chance.

In the spring and summer of 1992, De Niro's personal life once again became the stuff of headlines. Naomi Campbell was less and less reticent about discussing their affair. In January 1992, she'd given an interview to the English *Hello!* magazine in which, asked whom she was in love with, she responded, 'Robert De Niro. I'm not going to deny it any more.'

In May, they spent a week at the Ritz in Paris, slipping into their fifth-floor suite unnoticed, De Niro disguised by an unusually short hairstyle and horn-rimmed glasses, and Campbell dressed as a man, down to a fake moustache.

De Niro was already planning his directorial debut with *A Bronx Tale*, and Campbell badgered him to let her play the role of Jane, with whom its teenage hero falls in love. Campbell, tall and black, met all the requirements for the role save one – she couldn't act. De Niro's refusal to cast her further cracked an already fragmenting relationship.

Meanwhile, Helena Springs, now divorced, returned to Los Angeles, and demanded that De Niro acknowledge paternity of Nina.

De Niro was in Vancouver shooting an adaptation of Tobias Wolff's novel *One Boy's Life*, with British director Michael

Caton-Jones. His co-stars were Ellen Barkin and the young Leonardo DiCaprio, who was proving a handful. Nevertheless, he arranged for Nina to be flown there, accompanied by his assistant Robin Chambers, and they spent a weekend together.

The renewed contact warmed the relationship, which made Springs even more insistent on formalising De Niro's paternity. He started paying $5000 a month towards Nina's upkeep. All this was too much for Toukie Smith, who made it clear that her relationship with De Niro was most definitely at an end.

Every major distributor turned down *Mistress*. It had the bad luck to collide with Robert Altman's *The Player*, which opened in April 1992 and attacked many of the same targets. Even if they didn't resent the anti-Hollywood satire, most distributors found the story tortuous and were depressed by the epilogue: though Landisman's wife begs him to abandon the movie, move to New York and teach theatre, he clings to his hopes. He's screening *La Grande illusion* yet again when Roth rings. He's having lunch with a possible backer tomorrow, and if he could only come along . . .

After a long pause, Landisman says, 'What time?'

De Niro lamented that theatre-owners only wanted 'high concept' movies – genre pictures with clearly drawn characters and strong plots. 'I thought that someone like Barry Primus,' he said, 'who is a real artist, who really cares and is compassionate about people, should have more than the right to direct his own film compared to some people who are hacks and who do movies time and time again and they make money, enough money to keep moving from job to job, and they have nothing to say.'

Some people believed that De Niro had himself fallen into this category with many of his recent choices, but were too circumspect to say so. As one distributor admitted, 'No one will say anything negative about [*Mistress*] on the record because they don't want to jeopardise future deals.'

Tribeca eventually gave the film to Henry Jaglom, the wealthy independent director/producer who'd created an *ad hoc* network of smaller cinemas, unaligned with the majors, through which he filtered his own films out to the public. It was an admission of defeat.

De Niro had barely finished shooting *This Boy's Life* when the Springs paternity case broke in March 1992. Apparently thinking the result a foregone conclusion, he agreed to a blood test that would, he assumed, confirm his parenthood. To the astonishment of everyone, it proved negative.

De Niro called Springs to tell her the news. She was incredulous. He *had* to be the father, she insisted – though she had, she admitted, slept with one other man during the time she was seeing him. Asked why that man's blood hadn't been tested, Springs claimed he'd since died in a boating accident. Just to be sure, De Niro submitted to two more tests. They confirmed the first.

In May, De Niro's lawyers received notification that Springs would fight the case anyway, and had retained famed 'palimony' lawyer Marvin Mitchelson.

In a suit brought by the long-time companion of actor Lee Marvin, Mitchelson had established the principle that people in enduring relationships, even if not legally recognised, incurred the same financial responsibilities as did marriage and parenthood. De Niro's payments to Springs over the years, argued Mitchelson, and his long-standing interest in Nina constituted an enforceable relationship. He demanded that De Niro increase his monthly payments to $15,000. Since De Niro wasn't prepared to admit anything, the case was set down for hearing later in the year. Until then, De Niro kept paying $5000 a month.

A *New York Times* journalist who suggested to De Niro that he was acting in quickie productions to pay for his property purchases received a snarled, 'You know the answer to that, so don't even ask the question.' And indeed, it was hard to see any other reason why he should have taken on John McNaughton's *Mad Dog and Glory* in the summer of 1992.

Following *Cape Fear*, Martin Scorsese contracted with Universal to produce one film a year. The first, on which he took co-credit with his then wife, Barbara de Fina, came from an original screenplay by Richard Price, who had also adapted *The Color of Money*.

Mad Dog and Glory confronted De Niro for the first time with the new generation of film performers who'd trained in television rather than acting schools. They had none of his interest in transformation. If a director wanted them to look different, it was his job to do so with costume or lighting. Few felt like grappling with a challenging accent, and if they did so, it was generally badly. Like the stand-up comedians they most resembled, these performers made their living from being just what they appeared to be. Compared with Eddie Murphy, Arnold Schwarzenegger, Bruce Willis and Sly Stallone, De Niro looked like Laurence Olivier in bronze.

Bill Murray was an offbeat but interesting choice for the role of gang boss Frank Milo in *Mad Dog and Glory*, since his character drives the story. A graduate of *Saturday Night Live*, he worked harder than most to shake his comic image. After an unhappy try at drama in a 1984 adaptation of Somerset Maugham's *The Razor's Edge*, he'd settled on a tone of mocking seriousness masking a fundamental misanthropy. Murray characters didn't like people, but never said so to their faces. Bile was disguised as banter. It was a style that had worked for Walter Matthau and would function just as effectively for him.

By comparison, De Niro's character, Wayne 'Mad Dog' Dobie, is a cipher. An inoffensive photographer for the Chicago Police Force – his nickname is meant sarcastically; anybody less rabid would be hard to imagine – he saves Milo from a murderous young criminal. Grateful, but at the same time resentful of owing his life to a cop, Milo invites him to his club to hear him do his stand-up act mocking the Mafia.

That could have been the end of it had the club's barmaid Glory (Uma Thurman) not caught Dobie's eye. Quixotically, Milo sends her around to be his plaything for a week. But they fall in love, whereupon Milo, delighted to have Dobie in his debt, offers to sell her to him. When he can't raise the money, the two men duke it out on the street.

De Niro was offered his choice of the two main roles. Unde-
cided, he held a reading for the director, producer Steve Jones,
and Martin Scorsese. De Niro did both parts consecutively, and
those listening told him he carried more conviction as Dobie.
Murray inherited the flash role of Milo, and walked away with
the film.

Mad Dog and Glory is *Pretty Woman* from the seamy side.
De Niro is as dull as Richard Gere was glamorous, and, where
Julia Roberts was optimistic and resourceful, Uma Thurman
whines – not without reason – at the misfortune which has caused
her to sell herself to Milo to settle her brother's debt. The result
may be closer to life, but not to entertainment.

For the next year, rumours circulated that De Niro and the
leggy, lanky Thurman, then on the rebound from her marriage
to English actor Gary Oldman, were lovers. In 1994, the tabloids
announced that the couple, instead of appearing at Cannes to
promote their respective films, had checked into a Paris hotel. A
publicist claimed that the two 'became very good friends while
working together. They see each other when they're both in New
York. They have never dated but they like to joke and pretend
they are lovers to confuse the press.' De Niro a joker? Eyebrows
were raised.

So prolific was De Niro at this time that three of his films would
open in 1993, two of them, *Mad Dog and Glory* and *This Boy's
Life*, within a month of one another, in March and April.

Tobias Wolff's autobiographical *This Boy's Life* had kicked
about Hollywood until it came into the hands of Art Linson,
who recognised some similarities to *Alice Doesn't Live Here
Anymore* and commissioned that film's screenwriter, Robert Getchell, to adapt it. Like the teenage boy in *Alice*, the young Wolff
had locked horns with the man his mother chose to take up with.
In Wolff's case, however, the mother was too weak to defy her
new husband, Dwight Hansen, when he decided to sever his
stepson's association with local juvenile delinquents.

These were themes De Niro knew well from his own childhood,
and he instantly related to the script. Wolff, then teaching college

in Syracuse – another De Niro connection – was astonished when he decided to quiz him personally. 'He arrived carrying this enormous notebook,' said the writer. 'It was filled with about two hundred observations about Dwight which he had noted while reading the book. De Niro was interested in the tiniest, smallest detail about the man. What did he wear when he came out of the bathroom? Did he walk around the house naked? Did he wear a T-shirt? He wanted to know everything, accumulating details like a scholar.'

De Niro flew to Los Angeles to read with the ten actors under consideration to play his stepson. 'When the last actor finished,' recalled Art Linson, who videotaped the auditions, 'Bob reached for a phone, made two quick calls, moved to the door, and said, "I like the kid who was second to last."'

The boy was Leonardo DiCaprio, and the recordings confirmed De Niro's judgment. 'The tape revealed to us a sensitivity that watching the reading live never did,' said Linson. 'Bob's decision was made without hesitation; his instincts were impeccable.'

On the Vancouver locations, De Niro, despite his personal problems, was just as meticulous, trying on two hundred jackets before he found one which seemed right for the character, and spending hours mastering the macho way Hansen snapped a Zippo lighter open and closed.

It was harder to deal with the seventeen-year-old Leonardo DiCaprio. 'I think Michael [Caton-Jones] liked me', DiCaprio recalled. 'Then I had the big meeting with De Niro. I read a scene with him. To make an impression, I yelled some of the lines in his face. I was a smart-ass in a lot of ways. Very overconfident.'

Caton-Jones called him 'a smart-mouthed little fuck', the general opinion at the time. When DiCaprio interrupted a scene between De Niro and Ellen Barkin, Barkin told him to behave himself, as they were doing. DiCaprio retorted, 'Let's see. On the one hand, he did *Raging Bull*. On the other hand, you did *Switch*. And *you're* the one who is telling *me* what to do?'

De Niro's performance as Dwight Hansen was among his most complex in a decade, and in a better film might have revived his tarnished reputation. But *This Boy's Life* shows him as little more than a demagogue. As the *Washington Post* put it, 'De Niro is torn from the pages of the *Scouting Handbook* and *Reader's Digest*, with a Gary Larsonesque twist. He hates Democrats and homosexuals. In his eyes, the fist is mightier than the pen; and he's full of such expressions as "Shut your piehole." To him, DiCaprio is a lily-livered wimp who needs toughening.'

If one were looking for ironies in De Niro's life, there were plenty during 1992 and 1993.

The man whose childhood left him fundamentally preoccupied with the duty of a father towards his child was in court trying to extricate himself from his supposed responsibility for a ten-year-old daughter. At the same time, he'd just finished a film about the touchy relationship between a rebellious boy and his bullying stepfather, while preparing another film in which two men, one the real father, the other a surrogate, fight about who is to influence a boy. Then, in the middle of this emotional minefield, De Niro's own father would die.

A Bronx Tale, De Niro's first film as a director, grew from *Tales of the Bronx*, the one-man show by actor Chazz Palminteri, which in turn developed from a ten-minute monologue Palminteri had prepared for acting classes at the Theater West company in Los Angeles.

Born Calogero Lorenzo Palminteri in the Bronx in 1952, Palminteri was a bulky, tall man with the frame of a leg-breaker. He'd done small parts on Broadway and played thugs in a few Hollywood movies but hadn't yet made his mark as the gunman/playwright in Woody Allen's 1994 *Bullets Over Broadway* when De Niro heard him do *Tales of the Bronx*, taking all eighteen roles himself.

Palminteri's story takes place in the Fordham neighbourhood of New York, around East 187th Street, starting in 1960. Calogero is nine, the son of a bus driver, Lorenzo, who believes in living honestly and working hard. When Calogero sees someone killed on their street by the local gang boss, Sonny, he won't inform on the killer. Sonny takes the boy under his wing, to the fury of his father, who warns him off. For the rest of Calogero's adolescence the two men skirmish over his fate, until he becomes old enough to decide for himself

'From the moment I did the show,' Palminteri says, 'everybody wanted to make the movie. But the reality was, they didn't want me. I was offered $250,000, and though I only had a few hundred dollars in the bank at the time, I said, "I want to be in it, and I want to write the screenplay." They said, "No," and I said, "Forget it."'

On the eve of *Tales of the Bronx*'s transfer to New York, the top bidder told Palminteri, 'Sign this contract and you'll have a cheque for a million dollars tomorrow.' Palminteri asked, 'Am I in it?' Told that he wasn't, the actor refused. 'If the play bombs,' they told him, 'the cheque may not be here when you get back.' Palminteri replied, 'If it's a hit, you might end up paying more. Better get me while I'm cheap.'

Sonny was a more thoughtful figure than the mobsters in *GoodFellas*. Palminteri gives him some ideas from Macchiavelli's *The Prince*, and the same weary sense of history that informs the ageing Don Vito Corleone in *The Godfather II*.

Palminteri says, 'My father always told me, "It takes a lot more strength to get up in the morning and go to work than it does to pull a trigger."' Such worthy sentiments aren't on the same level as Macchiavelli's musing on whether it is better for a prince to be feared or loved, and it's always Sonny who has the best lines.

An inter-racial love story takes up the second part of the film, with Calogero besotted by Jane, a tall black girl from his school. Knowing De Niro's taste for such women, most people assumed he'd added it for the film, but it was in fact in the original play, as was the death of Calogero's friends when a Molotov cocktail attack on a black hangout goes wrong.

De Niro was a lot more forthcoming about the mechanics of acquiring and directing *A Bronx Tale* than he had ever been about any acting role. 'I wanted to do something for a long time, and I wanted to really write something, but I felt I hadn't found anything and I couldn't sit down and write. I had ideas; I'd always be making notes about things, but I just couldn't have the discipline to sit down and write.

'So the years are going by and I figure I better start doing something. As soon as I started Tribeca, Jane Rosenthal and I talked very seriously. I said, I have to direct a movie, so we have to make a concentrated effort to find something. Meanwhile I just heard indirectly through my trainer that somebody told him about *Tales of the Bronx*, so I told Jane about it and said, "When you're in California, go see it." She went to see it and told me, and the proviso of Chazz's was that he'd be in it because he really wrote it for himself. I said I don't want to come into a situation where I'm being given certain ingredients that I haven't chosen myself, so I don't know if I'd be interested.

'And I saw it and I liked Chazz very much and we talked a bit backstage, and I asked him, "Can I see a screenplay?" And he said, "Yeah, OK." This was a long process of months, we kept talking about it. Somewhere in there he said, "You know I have to play Sonny." I said, "That'll happen. Let me just have a reading of it at Tribeca, just to get a little bit closer idea of what it all is."

'So we sat around and had a reading, and I watched it with other people whose opinions I respected, Jane Rosenthal and so on, and I decided that I would do it and I told Jane I'd do it, 'cause as I was watching I was saying, I gotta do it; it's all unknown, it's all uncertain – you gotta just jump in and take a chance with it. So I committed to it; I said I just have to finish my other obligations so we'd have to wait a few years.'

De Niro didn't mention that his own son, eighteen-year-old Raphael, read the part of Calogero. He may have hoped to play the role himself.

Someone who made no secret of wanting a role in the film was Naomi Campbell, who saw herself as Jane. She had been taking lessons with voice coach Sam Chwat, who had helped De Niro with Max Cady's accent. When it came down to it, however, De Niro wouldn't compromise his film. It was, he told the press, 'a professional decision which had no bearing on their personal relationship', but within a few weeks Campbell was being seen on the arm of Adam Clayton, of the Irish rock band U2, whom she later married. When Campbell did finally made her film debut in 1996, in Spike Lee's *Girl 6*, her performance bore out De Niro's instincts. She was dreadful.

De Niro decided to take the role of the father. 'It would help get the movie made more easily,' he reasoned. '[The other actors] will be unknowns as far as I'm concerned. It's a good part for me to play, because I'd never done that type of thing, you always expect me to do the part that Chazz is playing.'

He asked advice from other actors who'd directed themselves, like Danny De Vito and Jack Nicholson, but mainly about technicians. He was more interested in what Palminteri had to say. 'Bob is a very collaborative person,' Palminteri says. 'He said, "You must be on the set even when you're not acting." Usually the writer, he gets a cup of coffee, he says hello, then they come and get him out of here! But Bob insisted that I be there. I was involved in the casting, I was involved in the locations, even at the end of the movie I was ready to go back to Los Angeles, and he said no, I want you to stay here and be involved in the editing, which was amazing. I was involved in the mixing at the end, which was really incredible.'

Palminteri also helped on casting, particularly the role of Eddie Mush, a minor criminal whom Sonny regards as a jinx. When Mush bets on a horse at the racetrack, Sonny tears up his tickets, even before the race is run: if Eddie Mush likes the horse, it has no chance.

De Niro, according to Palminteri, 'loved the character of Eddie Mush. We were having trouble casting the role, we could not find the character, it's such a strange character. Here's a guy who's been a born loser all his life. He's a jinx, and we had trouble casting this part. And it was Bob's idea, he said to me, "Where is the real Eddie Mush?" I said, "Well, he's probably in the neighbourhood still losing bets." So he said, "Let's find him." And we go down and there he was, with the *Racing Form*. This guy has done this all his life. He's been running from loan sharks, borrowing money, paying the other guy, so then when we finally cast him in the movie I turn to Bob and said, "I'm really nervous now because he might jinx the movie." Bob said, "Holy shit! I didn't realise that," and we got really nervous! We did put him in the movie, obviously, and the first day on the set it rained. It did! We had to go to a covered set. I looked at him and said, "I want to kill you!"'

De Niro began shooting *A Bronx Tale*, as he now called the film, on 31 August. Earlier that month, in a bad omen, *Mistress* had begun its limited release, to less than ecstatic reviews. Given that it was receiving, through Jaglom, the sort of circulation normally allocated to foreign films, it made only $1.1 million. Primus didn't direct another feature until *Out on my Feet* in 2001. Significantly, the money didn't come from Tribeca Productions.

As a director, De Niro applied many of the techniques he used in preparing his acting roles. 'He'd push me to come up with new ideas,' says Palminteri. 'He'd ask me to rewrite a scene. Then, when he saw it, he'd say, "Yeah, that's pretty good, but let's go back to the original." It's very exhausting. I didn't think anybody else worked like that except myself. I'm a workaholic, but he took it to a whole 'nother level.'

De Niro also encouraged the actors to try the technique he suggested to Walken in *The Deer Hunter* of thinking some lines rather than saying them aloud. 'Basically, he was telling us, "Keep your mind alive,"' says Palminteri. '"Live in the instant."'

Such care and attention to performances had its downside. Budgeted at $14 million, *A Bronx Tale* cost $21 million, in part because De Niro spent as much time as he felt was needed on a scene, even if that involved forty or fifty takes. Principal photography would eventually take five months.

In October, in the middle of production, the Springs case came to court, and De Niro closed down shooting for a week while he flew to LA. At the hearing before the Superior Court of Los Angeles, Marvin Mitchelson, with typical *chutzpah*, argued that Springs had gone through 'ten years of hell' with De Niro. This proved difficult to substantiate, however, since they'd met only occasionally after their first brief affair. De Niro had also made substantial contributions to the care of Nina. The judge reserved his decision.

Just when shooting on *Bronx Tale* ended, early in 1993, De Niro's father became ill, and was hospitalised. By coincidence, Scorsese's father was in the same hospital, and De Niro always visited both. 'My father never forgot that,' says Scorsese.

In March, *Mad Dog and Glory* was released, but only made $11 million and received poor reviews, adding another critical and box-office flop to the De Niro roster. *This Boy's Life* came out the following month, to better reviews but indifferent box office.

In between, the Los Angeles Superior Court handed down its decision about Nina Springs. The blood tests proved decisive. The judge ruled that De Niro had not 'bonded' with Nina. Their relationship was 'minimal in nature' and 'should not obligate him legally, morally or ethically to this child'. For a man who longed for a family, the victory was a Pyrrhic one, in which he lost more than he gained.

CHAPTER TWENTY ONE

In Cop Land

To Protect and to Serve

Motto of the Los Angeles Police Department

On 3 May 1993, Robert De Niro Sr died, aged seventy-one. Obituaries rated him a significant painter, though one whose small output, laborious methods and aloof nature barred him from wider appreciation. He was, as might have been expected, mentioned mainly as the father of Robert Jr. One of his last projects was a commission from Francis Ford Coppola to design a label for the wine produced in his Napa vineyards. Coppola then promptly 'lost' the drawing, which did not improve De Niro Sr's opinion of movie people.

During the last decade of his life, he'd come to terms with his son's fame, and even begun to enjoy it. Robert Jr coaxed him into letting him hang some of his paintings in the Tribeca Bar and Grill, and occasionally a member of the staff would ring upstairs to say, 'Your father is here.' De Niro would come down to find him entertaining a few friends, and admiring what was, in effect, a permanent show of his work.

His father's death underlined the extent to which the two men resembled one another, particularly in their solitary natures. 'No one, perhaps, is better suited to being an actor and less suited to being a personality,' wrote Elizabeth Kaye of De Niro Jr in the *New York Times Magazine*. 'He despises small talk and cannot do it, though he will discuss his work for hours.'

De Niro's emotional life reproduced that of his mother, who never remarried, as well as that of his father, who never entered into any long-term relationship, gay or otherwise. A sense that this was somehow an inevitable state of affairs suffused De Niro's work as an actor, just as it did his father's paintings of empty landscapes and people sitting alone.

De Niro turned fifty in August 1993. He was still editing *A Bronx Tale*, pushing to get it ready for its premiere at the Toronto Film Festival in September, when, unexpectedly, Chazz Palminteri arrived in his cutting room and told him the editing machines had broken down. Palminteri offered to take him out for dinner while they were being fixed, and steered him to a nearby restaurant. De Niro walked into a surprise party with seventy guests, including a contingent from Hollywood, with Mike Ovitz, Penny Marshall, Danny De Vito, Paul Schrader, Raul Julia and Harvey Keitel. Kenneth Branagh and his then-wife Emma Thompson had flown in from London (though Branagh was already involved with Helena Bonham Carter). Francis Ford Coppola supplied the wine, which was labelled with the 'lost' design by De Niro's father. Toukie Smith, Uma Thurman and Diahnne Abbott also showed up. Abbott couldn't resist cracking to De Niro, 'You were a lousy husband,' while acknowledging that he was her 'best friend' and 'a wonderful father to our children'.

In an article on Harvey Keitel, whose life was a battleground of broken marriages, child-support hearings and widely reported public brawls, *New York* magazine took the opportunity to anatomise Scorsese and De Niro too, as similarly driven, self-destructive workaholics, maimed socially and emotionally by early privations.

'For real working-class artists like them,' wrote the reporter, 'it was necessary to develop a remorseless sense of their careers – "If I'm not working, I'm nuts," Scorsese told me while shooting *Taxi Driver* in 1975. De Niro used to ride around town on a bicycle to audition in order to save money, and Keitel worked for eight years as a court stenographer. The desire to not repeat such experiences is understandably powerful, and the anxiety it causes can warp perception and behaviour, especially in the hyper-narcissistic force field of the movies.

'And so the strange tales: Scorsese's calculated distance from the children he's fathered (they might lessen his concentration), all being raised by ex-wives and girlfriends; De Niro's "obsessive" portrayals and pathological reluctance to express himself, even with pre-screened, surgically neutered celebrity journalists . . .'.

Given this perception, it's little wonder that De Niro decided to go to England in October 1993 to appear as Frankenstein's monster. Few more remote and alien figures existed in the actor's repertoire than the creature Victor Frankenstein cobbled together out of corpses in Mary Wollstonecraft Shelley's 1818 novel.

Francis Ford Coppola had been due to direct the film for TriStar, but passed the project to Kenneth Branagh, who also wanted to play the monster's creator. Various actors were considered to play the monster, including John Malkovich and Jeremy Irons; Gerard Depardieu too, though his reputation in the United States still hadn't recovered from a scandal over false accusations of rape, resurrected in 1991 when he was up for an Oscar. But as soon as De Niro expressed an interest, he became the front-runner.

Coppola brought Branagh to New York to meet De Niro. Their first encounter took place in a taxi *en route* to the Tribeca Center. De Niro was reassured when Branagh didn't 'turn up in some sort of Elizabethan suit with a box of sonnets under my arm'. Briefed by Coppola on De Niro's weaknesses, Branagh told him that 'my whole concept was to portray Frankenstein and his Creature as a kind of father and son relationship, and show the complexities of it all'. At the hint of a familial relationship between doctor and monster, De Niro's interest quickened.

A screenplay existed, written by newcomer Steph Lady, but Coppola's Zoetrope and TriStar commissioned a rewrite from Frank Darabont, who'd already scripted interesting sequels to *The Blob*, *The Fly* and *Nightmare on Elm Street*. Darabont re-inserted much of the original novel's narrative dropped from earlier films, including the framing story that takes place in the Arctic, where Dr Frankenstein pursues his creation.

Since this monster was no lumbering brute but rational, literate and articulate, Darabont also restored his Gothic revenge on Frankenstein, in which he engineers the hanging of the Baron's adoptive cousin for a murder she didn't commit, then kills Frankenstein's wife Elizabeth, tearing out her heart, and driving the Baron to try to revive her with the same methods that he used to make the monster.

At the same time, comic-book artist Bernie Wrightson executed a set of pen-and-ink 'concept' drawings which provided the cover and interior illustrations for the second revised draft of the screenplay, dated 8 February 1993.

This is as close as Darabont's conception came to being realised. He received co-credit as screenwriter with Steph Lady on the finished film, but Branagh rewrote most of the dialogue, altered some elements of the story, and pushed back the period from 1839 to 1794. Instead of the Industrial Revolution, with its emphasis on nuts-and-bolts technology, the setting became the Enlightenment, a period of philosophical theorising and speculation, electric with social and cultural change.

In itself, this wasn't a bad idea, but as Branagh tried to follow it through, creating a pre-industrial Europe in which Goethe might have been comfortable, he couldn't resist the temptation to inflate. The Frankenstein home, supposedly that of a moderately prosperous doctor, became a castle with vast unfurnished halls and a staircase that would not have shamed *Der Nibelung-enlied*. To live up to these spaces, Victor Frankenstein had to become an Errol Flynn conception of a scholar. Leaping bare-chested around his lab, he sprawls on top of the copper pressure-cooker in which he creates the monster, and slithers in galvanic fluid with his naked creation as he struggles to get him dried off.

Some of Branagh's additions were more ingenious. Frankenstein begins his work as assistant to Dr Waldman (John Cleese, in an unexpected dramatic role), who is murdered in the street during a cholera epidemic. The murderer is played by De Niro, whose corpse subsequently provides most of the parts needed to build the monster.

De Niro accepted the role of the monster on the basis of Darabont's script, not Branagh's rewrite, but over a period of months Branagh won him over. He had never faced quite so stringent a test of his belief in authenticity. Creating a creature that never existed, he had to build him from scratch on the basis of 'What would . . . ?' rather than 'What did . . . ?'

As part of his research, he delved into the physical aspects of death. Preparing for *Brazil*, he'd attended brain surgery. For *Frankenstein*, according to French journalist Yaron Svoray, he tried to locate 'snuff' films in which people were slaughtered and dismembered.

Svoray says he'd gone undercover in the porn film industry to research it for his book *Gods of Death*. De Niro, he claimed, was in Paris and asked him to find a snuff film 'because [he] was having trouble with a script that dealt with the subject'. Svoray said he told porn merchants that he had a client, but he'd need to see the film first. To De Niro, he suggested that, to avoid having to buy the film, they start watching it, but leave before it finished, telling the potential sellers it was 'boring'. De Niro and a friend did go to a small hotel to see the film, says Svoray, which showed a woman being dismembered. As agreed, De Niro said he wasn't impressed.

Svoray recalled, 'I said, "OK, then . . . Let's get out of here," expecting Robert to take my lead. To my surprise he shook his head. He told me to settle down; maybe there was something coming up that we would like.'

They watched the rest of the film, De Niro denouncing it as 'crap' which, in any event, he'd seen before. Svoray says he thought the film was real, and was disappointed that De Niro and his friend didn't agree. 'They asked questions,' he said, 'but not the right ones. They didn't ask how what they had seen could've been allowed to happen, or what they could do about it . . . Although I knew Robert and his friend had been affected by what they had seen, they were still Hollywood. They were interested in motivation; the psychology of what we had done.

They did not seem interested in the fact that they had just witnessed murder.'

According to Svoray, De Niro paid him about $10,000 to cover his expenses, and asked if he had any other snuff films. Svoray said he didn't. De Niro was on a plane back to New York the next day.

Svoray hoped De Niro would help him promote his book by making a statement against snuff films. Instead, De Niro's lawyer Stan Rosenfield, claiming his client was on holiday abroad and couldn't be contacted, issued a statement which neither confirmed nor denied the story, but did say that, if De Niro had seen the film, it wasn't so strange that he had responded to it in the way Svoray described. 'Bob plays life close to the vest,' said Rosenfield. 'He's not a public person. He often doesn't show strangers what he's feeling. When people try to interpret him, they end up misinterpreting him.'

The supposed snuff film was almost certainly one of the many fakes circulating in the porn world; nobody has yet produced a guaranteed authentic example. In that case, De Niro's dismissal of it is understandable. But his impulse to see such a film is entirely consistent with his method of preparing a role.

Frankenstein was shot on a taxing eighteen-week schedule at Shepperton Studios, outside London. On days when he played the monster, De Niro was picked up at 2.30 a.m., delivered to the studio by 3 a.m., but wouldn't be out of the make-up chair until 1 p.m. In most other films, only the monster's head and hands are visible, but this version contained scenes of him naked, which meant his body needed to be marked with winding ropes of unhealed purple scars.

Branagh claimed he learned something from working with De Niro – 'to take my time; that the only thing worth getting is something real. It didn't matter if you spoke it right, or moved in the right direction; unless something real happens, it's not worth it. He taught me selfishness. There's too much of a producer in me; I tend to think, "Come on, we spent two hours on this thing, let's move on, it's not worth that." Bob will doggedly work, work, work till it's right, even if that takes half a day.'

While he was in Europe, De Niro agreed to do a cameo in French director Agnes Varda's *Les Cent et une nuits*. Meant to celebrate the centenary of the movies, Varda's meandering film involved the ancient Simon Cinéma (Michel Piccoli), who lives in a country château surrounded by souvenirs of the movies. To keep his memory alive, he hires a girl to come every day and read to him, but she seldom gets the chance, since a series of celebrities drop by. They include Marcello Mastroianni, Harrison Ford, Anouk Aimée, and De Niro, who clowns in a rowing boat with Catherine Deneuve.

Also while he was in Paris, De Niro hung out at some of the city's more *branché* nightspots, in particular Les Bains-Douches, the owner of which was a friend. 'He comes whenever he's in Paris,' recalls Jacques Boko, the *physionomiste* or doorman/selector who controls who comes into the club. 'He goes out to dinner with the boss, who then calls here to say De Niro is coming, between 1 and 2 a.m. He doesn't show up in a big car. He comes with friends, people not famous, four or five, of different ages, young people too, and then the girls – beautiful girls, of course.

'De Niro goes up to the first floor and stays there, sitting down. He doesn't move. He's just there. He observes. He doesn't dance. He drinks. He drinks a lot. He doesn't pay. I've never seen him stick his hand in his pocket.'

Clubs like the Bains-Douches pride themselves on not being pick-up spots. Nobody remembers De Niro ever leaving with a woman.

The money De Niro earned from films like *Frankenstein* was crucial in propping up the Tribeca enterprises, of which only the basement Tribeca Bar and Grill made money. Not slow to see an opportunity, De Niro, with Coppola and Robin Williams, invested in a new restaurant opened by Drew Nieporent in San Francisco. 'Rubicon', named after the stream crossed by Julius Caesar when he marched on Rome, was also the name of the red wine Coppola manufactured in his vineyards. Nieporent opened another in New York and, in 2001, a Paris 'Nobu', directed by Japanese chef Nobuyuki Matsuhisa, who'd originally been proposed to launch a Japanese section in the Bar and Grill. All became money-spinners, in part because they bore the De Niro/ Williams showbiz cachet.

By comparison, Tribeca's film production was unglamorous and unprofitable. In 1992, it launched its TV anthology series *Tribeca Anthology*. A showcase for new talent and stories with a New York setting, it featured actors like Kevin Spacey and Laurence Fishburne, but audiences distrusted a series without continuing characters, and it was axed after seven episodes.

After that, the 'Tribeca Productions' label appeared on most of the films in which De Niro acted, and on occasional independent features, like *The Night we Never Met* (1993) and *Entropy* (1999), the former co-funded with Tribeca Center partners Miramax, but otherwise the Center shifted its efforts into educational projects designed to encourage film-making in New York.

His steady deal with Universal gave Martin Scorsese the breathing time he'd always lacked, and he was making the most of it, attacking the most ambitious projects of his career. He'd just finished an adaptation of Edith Wharton's *The Age of Innocence* and was sifting through other ideas when Nicholas Pileggi approached him with the idea that would become *Casino*.

It began with a 1980 report in the *Las Vegas Sun* about police being called to a domestic argument between a casino figure and his wife on the lawn of their Las Vegas home. The couple were Frank 'Lefty' Rosenthal, a key figure in the management of the Stardust casino, and his wife, formerly the topless dancer Geri McGee.

Over the previous twelve years, Rosenthal had risen from obscure Kansas City gambler to manager of one of America's biggest casinos. He'd done so without a licence from the Nevada gaming authorities, and with the overt help of thief and murderer Tony Spilotro, a close friend from the 'old neighbourhood' in Chicago whom Rosenthal had brought out to protect his back, and to share in the spoils.

Spilotro was a psychopath, charged at various times with thirty-five murders, but always acquitted, since no witnesses survived to testify. He also had the benefit of representation from legendary mob lawyer Oscar Goodman (who played himself in the film). At the head of a tight crew of thieves and killers, Spilotro looted Las Vegas, with Rosenthal at first complaisant, then powerless to stop him.

In the end, Spilotro's rule of terror alerted the FBI to a potential mob takeover of Las Vegas gaming, leading to the arrest of the five *capi* in Kansas City who were funding it. The reclusive mobsters decided to abandon their casinos, leaving Vegas to the big corporations. Everybody who might testify against them was murdered, including Spilotro, who with his brother was beaten with baseball bats and buried alive in a cornfield – a killing almost certainly monitored by FBI agents, who by then had bugged every car, house and restaurant in town, but who did nothing to save the Spilotros. A bomb was also planted, somewhat ineptly, in Rosenthal's car. He survived, to be made famous by *Casino*, and even launch his own website (Frankrosenthal.com).

Pileggi wanted to write a book about these events, then turn it into a film, but Scorsese persuaded him to reverse the order. Adapting and compressing, they turned the sprawling story of the mob's Las Vegas adventure into a 177-minute sprint through twelve hectic years. Scorsese called it 'the oldest story in the world. It's people doing themselves in by their own pride, and losing paradise. If they handled it right, they would still be there. Everybody would be happy, but it got out of hand.'

The film hinges on two relationships, both of which are soured by greed. The first is between Rosenthal, called Sam 'Ace' Rothstein in the film, and the Spilotro character, called Nicky Santoro. The second is that of Rothstein and his glamorous but corrupt wife Ginger.

Casino is *GoodFellas* on speed. Every technique used in the first film is re-employed, but bigger, brighter, louder. Instead of two people telling their story in voice-over, there are half a dozen. The wide-screen format of the first gives way to Cinemascope, the over-decorated suburban interiors to sprawling family homes furnished in marble and gold, the club and bar sequences to a repeated plunge into a rainbow torrent of neon.

Sam Rothstein is Scorsese's Icarus, the man who flies too close to the sun, a metaphor prefigured by the credits, when the gambler, blown out of his car, floats in slow motion through a bath of flame, hovering between his violent past and an uncertain future.

De Niro plays Rothstein to perfection, a nervous man who can hardly believe his good fortune in being handed the Tangiers, as Scorsese rechristens the Stardust, and who tries, single-handed, to protect his new toy from the greed of his friends, his mob backers, the local gaming commission, and the state senate.

He's almost successful, but his Achilles' heel is Ginger, the glamorous but rapacious prostitute with whom he falls in love and marries. Content at first to be the boss's wife, Ginger maintains the façade of what both acknowledge as a loveless marriage, but gradually old instincts assert themselves. She starts to hoard jewels and cash in a vault to which Rothstein, in a misplaced gesture of trust, gives her unlimited access. She also takes up with her old boyfriend, pimp and gambler Lester Diamond, played with unregenerate sleaziness by James Woods. The marriage deteriorates into recrimination, violence, and the confrontation on their front lawn that inspired the newspaper report read by Pileggi.

As Scorsese says, this is the oldest story in the world. What lifts *Casino* onto another level is the factual detail that supports it. The first thirty minutes are almost a documentary on the management of a big-time gambling operation. As Rothstein imposes his will on the Tangiers' slovenly management, Scorsese's camera follows every move, sometimes swooping down to a close-up of crimson dice bouncing in lazy slow motion across green baize, then soaring to peer down vertically on crowds milling around the slot machines like fish feeding on a reef.

Following Ginger, Scorsese catches her winning at craps for a delighted 'john', while at the same time stealing chips from his pile. When he protests about her leaving, perhaps taking his luck with her, she tosses all his winnings into the air for others to scramble for. Weaving through the casino, a blonde apparition of gold lamé, she slips bribes to parking attendants and pit bosses, grabs her car and speeds off along the fountaining neon of the main street. No wonder Rothstein falls for her.

Nicky Santoro's world is the underside of Ginger's. Barred from entering any casino because of his criminal past, Santoro hangs out in dark bars, warehouses and parking lots, or in the desert, where the secret meetings take place and the bodies are buried. Repeatedly, Scorsese returns us to the desert, showing individual figures almost lost in its glaring expanse – a reminder that, away from the neon, nobody's life is worth more than a single bullet.

In Santoro's world, all problems are soluble by violence. The hand of a card cheat is smashed with a hammer. A man who refuses to divulge the name of his confederates has his head put into a vice and squeezed until the skull caves in. Arguing over a pen, Santoro stabs it repeatedly into another man's face and neck, then kicks him senseless.

Santoro is a *tour de force* for Joe Pesci, the apotheosis of the psycho thug he played in *GoodFellas*, but Sharon Stone, in a role originally intended for Michelle Pfeiffer, is no less impressive as Ginger. A Cadillac of greed, she cruises the midnight-to-dawn world of Vegas, queen of all she surveys.

By comparison with these two larger-than-life characters, De Niro appears diminished, subdued. *Casino* is not his film. Watching his increasingly furrowed brow, and the way Scorsese marginalises him, placing him on the edge of the frame, or giving him absurd things to do, like answering calls in his office without his trousers on, exchanging banter on TV with singer Frankie Avalon, one almost expects him to launch into the 'I coulda been a contender' scene from *On the Waterfront*.

Casino finished shooting in the early summer of 1995. De Niro returned to New York. Now on the wrong side of fifty, and with his father recently dead, he had begun to ponder his legacy. The Tribeca Center was, at best, a limited success. His career was not flourishing as he wished; contemporaries like Dustin Hoffman, Al

Pacino and Robin Williams might not have his reputation, but all of them were more famous, and making more money.

At such moments, one's thoughts turn to children. Raphael was eighteen now. De Niro's adopted stepdaughter Drena remained with Diahnne Abbott, and he no longer had any real contact with Nina Nadeja Springs. A new family might give him the sense of belonging that he lacked. But with whom would he have such a family? He had no permanent partner, and nobody he cared to make into one.

Ex-girlfriend Toukie Smith offered a possible solution. Their first attempt at a child had miscarried. After that, they had tried, unsuccessfully, to adopt a child whose mother had died of AIDS. The course of action she proposed now offered De Niro a family relationship with the minimum possible intimacy and emotional investment. Since Smith, besides having suffered one miscarriage, was approaching the age where birth defects are more common, she suggested that, under conditions of great secrecy, she have a surrogate mother implanted with one of her eggs, which had been fertilised *in-vitro* with De Niro's sperm.

De Niro's next film, *Heat*, was a pet project of its director/writer Michael Mann, who brought it to Art Linson in hopes of persuading De Niro to take one of the two central roles, that of professional thief Neil McCauley, with Al Pacino opposite him as Vincent Hanna, the Los Angeles cop who destroys him.

The film was based on the life and death of the real Neil McCauley – Mann retained his name for the film – whom a policeman friend of Mann's shot and killed in 1963, shortly after the two had arranged to meet over coffee. Their amiable conversation revealed how much they had in common, and how little either was likely to change. Mann had filmed the story once before, in 1989, as the made-for-TV feature *LA Takedown*, with essentially the same screenplay but on a much reduced scale and with a cast of near-unknowns. Compressed to the dimensions of the TV screen, the story of two men and their teams playing a sophisticated game of hide and seek through the streets of Los Angeles had the intensity Mann brought to the series *Miami Vice*, which he developed. Like that series, conceived when an inspired TV executive scrawled 'MTV Cops' on a pad in the midst of a production meeting, the people of both *LA Takedown* and *Heat* live like princes, dressing in Armani, eating at the best restaurants, driving smart imported cars. Their spacious homes of glass and concrete open onto palm-filled canyons, the Pacific or, even more magisterially, the web of light that is night-time LA.

To Mann, who made few films and refined the look and sound of each in meticulous detail, the game of wits between these two men was a paradigm of twentieth-century professional life. Like Jean-Pierre Melville, the French director of *Le Samourai* (1967), whose stated aim in life was 'to become immortal, then to die', he found in their lives something of the infinite.

Isolation is part of their calling. Eady, the woman McCauley will fall in love with, is lonely herself, and is interested in others like her.

'You travel a lot?' she asks.

'Yeah.'

'Doesn't it get lonely?'

'I am alone,' McCauley says amiably. 'I'm not lonely.'

Neither McCauley nor Hanna is happy, but both draw strength from their expertise. McCauley, after years in prison, defines himself mainly by negatives. He's 'a needle, starting at zero, going the other way'. Like Alain Delon's affectless assassin in *Le Samourai*, he admits nothing to his life that might impede escape from it. Rule 1, learned from an old prisoner in jail, is 'Do not have any attachments. Do not have anything in your life you are not willing to walk out on in thirty seconds flat if you spot the heat around the corner.'

Inevitably, McAuley breaks this rule by falling in love with a 'civilian', graphic designer Eady (Amy Brennerman). Hoping to make one last score and retire with her, he is destroyed. In *LA Takedown*, Eady sees the botched bank robbery on TV and simply refuses to leave with McAuley, a scene played out on a hilltop with a burning palm tree blazing memorably if inexplicably in the background. Then McCauley has a chance to kill the man who informed on him and his team, and finds the temptation irresistible. He dies outside his hotel room, with Hanna holding his hand in mute respect.

In *Heat*, with more money to spend, Mann attenuates the action. Eady accompanies McAuley to the airport hotel where the informer is hiding, and waits outside while he bluffs his way in and kills the man. Hanna arrives in time to spot him leaving, and McCauley, unwilling to involve Eady, leads him away from the waiting car and onto the airfield, where they track one another along the edge of the runway until McCauley is killed, dying hand in hand with his adversary.

Both men exist only within the frame of their work. 'All I am is what I'm going after,' confesses Hanna. He says as much to McCauley when they meet, for the first and last time. On impulse, Hanna follows McCauley's car along the night-time freeway, stops him and says, 'What do you say I buy you a cup of coffee?'

Facing one another in the crowded restaurant, they exchange some weary and guarded truths. The conversation ends with a simple acknowledgment of what the audience has long realised – that they are just the same.

'Maybe we should both be doing something else, pal,' McCauley tells Hanna.

'I don't know how to do anything else.'

'Neither do I.'

'I don't much want to either.'

'Neither do I.'

The dialogue was just as true of the two actors as it was of the characters they played. They had never played a scene together before, but Mann found them instantly comfortable with one another. What could have been a locking of horns was instead a performance for four hands.

But neither, it has to be said, was as good as if he had been playing with a lesser partner. Normally, Pacino and De Niro devour their opposite numbers to reach a creative peak. The cautious fencing of the two best screen actors of their generation resembled the sole screen pairing of the two best dancers of theirs, Fred Astaire and Gene Kelly, in the number 'The Babbit and the Bromide' for *Ziegfeld Follies* in 1944. Individually, they were great. Together, each robbed the other, and the effect was disappointing.

As usual, Mann reserves his true attention for the background. Los Angeles has seldom looked so severely seductive, an icy arrangement of space that confirms the definition of architecture as 'frozen music'. (The actual music is provided by California's greatest proponents of the *avant garde* repertoire, the Kronos Quartet, and by the hermetic airport music of Brian Eno. It could hardly be bettered.)

In the film's most bravura sequence, McCauley and his crew break into a warehouse, unaware that Hanna's men are all around, observing them with long lenses, infra-red scanners and parabolic antennae. In one of the parked trailers opposite, a careless cop bumps the metal wall. McCauley steps out of the shadows, suddenly suspicious. Hanna watches the face of his opposite number in negative on the infra-red screen until, sensing the trap, he calls off the heist and his men walk off into the dark.

De Niro needed little training for the role of McCauley, though he did spend some time with professional thieves who resembled him. Talking to men who'd spent years in tiny cells, he learned that many took refuge in meticulous neatness, a fact he incorporated into the character of McCauley, who always wears a crisp white shirt, and lives in Spartan simplicity in a bleakly modern house.

After *Heat*, De Niro had a short-lived relationship with Ashley Judd, the hard-faced blonde who played the unfaithful wife of McAuley's henchman played by Val Kilmer. Then, on 20 October 1995, the surrogate mother chosen by him and Toukie Smith successfully gave birth to twins, Aaron Kendrick and Julian Henry. In a bland press statement, Smith and De Niro announced they 'will continue their separate personal and professional lives' but 'look forward to sharing the parenting of the children'. The news startled even the blasé staff of *People* magazine. Its head-shaking report commenced, 'Robert De Niro's storied love life grows curiouser and curiouser.' It was destined to become curiouser still.

* * *

The day after the birth of the twins, De Niro started work on *The Fan*, for British director Tony Scott.

The Fan began life as a modest film without major stars, to be produced at TriStar by Wendy Finerman, who made the Academy Award-winning *Forrest Gump*. Though Finerman's husand, Mark Canton, was head of Sony Pictures, the real power lay with Peter Guber, whose wild lifestyle and prodigious spending had almost ruined the Japanese's company's ill-judged attempt to make films in Hollywood.

Guber saw possibilities in *The Fan*, and grabbed it from TriStar for his own Mandalay Pictures. When he left Sony, the project went with him, but Canton, to whom Guber remained close, agreed to produce it if Guber could find some of the budget from another source. Guber returned triumphantly with $100 million obtained from a London bank, and *The Fan* went into production.

Rising black actor Wesley Snipes was paid $7 million to play baseball star Bobby Rayburn, and Guber brought in director Scott, the graduate from TV commercials who'd made *Top Gun* into a major hit. Further to enrich the project, Sony persuaded De Niro to play Gil Renard, the deranged fan who attaches himself to Rayburn.

On paper, the role of Renard was ideal for De Niro. Once again, it was a story of an older man taking a paternal though finally damaging interest in someone younger. A salesman for the hunting-knife company once run by his father, De Niro has a morbid preoccupation with its products. An expert in their use, he can throw one with enough force and accuracy to spit a bug on the opposite side of the room, and put the blade through a heavy door. But, with the company now managed by jerks who insist on selling trash, Renard perceives baseball, at which he was a high-school star, as the last repository of traditional values.

When he takes his son to a baseball game but abandons him there to make some business calls, the boy, who's little interested in the game, makes his own way home, and Renard's ex-wife gets a court order barring his access. He also loses his job. In reaction, he becomes fixated on his team's new star, the $40 million Rayburn. He starts talking to him via radio phone-in hostess Ellen Barkin, and, learning that he feels unlucky because another player refuses to relinquish the shirt with his lucky number, kills the man. When Rayburn's game still doesn't pick up, Renard kidnaps his son.

Watching Martin Scorsese had given De Niro some insight into obsession. Renard's 'lucky' shirt is number eleven, the number Scorsese believed brought him bad luck. Renard also puts his faith in lucky charms, in his case neckties, and repeats mantras like 'Positive things happen to positive thinkers.'

De Niro did the minimum amount of preparation for this ill-starred project, Scott saving all his scenes for an intensive two-week period. Supporting actors like Don Davis were told not to engage him in conversation or even meet his eye when he was on the set.

Once De Niro left, and the full extent of the film's potential failure became evident, Canton, Guber and Scott tried to pile in production values. $2 million was spent on inserting some Rolling Stones songs. Elaborate crowd shots, including a spectacularly empty finale, in which De Niro and Snipes face off on the rainswept ballpark, knife against baseball bat, pushed the budget to $70 million. 'How do you create any fiscal responsibility when the producer is married to the studio head?' queried a former Sony executive. Early cuts of the film were described by one executive as 'ugly, mean, and misogynistic – all cocksmanship', but Canton reportedly refused to listen to criticism. Persuaded to hold a test screening, he wouldn't let staff hand out the research cards which would have revealed what the audience thought. *The Fan* grossed a mere $20 million.

On Tuesday, 10 October, during work on *The Fan*, De Niro was accused of attacking TV cameraman Joseph Ligier as he tried to film him emerging from the Bowery Bar late on the previous Saturday night. 'He punched me in the nose and grabbed me by my hair,' Ligier said. 'He had me bent over a car. He kept saying, "Give me the video." I said, "No way." I had footage of Julia Roberts on the same tape.'

De Niro's spokesman Stan Rosenfield accused Ligier of being one of the 'video *paparazzi*' or 'stalkerazzi' who provoked celebrities into scenes, then sold the footage (Ligier admitted he had a deal to sell the tape to the tabloid TV show *Hard Copy*). De Niro surrendered to the police, was fingerprinted, photographed, and bailed over to appear in court later.

In the month before the case came up, Ligier offered to drop the charges for $300,000, which he later reduced to $150,000, then $110,000. Sensing a shakedown, De Niro told the police, who set up a fake drop in a chauffeured limousine. Once De Niro handed over the money, the driver was supposed to take him and Ligier to the police station for a formal withdrawal of charges. Instead, the meeting was recorded, and Ligier threatened with extortion charges.

Over the next year, De Niro became increasingly attached to Toukie Smith's two boys, who bore, everyone agreed, a strong physical resemblance to him. Most weekends, he could be seen pushing them around TriBeCa in a tandem stroller. He also took them and their mother for weekends in the rural retreat he'd recently bought in Ulster County, upstate New York. Smith resented the attention De Niro paid the boys, since it was assumed she'd raise them alone, with him footing the bills. Even in so legalistic a society as the one they moved in, the assumption had been so implicit that they hadn't bothered to spell out the relationship on paper. One spokesperson for Smith said, 'He was just supposed to be the biological father. That was the deal. They were supposed to be Toukie's kids. But now he's bonded with them.'

Smith, whose restaurant in the West Village had closed down, took De Niro to the Manhattan Family Court, asking for more child support. De Niro counter-argued that he wasn't getting sufficient 'quality time' with the boys. His lawyer even suggested he should have full custody of them. 'I can't believe he'd ever expect to get full custody,' said one of the lawyers involved. 'Courts rarely give it to a father – especially when you're a surrogate father who's off shooting movies most of the year.' When the smoke cleared, Smith had more money and De Niro more access. The pleasure of having children also apparently planted in his mind the idea that he might father more.

CHAPTER TWENTY TWO

Ageing Bull

> Taxi Driver *is a better* Blade Runner *than* Blade Runner.
> *New York is a nightmare LA/Tokyo of the future. De Niro*
> *is a sleepless alien who does a poor job of passing himself*
> *off as an earthling. He can't figure out human sexuality but*
> *he wants to get involved anyway.*

David Cronenberg

Heat opened in December 1995, but its good reviews did nothing to convince De Niro he should choose his roles with more care. The days of 'earning the right' to a character had passed.

Though its street-level Café and more expensive basement Grill continued profitable, the Tribeca Center's other activities were relative failures. New York film-making had, as De Niro hoped, revived in the nineties. Between 1993 and 1998 the total expenditure within the city on films and TV rose to $2.57 billion in 1998, when twenty-one feature films and 7680 days of TV were shot in the New York area. However, just as in the sixties, most films were either big-budget Hollywood productions, with casts and crew hired in California, or independent projects cutting every possible corner. The former had no need of permanent offices in an establishment like the Center, while the latter couldn't afford them.

Writing up her week's activities for the internet magazine *Slate*, producer Lynda Obst captured some of the *ad hoc* style of new Manhattan cinema and the anomalous position of De Niro within it: 'We're a studio movie trying to run and gun like an indie. We work in indie land, right near my *Slate* cohort Christine Vachon's office (or so I hear) and within walking distance of the TriBeCa screening room, restaurant, and everything else Robert De Niro owns downtown. (Everything there is, it seems. Unless it's about to be bought by [Miramax head] Harvey Weinstein for Gwyneth [Paltrow].) In the past, on *Sleepless*, *Fisher King*, *One Fine Day*, and *The Siege*, all unabashedly studio movies, our offices were in midtown. Now we're hipsters, competing with dot.commers for space. We work in a hole. I knew the neighbourhood of my production office on Laight Street was the real thing when I walked into a gaggle of drag queens being shot by Abel Ferrara. There's guerrilla film-making and then there's us, the *poseurs*.'

Recognising that film-making alone would not support the Center, De Niro and Jane Rosenthal diversified into the world of the 'dot.commers'. They marketed a video game, The Last Resort, where players inherit a decrepit holiday resort and have to fight off rapacious developers. James Belushi, Christopher Reeve and Cher were among the stars who voiced the characters, but the game did poorly against the more strident appeal of Tomb Raider. De Niro also joined the board of advisers of a website devoted to hip-hop music. Fellow members included rappers Heavy D and Q-Tip. A spokesman said De Niro would 'help develop contacts in the film industry. Who has better contacts? He thinks hip-hop is the next big thing.' In 2002 De Niro also invested in *We Will Rock You*, a London stage musical from the music of rock band Queen.

With Tribeca Productions forced by limited funds to find potential film properties from the fringes of publishing and the theatre, Rosenthal and De Niro had trouble convincing the studios to accept their projects unless De Niro was attached in a juicy part. Those they did get going, like a combined live-action and animated version of the sixties children's TV cartoon series *The Adventures of Rocky and Bullwinkle*, took years to knock into filmable shape.

As a performer, De Niro continued to command top salaries, if not the stratospheric fees of idols like Tom Cruise: $8 million for *Analyze This*, $13.5 million for *Meet the Parents*, $14 million for *Ronin* and $15 million for *The Score*. But these sums didn't come without cost, mostly to his ego. Now he was forced to accept scripts which he would have scorned a decade before. Moreover, where, in the eighties, producers would offer him a choice of the plum roles in a film, he was now often their second choice, taking over a part which another actor hadn't wanted or been able to play. The result was a coarsening of his work, and a descent into the clichés of genre film.

In 1996 alone, De Niro worked on three films, none of which deserved comparison with his best.

Based on a book by Lorenzo Carcaterra, *Sleepers* purported to tell the true story of four ex-inmates of a boys' correctional institution who, as adults, take revenge on the brutal guard who raped and brutalised them as children. When two of the boys, now career criminals, are arrested for shooting the guard, their two friends, fortuitously a newspaper reporter and the assistant district attorney assigned to prosecute his pals, connive to get them off, with the help of a broken-down lawyer, played perfunctorily by Dustin Hoffman. Central to the scheme is the local priest, Father Bobby (De Niro), who, once he understands the extent of the suffering endured by the boys, perjures himself on the stand.

De Niro's scenes, none of them central, comprised mainly him staring into the middle distance and looking thoughtful – shorthand for confronting a moral dilemma. Many critics were uneasy about the film's endorsement of vigilantism, and pressed Carcaterra for more details about the events on which he based the book. None were forthcoming, and *Sleepers* was downgraded from 'faction' to 'fiction'. De Niro claimed not to have been troubled by any such doubts. 'It all seemed credible to me. When I spoke to Carcaterra, I believed him. I know other people who didn't. But the important part, the thing he kept saying, was that young men get raped in prison, and that, I believe, is true. Anything you can imagine happening in prison does happen.'

By the time *The Fan* was released in August 1996, De Niro had finished yet another quickie role, in *Marvin's Room*. The brevity of his performance belies the time he spent setting up the film. Meryl Streep, who plays Lee, a woman who returns to her estranged family in the hope that one of them will contribute the bone marrow she needs to cure her of leukaemia, first heard of it five years earlier. 'Bob De Niro called me up,' she says. 'He had this woman who owned the film rights to Scott McPherson's play and who, since she owned it, got to say she wanted to direct it as well. She'd never directed before, either in movies or TV. I thought I should see the play first, so I took my son Henry, who was then twelve (he's now seventeen), and we loved it! We thought it was really interesting.

'I was to play Bessie [the sister who has stayed at home to nurse their aged father], Anjelica Huston was going to play Lee. It fell apart basically because I was afraid. Because of the nature of the play. Because it skirts a very fine line between real-felt tragedy and a purely comic sensibility. And I thought it would take too heavy a toll to do it.

'So I bailed. Years later, Bob came back to me about it; by then, he and [producer] Scott Rudin had bought the rights to the play, they had got a real director – Jerry Zaks – and it felt like a good thing. By that time, however, I didn't want to play Bessie. I had just shot [Barbet Schroeder's] *Before and After*. I had played all those good mothers and good people. . .So I just said, "Gimme the shitty one." '

Marvin's Room really belongs to Streep and Diane Keaton as the sisters, and Leonardo DiCaprio as the pyromaniac son. As the amiable, well-meaning but bumbling Dr Wally, De Niro gave a performance that could have come from any one of a hundred actors.

The same was true of *Cop Land*, another excursion into police corruption. The characters are all New York cops who, forbidden to live outside the city, exploit a loophole that allows transit police to have homes in more attractive and cheaper satellite towns like Garrison, New Jersey, and sign up as part-time 'staties'.

Garrison, so filled with police it's called 'Cop Land', is notionally controlled by broken-down sheriff Sylvester Stallone, who does little or nothing to block its real kingpin, NYPD investigator Harvey Keitel. When a cop kills innocent citizens in a drunken rage, then disappears, a supposed suicide, Stallone has to decide whether to kowtow to Keitel or inform on his pals to Internal Affairs investigator De Niro, who has three scenes, done, it seems, over a lazy weekend, reportedly as a favour to his friend and tenant, Harvey Weinstein, who personally delivered the script to him on holiday. The film became a classic illustration of the dictum that business and friendship don't mix.

De Niro next headed west to take another supporting role performance in Quentin Tarantino's *Jackie Brown*, an intricate and witty retelling of Elmore Leonard's novel *Rum Punch*, in which an ageing black flight attendant with too many connections to organised crime connives with a bail bondsman to swindle a cocaine dealer, under the very noses of the FBI.

Tarantino's direction is deft and funny, while his decision to use two almost-forgotten stars of the sixties, Robert Forster and Pam Grier, as the bondsman and his heroine, pays off superbly. Samuel L. Jackson is agreeably profane and ruthless as the dealer, and Michael Keaton no less expert as the FBI man. De Niro, however, has little or nothing to do as Louis Gara, an old prison pal of Jackson's who spends most of his time hanging around his friend's apartment, watching TV and, on one occasion, diddling Jackson's ditzy girlfriend (Bridget Fonda), who, later in the story, he shoots dead in exasperation.

Even less effort was required to play the Abel Magwitch character in a remake of *Great Expectations*. Updated to the 1990s and shifted to Florida and New York, Charles Dickens' epic of upward mobility and moral regeneration became a soap opera, with a young Florida redneck saving a runaway convict, who, escaping to Australia, secretly finances his training as a painter in New York. This being a Hollywood version, Ethan Hawke, now called 'Finn', not 'Pip', doesn't simply get to live the life of a spoiled young remittance man but becomes a famous and successful artist. De Niro spends his few scenes as Hawke's benefactor twinkling like Santa Claus from behind a heavy beard.

*   *   *

During 1996, De Niro revived a dormant relationship with Grace Hightower, an African-American ex-airline stewardess in her forties whom he'd first met some years before when she managed the restaurant Mr Chow's in New York: in an arresting version of 'meeting cute', she told him he'd arrived too late, and his reservation had gone to someone else.

By March, De Niro and Hightower were a couple. Rather than be separated from her while shooting *Jackie Brown*, he leased a five-bedroom house in Brentwood for $30,000 a month. 'It's probably the most private property in the world, with a big wall and a long driveway,' reported the *New York Times*. In this hideaway, De Niro proposed marriage, and presented Hightower with a large diamond and emerald ring. A few weeks later, the ring was on display, along with much of Hightower in a violet Armani dress with a startling décolletage, when De Niro accepted the Jacqueline Kennedy Onassis Medal of the Municipal Art Society of New York for helping revive TriBeCa, and for his new investments in restaurants in Harlem. Hightower and his mother listened as he said, 'I am fortunate to live and work in a neighbourhood I love.'

In September 1996, while lawyers drafted a pre-nuptial agreement, De Niro made a low-key visit to Israel to research a project that would prove prescient. In the wake of that year's bomb attack on the World Trade Center in New York, he contemplated a film on a character like the Saudi millionaire terrorist Osama bin Laden, widely assumed to have financed it. De Niro imagined a 'psychological actioner' in which he would play an agent who tracks and foils a similar international terrorist. The film was never made, but on 11 September 2001 TriBeCa would be rocked by the destruction of the World Trade Center in a second and far more catastrophic outrage. On that occasion, De Niro sent meals from his restaurants to feed the rescue workers, and visited the site to help out and sign autographs. He also appeared on the nationwide telecast *A Salute to Heroes* a week after the event, reading from Franklin Roosevelt's speech on the outbreak of World War II.

On 17 June 1997, De Niro and the forty-two-year-old

Hightower were married in a private ceremony. Guests included Joe Pesci and Harvey Keitel. Almost immediately, Hightower became pregnant.

Happiness may have had something to do with the good nature and genuine wit which De Niro brought to Barry Levinson's *Wag the Dog*, a political satire scripted by David Mamet which he shot in thirty filming days during the spring of 1997 on a modest $15 million budget. Tribeca already owned Larry Beinhart's novel *American Hero*, and Rosenthal and De Niro asked Mamet, who was writing something else for them, to adapt it. The title was Mamet's, though so few people knew the phrase that it had to be explained in laborious preliminary titles.

Still wearing his *Great Expectations* beard, De Niro plays Conrad Brean, a veteran political 'fixer' brought in to cover up a sexual indiscretion by an American President just a few weeks before he runs for re-election. Brean's solution is a well-tried one. As he points out to White House aide Winifred Ames (Anne Heche), in 1983, Ronald Reagan responded to the terrorist murder of hundreds of Marines in Beirut by invading inoffensive Grenada. A war pushes everything else off the front page, so Brean cooks up a war – or rather, 'the appearance of a war' – with Albania. To produce it, he recruits Hollywood producer Stanley Motss, played by Dustin Hoffman in a parody of Robert Evans, including the ex-Paramount studio head's languid drawl. Fending off the CIA, a cretinous Republican candidate, a nitpicking President and a psychotic hero, Motss and Brean save the administration, though Motss's demand to be credited for what Brean has called the 'pageant' spells his doom.

De Niro was still no more able to play comedy in *Wag the Dog* than he had been in *Bogart Slept Here*, but he'd learned enough to leave Mamet's lines alone, and to defer to the character actors with whom Levinson surrounded him, including Willie Nelson as a country and western songwriter, Denis Leary as 'The Fad King', expert on catching the public imagination, William H. Macy as the head of the CIA, and above all Hoffman as Motss. As in *Great Expectations*, De Niro mainly twinkles, but the effect here is to charm, not appall.

Various inspirations were suggested for the rumpled Brean, with his tweed hat, anonymous clothes and evasive manner. Levinson mentioned Republican spin-doctors Lyn Nofziger and Ed Rollins, but most people agree he was patterned on Bill Clinton's campaign adviser Dick Morris, who admitted to suggesting, after the downing of TWA Flight 800 in July 1996 and the pipe bomb at the Atlanta Olympics shortly afterwards, that Clinton blame terrorists because 'it could be worth four or five points in the polls'.

Cop Land, *Jackie Brown* and *Wag the Dog* were all released between August and December 1997. For most of this time, De Niro was in France, shooting *Ronin*, scripted once again by Mamet and directed by John Frankenheimer.

Ronin was the kind of film which Frankenheimer, with *The French Connection*, had proved he could do consummately well. The plot was as perfunctory as all the best shoot-'em-ups: a woman with connections to the IRA and plenty of money assembles a group of soldiers of fortune in Paris to acquire a briefcase being guarded by a no less skilful group of mercenaries in the south of France.

Once the amateurs have been shaken out of the team, an American, Sam, and a Frenchman, Vincent, played by De Niro and Jean Reno, lead the assault, which inevitably involves running gunfights and violent car chases through crowded city streets, multiple double-crosses, and at least three surprise endings – the concluding one being that De Niro is a CIA man planted to flush out the brain behind the scheme, rabid Irish patriot Seamus (Jonathan Pryce).

Ronin – the term for Japanese samurai who've lost their master – is a good title, though 'Mercenaries' would have been more accurate. (Certainly De Niro would not have been there but for the $14 million he was paid.) Stellan Skarsgård, who plays the team's IT man, later characterised the characters, agents made redundant by the end of the Cold War, as 'trenchcoats without a country'. Sam, Vincent and the rest are in it for the money, and care little what the mysterious briefcase contains. ('Sandwiches,'

Reno replied when journalists asked that question. In fact, the
props team found that chocolate bars gave it the right weight.)

De Niro, with a convict-crop crewcut and a wardrobe mostly
of black leather, is in his element as the pro who anticipates
every turn of the plot with a chess grandmaster's skill. When the
blowhard Sean Bean hints at his secret training with an elite
British Army unit, De Niro has him slinking home simply by
demanding repeatedly, 'What colour is the boathouse at Lindley?'
– a nonsense question that, like everything else in the film, doesn't
demand an answer.

'What he gives is total, total believability, total realism,' says
Frankenheimer of De Niro. 'He's like a Stradivarius violin. It's
so sensitive, and the sound that comes out of it is so much better
than what comes out of another violin.' *Ronin* is the proof that
even 'Pop Goes the Weasel' sounds better on a great instrument.

Sam and Vincent forge a laconic friendship reminiscent of that
between Yul Brynner and Steve McQueen in *The Magnificent
Seven*. A glance, or the offer of a cigarette, says all that's needed.
Natascha MacElphone as Deirdre, the contractor, fits neatly
between the pair. Watching their quarry from a parked car, she
and De Niro fall automatically into a clinch as a police patrol
cruises by, and return to it with interest when they've gone. When
Vincent takes Sam, wounded and on the run, to the home of an
old friend, Sam stays conscious and lucid long enough to extract
the bullet and sew himself up, then announces politely that he's
going to pass out, and does so.

The first screenplay for *Ronin* by the unknown John David
Zeik was rewritten by David Mamet. 'We didn't shoot a line of
Zeik's script,' insisted Frankenheimer. 'The credits should read
"Story by J.D. Zeik. Screenplay by David Mamet".' The Writers'
Guild felt otherwise, accepting Zeik's contention that Mamet
only enlarged the role of Sam to accommodate De Niro, added
the character of Deirdre, and rewrote some scenes. They ordered
that credit be shared. A furious Mamet took his name off the
film, substituting 'Richard Weisz'.

De Niro's time in France filming *Ronin* was, however, destined
to become best known in his story for different reasons.

In February, Frederic N'guyen, a magistrate investigating an $8000-a-night prostitution ring operating in Paris, sent the police to bring De Niro from his hotel to the Prefecture. He was detained there for nine hours, and quizzed about his relationship with three women, one of them an English model named Charmaine Sinclair – also known as Charmaine Synclair, Charmaine Garth, Marcia Budomir . . . – whom he admitted having entertained in Paris while making *Les Cent et une nuits*.

Sinclair was not so reticent. She confessed to having gone to Paris to stay with De Niro, but said that 'sex was never the most important thing [. . .] we just enjoyed the intimacy'. He told her, she said, that she had a better bottom than Naomi Campbell.

De Niro insisted this was not prostitution; he had never paid for sex in his life – 'Women throw themselves at me,' he said indignantly. His lawyer skated around the question with the skilful use of legalese. Paying for sex was not a crime in France, he pointed out. 'But if [the charge of having paid for sex] were true, I would point out that he was an unmarried man then.'

Prostitution isn't illegal in France, though pimping is, but nobody proved that De Niro had anything to do with either. Sinclair and De Niro's names simply appeared in an address book seized during the investigation. However, N'Guyen insisted he'd been within his rights to detain the actor.

Furious at the bad publicity, De Niro set his French lawyers onto N'Guyen and the press that reported his charges. 'I never paid for a woman in my life,' he said, threatening never to return to France, and to send back the award of Chevalier des Arts et Métiers with which he had been presented a year earlier. N'guyen responded no less vigorously. 'No matter how violent and defamatory the attacks on me are,' he said, 'it will all come out at the trial that I acted properly. I have twenty years of experience. I am doing everything according to the law. I know what I am doing.'

De Niro's French lawyer George Kiejman didn't deny that the address book might exist, and that De Niro's name could be in it. 'It's possible. If you know the number of women who are pretty and ravishing who have his phone number . . .'. But he insisted that N'guyen had ulterior motives in questioning his client: 'the name of Robert De Niro is like a jewel for a judge'. In June, a civil court ruled that two articles in the daily *France Soir* had transgressed France's notoriously strict privacy laws, and ordered the paper to pay De Niro $13,400 damages. Cases against the judge alleging 'violation of secrecy involving an investigation' and 'obstruction of freedom of movement' were still pending.

Hardly had the Sinclair scandal abated than De Niro was in the news again, as father of a baby boy, whom he and Hightower christened Elliot.

But the reports of his R & R in Paris had done their damage. By June, friends were anticipating the end of the short-lived marriage. De Niro leased two apartments in nearby buildings in New York – perhaps as boltholes, they speculated, should the relationship get worse. For her part, Hightower had her lawyer going over their pre-nuptial agreement with a magnifying glass.

Hightower complained that De Niro was never at home. 'She knew his behaviour patterns before she got married to him,' retorted a friend, but people in the Hightower camp hinted that De Niro was intentionally avoiding her: 'It's like he and Grace lead separate lives.' She was also upset that De Niro wanted baby Elliot cared for by the same nanny as his twins by Toukie Smith. 'She doesn't want those nannies taking care of Elliot,' said a friend. 'It's perfectly natural from a mother's point of view. But not from De Niro's.' As the marriage soured further, there would be uglier charges involving drug abuse.

It was during this period, around May 1998, that De Niro signed up for a film that, in every respect, marked a departure from his normal work. Director Joel Schumacher brought him his own screenplay for *Flawless* and proposed it as a joint production, with him directing and De Niro playing Walt Koontz, a homophobic security guard who, after a stroke, is forced to approach a gay transvestite for the singing lessons that will help him regain his voice. It's not clear if Schumacher was aware of Robert De Niro Sr's homosexuality, but for the actor the decision to make the film at all represented a major step towards acceptance and reconciliation. Shooting was set down to start in December.

Before then, De Niro was again in Hollywood, working on another comedy. The success of *Wag the Dog* reminded producers that, put next to a gifted comic, De Niro could radiate a reflected humour. With this in mind, Billy Crystal had sent him the screenplay of *Analyze This*, about psychiatrist Ben Sobel who, consulted by Mafia *capo* Paul Vitti, finds himself sucked deeper into the world of organised crime as he tries to unravel the mobster's emotional tangles.

This was an old joke. It appeared in George Armitage's 1997 film *Grosse Point Blank*, and was the central conceit of the most popular current series on cable TV, HBO's *The Sopranos*. De Niro rightly rejected the script as 'too broad and a little hokey'. Over months, the screenwriters refined it, adding subplots to draw attention away from the obviousness of the central premise.

In the finished version, Sobel has almost as many problems as his clients. Dominated by his father, also a psychiatrist, but a successful media figure on top of it, he's bored with his whining patients, and desperately needs to escape to Florida to get married. But once Vitti has decided that Sobel can help with the panic attacks that are impairing his control of the mob, the doctor can't escape him. Henchmen creep into his bedroom, accost him at Marineland, even disrupt his wedding when a would-be assassin falls six floors into the buffet lunch.

Crystal's timing as Sobel is good enough to carry a one-joke screenplay, but as Vitti, De Niro has to rely on mugging. Shrugging, grinning, grimacing, wrinkling his face in fury or admiration, he exhausts his meagre repertoire before the film is halfway through, and simply recycles the tricks until there's no more plot. But the film, for which De Niro was paid $8 million, grossed $106 million on the domestic market, and by 2002 a sequel, *Analyze That*, was on the screen.

On his return to New York, De Niro started work on *Flawless*. In the interim, Schumacher had cast the talented young Philip

Seymour Hoffman as Rusty, the drag queen who first helps Koontz for money, then out of genuine affection. De Niro had never made a film in which homosexuality was even a detail, let alone a primary theme. Moreover, the homophilia in *Flawless* isn't the love of one hard-bodied hunk for another, but of an overweight drag queen approaching middle age for the woman he is almost convinced he could become, given the necessary surgery and hormone shots.

From watching his own father, De Niro knew at first hand the loneliness and despair of the ageing gay, but wasn't, even at fifty-five years of age, sufficiently comfortable to confront it squarely. Relentlessly homophobic, Koontz is as maimed physically as he believes a homosexual to be maimed emotionally. Only when he's half paralysed does he drag himself upstairs to Rusty's cluttered apartment. Even then, the *rapprochement* is grudging and painful.

To keep the kids happy, Schumacher introduces a contrived sub-plot about drug dealers and missing money, but essentially *Flawless* is simply the story of a growing friendship between the two men. As they come closer, Walt doesn't embrace homosexuality but at least recognises its existence. And Rusty spends some of his hard-won cash not on surgery and hormones but on repairing Walt's wounds.

Roger Ebert wrote in the *Chicago Sun-Times*, 'De Niro is a great technical actor who may have been attracted to this material because of the chance to play a stroke victim. His performance not only gets Walt's symptoms right, but also shows sympathy for the man inside. [. . .] Too bad they're stuck in a jumbled plot, but as an odd couple, they work.' In fact, De Niro's performance as a stroke victim is clumsy, consisting of screwing up one side of his face and talking between motionless lips. If anything interested him about the role, it was the 'odd couple' element. Walt's affection for Rusty at the end of *Flawless* is literally the love that dare not speak its name, as was De Niro's love of his father while his father was alive; and even after his death, the best De Niro can manage is a mumble.

*   *   *

While De Niro was busy with his roster of small roles, Jane Rosenthal, in conjunction with NBC, was overseeing the only ambitious production to date in the so-far disappointing history of Tribeca Productions. Not surprisingly, the subject was organised crime. *Witness to the Mob*, a four-hour mini-series telecast in 1998, detailed the downfall of New York Mafia don John Gotti in the 1980s after his long-time lieutenant Salvatore 'Sammy the Bull' Gravano informed on him.

Nobody emerges with particular credit from the series, another contribution to the mythology of the mob and in particular of that loathed but apparently inevitable figure, the informer, a character already celebrated in *The Valachi Papers*, *Serpico*, *Prince of the City*, *GoodFellas* and *Donnie Brasco*. The trailer even made the link specific, describing *Witness to the Mob* as 'in the tradition of *The Godfather*, *GoodFellas* and *Donnie Brasco*'.

To reinforce a tenuous *Godfather* connection, Rosenthal and De Niro cast Abe Vigoda, who played Sal Tessio in Coppola's original film, as Paul Castellano, the ageing don bumped off by Gravano and his ambitious colleagues, while the first scene after the credits shows the young punks comparing their favourite *Godfather* lines, complete with Brando imitations.

But *Witness to the Mob* has none of the sense of history implicit in Coppola's trilogy. We never step outside the narrow world of these gangsters, and in fact see little of even that, except for the social club in Bensonhurst which was Gotti's headquarters, and a succession of bars and back rooms.

The most elaborate scenes take place in the real-life courtroom where Gravano gives his evidence against the background of a thirties mural depicting the majesty and even-handedness of the law – neither conspicuously on display in the cynical plea-bargaining without which he would never have taken the stand at all. In an additional irony, Bruce Cutler, Gotti's lawyer, whose spirited attack on the FBI's case is featured, and who, on Gotti's behalf, had criticised *GoodFellas*, would turn up in 2001 as an actor in Jim Herzfeld's *Fifteen Minutes*, playing opposite none other than De Niro.

With little money to spend, Irish director Thaddeus O'Sullivan, a cinematographer and 'underground' film-maker before he started directing, uses every cheat in the B-movie book. A single table with a view over Manhattan approximates a fancy restaurant, and a building site and some men in hard hats the Gravano construction empire that excites Gotti's resentment, precipitating his lieutenant's downfall, then his own.

Tom Sizemore, one of De Niro's 'crew' on *Heat*, gained twenty kilos to play Gotti, but never looks convincing in the don's trademark shiny silk suits and white overcoat, which bulge over the actor's ample paunch. Gravano is more credibly played by stumpy Nicholas Turturro, in part because the actor spent most of his screen career playing mobsters and cops, notably the principled and compassionate James Martinez in the TV series *NYPD Blue*. Turturro's voice-over goes some way to giving *Witness to the Mob* the cohesion O'Sullivan couldn't impose in shooting, but he is, as Raymond Chandler once said of the equally short Alan Ladd, 'a small boy's idea of a tough guy'.

Despite Rosanne Massa, sister of one of Gravano's victims, acting as 'technical adviser', *Witness to the Mob* gives Gravano a soft ride, showing him as Gotti's loyal underboss until the ostentatious *capo* turns on him out of jealousy. 'It's really trying to be a balanced story,' Jane Rosenthal told the press. 'As balanced as you can possibly be' – citing, as proof of even-handedness, that she and De Niro solicited no co-operation from either Gravano or Gotti. (Would it have been forthcoming? Not, according to reports of the time, without Tribeca paying more than they could afford, since both Gotti and Gravano had their own film deals going.)

Gravano still emerges as a hero, the voice-over repeatedly stressing how life on the street instilled toughness, courage and loyalty. In the final scene, he talks to a film crew in what is supposedly Arizona, where the FBI relocated him after his token three years in prison. He behaved honourably, he says, and now phlegmatically accepts that the families of the nineteen men he killed, which included his own brother-in-law, might come looking for him.

A closing title says he 'lives somewhere in the United States and continues to do business while defending himself against legal action'. In fact, Gravano became a major drug dealer in his adoptive state, using his restaurant in Scottsdale as a front, and made millions dealing Ecstasy. 'I own Arizona,' he boasted to a man whose drug business he wanted to take over. 'It's locked down. You can't sell pills here without going through me.' But the FBI, in a piece of poetic justice, had bugged the meeting, and Gravano ended up in prison.

People who knew De Niro attributed his growing lack of interest in acting to a corresponding enthusiasm for property development. As well as his restaurant empire, which was spreading to the west coast, London and Paris, he lent his name and money to a number of projects in TriBeCa.

The culmination of this wheeling and dealing seemed to have arrived in May 1999 when De Niro and Stephen Roth of Vornado Realty Trust announced a plan, with Miramax, to convert the derelict Brooklyn Navy Yard into film studios and sound stages at a cost of $140 million. The new complex would rival Hollywood, with all the economic fallout that such businesses customarily brought to an area. New York's Mayor Rudy Giuliani made the formal announcement. The new facility would 'contain twelve sound stages on a fifteen-acre portion of the Navy Yard, [which] will rival those on the west coast and serve as the preeminent east coast film and television production facility'.

The scheme made headlines, but financial journalists noted that De Niro and Roth were mainly pledging their names; the money would come from conventional banking sources, not noted for generosity. The doomsayers were proved right a few months later when it was announced that the deal was on hold, perhaps permanently.

As expected, De Niro's marriage to Grace Hightower didn't survive his restless lifestyle nor his taste for casual sex. In August 1999, he served her with divorce papers, then went straight to Wesley Snipes' apartment to celebrate Snipes' thirty-sixth birthday. While Quentin Tarantino and Rosie Perez danced, De Niro chatted up a pretty girl. She left before him, but when she got home she found his phone number in the pocket of her coat.

Before this, De Niro had finished work on the long-delayed *Adventures of Rocky and Bullwinkle*. Shooting ended in June 1999, though the film didn't open until a year later. Playwright Kenneth Lonergan adapted Jay Ward's animated series about the intrepid squirrel aviator (the advertising tag line, borrowed from *Superman*, promises, 'You'll Believe a Squirrel can Fly') and his offsider, Bullwinkle the moose. Director Les McAnuff came from theatre. He'd staged The Who's rock opera *Tommy* on Broadway, but his only film credit was for a 1998 adaptation of Balzac's *Cousin Bette*.

De Niro played Fearless Leader, a Nazi martinet with cheeks scarred from duelling and a Cherman accent that would have shamed 1930s stock German actor Sig Ruman. Always happier when he could be transformed physically, De Niro had his chin and nose built up, and his hair lacquered into black patent leather, but he made no secret of his scorn for the project. Inveigled onto Rosie O'Donnell's witless talk show to promote it, he announced bleakly, 'I was dragged into it by my partner, Jane Rosenthal.' Rubbing salt in the wound, O'Donnell ran a clip in which De Niro, talking to his minions via a video phone, reprises the 'Are you talking to me?' speech from *Taxi Driver*, but in a fake accent, and with laboured comic emphasis. Not since a drunken John Barrymore lurched through the self-parodying comic roles that ended his career had a great actor been made to look quite so absurd.

To see De Niro at the peak of his form during the years leading up to his sixtieth birthday, one needed only to watch his rare appearance on stage at the March 1999 Academy Awards ceremony, where he joined Martin Scorsese to help the ageing Elia Kazan accept his Oscar for lifetime achievement.

For the previous six months, De Niro had been active behind the scenes raising money for Bill Clinton's legal defence campaign. Not that De Niro was particularly political; his motivation seems have been personal loyalty to Clinton and in particular to his wife Hillary, who'd become a friend over the last two years of her husband's administration. De Niro himself kicked in only a meagre $5000, but enough celebs liked and sympathised with the Clintons to add $2.2 million to the $2.2 million already raised – still not nearly enough to wipe out the Clintons' combined legal and domestic debt of $9 million.

De Niro also lobbied House Republicans to vote against Clinton's impeachment – in vain, since he was impeached on 19 December 1998. A few days later, the Clintons, the most media-savvy presidential couple since John and Jackie Kennedy, left for a holiday in Park City, Utah, where they often stayed with Dreamworks SKG co-founder and animation expert Jeffrey Katzenberg.

De Niro's involvement with the Clintons appeared to be at an end, but political scandal has a long half-life, and only a few days before the Oscar award ceremony, the fact of his lobbying hit the headlines. A public relations adviser would have urged him to stay out of the spotlight. But if anyone gave De Niro this advice, he ignored it. Instead, as the ninety-year-old Elia Kazan shuffled on stage to receive his honorary Academy Award, De Niro and Scorsese flanked him.

To those who regarded Kazan as the ultimate turncoat, betrayer of the left-wing tradition of American cinema and theatre, the two men – Scorsese, unsmiling, tense, lips, as always, pressed tightly together, De Niro expressionless, almost dreamy, in a steep-sided convict-crop haircut assumed for his role as a navy instructor in *Men of Honor* – looked like a pair of leg-breakers sent by the mob, and Kazan an aged bookie about to be fitted for cement overshoes before being assigned to a watery grave.

Scorsese, standing next to De Niro a few steps behind Kazan during the ritual montage of film clips and the veteran director's unexpectedly chipper acceptance speech, seemed like someone following an act of will. Rationally, he had decided that Kazan, for all his political apostasy, deserved honour for having introduced the Hollywood of fevered melodrama and mindless diversion to the richness of the east-coast stage. His appearance was emblematic, not personal. He and Kazan touched only once, when Kazan, in a moment of confusion, looked around and reached out for the younger man. Awkwardly, Scorsese endured his embrace.

De Niro's behaviour was entirely different. As Kazan put his arm around Scorsese's neck, one corner of his mouth quirked in a smile. Those who knew him realised that he was giving a performance up there on the stage of the Shrine auditorium, one of his best.

Coaxed into throwing his weight against the prevailing anti-Kazan prejudice, De Niro's character had surrendered to the importuning of old friends like Scorsese, and to a sense of injustice that people without political convictions of any kind and mostly not even born in the days of the blacklist were condemning a director who, whatever his weaknesses, had remade the face of their craft.

The name of the character was 'The Actor Who Doesn't Care'. He'd researched the role; earned the right to play it. Now he entered into it as the priest enters into the sacrament – and, consuming the role, the role consumed him. Robert De Niro was doing what he was born to do – the only thing he really knew how to do well. He was being someone else.

After the awards, De Niro went into *Men of Honor*, formerly 'Navy Divers', directed by George Tillman, another relative newcomer, whose only previous film was the 1997 comedy *Soul Food*. Scott Smith wrote the screenplay, in which De Niro played an instructor at the navy diving school where Carl Brashear, the first African-American admitted to the programme, finds himself undergoing training. As Leslie Sunday, nicknamed 'Billy' after the 1920s temperance campaigner, De Niro is a composite of all the racist autocrats with whom Brashear had to contend, and offers the snarling, grimacing performance familiar from other films.

De Niro says he found playing a racist 'unsavoury' and 'uncomfortable', but explained, 'If I didn't do it as fully as I felt it should be done, there'd be no point in doing it. I was worried that maybe I'd go too far. But there are people who go that far.' Cuba Gooding Jr, who played Brashear as dignified, plucky and finally triumphant, was, as befits a new actor on the rise, accepting of his co-star's methods. 'De Niro, he wears his insecurity on his sleeve. I guess the word is vulnerable. He's a very vulnerable actor. He chooses not to try to do anything expressive emotionally until he truly believes it. And if that takes rehearsal time, then so be it.'

Less rehearsal was necessary for De Niro's next film, the comedy *Meet the Parents*. Fringe film-makers like Todd Phillips (*Road Trip*) and the Farrelly brothers (*Dumb and Dumber*, *There's Something About Mary*) had introduced mainstream audiences to the cinema of adolescent nightmare. Too young to be frightened of disease or concerned at the Human Condition, the twelve-to-eighteen-year-old American males who made up the primary audience fretted about the all-too-realistic horrors of farting at the dinner table, getting their penises snagged in their zippers, and being caught masturbating or picking their noses. Ever since, Hollywood had been falling over itself to catch up.

The source for *Meet the Parents* was an acclaimed but obscure 1992 short film of the same name by Greg Glienna and Mary Ruth Clarke. Jim Herzfeld and John Hamburg expanded and updated Glienna and Clarke's screenplay and story. Rosenthal and De Niro took the script to Universal and Dreamworks, which agreed to back it with Jay Roach, director of the highly successful *Austin Powers*, in charge.

Ben Stiller of *There's Something About Mary* played male nurse Greg Focker, who's invited to spend the weekend with the parents of his fiancée. De Niro was the mysterious father, Jack Byrnes, who though posing as a retired florist is actually an ex-CIA agent, ready to be convinced that his prospective son-in-law is a pervert, an idiot and probably a Communist.

Evidence of at least the first two is readily to hand. It's bad enough to be called 'Focker' and work as a nurse, but Greg also arrives with someone else's luggage – inevitably containing black lingerie and a whip. After that, gaffe follows gaffe. He deranges the house's sensitive plumbing, smashes the urn containing

Byrnes' mother's ashes, sets the house on fire and sprays everyone with sewage from an overflowing septic tank. The result looked like a film capable of making a modest profit. But De Niro's fee and the complicated physical action pushed the budget to $55 million – more than the cost of any similar film.

Meanwhile, De Niro continued to expand his restaurant holdings, which brought him into conflict with long-time partner Drew Nieporent. In March 2000, the *New York Post* reported: 'the two nabobs behind "Nobu" have been feuding and are abandoning plans to open two new Nobu restaurants together – one in London's Canary Wharf and another in Miami. Nieporent insisted that the two new Nobus would go ahead as planned. "I get along with everyone, and I stand behind what I've done," he says. "There are all kinds of projects under the Nobu mantle. Nobu [Matsuhisa] controls those decisions, not Robert De Niro."' Nobu London did open, and De Niro also talked with London hotelier Ian Schrager about restaurants for his hotels in London's St Martin's Lane and at New York's upcoming Astor Place Hotel.

In June, *The Adventures of Rocky and Bullwinkle* opened. The $76 million production grossed only $16 million on its first domestic weekend, and went downhill thereafter. Jane Rosenthal was stunned. 'We sat shiva out of respect for the dead,' she said ruefully. 'No one called for seventy-two hours. There was complete silence. The telephone doesn't ring.'

De Niro was already working on a new film which returned him to the milieu with which he was more familiar – cops, crime and the streets. The script, *Fifteen Minutes*, by *Meet the Parents*' Jim Herzfeld, who also directed, took its title from Andy Warhol's phrase that 'In the future, everyone will be famous for fifteen minutes.' De Niro plays the tough but media-smart NYPD detective Eddie Flemming, the sort of cop who gets on the cover of *People* and is featured on 'reality' TV shows, represented in this case by *Top Story*, fronted by Robert Hawkins. Hawkins is embodied in the improbable shape of Kelsey Grammer, best known as the genial psychiatrist hero of the series *Frasier*. Tired of his anodyne role as Frasier, Grammer longed for opportunities to show off his acting skills. These included a disastrous attempt at *Macbeth*, of which the best any critic could say was that he knew his lines. *Fifteen Minutes* promised a fundamental change of pace, but early advertising, unwilling to frighten off Grammer's fans, described his character only as 'an aggressive and steadfast host of a TV tabloid show'. In fact, Hawkins would emerge as a slimy blend of half a dozen such personalities with the worst characteristics of all of them.

Flemming finds himself the unwilling subject of Hawkins' interest when Oleg and Emil, gangsters from the old Soviet Union, in town to collect their share of a big score, decide that the United States is a country where anything goes and nobody ever gets punished, and begin exploiting the fact. Emil videos Oleg killing people, and offers the tapes to Grammer for $1 million. If arrested, they plan to plead insanity, claiming they were abused as children. Meanwhile, they watch themselves eagerly on TV while dining at Planet Hollywood, and Emil, a fan of *It's a Wonderful Life*, checks into hotels as 'Frank Capra'.

Matched with a young arson investigator, played by Edward Burns, Flemming pursues the killers, always aware that whatever he does will turn up on TV that night. But Herzfeld wouldn't or couldn't push his material into the satiric area of Paddy Chayefsky's *Network*, which pioneered such parodies of the mass media. Flemming stops Oleg and Emil, with, of all people, John Gotti's mouthpiece Bruce Cutler turning up to cut the TV deals, and, while handing Hawkins his comeuppance at the end, still makes a pitch for TV celebrity being a useful adjunct to criminology.

On 27 July 2000, Virginia Admiral died, aged eighty-five – ironically followed only eight days later, and at almost precisely the same age, as Sir Alec Guinness, with whom De Niro had so often been compared as a young actor. Obituaries paid tribute to her role in the renaissance of art in New York in the forties, her political activities, and her campaigning for low-cost housing for artists in Greenwich Village; but inevitably it was as the mother of Robert Jr that she was most remembered.

To complete a trilogy of disaster, in September De Niro and

Rosenthal presented Tribeca Productions' first annual 'Ruler's Edge' Awards, 'recognising individuals who break the rules of conventional entertainment wisdom when it comes to the internet'. The ceremony came as the climax of 'a two-day special event of panel discussions, keynote breakfasts, and short film and animation screenings designed to examine the convergence of film, technology and the internet'.

'Oddly, many of the winners of Tribeca Production's Ruler's Edge Awards didn't bother to show up to claim their kudos,' wrote media reporter R. Allen Lieder, who observed the conference. 'Pamela Anderson Lee won three of the awards for Most Influential Netizen, Most Sites and Entertainer of the Decade. William Shatner was absent for his bestowing of Best Celebrity Pitchman as was Cindy Margolis for Best Entrepreneurial Role Model, Shawn Fanning for Rascal of the Decade and the Humanitarian Award. Fifteen-year-old Ashley Power was given the Lifetime Achievement Award. You get the idea. With categories like these and winners to match, it's little wonder that the most notable show-ups were the Pets.com sock puppet and Gary Coleman (Best Marketing Campaign). The award itself was an engraved crystal-edged ruler.'

As the October release date of Meet the Parents approached, De Niro can have had few reasons to be optimistic. Yet the film grossed more than half its budget on its first weekend, the biggest October opening in Hollywood history, and built into one of the year's most profitable productions. 'Who would have imagined,' asked Jane Rosenthal, with understandable surprise, 'that Bob De Niro would turn out to be America's funniest man?' Universal and Dreamworks immediately offered Jim Herzfeld $1.1 million to script the sequel, Meet the Fockers.

A few weeks later, the American Museum of the Moving Image threw another tribute, this time to honour Rosenthal. De Niro attended with his stepdaughter Drena, whose film career, despite bit parts in Wag the Dog, Great Expectations, Entropy and Adventures of Rocky and Bullwinkle, had never taken off.

If people hoped for a long address, they were disappointed. De Niro's entire speech consisted of two sentences. 'Jane, for twelve years you've been a trusted friend and unbelievable business partner. Congratulations, and congratulations on *Meet the Parents*.' And even this was read from notes.

Now unexpectedly a box-office draw, De Niro had plenty of projects from which to choose. He agreed to team up with Eddie Murphy for a satire on cop buddy movies called *Showtime*. A comic reprise of *Fifteen Minutes*, with elements of *Beverly Hills Cop* and *48 Hours*, it would pair Murphy as a reckless rookie with tough old hand De Niro as stars of a 'reality' TV show designed to improve the force's public image.

He also signed for *City by the Sea*, a $60 million production to be directed by Michael Caton-Jones. The project, supposedly based on a true story, had begun with Al Pacino as the cop whose father was executed for murder, and who finds that the murderer in the case he's investigating is his own son. The 'city by the sea' is sleazy Long Beach, Long Island, where the manhunt takes place.

Most interesting of all, however, was Martin Scorsese's *Gangs of New York*, set in New York in the 1850s, and based on a screenplay by ex-critic Jay Cocks. Production had been delayed for five years, first as Scorsese shifted the location from Rome to Hollywood and back again, then in problems over money, which Disney/Touchstone finally remedied, but most recently at the whim of its primary star, Leonardo DiCaprio, who was to play the head of an Irish street gang called the Dead Rabbits. 'Robert De Niro will be his main adversary,' explained Scorsese, 'one of the tougher ones, a leader of a gang called the Native Americans, who are anti-immigration, anti-Irish, anti-Catholic.' The story, Scorsese said, 'is about the ethnic struggle for power, and how the gang element is reflected in the politicians and the police force'.

When DiCaprio finally committed, it was De Niro's turn to back out. At first, he'd been unwilling to return to Europe in the wake of the call-girl investigation in Paris. Then, following his divorce from Grace Hightower, he was concerned that any absence for a long period might prejudice his chance of getting custody of their son. 'It's only a matter of time before he signs on,' said a source close to Scorsese, who had added Daniel Day-Lewis to the cast; but at this point Disney began to have new doubts about the script, and Scorsese began working on a film of Nick Tosches' biography of the singer and actor Dean Martin while De Niro became involved in a new cop film, *The Score*, for Peter Guber's open-handed Mandalay Pictures.

Once again, the film was a retread. The first casting for the main character of Nick, the big-time burglar who comes out of retirement for One Last Big Job, had been Michael Douglas, but once he took up with young Welsh actress Catherine Zeta Jones, Douglas preferred a project in which they could appear together – the remake of *Dial M for Murder*, *A Perfect Murder*. Guber offered $15 million for De Niro to step into Douglas's shoes, with the added bonus of playing opposite Marlon Brando as the thief's fence and oldest friend.

Director Frank Oz started shooting in Montreal in March 2000. De Niro is Nick, the ageing burglar who's retired to run a jazz club, but who is lured back one final time out of loyalty to Max (an elephantine Marlon Brando), who owes a gang boss $4 million. Equally true to the stereotype, the deal quickly goes sour, responsibility resting with a young punk (Edward Norton, showing an unexpected lean menace reminiscent of John Cusack) who has found a way to rob the Montreal Customs House of a $30 million French sceptre.

Squinting from under a corrugated brow, his now-standard method of indicating deep feeling, De Niro ploughs through shoals of red herrings in search of a way to steal this unlikely McGuffin. Warned on every side, particularly by his girlfriend Diane (Angela Bassett), that he is heading for disaster, and reminded by everyone that he swore never to commit a crime in his own home town, he persists, for no motives more complex than a wish to pay off the mortgage on what is apparently a very profitable business anyway.

A sense of *déjà vu* afflicts one at every turn of the plot. It's not just that De Niro's character in *New York, New York* owned a jazz club, that the plot reprises *Heat*, or that having a black girlfriend reminds us of the actor's sexual tastes; his lines, his expressions, his clothes, his entire demeanour recall other films in a way that was never true of *Raging Bull*, *The King of Comedy*, *The Untouchables*, even *Bloody Mama* or *Bang the Drum Slowly*. An actor accustomed to having his roles, like his suits, tailored to his exact dimensions, was wearing something off the peg, and, at that, from K-Mart rather than Brooks Brothers. That Nick spends most of his more physically harrowing scenes in a ski-mask also suggests that a stuntman doubled De Niro, negating one of his last claims to superiority over less committed colleagues.

If there are acting honours in *The Score* they go to Edward Norton as Jack Teller, who thinks up the heist. In every way, his is a De Niro performance – part-time a criminal mastermind, at others a mentally handicapped janitor, sometimes charming, sometimes malicious, he builds a performance in the way once characteristic of De Niro, but now, in his career, apparently a thing of the past.

Opposite Brando at last, De Niro makes little of the opportunity. Lumbering, blimpish, speaking in a papery wheeze, Brando lacks the rumbling voice that made Orson Welles imposing even at his most obese. Not for the first time, he treated the production as his plaything, mischievously stirring up trouble among cast and crew. His particular target was director Oz, a journeyman without the strength to oppose the legend. Brando let it be known to the press that he preferred De Niro's direction, and wanted him to take over the film. De Niro, as usual, was silent.

In July 2001, De Niro's divorce from Grace Hightower became final. The judge hearing the case noted that there was little to be decided, since the two had worked out most of their differences in the previous two years. Hightower's last-minute suggestion that De Niro should take a drug test appears to have been a stratagem to gain some final financial advantage. Whatever the reason, De Niro walked away from this entanglement, as he has walked away from every such emotional impediment in his life.

But for the events of 11 September 2001, the zone of affectless anomie he habitually inhabited might have remained his permanent home. Instead, the ruin of New York and, worse, that part of New York below 14th Street where he had been born, raised and elected to live and work, jolted him fundamentally. Within days, the kitchens of Nobu and the Tribeca Bar and Grill were ferrying meals to the firefighters and construction workers at Ground Zero. Nobody was more visible on television than De Niro in the days following the attack. And within a few months he also agreed, at the behest of *Vanity Fair* editor Graydon Parker, one of its producers, to host and narrate the two-hour CBS TV documentary *9/11*. Compiled from footage shot inside the stricken buildings by French film-makers Jules and Gedeon Naudet, this documentary about the terrorist attack and its aftermath was broadcast in April 2002. Watched by more than half the households in New York, it drew, said a network spokesman (without evident irony), the largest audience for any broadcast event not involving sports.

To some commentators, De Niro's assumption of the mantle of spokesman for New York and his adoption of what critic David Thomson called 'the Giuliani spirit' marked yet another departure from his persona as an actor – one he'd found more and more galling with the years. Having always seen him as an extension of his dour, repressed father, they now realised he had inherited as well the pragmatism of his mother – who, they were quick to point out, also abandoned art to concentrate on business and New York politics. 'Man of the People' might yet turn out to be Robert De Niro's most memorable and enduring role.

Filmography

THE WEDDING PARTY (1963/1968)
Director, producer, writer and editor Cynthia Munroe, Wilford Leach and Brian De Palma; photography Peter Powell; music John Henry McDowell.
Cast: Jill Clayburgh, Charles Pfluger, Valda Satterfield, Raymond McNally, Jennifer Salt, John Braswell, Judy Thomas, Robert De Niro (as 'Robert De Nero'), William Finley.

TROIS CHAMBRES À MANHATTAN (1965)
Director Marcel Carné; writers Jacques Sigurd and Marcel Carné; photography Eugen Schuftan.
Cast: Annie Girardot, Roland Lesaffre, Maurice Ronet, Gabrielle Ferzetti.
De Niro has a walk-on appearance.

GREETINGS (1968)
Director Brian De Palma; producer Charles Hirsch; screenplay Brian De Palma and Charles Hirsch; photography Robert Fiore; editor Brian De Palma; music Children of Paradise.
Cast: Jonathan Warden, Robert De Niro (as Jon Rubin), Gerrit Graham, Richard Hamilton, Megan McCormick, Allen Garfield.

SAM'S SONG (1969)
Director Jordan Leondopoulas; producer Christopher C. Dewey; screenplay Jordan Leondopoulas; photography Alex Phillips Jr; editor Arline Garson; music Gershon Kingsley.
Cast: Robert De Niro (as Sam), Jared Mickey, Jennifer Warren, Martin Kelley, Viva.
See also *The Swap* (1979).

BLOODY MAMA (1970)

Director and producer Roger Corman; co-producers Samuel Z. Arkoff and James H. Nicholson; screenplay Robert Thom from a story by Thom and Don Peters; photography John Alonzo; editor Eve Newman; music Don Randi.

Cast: Shelley Winters, Pat Hingle, Don Stroud, Diane Varsi, Bruce Dern, Clint Kimbrough, Robert Walden, Robert De Niro (as Lloyd Barker), Alex Nicol, Pamela Dunlap, Scatman Crothers, Lisa Jill.

HI, MOM! (1970)

Director Brian De Palma; producer Charles Hirsch; screenplay Brian De Palma from a story by De Palma and Hirsch; photography Robert Elfstrom; editor Paul Hirsch; music Eric Kaz.

Cast: Robert De Niro (as Jon Rubin), Allen Garfield, Lara Parker, Jennifer Salt, Gerrit Graham, Charles Durning.

JENNIFER ON MY MIND (1971)

Director Noel Black; producer Bernard Schwartz; screenplay Erich Segal; photography Andy Laszlo; editor Jack Wheeler; music Stephen J. Lawrence.

Cast: Tippy Walker, Michael Brandon, Lou Gilbert, Steve Vinovich, Peter Bonerz, Renee Taylor, Chuck McCann, Bruce Kornbluth, Barry Bostwick, Jeff Conaway, Robert De Niro (as Mardigian), Erich Segal.

BORN TO WIN (1971. Also known as *Addict* and *Born to Lose*.)

Director Ivan Passer; producer Philip Langner; co-producers George Segal and Jerry Tokofsky; screenplay David Scott Milton; cinematographers Jack Priestly and Richard Kratina; editor Ralph Rosenbaum; music William S. Fisher.

Cast: George Segal, Karen Black, Jay Fletcher, Hector Elizondo, Marcia Jean Kurtz, Irving Selbst, Robert De Niro (as Danny), Paula Prentiss, Sylvia Sims.

THE GANG THAT COULDN'T SHOOT STRAIGHT (1971)
Director James Goldstone; producers Robert Chartoff and Irwin Winkler; screenplay Waldo Salt; photography Owen Roizman; editor Edward A. Biery; music Dave Grusin.
Cast: Jerry Orbach, Leigh Taylor-Young, Jo Van Fleet, Lionel Stander, Robert De Niro (as Mario), Irving Selbst, Hervé Villechaize.

BANG THE DRUM SLOWLY (1973)
Director John Hancock; producers Maurice and Lois Rosenfield; screenplay Mark Harris from his own novel; cinematographer Richard Shore; editor Richard Marks; music Stephen Lawrence.
Cast: Robert De Niro (as Bruce Pearson), Michael Moriarty, Vincent Gardenia, Phil Foster, Anne Wedgwood.

MEAN STREETS (1973)
Director Martin Scorsese; producer Jonathan T. Taplin; executive producer E. Lee Perry; screenplay Martin Scorsese and Mardik Martin; photography Kent Wakeford; editor Sidney Levin.
Cast: Harvey Keitel, Robert De Niro (as Johnny Boy), David Proval, Amy Robinson, Richard Romanus, Cesare Danova.

THE GODFATHER PART II (1974)
Director and producer Francis Ford Coppola; co-producers Gray Frederickson and Fred Roos; screenplay Francis Ford Coppola and Mario Puzo; photography Gordon Willis; editors Peter Zinner, Barry Malkin and Richard Marks; music Nino Rota with additional music by Carmine Coppola.
Cast: Al Pacino, Robert De Niro (as Vito Corleone), Diane Keaton, Robert Duvall, John Cazale, Talia Shire, Lee Strasberg, Michael V. Gazzo.

THE LAST TYCOON (1976)
Director Elia Kazan; producer Sam Spiegel; screenplay Harold Pinter based on the unfinished novel by F. Scott Fitzgerald; photography Victor Kemper; editor Richard Marks; music Maurice Jarre.

Cast: Robert De Niro (as Monroe Stahr), Tony Curtis, Robert Mitchum, Jeanne Moreau, Jack Nicholson, Donald Pleasence, Ingrid Boulting.

TAXI DRIVER (1976)
Director Martin Scorsese; producers Michael and Julia Phillips; screenplay Paul Schrader; photography Michael Chapman; editors Marcia Lucas, Tom Rolf and Melvin Shapiro; music Bernard Herrmann.
Cast: Robert De Niro (as Travis Bickle), Cybill Shepherd, Jodie Foster, Peter Boyle, Albert Brooks, Leonard Harris, Harvey Keitel, Martin Scorsese.

1900 (NOVECENTO) (1977)
Director Bernardo Bertolucci; producer Alberto Grimaldi; screenplay Franco Arcali, Bernardo Bertolucci, Giuseppe Bertolucci; photography Vittorio Storaro; editor Franco Arcali; music Ennio Morricone.
Cast: Robert De Niro (as Alfredo Berlinghieri), Gérard Depardieu, Dominique Sanda, Burt Lancaster, Donald Sutherland, Sterling Hayden.

NEW YORK, NEW YORK (1977)
Director Martin Scorsese; producers Irwin Winkler and Robert Chartoff; screenplay Earl MacRauch and Mardik Martin; story Earl MacRauch; photography Laszlo Kovacs; editors Irving Lerner, Marcia Lucas, Tom Rolf, B. Lovitt and David Ramirez; musical director Ralph Burns; new songs by John Kander and Freb Ebb; choreography Ron Field.
Cast: Liza Minnelli, Robert De Niro (as Jimmy Doyle), Lionel Stander, Barry Primus, Mary Kay Place, Georgie Auld.

THE DEER HUNTER (1978)
Director Michael Cimino; producers Barry Spikings, Michael Deeley, Michael Cimino and John Peverall; screenplay Deric Washburn from a story by Cimino, Washburn, Louis Garfinkle

and Quinn K. Redeker; photography Vilmos Zsigmond; editor Peter Zinner; music Stanley Myers.

Cast: Robert De Niro (as Michael Vronsky), John Cazale, John Savage, Christopher Walken, Meryl Streep, George Dzundza, Chuck Aspegren.

THE SWAP (1979. See *Sam's Song*.)
Director Jordan Leondopoulas; producer Christopher C. Dewey; screenplay Jordan Leondopoulas; photography Alex Phillips Jr; editor Arline Garson; music Gershon Kingsley.

Cast: As for *Sam's Song* with the addition of Sybil Danning, James Brown and Lisa Blount.

RAGING BULL (1980)
Director Martin Scorsese; producers Irwin Winkler and Robert Chartoff; screenplay Paul Schrader and Mardik Martin, based on the book by Jake La Motta with Joseph Carter and Pete Savage; photography Michael Chapman; editor Thelma Schoonmaker; music Pietro Mascagni.

Cast: Robert De Niro (as Jake La Motta), Cathy Moriarty, Joe Pesci, Frank Vincent, Nicholas Colasanto, Theresa Saldana, Martin Scorsese.

TRUE CONFESSIONS (1981)
Director Ulu Grosbard; producers Irwin Winkler and Robert Chartoff; screenplay John Gregory Dunne and Joan Didion from the novel by Dunne; photography Owen Roizman; editor Lynzee Klingman; music Georges Delerue.

Cast: Robert De Niro (as Monsignor Desmond Spellacy), Robert Duvall, Burgess Meredith, Charles Durning, Ed Flanders, Cyril Cusack.

KING OF COMEDY (1983)
Director Martin Scorsese; producer Arnon Milchan; screenplay Paul D. Zimmermann; photography Fred Shuler; editor Thelma Schoonmaker; music Robbie Robertson.

Cast: Robert De Niro (as Rupert Pupkin), Jerry Lewis, Diahnne Abbott, Sandra Bernhard, Shelley Hack.

FALLING IN LOVE (1984)

Director Ulu Grosbard; producer Marvin Worth; screenplay Michael Christofer; photography Peter Suschitzky; editor Michael Kahn; music Dave Grusin.
Cast: Robert De Niro (as Frank Raftis), Meryl Streep, Jane Kaczmarek, George Martin, David Glennon, Dianne Wiest, Harvey Keitel.

ONCE UPON A TIME IN AMERICA (1984)

Director Sergio Leone; producer Arnon Milchan; screenplay Sergio Leone, Leonardo Benvenuti, Piero De Bernardi, Enrico Medioli, Franco Arcalli, Franco Ferrini and Stuart Kaminsky; photography Tonino Delli Colli; editor Nino Baragli; music Ennio Morricone.
Cast: Robert De Niro (as David 'Noodles' Aaronson), James Woods, Elizabeth McGovern, Treat Williams, Tuesday Weld, Burt Young, Danny Aiello.

BRAZIL (1985)

Director Terry Gilliam; producer Arnon Milchan; screenplay Gilliam, Tom Stoppard and Charles McKeown; photography Roger Pratt; editor Julian Doyle; music Michael Kamen.
Cast: Jonathan Pryce, Robert De Niro (as Archibald 'Harry' Tuttle), Katherine Helmond, Ian Holm, Bob Hoskins, Michael Palin.

THE MISSION (1986)

Director Roland Joffe; producers Fernando Ghia and David Puttnam; screenplay Robert Bolt; photography Chris Menges; editor Jim Clark; music Ennio Morricone.
Cast: Robert De Niro (as Mendoza), Jeremy Irons, Ray McAnally, Aidan Quinn, Liam Neeson, Cherie Lunghi, Ronald Pickup, Daniel Berrigan.

ANGEL HEART (1986)

Director Alan Parker; producers Alan Marshall and Elliott Kastner; screenplay Alan Parker from the novel *Falling Angel* by William Hjortsberg; photography Michael Seresin; editor Gerry Hambling; music Trevor Jones.

Cast: Mickey Rourke, Robert De Niro (as Louis Cyphre), Lisa Bonet, Charlotte Rampling.

DEAR AMERICA (1987)

Director Bill Couturie; producers Bill Couturie and Thomas Bird; screenplay by Richard Dewhurst and Bill Couturie based on the book *Dear America, Letters Home from Vietnam.*

Voice cast includes narration by Robert De Niro, Michael J. Fox, Ellen Burstyn, Kathleen Turner, Tom Berenger, Willem Dafoe, Sean Penn and others.

THE UNTOUCHABLES (1987)

Director Brian De Palma; producer Art Linson; screenplay David Mamet; photography Stephen H. Burum; editors Jerry Greenberg and Bill Pankow; music Ennio Morricone.

Cast: Kevin Costner, Sean Connery, Charles Martin Smith, Andy Garcia, Robert De Niro (as Al Capone), Richard Bradford.

MIDNIGHT RUN (1988)

Director and producer Martin Brest; executive producer William S. Gilmore; screenplay George Gallo; photography Donald Thorin; editors Billy Weber, Chris Lebenzon and Michael Tronick; music Danny Elfman.

Cast: Robert De Niro (as Jack Walsh), Charles Grodin, Yaphet Kotto, John Ashton, Dennis Farina, Joe Pantoliano.

JACKNIFE (1989)

Director David Jones; producers Robert Schaffel and Carol Baum; screenplay Stephen Metcalfe from his play *Strange Snow*; photography Brian West; editor John Bloom; music Bruce Broughton.

Cast: Robert De Niro (as Joseph 'Megs' Megessey), Ed Harris, Kathy Baker, Charles Dutton, Loudon Wainwright III.

WE'RE NO ANGELS (1989)
Director Neil Jordan; producer Art Linson; executive producer Robert De Niro; screenplay David Mamet from the 1955 screenplay by Ranald McDougall; photography Philippe Rousselot; editors Mick Audsley and Joke Van Wijk; music George Fenton.
Cast: Robert De Niro (as Ned), Sean Penn, Demi Moore, Hoyt Axton, Bruno Kirby, Ray McAnally.

AWAKENINGS (1990)
Director Penny Marshall; producers Walter F. Parkes and Lawrence Lasker; screenplay Steve Zaillian based on the book by Oliver Sacks; photography Miroslav Ondricek; editors Jerry Greenberg and Battle Davis; music Randy Newman.
Cast: Robert De Niro (as Leonard Lowe), Robin Williams, Julie Kavner, Ruth Nelson, John Heard, Penelope Ann Miller, Dexter Gordon, Max Von Sydow.

GOODFELLAS (1990)
Director Martin Scorsese; producer Irwin Winkler; executive producer Barbara De Fina; screenplay Martin Scorsese and Nicholas Pileggi based on the book *Wiseguy* by Nicholas Pileggi; photography Michael Ballhaus; editor Thelma Schoonmaker.
Cast: Robert De Niro (as Jimmy 'The Gent' Conway), Ray Liotta, Joe Pesci, Lorraine Bracco, Paul Sorvino.

STANLEY AND IRIS (1990)
Director Martin Ritt; producers Arlene Sellars and Alex Winitsky; executive producer Patrick Palmer; screenplay Irving Ravetch and Harriet Frank Jr from the novel *Union Street* by Pat Barker; photography Donald McAlpine; editor Sidney Levin; music John Williams.
Cast: Jane Fonda, Robert De Niro (as Stanley Everett Cox), Swoosie Kurtz, Martha Plimpton, Harley Cross, Jamey Sheridan.

GUILTY BY SUSPICION (1991)

Director Irwin Winkler; producer Arnon Milchan; screenplay Irwin Winkler; photography Michael Ballhaus; editor Priscilla Nedd; music James Newton Howard.

Cast: Robert De Niro (as David Merrill), Annette Bening, George Wendt, Patricia Wettig, Sam Wanamaker, Martin Scorsese, Barry Primus.

BACKDRAFT (1991)

Director Ron Howard; producers Richard B. Lewis, John Watson and Pen Densham; screenplay Gregory Widen; photography Mikael Salomon; editors Daniel Hanley and Michael Hill; music Hans Zimmer.

Cast: Kurt Russell, William Baldwin, Jennifer Jason Leigh, Scott Glenn, Rebecca De Mornay, Robert De Niro (as Donald Rimgale), Donald Sutherland, J.T. Walsh, Jason Gedrick.

CAPE FEAR (1991)

Director Martin Scorsese; producer Barbara De Fina; executive producers Kathleen Kennedy and Frank Marshall; screenplay Wesley Strick from the original screenplay by James R. Webb; photography Freddie Francis; editor Thelma Schoonmaker; music Bernard Herrmann adapted and arranged by Elmer Bernstein.

Cast: Robert De Niro (as Max Cady), Nick Nolte, Jessica Lange, Juliette Lewis, Joe Don Baker, Robert Mitchum, Gregory Peck, Martin Balsam.

MISTRESS (1992)

Director Barry Primus; producers Meir Teper and Robert De Niro; screenplay Barry Primus and J.F. Lawton from a story by Primus; photography Sven Kirsten; editor Steven Weisberg; music Galt MacDermot.

Cast: Robert Wuhl, Martin Landau, Jace Alexander, Robert De Niro (as Evan M. Wright), Laurie Metcalf, Eli Wallach, Danny Aiello, Christopher Walken.

NIGHT AND THE CITY (1992)

Director Irwin Winkler; producers Jane Rosenthal and Irwin Winkler; screenplay Richard Price based on a script by Jo Eisenger; photography Tak Fujimoto; editor David Brenner; music James Newton Howard.

Cast: Robert De Niro (as Harry Fabian), Jessica Lange, Cliff Gorman, Alan King, Jack Warden, Eli Wallach, Barry Primus.

MAD DOG AND GLORY (1993)

Director John McNaughton; producers Barbara De Fina and Martin Scorsese; co-producer Steven A. Jones; executive producer/writer Richard Price; photography Robby Müller; editors Craig McKay and Elena Maganini; music Elmer Bernstein.

Cast: Robert De Niro (as Wayne 'Mad Dog' Dobie), Uma Thurman, Bill Murray, David Caruso, Mike Starr, Tom Towles, Kathy Baker.

THIS BOY'S LIFE (1993)

Director Michael Caton-Jones; producer Art Linson; executive producers Peter Guber and Jon Peters; screenplay Robert Getchell from Tobias Wolff's book; photography David Watkin; editor Jim Clark; music Carter Burwell.

Cast: Robert De Niro (as Dwight Hansen), Ellen Barkin, Leonardo DiCaprio, Johan Blechman.

A BRONX TALE (1993)

Director Robert De Niro; producers Robert De Niro, Jane Rosenthal and Jon Kilik; screenplay Chazz Palminteri from his own play; photography Reynaldo Villalobos; editors David Ray and R.Q. Lovett; music Butch Barbella.

Cast: Robert De Niro (as Lorenzo Anello), Chazz Palminteri, Lillo Brancato, Francis Capra, Joe Pesci, Taral Hicks, Katherine Narducci.

MARY SHELLEY'S FRANKENSTEIN (1994)
Director Kenneth Branagh; producer Francis Ford Coppola; screenplay by Frank Darabont from the novel by Mary Shelley; photography Roger Pratt; music Patrick Doyle.
Cast: Robert De Niro (as The Creature), Kenneth Branagh, Helena Bonham Carter, Aidan Quinn, John Cleese, Thomas Hulce, Cherie Lunghi, Ian Holm, Richard Briers.

CASINO (1995)
Director Martin Scorsese; producer Barbara De Fina; screenplay Nicholas Pileggi and Martin Scorsese based on the book by Nicholas Pileggi; photography Robert Richardson; editor Thelma Schoonmaker.
Cast: Robert De Niro (as Sam 'Ace' Rothstein), Sharon Stone, Joe Pesci, Don Rickles, Kevin Pollack, James Woods.

HEAT (1995)
Director Michael Mann; producers Michael Mann and Art Linson; screenplay Michael Mann; photography Dante Spinotti; editors Dov Hoenig and Pasquale Buba; music Elliot Goldenthal.
Cast: Robert De Niro (as Neil McAuley), Al Pacino, Val Kilmer, Ashley Judd, Jon Voight.

SLEEPERS (1996)
Directed, written and produced by Barry Levinson; photography by Michael Ballhaus; editor Stu Linder.
Cast: Kevin Bacon, Billy Crudup, Robert De Niro (as Father Bobby), Minnie Driver, Ron Eldard, Vittorio Gassman, Dustin Hoffman, Jason Patric, Brad Pitt, Brad Renfro.

MARVIN'S ROOM (1996)
Director Jerry Zaks; producers Scott Rudin and Jane Rosenthal; executive producer Robert De Niro; screenplay Scott McPherson; photography Piotr Sobocinski; editor Jim Clark.
Cast: Meryl Streep, Diane Keaton, Leonardo DiCaprio, Robert De Niro (as Dr Wally), Hume Cronyn, Gwen Verdon.

THE FAN (1996)

Director Tony Scott; producer Wendy Finerman; screenplay Phoef Sutton; photography Darik Wolski; editor Chris Wagner.
Cast: Robert De Niro (as Gil Renard), Wesley Snipes, Ellen Barkin, John Leguizamo, Benicio Del Toro.

LES CENT EN UNE NUITS (1995)

Director and screenplay Agnes Varda; producer Dominique Vignet; photography Eric Gautier.
Cast: Michel Piccoli, Marcello Mastroianni, Anouk Aimée, many others. De Niro has a cameo with Catherine Deneuve.

COP LAND (1997)

Director and screenplay James Mangold; producer Christopher Goode; photography Eric Edwards; music Bruce Springsteen and Howard Shore.
Cast: Sylvester Stallone, Harvey Keitel, Ray Liotta, Cathy Moriarty, Robert De Niro (as Lt Moe Tilden, Internal Affairs).

WAG THE DOG (1997)

Director Barry Levinson; producers Robert De Niro, Jane Rosenthal and Barry Levinson; screenplay Hilary Henkin and David Mamet from Larry Beinhart's novel *American Hero*; photography Robert Richardson; music Mark Knopfler.
Cast: Dustin Hoffman, Robert De Niro (as Conrad Brean), Anne Heche, Denis Leary, Willie Nelson.

JACKIE BROWN (1997)

Director and screenplay Quentin Tarantino, from Elmore Leonard's novel *Rum Punch*; producer Lawrence Bender; photography Guillermo Navarro; music Joseph Julian Gonzalez.
Cast: Pam Grier, Samuel L. Jackson, Robert Forster, Bridget Fonda, Michael Keaton, Robert De Niro (as Louis Gara).

GREAT EXPECTATIONS (1998)
Director Alfonso Cuaron; screenplay Mitch Glazer from Charles Dickens' novel; producers Art and John Linson; photography Emmanuel Lubezki.
Cast: Ethan Hawke, Gwyneth Paltrow, Hank Azaria, Chris Cooper, Anne Bancroft, Robert De Niro (as Arthur Lustig).

RONIN (1998)
Director John Frankenheimer; screenplay J.D. Zeik and 'Richard Weisz' (David Mamet); producer Frank Mancuso Jr; photography Robert Fraisse; music Elia Cmiral.
Cast: Robert De Niro (as Sam), Jean Reno, Natascha McElhone, Stellan Skarsgård, Sean Bean, Skipp Sudduth, Michael Lonsdale, Jonathan Pryce.

ANALYZE THIS (1999)
Director Harold Ramis; screenplay Harold Ramis and Kenneth Lonergan from a story by Lonergan and Peter Tolan; producers Jane Rosenthal and Paula Weinstein; photography Stuart Dryburgh; music Howard Shore.
Cast: Robert De Niro (as Paul Vitti), Billy Crystal, Lisa Kudrow, Chazz Palminteri, Joe Viterelli.

FLAWLESS (1999)
Director, screenplay and co-producer Joel Schumacher; producer Jane Rosenthal; photography Declan Quinn; music Bruce Roberts.
Cast: Robert De Niro (as Walt Koontz), Philip Seymour Hoffman, Barry Miller, Christopher Bauer, Skipp Sudduth, Wilson Jermaine Heredia, Nashom Benjamin, Scott Allen Cooper.

THE ADVENTURES OF ROCKY AND BULLWINKLE (2000)
Director Des McAnuff; screenplay Kenneth Lonergan, based on characters created by Jay Ward; producers Robert De Niro, Jane Rosenthal and Brad Epstein; photography Thomas E. Ackerman; music Lavant Coppock, Lisa McClowry and Mark Mothersbaugh.
Cast: Rene Russo, Jason Alexander, Piper Perabo, Randy Quaid,

Robert De Niro (as Fearless Leader), Janeane Garofalo, Carl Reiner.

MEN OF HONOR (2000)
Director George Tillman Jr; screenplay Scott Marshall Smith; producers Bill Bardalato and Robert Tietel; photography Anthony B. Richmond; music Mark Isham.
Cast: Robert De Niro (as Leslie W. 'Billy' Sunday), Cuba Gooding Jr, Charlize Theron, Aunjanue Ellis, Hal Holbrook, Michael Rapaport, Powers Boothe, David Keith.

MEET THE PARENTS (2000)
Director Jay Roach; screenplay James Herzfeld and John Hamburg from the original story and screenplay by Greg Glienna and Mary Ruth Clarke; producers Robert De Niro, Jane Rosenthal, Amy Sayres and Jim Vincent; photography Peter James; music Randy Newman.
Cast: Robert De Niro (as Jack Byrnes), Ben Stiller, Teri Polo, Blythe Danner, Nicole DeHuff, Jon Abrahams, Thomas McCarthy, Phyllis George, James Rebhorn.

FIFTEEN MINUTES (2001)
Director and screenplay John Herzfeld; producers Keith Addis and David Blocker; photography Jacques-Yves Escoffier; music Anthony Marineli and J. Peter Robinson.
Cast: Robert De Niro (as Eddie Flemming), Edward Burns, Kelsey Grammer, Avery Brooks, Melina Kanakaredes, Karel Roden, Oleg Taktarov, Vera Farmiga, John DiResta, James Handy.

THE SCORE (2001)
Director Frank Oz (uncredited Robert De Niro); screenplay Lem Dobbs and Scott Marshall Smith from a story by Daniel E. Taylor and Kario Salem; photography Rob Hahn; music Howard Shore.
Cast: Robert De Niro (as Nick Wells), Edward Norton, Marlon Brando, Angela Bassett, Gary Farmer, Paul Soles, Jamie Harrold.

CITY BY THE SEA (2002)
Director Michael Caton-Jones; screenplay Ken Hixon from an article by Michael McAlary; producers Matthew Baer, Brad Grey and Elie Samaha; photography Declan Quinn, Karl Walter Lindenlaub.
Cast: Robert De Niro (as Vincent Lamarca), James Franco, Eliza Dushku, George Dzundza.

SHOWTIME (2002)
Director Tom Dey; screenplay Miles Millar, Keith Sharon and Alfred Gough from a story by Jorge Saralegui; producers Bruce Berman and Jane Rosenthal; photography Thomas Kloss; music Alan Silvestri.
Cast: Robert De Niro (as Mitch Preston), Ken Hudson, Eddie Murphy, Rene Russo, William Shatner, Mel Rodriguez, Jullian Dulce Vida.

MEET THE FOCKERS (2003)
Director Jay Roach; screenplay James Herzfeld; music Randy Newman.
Cast: Robert De Niro (as Jack Byrnes), Ben Stiller, Blythe Danner, Teri Polo.

Index